Daily Office Readings

Year One, Volume 1

Compiled and edited by
The Reverend Terence L. Wilson

The Church Hymnal Corporation
800 Second Avenue, New York, NY 10017

Introduction

Daily Office Readings (DOR) is published in four volumes, two for each year of the Daily Office Lectionary. The selection of the readings is in strict accordance with the Daily Office Lectionary of *The Book of Common Prayer,* pages 936-1000, and has been drawn from *The Common Bible* (Revised Standard Version, an Ecumenical Edition), whose accuracy and wide ecumenical acceptance are generally recognized. The texts in this book may, of course, be replaced by corresponding passages from any of the other versions of the Bible authorized for public worship in this Church.

The readings have been edited for liturgical use, as were the readings in *Lectionary Texts,* in accordance with the suggestions in BCP, page 888. All alternatives cited have been included. In only a very few cases where exactly the same passages are to be read, rather than reprinting an entire passage, page references to a preceding page are given.

All optional passages have also been included. Those which may be omitted (cited in parentheses in the Daily Office Lectionary), have been set off in separate indented paragraphs, and marked with a vertical bar line at the margin. In some of the passages, an opening phrase may have been needed to clarify the context and is printed in italics and set off in brackets. The italicized words should be omitted when the preceding section is read and the continuity of the entire reading is clear.

In this book, citations from the Psalter are placed at the point where psalmody is normally used in the reading of the Daily Offices, before the Lessons. Citations for Morning Prayer are given first, for Evening Prayer second, separated by the ❖ Where the citation is only for either Morning Prayer or Evening Prayer, the Office is named. This is especially the case in the readings for Holy Days. Page numbers refer to BCP Psalter unless otherwise noted, and are enclosed in brackets. Optional psalmody is enclosed in parentheses; this is true when either an entire Psalm or only part of a Psalm is optional.

The Lessons for Daily Office Holy Days applicable for the part of the year covered by each volume are included at the back of the volume.

For ease of reference, footlines on each page identify the day found on that page.

Because of the importance of the Daily Office in the Anglican tradition, it is hoped these volumes will make the Offices easier to recite, aiding the use of the Office for private or public prayers. These volumes eliminate the need to find three readings for each day in the Bible and to track down those readings which skip around within a given passage.

DOR should make it more possible for the laity and clergy alike to develop the habit of reciting the Offices by eliminating much of the work involved. They will also be invaluable for those who are traveling.

The publishers hope this book will enrich participation in worship by all the people, and will assist the clergy and other ministers in worthily proclaiming the Word of God at the daily recitation of the Offices.

Daily Office Readings

Year One, Volume 1
Advent through Trinity Sunday

Week of 1 Advent

Sunday

Psalm 146 [page 803], *Psalm 147* [page 804] ❖
Psalm 111 [page 754], *Psalm 112* [page 755],
Psalm 113 [page 756]

A Reading (Lesson) from the Book of Isaiah [1:1-9]

The vision of Isaiah the son of Amoz, which he saw
concerning Judah and Jerusalem in the days of Uzzi'ah,
Jotham, Ahaz, and Hezeki'ah, kings of Judah. Hear, O
heavens, and give ear, O earth; for the Lord has spoken:
"Sons have I reared and brought up, but they have rebelled
against me. The ox knows its owner, and the ass its
master's crib; but Israel does not know, my people does
not understand." Ah, sinful nation, a people laden with
iniquity, offspring of evildoers, sons who deal corruptly!
They have forsaken the Lord, they have despised the Holy
One of Israel, they are utterly estranged. Why will you still
be smitten, that you continue to rebel? The whole head is
sick, and the whole heart faint. From the sole of the foot
even to the head, there is no soundness in it, but bruises
and sores and bleeding wounds; they are not pressed out,
or bound up, or softened with oil. Your country lies

desolate, your cities are burned with fire; in your very presence aliens devour your land; it is desolate, as overthrown by aliens. And the daughter of Zion is left like a booth in a vineyard, like a lodge in a cucumber field, like a besieged city. If the Lord of hosts had not left us a few survivors, we should have been like Sodom, and become like Gomor'rah.

A Reading (Lesson) from the Second Letter of Peter
[3:1-10]

This is now the second letter that I have written to you, beloved, and in both of them I have aroused your sincere mind by way of reminder; that you should remember the predictions of the holy prophets and the commandment of the Lord and Savior through your apostles. First of all you must understand this, that scoffers will come in the last days with scoffing, following their own passions and saying, "Where is the promise of his coming? For ever since the fathers fell asleep, all things have continued as they were from the beginning of creation." They deliberately ignore this fact, that by the word of God heavens existed long ago, and an earth formed out of water and by means of water, through which the world that then existed was deluged with water and perished. But by the same word the heavens and earth that now exist have been stored up for fire, being kept until the day of judgment and destruction of ungodly men. But do not ignore this one fact, beloved, that with the Lord one day is as a thousand years, and a thousand years as one day. The Lord is not slow about his promise as some count slowness, but is forebearing toward you, not wishing that any should perish, but that all should reach repentance. But the day of the Lord will come like a thief, and then the heavens will pass away with a loud noise, and the elements will be dissolved with fire, and the earth and the works that are upon it will be burned up.

A Reading (Lesson) from the Gospel according to Matthew
[25:1-13]

Jesus said to the disciples, "The kingdom of heaven shall be compared to ten maidens who took their lamps and went to meet the bridegroom. Five of them were foolish, and five were wise. For when the foolish took their lamps, they took no oil with them; but the wise took flasks of oil with their lamps. As the bridegroom was delayed, they all slumbered and slept. But at midnight there was a cry, 'Behold, the bridegroom! Come out to meet him.' Then all those maidens rose and trimmed their lamps. And the foolish said to the wise, 'Give us some of your oil, for our lamps are going out.' But the wise replied, 'Perhaps there will not be enough for us and for you; go rather to the dealers and buy for yourselves.' And while they went to buy, the bridegroom came, and those who were ready went in with him to the marriage feast; and the door was shut. Afterward the other maidens came also, saying, 'Lord, lord, open to us.' But he replied, 'Truly, I say to you, I do not know you.' Watch therefore, for you know neither the day nor the hour."

Monday

Psalm 1 [page 585],   *Psalm 2* [page 586],
Psalm 3 [page 587]   ❖   *Psalm 4* [page 587],
Psalm 7 [page 590]

A Reading (Lesson) from the Book of Isaiah [1:10-20]

Hear the word of the Lord, you rulers of Sodom! Give ear to the teaching of our God, you people of Gomor'rah! "What to me is the multitude of your sacrifices? says the Lord; I have had enough of burnt offerings of rams and the fat of fed beasts; I do not delight in the blood of bulls, or of lambs, or of he-goats. When you come to appear before me, who requires of you this trampling of my courts?

Bring no more vain offerings; incense is an abomination to me. New moon and sabbath and the calling of assemblies — I cannot endure iniquity and solemn assembly. Your new moons and your appointed feasts my soul hates; they have become a burden to me, I am weary of bearing them. When you spread forth your hands, I will hide my eyes from you; even though you make many prayers, I will not listen; your hands are full of blood. Wash yourselves; make yourselves clean; remove the evil of your doings from before my eyes; cease to do evil, learn to do good; seek justice, correct oppression; defend the fatherless, plead for the widow. Come now, let us reason together, says the Lord: though your sins are like scarlet, they shall be as white as snow; though they are red like crimson, they shall become like wool. If you are willing and obedient, you shall eat the good of the land; But if you refuse and rebel, you shall be devoured by the sword; for the mouth of the Lord has spoken."

A Reading (Lesson) from the First Letter of Paul to the Thessalonians [1:1-10]

Paul, Silva'nus, and Timothy, To the church of the Thessalo'nians in God the Father and the Lord Jesus Christ: Grace to you and peace. We give thanks to God always for you all, constantly mentioning you in our prayers, remembering before our God and Father your work of faith and labor of love and steadfastness of hope in our Lord Jesus Christ. For we know, brethren beloved by God, that he has chosen you; for our gospel came to you not only in word, but also in power and in the Holy Spirit and with full conviction. You know what kind of men we proved to be among you for your sake. And you became imitators of us and of the Lord, for you received the word in much affliction, with joy inspired by the Holy Spirit; so that you became an example to all the believers in Macedo'nia and in Acha'ia. For not only has the word of the Lord sounded forth from you in Macedo'nia and

Acha'ia, but your faith in God has gone forth everywhere, so that we need not say anything. For they themselves report concerning us what a welcome we had among you, and how you turned to God from idols, to serve a living and true God, and to wait for his Son from heaven, whom he raised from the dead, Jesus who delivers us from the wrath to come.

A Reading (Lesson) from the Gospel according to Luke [20:1-8]

One day, as Jesus was teaching the people in the temple and preaching the gospel, the chief priests and the scribes with the elders came up and said to him, "Tell us by what authority you do these things, or who it is that gave you this authority." He answered them, "I also will ask you a question; now tell me, Was the baptism of John from heaven or from men?" And they discussed it with one another, saying, "If we say, 'From heaven,' he will say, 'Why did you not believe him?' But if we say, 'From men,' all the people will stone us; for they are convinced that John was a prophet." So they answered that they did not know whence it was. And Jesus said to them, "Neither will I tell you by what authority I do these things."

Tuesday

Psalm 5 [page 588], *Psalm 6* [page 589] ❖
Psalm 10 [page 594], *Psalm 11* [page 596]

A Reading (Lesson) from the Book of Isaiah [1:21-31]

How the faithful city has become a harlot, she that was full of justice! Righteousness lodged in her, but now murderers. Your silver has become dross, your wine mixed with water. Your princes are rebels and companions of thieves. Every one loves a bribe and runs after gifts. They do not defend the fatherless, and the widow's cause does not come to them. Therefore the Lord says, the Lord of hosts, the Mighty One of Israel: "Ah, I will vent my wrath on my enemies, and avenge myself on my foes. I will turn my hand against you and will smelt away your dross as with lye and remove all your alloy. And I will restore your judges as at the first, and your counselors as at the beginning. Afterward you shall be called the city of righteousness, the faithful city." Zion shall be redeemed by justice, and those in her who repent, by righteousness. But rebels and sinners shall be destroyed together, and those who forsake the Lord shall be consumed. For you shall be ashamed of the oaks in which you delighted; and you shall blush for the gardens which you have chosen. For you shall be like an oak whose leaf withers, and like a garden without water. And the strong shall become tow, and his work a spark, and both of them shall burn together, with none to quench them.

A Reading (Lesson) from the First Letter of Paul to the Thessalonians [2:1-12]

You yourselves know, brethren, that our visit to you was not in vain; but though we had already suffered and been shamefully treated at Philippi, as you know, we had courage in our God in the face of great opposition. For our appeal does not spring from error or uncleanness, nor is it made with guile; but just as we have been approved by God to be entrusted with the gospel, so we speak, not to please men, but to please God who tests our hearts. For we never used either words of flattery, as you know, or a cloak for greed, as God is witness; nor did we seek glory from men, whether from you or from others, though we might have made demands as apostles of Christ. But we were gentle among you, like a nurse taking care of her children. So, being affectionately desirous of you, we were ready to share with you not only the gospel of God but also our own selves, because you had become very dear to us. For you remember our labor and toil, brethren; we worked night and day, that we might not burden any of you, while we preached to you the gospel of God. You are witnesses, and God also, how holy and righteous and blameless was our behavior to you believers; for you know how, like a father with his children, we exhorted each one of you and encouraged you and charged you to lead a life worthy of God, who calls you into his own kingdom and glory.

A Reading (Lesson) from the Gospel according to Luke [20:9-18]

Jesus began to tell the people this parable: "A man planted a vineyard, and let it out to tenants, and went into another country for a long while. When the time came, he sent a servant to the tenants, that they should give him some of the fruits of the vineyard; but the tenants beat him, and sent him away empty-handed. And he sent another servant; him also they treated shamefully, and sent him away empty-handed. And he sent yet a third; this one they wounded and cast out. Then the owner of the vineyard said, 'What shall I do? I will send my beloved son; it may be they will respect him.' But when the tenants saw him, they said to themselves, 'This is the heir; let us kill him, that the inheritance may be ours.' And they cast him out of the vineyard and killed him. What then will the owner of the vineyard do to them? He will come and destroy those tenants, and give the vineyard to others." When they heard this, they said, "God forbid!" But he looked at them and said, "What then is this that is written: 'The very stone which the builders rejected has become the head of the corner'? Every one who falls on that stone will be broken to pieces; but when it falls on any one it will crush him."

Wednesday

Psalm 119:1-24 [page 763] ❖ *Psalm 12* [page 597], *Psalm 13* [page 597], *Psalm 14* [page 598]

A Reading (Lesson) from the Book of Isaiah [2:1-11]

The word which Isaiah the son of Amoz saw concerning
Judah and Jerusalem. It shall come to pass in the latter
days that the mountain of the house of the Lord shall be
established as the highest of the mountains, and shall be
raised above the hills; and all the nations shall flow to it,
and many peoples shall come, and say: "Come, let us go
up to the mountain of the Lord, to the house of the God of
Jacob; that he may teach us his ways and that we may
walk in his paths." For out of Zion shall go forth the law,
and the word of the Lord from Jerusalem. He shall judge
between the nations, and shall decide for many peoples;
and they shall beat their swords into plowshares, and their
spears into pruning hooks; nation shall not lift up sword
against nation, neither shall they learn war any more. O
house of Jacob, come, let us walk in the light of the Lord.
For thou hast rejected thy people, the house of Jacob,
because they are full of diviners from the east and of
soothsayers like the Philistines, and they strike hands with
foreigners. Their land is filled with silver and gold, and
there is no end to their treasures; their land is filled with
horses, and there is no end to their chariots. Their land is
filled with idols; they bow down to the work of their
hands, to what their own fingers have made. So man is
humbled, and men are brought low—forgive them not!
Enter into the rock, and hide in the dust from before the
terror of the Lord, and from the glory of his majesty. The
haughty looks of man shall be brought low, and the pride
of men shall be humbled; and the Lord alone will be
exalted in that day.

*A Reading (Lesson) from the First Letter of Paul
to the Thessalonians* [2:13-20]

We also thank God constantly for this, that when you
received the word of God which you heard from us, you
accepted it not as the word of men but as what it really is,

the word of God, which is at work in you believers. For you, brethren, became imitators of the churches of God in Christ Jesus which are in Judea; for you suffered the same things from your own countrymen as they did from the Jews, who killed both the Lord Jesus and the prophets, and drove us out, and displease God and oppose all men by hindering us from speaking to the Gentiles that they may be saved—so as always to fill up the measure of their sins. But God's wrath has come upon them at last! But since we were bereft of you, brethren, for a short time, in person not in heart, we endeavored the more eagerly and with great desire to see you face to face; because we wanted to come to you—I, Paul, again and again—but Satan hindered us. For what is our hope or joy or crown of boasting before our Lord Jesus at his coming? Is it not you? For you are our glory and joy.

A Reading (Lesson) from the Gospel according to Luke
[20:19-26]

The scribes and the chief priests tried to lay hands on Jesus at that very hour, but they feared the people; for they perceived that he had told this parable against them. So they watched him, and sent spies, who pretended to be sincere, that they might take hold of what he said, so as to deliver him up to the authority and jurisdiction of the governor. They asked him, "Teacher, we know that you speak and teach rightly, and show no partiality, but truly teach the way of God. Is it lawful for us to give tribute to Caesar, or not?" But he perceived their craftiness, and said to them, "Show me a coin. Whose likeness and inscription has it?" They said, "Caesar's." He said to them, "Then render to Caesar the things that are Caesar's, and to God the things that are God's." And they were not able in the presence of the people to catch him by what he said; but marveling at his answer they were silent.

Thursday

Psalm 18:1-20 [page 602] ❖ *Psalm 18:21-50* [page 604]

A Reading (Lesson) from the Book of Isaiah [2:12-22]

The Lord of hosts has a day against all that is proud and lofty, against all that is lifted up and high; against all the cedars of Lebanon, lofty and lifted up; and against all the oaks of Bashan; against all the high mountains, and against all the lofty hills; against every high tower, and against every fortified wall; against all the ships of Tarshish, and against all the beautiful craft. And the haughtiness of man shall be humbled, and the pride of men shall be brought low; and the Lord alone will be exalted in that day. And the idols shall utterly pass away. And men shall enter the caves of the rocks and the holes of the ground, from before the terror of the Lord, and for the glory of his majesty, when he rises to terrify the earth. In that day men will cast forth their idols of silver and their idols of gold, which they made for themselves to worship, to the moles and to the bats, to enter the caverns of the rocks and the clefts of the cliffs, from before the terror of the Lord, and from the glory of his majesty, when he rises to terrify the earth. Turn away from man in whose nostrils is breath, for of what account is he?

A Reading (Lesson) from the First Letter of Paul to the Thessalonians [3:1-13]

When we could bear it no longer, we were willing to be left at Athens alone, and we sent Timothy, our brother and God's servant in the gospel of Christ, to establish you in your faith and to exhort you, that no one be moved by these afflictions. You yourselves know that this is to be our lot. For when we were with you, we told you beforehand that we were to suffer affliction; just as it has come to pass, and as you know. For this reason, when I could bear it no longer, I sent that I might know your faith, for fear that somehow the tempter had tempted you and that our labor would be in vain. But now that Timothy has come to us from you, and has brought us the good news of your faith and love and reported that you always remember us kindly and long to see us, as we long to see you—for this reason, brethren, in all our distress and affliction we have been comforted about you through your faith; for now we live, if you stand fast in the Lord. For what thanksgiving can we render to God for you, for all the joy which we feel for your sake before our God, praying earnestly night and day that we may see you face to face and supply what is lacking in your faith? Now may our God and Father himself, and our Lord Jesus, direct our way to you; and may the Lord make you increase and abound in love to one another and to all men, as we do to you, so that he may establish your hearts unblamable in holiness before our God and Father, at the coming of our Lord Jesus with all his saints.

A Reading (Lesson) from the Gospel according to Luke
[20:27-40]

There came to Jesus some Sad'ducees, those who say that there is no resurrection, and they asked him a question, saying, "Teacher, Moses wrote for us that if a man's brother dies, having a wife but no children, the man must take the wife and raise up children for his brother. Now there were seven brothers; the first took a wife, and died without children; and the second and the third took her, and likewise all seven left no children and died. Afterward the woman also died. In the resurrection, therefore, whose wife will the woman be? For the seven had her as wife." And Jesus said to them, "The sons of this age marry and are given in marriage; but those who are accounted worthy to attain to that age and to the resurrrection from the dead neither marry nor are given in marriage, for they cannot die any more, because they are equal to angels and are sons of God, being sons of the resurrection. But that the dead are raised, even Moses showed, in the passage about the bush, where he calls the Lord the God of Abraham and the God of Isaac and the God of Jacob. Now he is not God of the dead, but of the living; for all live to him." And some of the scribes answered, "Teacher, you have spoken well." For they no longer dared to ask him any question.

Friday

Psalm 16 [page 599], *Psalm 17* [page 600] ❖
Psalm 22 [page 610]

A Reading (Lesson) from the Book of Isaiah [3:8-15]

Jerusalem has stumbled, and Judah has fallen; because their speech and their deeds are against the Lord, defying his glorious presence. Their partiality witnesses against them; they proclaim their sin like Sodom, they do not hide it. Woe to them! For they have brought evil upon themselves. Tell the righteous that it shall be well with them, for they shall eat the fruit of their deeds. Woe to the wicked! It shall be ill with him, for what his hands have done shall be done to him. My people—children are their oppressors, and women rule over them. O my people, your leaders mislead you, and confuse the course of your paths. The Lord has taken his place to contend, he stands to judge his people. The Lord enters into judgment with the elders and princes of his people: "It is you who have devoured the vineyard, the spoil of the poor is in your houses. What do you mean by crushing my people, by grinding the face of the poor?" says the Lord God of hosts.

A Reading (Lesson) from the First Letter of Paul to the Thessalonians [4:1-12]

Finally, brethren, we beseech and exhort you in the Lord Jesus, that as you learned from us how you ought to live and to please God, just as you are doing, you do so more and more. For you know what instructions we gave you through the Lord Jesus. For this is the will of God, your sanctification: that you abstain from unchastity; that each of you know how to take a wife for himself in holiness and honor not in the passion of lust like heathen who do not know God; that no man transgress, and wrong his brother in this matter, because the Lord is an avenger in all these things, as we solemnly forewarned you. For God has not called us for uncleanness, but in holiness. Therefore whoever disregards this, disregards not man but God, who gives his Holy Spirit to you. But concerning love of the brethren you have no need to have any one write to you, for you yourselves have been taught by God to love one another; and indeed you do love all the brethren throughout Macedo'nia. But we exhort you, brethren, to do so more and more, to aspire to live quietly, to mind your own affairs, and to work with your hands, as we charged you; so that you may command the respect of outsiders, and be dependent on nobody.

A Reading (Lesson) from the Gospel according to Luke
[20:41—21:4]

Jesus said to the scribes, "How can they say that the Christ is David's son? For David himself says in the Book of Psalms, 'The Lord said to my Lord, Sit at my right hand, till I make thy enemies a stool for thy feet.' David thus calls him Lord; so how is he his son?" And in the hearing of all the people he said to his disciples, "Beware of the scribes, who like to go about in long robes, and love salutations in the market places and the best seats in the synagogues and the places of honor at feasts, who devour widows' houses and for a pretense make long prayers. They will receive the greater condemnation." He looked up and saw the rich putting their gifts into the treasury; and he saw a poor widow put in two copper coins. And he said, "Truly I tell you, this poor widow has put in more than all of them; for they all contributed out of their abundance, but she out of her poverty put in all the living that she had."

Saturday

Psalm 20 [page 608], *Psalm 21:1-7(8-14)* [page 608] ❖
Psalm 110:1-5(6-7) [page 753], *Psalm 116* [page 759],
Psalm 117 [page 760]

A Reading (Lesson) from the Book of Isaiah [4:2-6]

In that day the branch of the Lord shall be beautiful and glorious, and the fruit of the land shall be the pride and glory of the survivors of Israel. And he who is left in Zion and remains in Jerusalem will be called holy, every one who has been recorded for life in Jerusalem, when the Lord shall have washed away the filth of the daughters of Zion and cleansed the bloodstains of Jerusalem from its midst by a spirit of judgment and by a spirit of burning. Then the Lord will create over the whole site of Mount Zion and over her assemblies a cloud by day, and smoke and the shining of a flaming fire by night; for over all the glory there will be a canopy and a pavilion. It will be a shade by day from the heat, and for a refuge and a shelter from the storm and the rain.

A Reading (Lesson) from the First Letter of Paul to the Thessalonians [4:13-18]

We would not have you ignorant, brethren, concerning those who are asleep, that you may not grieve as others do who have no hope. For since we believe that Jesus died and rose again, even so, through Jesus, God will bring with him those who have fallen asleep. For this we declare to you by the word of the Lord, that we who are alive, who are left until the coming of the Lord, shall not precede those who have fallen asleep. For the Lord himself will descend from heaven with a cry of command, with the archangel's call, and with the sound of the trumpet of God. And the dead in Christ will rise first; then we who are alive, who are left, shall be caught up together with them in the clouds to meet the Lord in the air; and so we shall always be with the Lord. Therefore comfort one another with these words.

A Reading (Lesson) from the Gospel according to Luke
[21:5-19]

As some spoke of the temple, how it was adorned with noble stones and offerings, Jesus said, "As for these things which you see, the days will come when there shall not be left here one stone upon another that will not be thrown down." And they asked him, "Teacher, when will this be, and what will be the sign when this is about to take place?" And he said, "Take heed that you are not led astray; for many will come in my name, saying, 'I am he!' and, 'The time is at hand!' Do not go after them. And when you hear of wars and tumults, do not be terrified; for this must first take place, but the end will not be at once." Then he said to them, "Nation will rise against nation, and kingdom against kingdom; there will be great earthquakes, and in various places famines and pestilences; and there will be terrors and great signs from heaven. But before all this they will lay their hands on you and persecute you, delivering you up to the synagogues and prisons, and you will be brought before kings and governors for my name's sake. This will be a time for you to bear testimony. Settle it therefore in your minds, not to meditate beforehand how to answer; for I will give you a mouth and wisdom, which none of your adversaries will be able to withstand or contradict. You will be delivered up even by parents and brothers and kinsmen and friends, and some of you they will put to death; and you will be hated by all for my name's sake. But not a hair of your head will perish. By your endurance you will gain your lives."

Week of 2 Advent

Sunday

Psalm 148 [page 805],   *Psalm 149* [page 807],
Psalm 150 [page 807],   ❖   *Psalm 114* [page 756],
Psalm 115 [page 757]

A Reading (Lesson) from the Book of Isaiah [5:1-7]

Let me sing for my beloved a love song concerning his
vineyard: My beloved had a vineyard on a very fertile hill.
He digged it and cleared it of stones, and planted it with
choice vines; he built a watchtower in the midst of it, and
hewed out a wine vat in it; and he looked for it to yield
grapes, but it yielded wild grapes. And now, O inhabitants
of Jerusalem and men of Judah, judge, I pray you, between
me and my vineyard. What more was there to do for my
vineyard, that I have not done in it? When I looked for it to
yield grapes, why did it yield wild grapes? And now I will
tell you what I will do to my vineyard. I will remove its
hedge, and it shall be devoured; I will break down its wall,
and it shall be trampled down. I will make it a waste; it
shall not be pruned or hoed, and briers and thorns shall
grow up; I will also command the clouds that they rain no
rain upon it. For the vineyard of the Lord of hosts is the
house of Israel, and the men of Judah are his pleasant
planting; and he looked for justice, but behold, bloodshed;
for righteousness, but behold, a cry!

A Reading (Lesson) from the Second Letter of Peter
[3:11-18]

Since all these things are thus to be dissolved, what sort of
persons ought you to be in lives of holiness and godliness,
waiting for and hastening the coming of the day of God,
because of which the heavens will be kindled and
dissolved, and the elements will melt with fire! But

according to his promise we wait for new heavens and a new earth in which righteousness dwells. Therefore, beloved, since you wait for these, be zealous to be found by him without spot or blemish, and at peace. And count the forbearance of our Lord as salvation. So also our beloved brother Paul wrote to you according to the wisdom given him, speaking of this as he does in all his letters. There are some things in them hard to understand, which the ignorant and unstable twist to their own destruction, as they do the other scriptures. You therefore, beloved, knowing this beforehand, beware lest you be carried away with the error of lawless men and lose your own stability. But grow in the grace and knowledge of our Lord and Savior Jesus Christ. To him be the glory both now and to the day of eternity. Amen.

A Reading (Lesson) from the Gospel according to Luke
[7:28-35]

Jesus spoke to the crowds concerning John: "I tell you, among those born of women none is greater than John; yet he who is least in the kingdom of God is greater than he." (When they heard this all the people and the tax collectors justified God, having been baptized with the baptism of John; but the Pharisees and the lawyers rejected the purpose of God for themselves, not having been baptized by him.) "To what then shall I compare the men of this generation, and what are they like? They are like children sitting in the market place and calling to one another, 'We piped to you, and you did not dance; we wailed, and you did not weep.' For John the Baptist has come eating no bread and drinking no wine; and you say, 'He has a demon.' The Son of man has come eating and drinking; and you say, 'Behold, a glutton and a drunkard, a friend of tax collectors and sinners!' Yet wisdom is justified by all her children."

Monday

Psalm 25 [page 614] ❖ *Psalm 9* [page 593],
Psalm 15 [page 599]

A Reading (Lesson) from the Book of Isaiah [5:8-12,18-23]

Woe to those who join house to house, who add field to field, until there is no more room, and you are made to dwell alone in the midst of the land. The lord of hosts has sworn in my hearing: "Surely many houses shall be desolate, large and beautiful houses, without inhabitant. For ten acres of vineyard shall yield but one bath, and a homer of seed shall yield but an ephah." Woe to those who rise early in the morning, that they may run after strong drink, who tarry late into the evening till wine inflames them! They have lyre and harp, timbrel and flute and wine at their feasts; but they do not regard the deeds of the Lord, or see the work of his hands. Woe to those who draw iniquity with cords of falsehood, who draw sin as with cart ropes, who say: "Let him make haste, let him speed his work that we may see it; let the purpose of the Holy One of Israel draw near, and let it come, that we may know it!" Woe to those who call evil good and good evil, who put darkness for light and light for darkness, who put bitter for sweet and sweet for bitter! Woe to those who are wise in their own eyes, and shrewd in their own sight! Woe to those who are heroes at drinking wine, and valiant men in mixing strong drink, who acquit the guilty for a bribe, and deprive the innocent of his right!

A Reading (Lesson) from the First Letter of Paul to the Thessalonians [5:1-11]

As to the times and the seasons, brethren, you have no need to have anything written to you. For you yourselves know well that the day of the Lord will come like a thief in the night. When people say, "There is peace and security," then sudden destruction will come upon them as travail comes upon a woman with child, and there will be no escape. But you are not in darkness, brethren, for that day to surprise you like a thief. For you are all sons of light and sons of the day; we are not of the night or of the darkness. So then let us not sleep, as others do, but let us keep awake and be sober. For those who sleep sleep at night, and those who get drunk are drunk at night. But, since we belong to the day, let us be sober, and put on the breastplate of faith and love, and for a helmet the hope of salvation. For God has not destined us for wrath, but to obtain salvation through our Lord Jesus Christ, who died for us so that whether we wake or sleep we might live with him. Therefore encourage one another and build one another up, just as you are doing.

A Reading (Lesson) from the Gospel according to Luke [21:20-28]

In the hearing of all the people Jesus said to his disciples, "When you see Jerusalem surrounded by armies, then know that its desolation has come near. Then let those who are in Judea flee to the mountains, and let those who are inside the city depart, and let not those who are out in the country enter it; for these are days of vengeance, to fulfil all that is written. Alas for those who are with child and for those who give suck in those days! For great distress shall be upon the earth and wrath upon this people; they will fall by the edge of the sword, and be led captive among all nations; and Jerusalem will be trodden down by the Gentiles, until the times of the Gentiles are fulfilled. And there will be signs in sun and moon and stars, and upon the earth distress of nations in perplexity at the roaring of the sea and the waves, men fainting with fear and with foreboding of what is coming on the world; for the powers of the heavens will be shaken. And then they will see the Son of man coming in a cloud with power and great glory. Now when these things begin to take place, look up and raise your heads, because your redemption is drawing near."

Tuesday

Psalm 26 [page 616],   *Psalm 28* [page 619]   ❖
Psalm 36 [page 632],   *Psalm 39* [page 638]

A Reading (Lesson) from the Book of Isaiah [5:13-17,24-25]

My people go into exile for want of knowledge; their
honored men are dying of hunger, and their multitude is
parched with thirst. Therefore Sheol has enlarged its
appetite and opened its mouth beyond measure, and the
nobility of Jerusalem and her multitude go down, her
throng and he who exults in her. Man is bowed down, and
men are brought low, and the eyes of the haughty are
humbled. But the Lord of hosts is exalted in justice, and
the Holy God shows himself holy in righteousness. Then
shall the lambs graze as in their pasture, fatlings and kids
shall feed among the ruins. Therefore, as the tongue of fire
devours the stubble, and as dry grass sinks down in the
flame, so their root will be as rottenness, and their blossom
go up like dust; for they have rejected the law of the Lord
of hosts, and have despised the word of the Holy One of
Israel. Therefore the anger of the Lord was kindled against
his people, and he stretched out his hand against them and
smote them, and the mountains quaked; and their corpses
were as refuse in the midst of the streets. For all this his
anger is not turned away and his hand is stretched out still.

*A Reading (Lesson) from the First Letter of Paul
to the Thessalonians* [5:12-28]

We beseech you, brethren, to respect those who labor
among you and are over you in the Lord and admonish
you, and to esteem them very highly in love because of
their work. Be at peace among yourselves. And we exhort
you, brethren, admonish the idlers, encourage the
fainthearted, help the weak, be patient with them all. See

that none of you repays evil for evil, but always seek to do good to one another and to all. Rejoice always, pray constantly, give thanks in all circumstances; for this is the will of God in Christ Jesus for you. Do not quench the Spirit, do not despise prophesying, but test everything; hold fast what is good, abstain from every form of evil. May the God of peace himself sanctify you wholly; and may your spirit and soul and body be kept sound and blameless at the coming of our Lord Jesus Christ. He who calls you is faithful, and he will do it. Brethren, pray for us. Greet all the brethren with a holy kiss. I adjure you by the Lord that this letter be read to all the brethren. The grace of our Lord Jesus Christ be with you.

A Reading (Lesson) from the Gospel according to Luke
[21:29-38]

In the hearing of all the people, Jesus told the disciples a parable: "Look at the fig tree, and all the trees; as soon as they come out in leaf, you see for yourselves and know that the summer is already near. So also, when you see these things taking place, you know that the kingdom of God is near. Truly, I say to you, this generation will not pass away till all has taken place. Heaven and earth will pass away, but my words will not pass away. But take heed to yourselves lest your hearts be weighted down with dissipation and drunkenness and cares of this life, and that day come upon you suddenly like a snare; for it will come upon all who dwell upon the face of the whole earth. But watch at all times, praying that you may have strength to escape all these things that will take place, and to stand before the Son of man." And every day he was teaching in the temple, but at night he went out and lodged on the mount called Olivet. And early in the morning all the people came to him in the temple to hear him.

Wednesday

Psalm 38 [page 636] ❖ *Psalm 119:25-48* [page 765]

A Reading (Lesson) from the Book of Isaiah [6:1-13]

In the year that King Uzzi'ah died I saw the Lord sitting upon a throne, high and lifted up; and his train filled the temple. Above him stood the seraphim; each had six wings: with two he covered his face, and with two he covered his feet, and with two he flew. And one called to another and said: "Holy, holy, holy is the Lord of hosts; the whole earth is full of his glory." And the foundations of the thresholds shook at the voice of him who called, and the house was filled with smoke. And I said: "Woe is me! For I am lost; for I am a man of unclean lips, and I dwell in the midst of a people of unclean lips; for my eyes have seen the King, the Lord of hosts!" Then flew one of the seraphim to me, having in his hand a burning coal which he had taken with tongs from the altar. And he touched my mouth, and said: "Behold, this has touched your lips; your guilt is taken away, and your sin forgiven." And I heard the voice of the Lord saying, "Whom shall I send, and who will go for us?" Then I said, "Here am I! Send me." And he said, "Go, and say to this people: 'Hear and hear, but do not understand; see and see, but do not perceive.' Make the heart of this people fat, and their ears heavy, and shut their eyes; lest they see with their eyes, and hear with their ears, and understand with their hearts, and turn and be healed." Then I said, "How long, O Lord?" And he said: "Until cities lie waste without inhabitant, and houses without men, and the land is utterly desolate, and the Lord removes men far away, and the forsaken places are many in the midst of the land. And though a tenth remain in it, it will be burned again, like a terebinth or an oak, whose stump remains standing when it is felled." The holy seed is its stump.

A Reading (Lesson) from the Second Letter of Paul to the Thessalonians [1:1-12]

Paul, Silva'nus, and Timothy, To the church of the Thessalo'nians in God our Father and the Lord Jesus Christ: Grace to you and peace from God the Father and the Lord Jesus Christ. We are bound to give thanks to God always for you, brethren, as is fitting, because your faith is growing abundantly, and the love of every one of you for one another is increasing. Therefore we ourselves boast of you in the churches of God for your steadfastness and faith in all your persecutions and in the afflictions which you are enduring. This is evidence of the righteous judgment of God, that you may be made worthy of the kingdom of God, for which you are suffering—since indeed God deems it just to repay with affliction those who afflict you, and to grant rest with us to you who are afflicted, when the Lord Jesus is revealed from heaven with his mighty angels in flaming fire, inflicting vengeance upon those who do not know God and upon those who do not obey the gospel of our Lord Jesus. They shall suffer the punishment of eternal destruction and exclusion from the presence of the Lord and from the glory of his might, when he comes on that day to be glorified in his saints, and to be marveled at in all who have believed, because our testimony to you was believed. To this end we always pray for you, that our God may make you worthy of his call, and may fulfil every good resolve and work of faith by his power, so that the name of our Lord Jesus may be glorified in you, and you in him, according to the grace of our God and the Lord Jesus Christ.

A Reading (Lesson) from the Gospel according to John [7:53—8:11]

They each went to his own house, but Jesus went to the Mount of Olives. Early in the morning he came again to the temple; all the people came to him, and he sat down and taught them. The scribes and the Pharisees brought a woman who had been caught in adultery, and placing her in the midst they said to him, "Teacher, this woman has been caught in the act of adultery. Now in the law Moses commanded us to stone such. What do you say about her?" This they said to test him, that they might have some charge to bring against him. Jesus bent down and wrote with his finger on the ground. And as they continued to ask him, he stood up and said to them, "Let him who is without sin among you be the first to throw a stone at her." And once more he bent down and wrote with his finger on the ground. But when they heard it, they went away, one by one, beginning with the eldest, and Jesus was left alone with the woman standing before him. Jesus looked up and said to her, "Woman, where are they? Has no one condemned you?" She said, "No one, Lord." And Jesus said, "Neither do I condemn you; go, and do not sin again."

Thursday

Psalm 37:1-18 [page 633]   ❖   *Psalm 37:19-42* [page 634]

A Reading (Lesson) from the Book of Isaiah [7:1-9]

In the days of Ahaz the son of Jotham, son of Uzzi'ah, king of Judah, Rezin the king of Syria and Pekah the son of Remali'ah the king of Israel came to Jerusalem to wage war against it, but they could not conquer it. When the house of David was told, "Syria is in league with E'phraim," his heart and the heart of his people shook as the trees of the forest shake before the wind. And the Lord said to Isaiah, "Go forth to meet Ahaz, you and She'ar-jash'ub your son, at the end of the conduit of the upper pool on the highway to the Fuller's Field, and say to him, 'Take heed, be quiet, do not fear, and do not let your heart be faint because of these two smoldering stumps of firebrands, at the fierce anger of Rezin and Syria and the son of Remali'ah. Because Syria, with E'phraim and the son of Remali'ah, has devised evil against you, saying, "Let us go up against Judah and terrify it, and let us conquer it for ourselves, and set up the son of Ta'be-el as king in the midst of it," thus says the Lord God: It shall not stand, and it shall not come to pass. For the head of Syria is Damascus, and the head of Damascus is Rezin. (Within sixty-five years E'phraim will be broken to pieces so that it will no longer be a people.) And the head of E'phraim is Samar'ia, and the head of Samar'ia is the son of Remali'ah. If you will not believe, surely you shall not be established.' "

A Reading (Lesson) from the Second Letter of Paul to the Thessalonians [2:1-12]

Now concerning the coming of our Lord Jesus Christ and our assembling to meet him, we beg you, brethren, not to be quickly shaken in mind or excited, either by spirit or by word, or by letter purporting to be from us, to the effect that the day of the Lord has come. Let no one deceive you in any way; for that day will not come, unless the rebellion comes first, and the man of lawlessness is revealed, the son of perdition, who opposes and exalts himself against every so-called god or object of worship, so that he takes his seat in the temple of God, proclaiming himself to be God. Do you not remember that when I was still with you I told you this? And you know what is restraining him now so that he may be revealed in his time. For the mystery of lawlessness is already at work; only he who now restrains it will do so until he is out of the way. And then the lawless one will be revealed, and the Lord Jesus will slay him with the breath of his mouth and destroy him by his appearing and his coming. The coming of the lawless one by the activity of Satan will be with all power and with pretended signs and wonders, and with all wicked deception for those who are to perish, because they refused to love the truth and so be saved. Therefore God sends upon them a strong delusion, to make them believe what is false, so that all may be condemned who did not believe the truth but had pleasure in unrighteousness.

A Reading (Lesson) from the Gospel according to Luke
[22:1-13]

Now the feast of Unleavened Bread drew near, which is
called the Passover. And the chief priests and the scribes
were seeking how to put him to death; for they feared the
people. Then Satan entered into Judas called Iscariot, who
was of the number of the twelve; he went away and
conferred with the chief priests and officers how he might
betray him to them. And they were glad, and engaged to
give him money. So he agreed, and sought an opportunity
to betray him to them in the absence of the multitude.
Then came the day of Unleavened Bread, on which the
passover lamb had to be sacrificed. So Jesus sent Peter and
John, saying, "Go and prepare the passover for us, that we
may eat it." They said to him, "Where will you have us
prepare it? He said to them, "Behold, when you have
entered the city, a man carrying a jar of water will meet
you; follow him into the house which he enters, and tell
the householder, 'The Teacher says to you, Where is the
guest room, where I am to eat the passover with my
disciples?'" And he will show you a large upper room
furnished; there make ready." And they went, and found it
as he had told them; and they prepared the passover.

Friday

Psalm 31 [page 662]   ❖   *Psalm 35* [page 629]

A Reading (Lesson) from the Book of Isaiah [7:10-25]

Again the Lord spoke to Ahaz, "Ask a sign of the Lord
your God; let it be deep as Sheol or high as heaven." But
Ahaz said, "I will not ask, and I will not put the Lord to
the test." And he said, "Hear then, O house of David! Is it
too little for you to weary men, that you weary my God
also? Therefore the Lord himself will give you a sign.
Behold, a young woman shall conceive and bear a son, and

shall call his name Imman'u-el. He shall eat curds and honey when he knows how to refuse evil and choose the good. For before the child knows how to refuse the evil and choose the good, the land before whose two kings you are in dread will be deserted. The Lord will bring upon you and upon your people and upon your father's house such days as have not come since the day that E'phraim departed from Judah—the king of Assyria." In that day the Lord will whistle for the fly which is at the sources of the streams of Egypt, and for the bee which is in the land of Assyria. And they will all come and settle in the steep ravines, and in the clefts of the rocks, and on all the thornbushes, and on all the pastures. In that day the Lord will shave with a razor which is hired beyond the River—with the king of Assyria—the head and the hair of the feet, and it will sweep away the beard also. In that day a man will keep alive a young cow and two sheep; and because of the abundance of milk which they give, he will eat curds; for every one that is left in the land will eat curds and honey. In that day every place where there used to be a thousand vines, worth a thousand shekels of silver, will become briers and thorns. With bow and arrows men will come there, for all the land will be briers and thorns; and as for all the hills which used to be hoed with a hoe, you will not come there for fear of briers and thorns; but they will become a place where cattle are let loose and where sheep tread.

A Reading (Lesson) from the Second Letter of Paul to the Thessalonians [2:13—3:5]

We are bound to give thanks to God always for you, brethren beloved by the Lord, because God chose you from the beginning to be saved, through sanctification by the Spirit and belief in the truth. To this he called you through our gospel, so that you may obtain the glory of our Lord Jesus Christ. So then, brethren, stand firm and hold to the traditions which you were taught by us, either by word of mouth or by letter. Now may our Lord Jesus Christ himself, and God our Father, who loved us and gave us eternal comfort and good hope through grace, comfort your hearts and establish them in every good work and word. Finally, brethren, pray for us, that the word of the Lord may speed on and triumph, as it did among you, and that we may be delivered from wicked and evil men; for not all have faith. But the lord is faithful; he will strengthen you and guard you from evil. And we have confidence in the Lord about you, that you are doing and will do the things which we command. May the Lord direct your hearts to the love of God and to the steadfastness of Christ.

A Reading (Lesson) from the Gospel according to Luke
[22:14-30]

When the hour for the passover came, Jesus sat at table, and the apostles with him. And he said to them, "I have earnestly desired to eat this passover with you before I suffer; for I tell you I shall not eat it until it is fulfilled in the kingdom of God." And he took a cup, and when he had given thanks he said, "Take this, and divide it among yourselves; for I tell you that from now on I shall not drink of the fruit of the vine until the kingdom of God comes." And he took bread, and when he had given thanks he broke it and gave it to them, saying, "This is my body which is given for you. Do this in remembrance of me." And likewise the cup after supper, saying, "This cup which is poured out for you is the new covenant in my blood. But behold the hand of him who betrays me is with me on the table. For the Son of man goes as it has been determined; but woe to that man by whom he is betrayed!" And they began to question one another, which of them it was that would do this. A dispute also arose among them, which of them was to be regarded as the greatest. And he said to them, "The kings of the Gentiles exercise lordship over them; and those in authority over them are called benefactors. But not so with you; rather let the greatest among you become as the youngest, and the leader as one who serves. For which is greater, one who sits at table, or one who serves? Is it not the one who sits at table? But I am among you as one who serves. You are those who have continued with me in my trials; and I assign to you, as my Father assigned to me, a kingdom, that you may eat and drink at my table in my kingdom, and sit on thrones judging the twelve tribes of Israel."

Saturday

Psalm 30 [page 621], *Psalm 32* [page 624] ❖
Psalm 42 [page 643], *Psalm 43* [page 644]

A Reading (Lesson) from the Book of Isaiah [8:1-15]

The Lord said to me, "Take a large tablet and write upon it in common characters, 'Belonging to Ma′her-shal′al-hash-baz.'" And I got reliable witnesses, Uri′ah the priest and Zechari′ah the son of Jeberechi′ah, to attest for me. And I went to the prophetess, and she conceived and bore a son. Then the Lord said to me, "Call his name Ma′her-shal′al-hash-baz; for before the child knows how to cry 'My father' or 'My mother,' the wealth of Damascus and the spoil of Samar′ia will be carried away before the king of Assyria." The Lord spoke to me again: "Because this people have refused the waters of Shilo′ah that flow gently, and melt in fear before Rezin and the son of Remali′ah; therefore, behold, the Lord is bringing up against them the waters of the River, mighty and many, the king of Assyria and all his glory; and it will rise over all its channels and go over all its banks; and it will sweep on into Judah, it will overflow and pass on, reaching even to the neck; and its outspread wings will fill the breadth of your land, O Imman′u-el." Be broken, you peoples, and be dismayed; give ear, all you far countries; gird yourselves and be dismayed; gird yourselves and be dismayed. Take counsel together, but it will come to nought; speak a word, but it will not stand, for God is with us. For the Lord spoke thus to me with his strong hand upon me, and warned me not to walk in the way of this people, saying: "Do not call conspiracy all that this people call conspiracy, and do not fear what they fear, nor be in dread. But the Lord of hosts, him you shall regard as holy; let him be your fear, and let him be your dread. And he will become a sanctuary, and a stone of offense, and a rock of stumbling to both houses of Israel, a trap and a snare to the inhabitants of Jerusalem. And many shall stumble thereon; they shall fall and be broken; they shall be snared and taken."

A Reading (Lesson) from the Second Letter of Paul to the Thessalonians [3:6-18]

We command you, brethren, in the name of our Lord Jesus Christ, that you keep away from any brother who is living in idleness and not in accord with the tradition that you received from us. For you yourselves know how you ought to imitate us; we were not idle when we were with you, we did not eat any one's bread without paying, but with toil and labor we worked night and day, that we might not burden any of you. It was not because we have not that right, but to give you in our conduct an example to imitate. For even when we were with you, we gave you this command: If any one will not work, let him not eat. For we hear that some of you are living in idleness, mere busybodies, not doing any work. Now such persons we command and exhort in the Lord Jesus Christ to do their work in quietness and to earn their own living. Brethren, do not be weary in well-doing. If any one refuses to obey what we say in this letter, note that man, and have nothing to do with him, that he may be ashamed. Do not look on him as an enemy, but warn him as a brother. Now may the

Lord of peace himself give you peace at all times in all ways. The Lord be with you all. I, Paul, write this greeting with my own hand. This is the mark in every letter of mine; it is the way I write. The grace of our Lord Jesus Christ be with you all.

A Reading (Lesson) from the Gospel according to Luke [22:31-38]

Jesus said to Peter, "Simon, Simon, behold, Satan demanded to have you, that he might sift you like wheat, but I have prayed for you that your faith may not fail; and when you have turned again, strengthen your brethren." And he said to him, "Lord, I am ready to go with you to prison and to death." He said, "I tell you, Peter, the cock will not crow this day, until you three times deny that you know me." And he said to them, "When I sent you out with no purse or bag or sandals, did you lack anything?" They said, "Nothing." He said to them, "But now, let him who has a purse take it, and likewise a bag. And let him who has no sword sell his mantle and buy one. For I tell you that this scripture must be fulfilled in me, 'And he was reckoned with transgressors'; for what is written about me has its fulfilment." And they said, "Look, Lord, here are two swords." And he said to them, "It is enough."

Week of 3 Advent

Sunday

Psalm 63:1-8(9-11) [page 670],
Psalm 98 [page 727]   ❖   *Psalm 103* [page 733]

A Reading (Lesson) from the Book of Isaiah [13:6-13]

Wail, for the day of the Lord is near; as destruction from the Almighty it will come! Therefore all hands will be feeble, and every man's heart will melt, and they will be dismayed. Pangs and agony will seize them; they will be in anguish like a woman in travail. They will look aghast at one another; their faces will be aflame. Behold, the day of the Lord comes, cruel, with wrath and fierce anger, to make the earth a desolation and to destroy its sinners from it. For the stars of the heavens and their constellations will not give their light; the sun will be dark at its rising and the moon will not shed its light. I will punish the world for its evil, and the wicked for their iniquity; I will put an end to the pride of the arrogant, and lay low the haughtiness of the ruthless. I will make men more rare than fine gold, and mankind than the gold of Ophir. Therefore I will make the heavens tremble, and the earth will be shaken out of its place, at the wrath of the Lord of hosts in the day of his fierce anger.

A Reading (Lesson) from the Letter to the Hebrews
[12:18-29]

You have not come to what may be touched, a blazing fire, and darkness, and gloom, and a tempest, and the sound of a trumpet, and a voice whose words made the hearers entreat that no further messages be spoken to them. For they could not endure the order that was given, "If even a beast touches the mountain, it shall be stoned." Indeed, so terrifying was the sight that Moses said, "I tremble with fear." But you have come to Mount Zion and to the city of the living God, the heavenly Jerusalem, and to innumerable angels in festal gathering, and to the assembly of the first-born who are enrolled in heaven, and to a judge who is God of all, and to the spirits of just men made perfect, and to Jesus the mediator of a new covenant, and to the sprinkled blood that speaks more graciously than the blood of Abel. See that you do not refuse him who is speaking. For if they did not escape when they refused him who warned them on earth, much less shall we escape if we reject him who warns from heaven. His voice then shook the earth; but now he has promised, "Yet once more I will shake not only the earth but also the heaven." This phrase, "Yet once more," indicates the removal of what is shaken, as of what has been made, in order that what cannot be shaken may remain. Therefore let us be grateful for receiving a kingdom that cannot be shaken, and thus let us offer to God acceptable worship, with reverence and awe; for our God is a consuming fire.

A Reading (Lesson) from the Gospel according to John [3:22-30]

After speaking with Nicode'mus Jesus and his disciples went into the land of Judea; there he remained with them and baptized. John also was baptizing at Ae'non near Salim, because there was much water there; and people came and were baptized. For John had not yet been put in prison. Now a discussion arose between John's disciples and a Jew over purifying. And they came to John, and said to him, "Rabbi, he who was with you beyond the Jordan, to whom you bore witness, here he is, baptizing, and all are going to him." John answered, "No one can receive anything except what is given him from heaven. You yourselves bear me witness, that I said, I am not the Christ, but I have been sent before him. He who has the bride is the bridegroom; the friend of the bridegroom who stands and hears him, rejoices greatly at the bridegroom's voice; therefore this joy of mine is now full. He must increase, but I must decrease."

Monday

Psalm 41 [page 641], *Psalm 52* [page 657] ❖
Psalm 44 [page 645]

A Reading (Lesson) from the Book of Isaiah [8:16—9:1]

Bind up the testimony, seal the teaching among my disciples. I will wait for the Lord, who is hiding his face from the house of Jacob, and I will hope in him. Behold, I and the children whom the Lord has given me are signs and portents in Israel from the Lord of hosts, who dwells on Mount Zion. And when they say to you, "Consult the mediums and the wizards who chirp and mutter," should not a people consult their God? Should they consult the dead on behalf of the living? To the teaching and to the testimony! Surely for this word which they speak there is no dawn. They will pass through the land, greatly distressed and hungry; and when they are hungry, they will be enraged and will curse their king and their God, and turn their faces upward; and they will look to the earth, but behold, distress and darkness, the gloom of anguish; and they will be thrust into thick darkness. But there will be no gloom for her that was in anguish. In the former time he brought into contempt the land of Zeb'ulun and the land of Naph'tali, but in the latter time he will make glorious the way of the sea, the land beyond the Jordan, Galilee of the nations.

A Reading (Lesson) from the Second Letter of Peter
[1:1-11]

Simeon Peter, a servant and apostle of Jesus Christ, To those who have obtained a faith of equal standing with ours in the righteousness of our God and Savior Jesus Christ: May grace and peace be multiplied to you in the knowledge of God and of Jesus our Lord. His divine power has granted to us all things that pertain to life and godliness, through the knowledge of him who called us to his own glory and excellence, by which he has granted to us his precious and very great promises, that through these you may escape from the corruption that is in the world because of passion, and become partakers of the divine nature. For this very reason make every effort to supplement your faith with virtue, and virtue with knowledge, and knowledge with self-control, and self-control with steadfastness, and steadfastness with godliness, and godliness with brotherly affection, and brotherly affection with love. For if these things are yours and abound, they keep you from being ineffective or unfruitful in the knowledge of our Lord Jesus Christ. For whoever lacks these things is blind and shortsighted and has forgotten that he was cleansed from his old sins. Therefore, brethren, be the more zealous to confirm your call and election, for if you do this you will never fall; so there will be richly provided for you an entrance into the eternal kingdom of our Lord and Savior Jesus Christ.

A Reading (Lesson) from the Gospel according to Luke [22:39-53]

Jesus came out of the upper room, and went, as was his custom, to the Mount of Olives; and the disciples followed him. And when he came to the place he said to them, "Pray that you may not enter into temptation." And he withdrew from them about a stone's throw, and knelt down and prayed, "Father, if thou art willing, remove this cup from me; nevertheless not my will, but thine, be done," And when he rose from prayer, he came to the disciples and found them sleeping for sorrow, and he said to them, "Why do you sleep? Rise and pray that you may not enter into temptation." While he was still speaking, there came a crowd, and the man called Judas, one of the twelve, was leading them. He drew near to Jesus to kiss him; but Jesus said to him, "Judas, would you betray the Son of man with a kiss?" And when those who were about him saw what would follow, they said, "Lord, shall we strike with the sword?" And one of them struck the slave of the high priest and cut off his right ear. But Jesus said, "No more of this!" And he touched his ear and healed him. Then Jesus said to the chief priests and officers of the temple and elders, who had come out against him, "Have you come out as against a robber, with swords and clubs? When I was with you day after day in the temple, you did not lay hands on me. But this is your hour, and the power of darkness."

Tuesday

Psalm 45 [page 647] ❖ *Psalm 47* [page 650],
Psalm 48 [page 651]

A Reading (Lesson) from the Book of Isaiah [9:1-7]

There will be no gloom for her that was in anguish. In the
former time he brought into contempt the land of Zeb'ulun
and the land of Naph'tali, but in the latter time he will
make glorious the way of the sea, the land beyond the
Jordan, Galilee of the nations. The people who walked in
darkness have seen a great light; those who dwelt in a land
of deep darkness, on them has light shined. Thou hast
multiplied the nation, thou hast increased its joy; they
rejoice before thee as with joy at the harvest, as men rejoice
when they divide the spoil. For the yoke of his burden, and
the staff for his shoulder, the rod of his oppressor, thou
hast broken as on the day of Mid'ian. For every boot of the
tramping warrior in battle tumult and every garment
rolled in blood will be burned as fuel for the fire. For to us
a child is born, to us a son is given; and the government
will be upon his shoulder, and his name will be called
"Wonderful Counselor, Mighty God, Everlasting Father,
Prince of Peace." Of the increase of his government and of
peace there will be no end, upon the throne of David, and
over his kingdom, to establish it, and to uphold it with
justice and with righteousness from this time forth and for
evermore. The zeal of the Lord of hosts will do this.

A Reading (Lesson) from the Second Letter of Peter
[1:12-21]

I intend always to remind you of these things, though you
know them and are established in the truth that you have. I
think it right, as long as I am in this body, to arouse you by
way of reminder, since I know that the putting off of my
body will be soon, as our Lord Jesus Christ showed me.

And I will see to it that after my departure you may be able at any time to recall these things. For we did not follow cleverly devised myths when we made known to you the power and coming of our Lord Jesus Christ, but we were eyewitnesses of his majesty. For when he received honor and glory from God the Father and the voice was borne to him by the Majestic Glory, "This is my beloved Son, with whom I am well pleased," we heard this voice borne from heaven, for we were with him on the holy mountain. And we have the prophetic word made more sure. You will do well to pay attention to this as to a lamp shining in a dark place, until the day dawns and the morning star rises in your hearts. First of all you must understand this, that no prophecy of scripture is a matter of one's own interpretation, because no prophecy ever came by the impulse of man, but men moved by the Holy Spirit spoke from God.

A Reading (Lesson) from the Gospel according to Luke
[22:54-69]

The crowd then seized Jesus and led him away, bringing him into the high priest's house. Peter followed at a distance; and when they had kindled a fire in the middle of the courtyard and sat down together, Peter sat among them. Then a maid, seeing him as he sat in the light and gazing at him, said, "This man also was with him." But he denied it, saying, "Woman, I do not know him." And a little later some one else saw him and said, "You also are one of them." But Peter said, "Man, I am not." And after an interval of about an hour, still another insisted, saying, "Certainly this man also was with him; for he is a Galilean." But Peter said, "Man, I do not know what you are saying." And immediately, while he was still speaking, the cock crowed. And the Lord turned and looked at Peter. And Peter remembered the word of the Lord, how he had said to him, "Before the cock crows today, you will deny me three times." And he went out and wept bitterly. Now the men who were holding Jesus mocked him and beat him; they also blindfolded him and asked him, "Prophesy! Who is it that struck you?" And they spoke many other words against him, reviling him. When day came, the assembly of the elders of the people gathered together, both chief priests and scribes; and they led him away to their council, and they said, "If you are the Christ, tell us." But he said to them, "If I tell you, you will not believe; and if I ask you, you will not answer. But from now on the Son of man shall be seated at the right hand of the power of God."

Wednesday

Psalm 119:49-72 [page 767]   ❖
Psalm 49 [page 652],   *(Psalm 53* [page 658])

A Reading (Lesson) from the Book of Isaiah [9:8-17]

The Lord has sent a word against Jacob, and it will light upon Israel; and all the people will know, E'phraim and the inhabitants of Samar'ia, who say in pride and in arrogance of heart: "The bricks have fallen, but we will build with dressed stones; the sycamores have been cut down, but we will put cedars in their place." So the Lord raises adversaries against them, and stirs up their enemies. The Syrians on the east and the Philistines on the west devour Israel with open mouth. For all this his anger is not turned away and his hand is stretched out still. The people did not turn to him who smote them, nor seek the Lord of hosts. So the Lord cut off from Israel head and tail, palm branch and reed in one day—the elder and honored man is the head, and the prophet who teaches lies is the tail; for those who lead this people lead them astray, and those who are led by them are swallowed up. Therefore the Lord does not rejoice over their young men, and has no compassion on their fatherless and widows; for every one is godless and an evildoer, and every mouth speaks folly. For all this his anger is not turned away and his hand is stretched out still.

A Reading (Lesson) from the Second Letter of Peter
[2:1-10a]

False prophets also arose among the people, just as there
will be false teachers among you, who will secretly bring in
destructive heresies, even denying the Master who bought
them, bringing upon themselves swift destruction. And
many will follow their licentiousness, and because of them
the way of truth will be reviled. And in their greed they will
exploit you with false words; from of old their
condemnation has not been idle, and their destruction has
not been asleep. For if God did not spare the angels when
they sinned, but cast them into hell and committed them to
pits of nether gloom to be kept until the judgment; if he did
not spare the ancient world, but preserved Noah, a herald
of righteousness, with seven other persons, when he
brought a flood upon the world of the ungodly; if by
turning the cities of Sodom and Gomor'rah to ashes he
condemned them to extinction and made them an example
of those who were to be ungodly; and if he rescued
righteous Lot, greatly distressed by the licentiousness of
the wicked (for by what that righteous man saw and heard
as he lived among them, he was vexed in his righteous soul
day after day with their lawless deeds), then the Lord
knows how to rescue the godly from trial, and to keep the
unrighteous under punishment until the day of judgment,
and especially those who indulge in the lust of defiling
passion and despise authority.

A Reading (Lesson) from the Gospel according to Mark
[1:1-8]

The beginning of the gospel of Jesus Christ, the son of
God. As it is written in Isaiah the prophet, "Behold, I send
my messenger before thy face, who shall prepare thy way;
the voice of one crying in the wilderness: Prepare the way
of the Lord, make his paths straight—" John the baptizer
appeared in the wilderness, preaching a baptism of

repentance for the forgiveness of sins. And there went out to him all the country of Judea, and all the people of Jerusalem; and they were baptized by him in the river Jordan, confessing their sins. Now John was clothed with camel's hair, and had a leather girdle around his waist, and ate locusts and wild honey. And he preached, saying, "After me comes he who is mightier than I, the thong of whose sandals I am not worthy to stoop down and untie. I have baptized you with water; but he will baptize you with the Holy Spirit."

Thursday

Psalm 50 [page 654] ❖ *(Psalm 59* [page 665],
Psalm 60 [page 667]) *or* *Psalm 33* [page 626]

A Reading (Lesson) from the Book of Isaiah [9:18—10:4]

Wickedness burns like a fire, it consumes briers and thorns; it kindles the thickets of the forest, and they roll upward in a column of smoke. Through the wrath of the Lord of hosts the land is burned, and the people are like fuel for the fire; no man spares his brother. They snatch on the right, but are still hungry, and they devour on the left, but are not satisfied; each devours his neighbor's flesh, Manas'seh E'phraim, and E'phraim Manas'seh, and together they are against Judah. For all this his anger is not turned away and his hand is stretched out still. Woe to those who decree iniquitous decrees, and the writers who keep writing oppression, to turn aside the needy from justice and to rob the poor of my people of their right, that widows may be their spoil, and that they may make the fatherless their prey! What will you do on the day of punishment, in the storm which will come from afar? To whom will you flee for help, and where will you leave your wealth? Nothing remains but to crouch among the prisoners or fall among the slain. For all this his anger is not turned away and his hand is stretched out still.

A Reading (Lesson) from the Second Letter of Peter
[2:10b-16]

Bold and wilful, they are not afraid to revile the glorious
ones, whereas angels, though greater in might and power,
do not pronounce a reviling judgment upon them before
the Lord. But these, like irrational animals, creatures of
instinct, born to be caught and killed, reviling in matters of
which they are ignorant, will be destroyed in the same
destruction with them, suffering wrong for their
wrongdoing. They count it pleasure to revel in the
daytime. They are blots and blemishes, reveling in their
dissipation, carousing with you. They have eyes full of
adultery, insatiable for sin. They entice unsteady souls.
They have hearts trained in greed. Accursed children!
Forsaking the right way they have gone astray; they have
followed the way of Balaam, the son of Be'or, who loved
gain from wrongdoing, but was rebuked for his own
transgression; a dumb ass spoke with human voice and
restrained the prophet's madness.

A Reading (Lesson) from the Gospel according to Matthew
[3:1-12]

In those days came John the Baptist, preaching in the
wilderness of Judea, "Repent, for the kingdom of heaven is
at hand." For this is he who was spoken of by the prophet
Isaiah when he said, "The voice of one crying in the
wilderness: Prepare the way of the Lord, make his paths
straight." Now John wore a garment of camel's hair, and a
leather girdle around his waist; and his food was locusts
and wild honey. Then went out to him Jerusalem and all
Judea and all the region about the Jordan, and they were
baptized by him in the river Jordan, confessing their sins.
But when he saw many of the Pharisees and Sad'ducees
coming for baptism, he said to them, "You brood of
vipers! Who warned you to flee from the wrath to come?
Bear fruit that befits repentance, and do not presume to say

to yourselves, 'We have Abraham as our father'; for I tell you, God is able from these stones to raise up children to Abraham. Even now the axe is laid to the root of the trees; every tree therefore that does not bear good fruit is cut down and thrown into the fire. I baptize you with water for repentance, but he who is coming after me is mightier than I, whose sandals I am not worthy to carry; he will baptize you with the Holy Spirit and with fire. His winnowing fork is in his hand, and he will clear his threshing floor and gather his wheat into the granary, but the chaff he will burn with unquenchable fire."

Friday

Psalm 40 [page 640],   *Psalm 54* [page 659]   ❖
Psalm 51 [page 656]

A Reading (Lesson) from the Book of Isaiah [10:5-19]

Ah, Assyria, the rod of my anger, the staff of my fury! Against a godless nation I send him, and against the people of my wrath I command him, to take spoil and seize plunder, and to tread them down like the mire of the streets. But he does not so intend, and his mind does not so think; but it is in his mind to destroy, and to cut off nations not a few; for he says: "Are not my commanders all kings? Is not Calno like Car'chemish? Is not Hamath like Arpad? Is not Samar'ia like Damascus? As my hand has reached to the kingdoms of the idols whose graven images were greater than those of Jerusalem and Samar'ia, shall I not do to Jerusalem and her idols as I have done to Samar'ia and her images?" When the Lord has finished all his work on Mount Zion and on Jerusalem he will punish the arrogant boasting of the king of Assyria and his haughty pride. For he says: "By the strength of my hand I have done it, and by my wisdom, for I have understanding; I have removed the boundaries of peoples, and have plundered their treasures; like a bull I have brought down those who sat on thrones. My hand has found like a nest the wealth of the peoples; and as men gather eggs that have been forsaken so I have gathered all the earth; and there was none that moved a wing, or opened the mouth, or chirped." Shall the axe vaunt itself over him who hews with it, or the saw magnify itself against him who wields it? As if a rod should wield him who lifts it, or as if a staff should lift him who is not wood! Therefore the Lord, the Lord of hosts, will send wasting sickness among his stout warriors, and under his glory a burning will be kindled, like the burning of fire. The light of Israel will become a fire, and his Holy One a flame; and it will burn and devour his thorns and briers in one day. The glory of his forest and of his fruitful land the Lord will destroy, both soul and body, and it will be as when a sick man wastes away. The remnant of the trees of his forest will be so few that a child can write them down.

A Reading (Lesson) from the Second Letter of Peter
[2:17-22]

These are waterless springs and mists driven by a storm; for them the nether gloom of darkness has been reserved. For, uttering loud boasts of folly, they entice with licentious passions of the flesh men who have barely escaped from those who live in error. They promise them freedom, but they themselves are slaves of corruption; for whatever overcomes a man, to that he is enslaved. For if, after they have escaped the defilements of the world through the knowledge of our Lord and Savior Jesus Christ, they are again entangled in them and overpowered, the last state has become worse for them than the first. For it would have been better for them never to have known the way of righteousness than after knowing it to turn back from the holy commandment delivered to them. It has happened to them according to the true proverb, The dog turns back to his own vomit, and the sow is washed only to wallow in the mire.

A Reading (Lesson) from the Gospel according to Matthew
[11:2-15]

When John heard in prison about the deeds of the Christ,
he sent word by his disciples and said to him, "Are you he
who is to come, or shall we look for another?" And Jesus
answered them, "Go and tell John what you hear and see:
the blind receive their sight and the lame walk, lepers are
cleansed and the deaf hear, and the dead are raised up, and
the poor have good news preached to them. And blessed is
he who takes no offense at me." As they went away, Jesus
began to speak to the crowd concerning John: "What did
you go out into the wilderness to behold? A reed shaken by
the wind? Why then did you go out? To see a man clothed
in soft raiment? Behold, those who wear soft raiment are
in kings' houses. Why then did you go out? To see a
prophet? Yes, I tell you, and more than a prophet. This is
he of whom it is written, 'Behold, I send my messenger
before thy face, who shall prepare thy way before thee.'
Truly, I say to you, among those born of women there has
risen no one greater than John the Baptist; yet he who is
least in the kingdom of heaven is greater than he. From the
days of John the Baptist until now the kingdom of heaven
has suffered violence, and men of violence take it by force.
For all the prophets and the law prophesied until John;
and if you are willing to accept it, he is Eli'jah who is to
come. He who has ears to hear, let him hear."

Saturday

Psalm 55 [page 660]   ❖   *Psalm 138* [page 793],
Psalm 139:1-17(18-23) [page 794]

A Reading (Lesson) from the Book of Isaiah [10:20-27]

In that day the remnant of Israel and the survivors of the
house of Jacob will no more lean upon him that smote
them, but will lean upon the Lord, the Holy One of Israel,

in truth. A remnant will return, the remnant of Jacob, to the mighty God. For though your people Israel be as the sand of the sea, only a remnant of them will return. Destruction is decreed, overflowing with righteousness. For the Lord, the Lord of hosts, will make a full end, as decreed, in the midst of all the earth. Therefore thus says the Lord, the Lord of hosts: "O my people, who dwell in Zion, be not afraid of the Assyrians when they smite with the rod and lift up their staff against you as the Egyptians did. For in a very little while my indignation will come to an end, and my anger will be directed to their destruction. And the Lord of hosts will wield against them a scourge, as when he smote Mid′ian at the rock of Oreb; and his rod will be over the sea, and he will lift it as he did in Egypt. And in that day his burden will depart from your shoulder, and his yoke will be destroyed from your neck."

A Reading (Lesson) from the Letter of Jude [17-25]

You must remember, beloved, the predictions of the apostles of our Lord Jesus Christ; they said to you, "In the last time there will be scoffers, following their own ungodly passions." It is these who set up divisions, worldly people, devoid of the Spirit. But you, beloved, build yourselves up on your most holy faith; pray in the Holy Spirit; keep yourselves in the love of God; wait for the mercy of our Lord Jesus Christ unto eternal life. And convince some, who doubt; save some, by snatching them out of the fire; on some have mercy with fear, hating even the garment spotted by the flesh. Now to him who is able to keep you from falling and to present you without blemish before the presence of his glory with rejoicing, to the only God, our Savior through Jesus Christ our Lord, be glory, majesty, dominion, and authority, before all time and now and for ever. Amen.

A Reading (Lesson) from the Gospel according to Luke [3:1-9]

In the fifteenth year of the reign of Tibe'ri-us Caesar, Pontius Pilate being governor of Judea, and Herod being tetrarch of Galilee, and his brother Philip tetrarch of the region of Iturae'a and Trachoni'tis, and Lysa'ni-as tetrarch of Abile'ne, in the high-priesthood of Annas and Ca'iaphas, the word of God came to John the son of Zechari'ah in the wilderness; and he went into all the region about the Jordan, preaching a baptism of repentance for the forgiveness of sins. As it is written in the book of the words of Isaiah the prophet, "The voice of one crying in the wilderness: Prepare the way of the Lord, make his paths straight. Every valley shall be filled, and every mountain and hill shall be brought low, and the crooked shall be made straight, and the rough ways shall be made smooth; and all flesh shall see the salvation of God." He said therefore to the multitudes that came out to be baptized by him, "You brood of vipers! Who warned you to flee from the wrath to come? Bear fruits that befit repentance, and do not begin to say to yourselves, 'We have Abraham as our father': for I tell you, God is able from these stones to raise up children to Abraham. Even now the axe is laid to the root of the trees; every tree therefore that does not bear good fruit is cut down and thrown into the fire."

Week of 4 Advent

Sunday

Psalm 24 [page 613],   *Psalm 29* [page 620]   ❖
Psalm 8 [page 592],   *Psalm 84* [page 707]

A Reading (Lesson) from the Book of Isaiah [42:1-12]

Behold my servant, whom I uphold, my chosen, in whom my soul delights; I have put my Spirit upon him, he will bring forth justice to the nations. He will not cry or lift up his voice, or make it heard in the street; a bruised reed he will not break, and a dimly burning wick he will not quench; he will faithfully bring forth justice. He will not fail or be discouraged till he has established justice in the earth; and the coastlands wait for his law. Thus says God, the Lord, who created the heavens and stretched them out, who spread forth the earth and what comes from it, who gives breath to the people upon it and spirit to those who walk in it: "I am the Lord, I have called you in righteousness, I have taken you by the hand and kept you; I have given you as a covenant to the people, a light to the nations, to open the eyes that are blind, to bring out the prisoners from the dungeon, from the prison those who sit in darkness. I am the Lord, that is my name; my glory I give to no other, nor my praise to graven images. Behold, the former things have come to pass, and new things I now declare; before they spring forth I tell you of them." Sing to the Lord a new song, his praise from the end of the earth! Let the sea roar and all that fills it, the coastlands and their inhabitants. Let the desert and its cities lift up their voice, the villages that Kedar inhabits; let the inhabitants of Sela sing for joy, let them shout from the top of the mountains. Let them give glory to the Lord, and declare his praise in the coastlands.

A Reading (Lesson) from the Letter of Paul to the Ephesians [6:10-20]

Be strong in the Lord and in the strength of his might. Put on the whole armor of God, that you may be able to stand against the wiles of the devil. For we are not contending against flesh and blood, but against the principalities, against the powers, against the world rulers of this present darkness, against the spiritual hosts of wickedness in the heavenly places. Therefore take the whole armor of God, that you may be able to withstand in the evil day, and having done all, to stand. Stand therefore, having girded your loins with truth, and having put on the breastplate of righteousness, and having shod your feet with the equipment of the gospel of peace; besides all these, taking the shield of faith, with which you can quench all the flaming darts of the evil one. And take the helmet of salvation, and the sword of the Spirit, which is the word of God. Pray at all times in the Spirit, with all prayer and supplication. To that end keep alert with all perseverance, making supplication for all the saints, and also for me, that utterance may be given me in opening my mouth boldly to proclaim the mystery of the gospel, for which I am an ambassador in chains; that I may declare it boldly, as I ought to speak.

A Reading (Lesson) from the Gospel according to John [3:16-21]

For God so loved the world that he gave his only Son, that whoever believes in him should not perish but have eternal life. For God sent the Son into the world, not to condemn the world, but that the world might be saved through him. He who believes in him is not condemned; he who does not believe is condemned already, because he has not believed in the name of the only Son of God. And this is the judgment, that the light has come into the world, and men loved darkness rather than light, because their deeds were evil. For every one who does evil hates the light, and does not come to the light, lest his deeds should be exposed. But he who does what is true comes to the light, that it may be clearly seen that his deeds have been wrought in God.

Monday

Psalm 61 [page 668],   *Psalm 62* [page 669]   ❖
Psalm 112 [page 755],   *Psalm 115* [page 757]

A Reading (Lesson) from the Book of Isaiah [11:1-9]

There shall come forth a shoot from the stump of Jesse,
and a branch shall grow out of his roots. And the Spirit of
the Lord shall rest upon him, the spirit of wisdom and
understanding, the spirit of counsel and might, the spirit of
knowledge and the fear of the Lord. And his delight shall
be in the fear of the Lord. He shall not judge by what his
eyes see, or decide by what his ears hear; but with
righteousness he shall judge the poor, and decide with
equity for the meek of the earth; and he shall smite the
earth with the rod of his mouth, and with the breath of his
lips he shall slay the wicked. Righteousness shall be the
girdle of his waist, and faithfulness the girdle of his loins.
The wolf shall dwell with the lamb, and the leopard shall
lie down with the kid, and the calf and the lion and the
fatling together, and a little child shall lead them. The cow
and the bear shall feed; their young shall lie down
together; and the lion shall eat straw like the ox. The
sucking child shall play over the hole of the asp, and the
weaned child shall put his hand on the adders den. They
shall not hurt or destroy in all my holy mountain; for the
earth shall be full of the knowledge of the Lord as the
waters cover the sea.

A Reading (Lesson) from the Revelation to John [20:1-10]

I saw an angel coming down from heaven, holding in his
hand the key of the bottomless pit and a great chain. And
he seized the dragon, that ancient serpent, who is the Devil
and Satan, and bound him for a thousand years, and threw
him into the pit, and shut it and sealed it over him, that he
should deceive the nations no more, till the thousand years
were ended. After that he must be loosed for a little while.
Then I saw thrones, and seated on them were those to
whom judgment was committed. Also I saw the souls of
those who had been beheaded for their testimony to Jesus
and for the word of God, and who had not worshiped the

beast or its image and had not received its mark on their foreheads or their hands. They came to life, and reigned with Christ a thousand years. The rest of the dead did not come to life until the thousand years were ended. This is the first resurrection. Blessed and holy is he who shares in the first resurrection! Over such the second death has no power, but they shall be priests of God and of Christ, and they shall reign with him a thousand years. And when the thousand years are ended, Satan will be loosed from his prison and will come out to deceive the nations which are at the four corners of the earth, that is, Gog and Magog, to gather them for battle; their number is like the sand of the sea. And they marched up over the broad earth and surrounded the camp of the saints and the beloved city; but fire came down from heaven and consumed them, and the devil who had deceived them was thrown into the lake of fire and sulphur where the beast and the false prophet were, and they will be tormented day and night for ever and ever.

A Reading (Lesson) from the Gospel according to John [5:30-47]

Jesus said to the Jews, "I can do nothing on my own authority; as I hear, I judge; and my judgment is just, because I seek not my own will but the will of him who sent me. If I bear witness to myself, my testimony is not true; there is another who bears witness to me, and I know that the testimony which he bears to me is true. You sent to John, and he has borne witness to the truth. Not that the testimony which I receive is from man; but I say this that you may be saved. He was a burning and shining lamp, and you were willing to rejoice for a while in his light. But the testimony which I have is greater than that of John; for the works which the Father has granted me to accomplish, these very works which I am doing, bear me witness that the Father has sent me. And the Father who sent me has himself borne witness to me. His voice you have never heard, his form you have never seen; and you do not have his word abiding in you, for you do not believe him whom he has sent. You search the scriptures, because you think that in them you have eternal life; and it is they that bear witness to me; yet you refuse to come to me that you may have life. I do not receive glory from men. But I know that you have not the love of God within you. I have come in my Father's name, and you do not receive me; if another comes in his own name, him you will receive. How can you believe, who receive glory from one another and do not seek the glory that comes from the only God? Do not think that I shall accuse you to the Father; it is Moses who accuses you, on whom you set your hope. If you believed Moses, you would believe me, for he wrote of me. But if you do not believe his writings, how will you believe my words?"

Tuesday

Psalm 66 [page 673],   *Psalm 67* [page 675]   ❖
Psalm 116 [page 759],   *Psalm 117* [page 760]

A Reading (Lesson) from the Book of Isaiah [11:10-16]

In that day the root of Jesse shall stand as an ensign to the peoples; him shall the nations seek, and his dwellings shall be glorious. In that day the Lord will extend his hand yet a second time to recover the remnant which is left of his people, from Assyria, from Egypt, from Pathros, from Ethiopia, from Elam, from Shinar, from Hamath, and from the coastlands of the sea. He will raise an ensign for the nations, and will assemble the outcasts of Israel, and gather the dispersed of Judah from the four corners of the earth. The jealousy of E'phraim shall depart, and those who harass Judah shall be cut off; E'phraim shall not be jealous of Judah, and Judah shall not harass E'phraim. But they shall swoop down upon the shoulder of the Philistines in the west, and together they shall plunder the people of the east. They shall put forth their hand against Edom and Moab, and the Ammonites shall obey them. And the Lord will utterly destroy the tongue of the sea of Egypt; and will wave his hand over the river with his scorching wind, and smite it into seven channels that men may cross dryshod. And there will be a highway from Assyria for the remnant which is left of his people, as there was for Israel when they came up from the land of Egypt.

A Reading (Lesson) from the Revelation to John
[20:11—21:8]

I saw a great white throne and him who sat upon it; from his presence earth and sky fled away, and no place was found for them. And I saw the dead, great and small, standing before the throne, and books were opened. Also another book was opened, which is the book of life. And the dead were judged by what was written in the books, by what they had done. And the sea gave up the dead in it, Death and Hades gave up the dead in them, and all were judged by what they had done. Then Death and Hades were thrown into the lake of fire. This is the second death, the lake of fire; and if any one's name was not found written in the book of life, he was thrown into the lake of fire. Then I saw a new heaven and a new earth; for the first heaven and the first earth had passed away, and the sea was no more. And I saw the holy city, new Jerusalem, coming down out of heaven from God, prepared as a bride adorned for her husband; and I heard a loud voice from the throne saying, "Behold, the dwelling of God is with men. He will dwell with them, and they shall be his people, and God himself will be with them; he will wipe away every tear from their eyes, and death shall be no more, neither shall there be mourning nor crying nor pain any more, for the former things have passed away." And he who sat upon the throne said, "Behold, I make all things new." Also he said, "Write this for these words are trustworthy and true." And he said to me, "It is done! I am the Alpha and the Omega, the beginning and the end. To the thirsty I will give from the fountain of the water of life without payment. He who conquers shall have this heritage, and I will be his God and he shall be my son. But as for the cowardly, the faithless, the polluted, as for the murderers, fornicators, sorcerers, idolators, and all liars, their lot shall be in the lake that burns with fire and sulphur, which is the second death."

A Reading (Lesson) from the Gospel according to Luke [1:5-25]

In the days of Herod, king of Judea, there was a priest named Zechari'ah, of the division of Abi'jah; and he had a wife of the daughters of Aaron, and her name was Elizabeth. And they were both righteous before God, walking in all the commandments and ordinances of the Lord blameless. But they had no child, because Elizabeth was barren, and both were advanced in years. Now while he was serving as priest before God when his division was on duty, according to the custom of the priesthood, it fell to him by lot to enter the temple of the Lord and burn incense. And the whole multitude of the people were praying outside at the hour of incense. And there appeared to him an angel of the Lord standing on the right side of the altar of incense. And Zechari'ah was troubled when he saw him, and fear fell upon him. But the angel said to him, "Do not be afraid, Zechari'ah, for your prayer is heard, and your wife Elizabeth will bear you a son, and you shall call his name John. And you will have joy and gladness, and many will rejoice at his birth; for he will be great before the Lord, and he shall drink no wine nor strong drink, and he will be filled with the Holy Spirit, even from his mother's womb. And he will turn many of the sons of Israel to the Lord their God, and he will go before him in the spirit and power of Eli'jah, to turn the hearts of the fathers to the children, and the disobedient to the wisdom of the just, to make ready for the Lord a people prepared." And Zechari'ah said to the angel, "How shall I know this? For I am an old man, and my wife is advanced in years." And the angel answered him, "I am Gabriel, who stand in the presence of God; and I was sent to speak to you, and t bring you this good news. And behold, you will be silent and unable to speak until the day that these things come to pass, because you did not believe my words, which will be fulfilled in their time." And the people were waiting for Zechari'ah, and they wondered at his delay in the temple. And when he came out, he could not speak to them, and they perceived that he had seen a vision in the temple; and he made signs to them and remained dumb. And when his time of service was ended, he went to his home. After these days his wife Elizabeth conceived, and for five months she hid herself, saying, "Thus the Lord has done to me in the days when he looked on me, to take away my reproach among men."

Wednesday

Psalm 72 [page 685] ❖ *Psalm 111* [page 754],
Psalm 113 [page 756]

A Reading (Lesson) from the Book of Isaiah [28:9-22]

"Whom will he teach knowledge, and to whom will he explain the message? Those who are weaned from the milk, those taken from the breast? For it is precept upon precept, precept upon precept, line upon line, line upon line, here a little, there a little." Nay, but by men of strang lips and with an alien tongue the Lord will speak to this people, to whom he has said, "This is rest; give rest to the weary; and this is repose"; yet they would not hear. Therefore the word of the Lord will be to them precept upon precept, precept upon precept, line upon line, line upon line, here a little, there a little; that they may go, and fall backward, and be broken, and snared, and taken. Therefore hear the word of the Lord, you scoffers, who rule this people in Jerusalem! Because you have said, "We have made a covenant with death, and with Sheol we have an agreement; when the overwhelming scourge passes through it will not come to us; for we have made lies our refuge, and in falsehood we have taken shelter"; therefore thus says the Lord God, "Behold, I am laying in Zion for a foundation a stone, a tested stone, a precious cornerstone, of a sure foundation: 'He who believes will not be in haste.' And I will make justice the line, and righteousness the plummet; and hail will sweep away the refuge of lies, and waters will overwhelm the shelter." Then your covenant with death will be annulled, and your agreement with Sheol will not stand; when the overwhelming scourge passes through you will be beaten down by it. As often as it passes through it will take you; for morning by morning it will pass through, by day and by night; and it will be sheer terror to understand the message. For the bed is too short to stretch oneself on it, and the covering too narrow to wrap oneself in it. For the Lord will rise up as on Mount Pera'zim, he will be wroth as in the valley of Gibeon; to do his deed—strange is his deed! and to work his work—alien is his work! Now therefore do not scoff, lest your bonds be made strong; for I have heard a decree of destruction from the Lord God of hosts upon the whole land.

A Reading (Lesson) from the Revelation to John [21:9-21]

Then came one of the seven angels who had the seven bowls full of the seven last plagues, and spoke to me, saying, "Come, I will show you the Bride, the wife of the Lamb." And in the Spirit he carried me away to a great, high mountain, and showed me the holy city Jerusalem coming down out of heaven from God, having the glory of God, its radiance like a most rare jewel, like a jasper, clear as crystal. It had a great, high wall, with twelve gates, and at the gates twelve angels, and on the gates the names of the twelve tribes of the sons of Israel were inscribed; on th east three gates, on the north three gates, on the south three gates, and on the west three gates. And the wall of the city had twelve foundations, and on them the twelve names of the twelve apostles of the Lamb. And he who talked to me had a measuring rod of gold to measure the city and its gates and walls. The city lies foursquare, its length the same as its breadth; and he measured the city with his rod, twelve thousand stadia; its length and breadth and height are equal. He also measured its wall, a hundred and forty-four cubits by a man's measure, that is, an angel's. The wall was built of jasper, while the city was pure gold, clear as glass. The foundations of the wall of th city were adorned with every jewel; the first was jasper, th second sapphire, the third agate, the fourth emerald, the fifth onyx, the sixth carnelian, the seventh chrysolite, the eighth beryl, the ninth topaz, the tenth chrysoprase, the eleventh jacinth, the twelfth amethyst. And the twelve gates were twelve pearls, each of the gates made of a singl pearl, and the street of the city was pure gold, transparent as glass.

A Reading (Lesson) from the Gospel according to Luke
[1:26-38]

In the sixth month the angel Gabriel was sent from God t a city of Galilee named Nazareth, to a virgin betrothed to man whose name was Joseph, of the house of David; and the virgin's name was Mary. And he came to her and said, "Hail, O favored one, the Lord is with you!" But she was greatly troubled at the saying, and considered in her mind what sort of greeting this might be. And the angel said to her, "Do not be afraid, Mary, for you have found favor with God. And behold, you will conceive in your womb and bear a son, and you shall call his name Jesus. He will be great, and will be called the Son of the Most High; and the Lord God will give to him the throne of his father David, and he will reign over the house of Jacob for ever; and of his kingdom there will be no end." And Mary said to the angel, "How shall this be, since I have no husband?" And the angel said to her, "The Holy Spirit will come upon you, and the power of the Most High will overshadow you; therefore the child to be born will be called holy, the Son of God. And behold, your kinswoman Elizabeth in her old age has also conceived a son; and this is the sixth month with her who was called barren. For with God nothing will be impossible." And Mary said, "Behold, I am the handmaid of the Lord; let it be to me according to your word." And the angel departed from her.

Thursday

Psalm 80 [page 702] ❖ *Psalm 146* [page 803], *Psalm 147* [page 804]

A Reading (Lesson) from the Book of Isaiah [29:13-24]

The Lord said: "Because this people draw near with their mouth and honor me with their lips, while their hearts are far from me, and their fear of me is a commandment of men learned by rote; therefore, behold, I will again do marvelous things with this people, wonderful and marvelous; and the wisdom of their wise men shall perish, and the discernment of their discerning men shall be hid." Woe to those who hide deep from the Lord their counsel, whose deeds are in the dark, and who say, "Who sees us? Who knows us?" You turn things upside down! Shall the potter be regarded as the clay; that the thing made should say of its maker, "He did not make me"; or the thing formed say of him who formed it, "He has no understanding"? Is it not yet a very little while until Lebanon shall be turned into a fruitful field, and the fruitful field shall be regarded as a forest? In that day the deaf shall hear the words of a book, and out of their gloom and darkness the eyes of the blind shall see. The meek shall obtain fresh joy in the Lord, and the poor among men shall exult in the Holy One of Israel. For the ruthless shall come to nought and the scoffer cease, and all who watch to do evil shall be cut off, who by a word make a man out to be an offender, and lay a snare for him who reproves in the gate, and with an empty plea turn aside him who is in the right. Therefore thus says the Lord, who redeemed Abraham, concerning the house of Jacob: "Jacob shall no more be ashamed, no more shall his face grow pale. For when he sees his children, the work of my hands, in his midst, they will sanctify my name; they will sanctify the Holy One of Jacob, and will stand in awe of the God of Israel. And those who err in spirit will come to understanding, and those who murmur will accept instruction."

A Reading (Lesson) from the Revelation to John
[21:22—22:5]

I saw no temple in the city, for its temple is the Lord God the Almighty and the Lamb. And the city has no need of sun or moon to shine upon it, for the glory of God is its light, and its lamp is the Lamb. By its light shall the nations walk; and the kings of the earth shall bring their glory into it, and its gates shall never be shut by day—and there shall be no night there; they shall bring into it the glory and the honor of the nations. But nothing unclean shall enter it, nor any one who practices abomination or falsehood, but only those who are written in the Lamb's book of life. Then he showed me the river of the water of life, bright as crystal, flowing from the throne of God and of the Lamb through the middle of the street of the city; also, on either side of the river, the tree of life with its twelve kinds of fruit, yielding its fruit each month; and the leaves of the tree were for the healing of the nations. There shall no more be anything accursed, but the throne of God and of the Lamb shall be in it, and his servants shall worship him; they shall see his face, and his name shall be on their foreheads. And night shall be no more; they need no light of lamp or sun, for the Lord God will be their light, and they shall reign for ever and ever.

A Reading (Lesson) from the Gospel according to Luke
[1:39-48a(48b-56)]

In those days Mary arose and went with haste into the hill country, to a city of Judah, and she entered the house of Zechari'ah and greeted Elizabeth. And when Elizabeth heard the greeting of Mary, the babe leaped in her womb; and Elizabeth was filled with the Holy Spirit and she exclaimed with a loud cry, "Blessed are you among women, and blessed is the fruit of your womb! And why is this granted me, that the mother of my Lord should come to me? For behold, when the voice of your greeting came to my ears, the babe in my womb leaped for joy. And blessed is she who believed that there would be a fulfilment of what was spoken to her from the Lord." And Mary said, "My soul magnifies the Lord, and my spirit rejoices in God my Savior, for he has regarded the low estate of his handmaiden.

For behold, henceforth all generations will call me blessed; for he who is mighty has done great things for me, and holy is his name. And his mercy is on those who fear him from generation to generation. He has shown strength with his arm, he has scattered the proud in the imagination of their hearts, he has put down the mighty from their thrones, and exalted those of low degree; he has filled the hungry with good things, and the rich he has sent empty away. He has helped his servant Israel, in remembrance of his mercy, as he spoke to our fathers, to Abraham and to his posterity for ever." And Mary remained with her about three months, and returned to her home.

Friday

Psalm 93 [page 722], *Psalm 96* [page 725] ❖
Psalm 148 [page 805], *Psalm 150* [page 807]

A Reading (Lesson) from the Book of Isaiah [33:17-22]

Your eyes will see the king in his beauty; they will behold a land that stretches afar. Your mind will muse on the terror: "Where is he who counted, where is he who weighed tribute? Where is he who counted the towers?" You will see no more the insolent people, the people of an obscure speech which you cannot comprehend, stammering in a tongue which you cannot understand. Look upon Zion, the city of our appointed feasts! Your eyes will see Jerusalem, a quiet habitation, an immovable tent, whose stakes will never be plucked up, nor will any of its cords be broken. But there the Lord in majesty will be for us a place of broad rivers and streams, where no galley with oars can go, nor stately ship can pass. For the Lord is our judge, the Lord is our ruler, the Lord is our king; he will save us.

A Reading (Lesson) from the Revelation to John
[22:6-11,18-20]

He who talked to me said to me, "These words are trustworthy and true. And the Lord, the God of the spirits of the prophets, has sent his angel to show his servants what must soon take place. And behold, I am coming soon." Blessed is he who keeps the words of the prophecy of this book. I John am he who heard and saw these things And when I heard and saw them, I fell down to worship at the feet of the angel who showed them to me; but he said to me, "You must not do that! I am a fellow servant with you and your brethren the prophets, and with those who keep the words of this book. Worship God." And he said to me, "Do not seal up the words of the prophecy of this book for the time is near. Let the evildoer still do evil, and the filthy still be filthy, and the righteous still do right, and the holy still be holy." I warn every one who hears the words of the prophecy of this book: if any one adds to them, God will add to him the plagues described in this book, and if any one takes away from the words of the book of this prophecy, God will take away his share in the tree of life and in the holy city, which are described in this book. He who testifies to these things says, "Surely I am coming soon." Amen. Come, Lord Jesus!

A Reading (Lesson) from the Gospel according to Luke [1:57-66]

Now the time came for Elizabeth to be delivered, and she gave birth to a son. And her neighbors and kinsfolk heard that the Lord had shown great mercy to her, and they rejoiced with her. And on the eighth day they came to circumcise the child; and they would have named him Zechari'ah after his father, but his mother said, "Not so; he shall be called John." And they said to her, "None of your kindred is called by this name." And they made signs to his father, inquiring what he would have him called. And he asked for a writing tablet, and wrote, "His name is John." And they all marveled. And immediately his mouth was opened and his tongue loosed, and he spoke, blessing God. And fear came on all their neighbors. And all these things were talked about through all the hill country of Judea; and all who heard them laid them up in their hearts, saying, "What then will this child be?" For the hand of the Lord was with him.

December 24

(Morning Prayer)   *Psalm 45* [page 647],   *Psalm 46* [page 649]

A Reading (Lesson) from the Book of Isaiah [35:1-10]

The wilderness and the dry land shall be glad, the desert shall rejoice and blossom; like the crocus it shall blossom abundantly, and rejoice with joy and singing. The glory of Lebanon shall be given to it, the majesty of Carmel and Sharon. They shall see the glory of the Lord, the majesty of our God. Strengthen the weak hands, and make firm the feeble knees. Say to those who are of a fearful heart, "Be strong, fear not! Behold, your God will come with vengeance, with the recompense of God. He will come and save you." Then the eyes of the blind shall be opened, and the ears of the deaf unstopped; then shall the lame man leap like a hart, and the tongue of the dumb sing for joy. For waters shall break forth in the wilderness, and streams in the desert; the burning sand shall become a pool, and the thirsty ground springs of water; the haunt of jackals shall become a swamp, the grass shall become reeds and rushes. And a highway shall be there, and it shall be called the Holy Way; the unclean shall not pass over it, and fools shall not err therein. No lion shall be there, nor shall any ravenous beast come up on it; they shall not be found there, but the redeemed shall walk there. And the ransomed of the Lord shall return, and come to Zion with singing; everlasting joy shall be upon their heads; they shall obtain joy and gladness, and sorrow and sighing shall flee away.

A Reading (Lesson) from the Revelation to John
[22:12-17,21]

"Behold, I am coming soon, bringing my recompense, to repay every one for what he has done. I am the Alpha and the Omega, the first and the last, the beginning and the end." Blessed are those who wash their robes, that they may have the right to the tree of life and that they may enter the city by the gates. Outside are the dogs and sorcerers and fornicators and murderers and idolaters, and every one who loves and practices falsehood. "I Jesus have sent my angel to you with this testimony for the churches. am the root and the offspring of David, the bright morning star." The Spirit and the Bride say, "Come." And let him who hears say, "Come." And let him who is thirsty come, let him who desires take the water of life without price. The grace of the Lord Jesus be with all the saints. Amen.

A Reading (Lesson) from the Gospel according to Luke [1:67-80]

John's father Zechari'ah was filled with the Holy Spirit, and prophesied, saying, "Blessed be the Lord God of Israel, for he has visited and redeemed his people, and has raised up a horn of salvation for us in the house of his servant David, as he spoke by the mouth of his holy prophets from of old, that we should be saved from our enemies, and from the hand of all who hate us; to perform the mercy promised to our fathers, and to remember his holy covenant, the oath which he swore to our father Abraham, to grant us that we, being delivered from the hand of our enemies, might serve him without fear, in holiness and righteousness before him all the days of our life. And you, child, will be called the prophet of the Most High; for you will go before the Lord to prepare his ways, to give knowledge of salvation to his people in the forgiveness of their sins, through the tender mercy of our God, when the day shall dawn upon us from on high to give light to those who sit in darkness and in the shadow of death, to guide our feet into the way of peace." And the child grew and became strong in spirit, and he was in the wilderness till the day of his manifestation to Israel.

Christmas Eve

(Evening Prayer)   *Psalm 89:1-29* [page 713]

A Reading (Lesson) from the Book of Isaiah [59:15b-21]

The Lord saw it, and it displeased him that there was no justice. He saw that there was no man, and wondered that there was no one to intervene; then his own arm brought him victory, and his righteousness upheld him. He put on righteousness as a breastplate, and a helmet of salvation upon his head; he put on garments of vengeance for clothing, and wrapped himself in fury as a mantle. According to their deeds, so will he repay, wrath to his adversaries, requital to his enemies; to the coastlands he will render requital. So they shall fear the name of the Lord from the west, and his glory from the rising of the sun; for he will come like a rushing stream, which the wind of the Lord drives. "And he will come to Zion as Redeemer, to those in Jacob who turn from transgression, says the Lord. And as for me, this is my covenant with them, says the Lord: my spirit which is upon you, and my words which I have put in your mouth, shall not depart out of your mouth, or out of the mouth of your children, or out of the mouth of your children's children, says the Lord, from this time forth and for evermore."

A Reading (Lesson) from the Letter of Paul to the Philippians [2:5-11]

Have this mind among yourselves, which is yours in Christ Jesus, who, though he was in the form of God, did not count equality with God a thing to be grasped, but emptied himself, taking the form of a servant, being born in the likeness of men. And being found in human form he humbled himself and became obedient unto death, even death on a cross. Therefore God has highly exalted him and bestowed on him the name which is above every name, that at the name of Jesus every knee should bow, in heaven and on earth and under the earth, and every tongue confess that Jesus Christ is Lord, to the glory of God the Father.

Christmas Day and Following

Christmas Day

Psalm 2 [page 586], *Psalm 85* [page 708] ❖
Psalm 110:1-5(6-7) [page 753], *Psalm 132* [page 785]

A Reading (Lesson) from the Book of Zechariah [2:10-13]

Thus said the Lord of hosts: "Sing and rejoice, O daughter of Zion; for lo, I come and I will dwell in the midst of you, says the Lord. And many nations shall join themselves to the Lord in that day, and shall be my people; and I will dwell in the midst of you, and you shall know that the Lord of hosts has sent me to you. And the Lord will inherit Judah as his portion in the holy land, and will again choose Jerusalem." Be silent, all flesh, before the Lord; for he has roused himself from his holy dwelling.

A Reading (Lesson) from the First Letter of John [4:7-16]

Beloved, let us love one another; for love is of God, and he who loves is born of God and knows God. He who does not love does not know God; for God is love. In this the love of God was made manifest among us, that God sent his only Son into the world, so that we might live through him. In this is love, not that we loved God but that he loved us and sent his Son to be the expiation for our sins. Beloved, if God so loved us, we also ought to love one another. No man has ever seen God; if we love one another, God abides in us and his love is perfected in us. By this we know that we abide in him and he in us, because he has given us of his own Spirit. And we have seen and testify that the Father has sent his Son as the Savior of the world. Whoever confesses that Jesus is the Son of God, God abides in him, and he in God. So we know and believe the love God has for us. God is love, and he who abides in love abides in God, and God abides in him.

A Reading (Lesson) from the Gospel according to John
[3:31-36]

He who comes from above is above all; he who is of the earth belongs to the earth, and of the earth he speaks; he who comes from heaven is above all. He bears witness to what he has seen and heard, yet no one receives his testimony; he who receives his testimony sets his seal to this, that God is true. For he whom God has sent utters the words of God, for it is not by measure that he gives the Spirit; the Father loves the Son, and has given all things into his hand. He who believes in the Son has eternal life; he who does not obey the Son shall not see life, but the wrath of God rests upon him.

First Sunday after Christmas

Psalm 93 [page 722],   *Psalm 96* [page 725]   ❖
Psalm 34 [page 627]

A Reading (Lesson) from the Book of Isaiah [62:6-7,10-12]

Upon your walls, O Jerusalem, I have set watchmen; all the day and all the night they shall never be silent. You who put the Lord in remembrance, take no rest, and give him no rest until he establishes Jerusalem and makes it a praise in the earth. Go through, go through the gates, prepare the way for the people; build up, build up the highway, clear it of stones, lift up an ensign over the peoples. Behold, the Lord has proclaimed to the end of the earth: Say to the daughter of Zion, "Behold, your salvation comes; behold, his reward is with him, and his recompense before him." And they shall be called The holy people, The redeemed of the Lord; and you shall be called Sought out, a city not forsaken.

A Reading (Lesson) from the Letter to the Hebrews
[2:10-18]

It was fitting that he, for whom and by whom all things exist, in bringing many sons to glory, should make the pioneer of their salvation perfect through suffering. For he who sanctifies and those who are sanctified have all one origin. That is why he is not ashamed to call them brethren, saying, "I will proclaim thy name to my brethren, in the midst of the congregation I will praise thee." And again, "I will put my trust in him." And again, "Here am I, and the children God has given me." Since therefore the children share in flesh and blood, he himself likewise partook of the same nature, that through death he might destroy him who has the power of death, that is, the devil, and deliver all those who through fear of death were subject to lifelong bondage. For surely it is not with angels that he is concerned but with the descendants of Abraham. Therefore he had to be made like his brethren in every respect, so that he might become a merciful and faithful high priest in the service of God, to make expiation for the sins of the people. For because he himself has suffered and been tempted, he is able to help those who are tempted.

A Reading (Lesson) from the Gospel according to Matthew
[1:18-25]

Now the birth of Jesus Christ took place in this way. When his mother Mary had been betrothed to Joseph, before they came together she was found to be with child of the Holy Spirit; and her husband Joseph, being a just man and unwilling to put her to shame, resolved to divorce her quietly. But as he considered this, behold, an angel of the Lord appeared to him in a dream, saying, "Joseph, son of David, do not fear to take Mary your wife, for that which is conceived in her is of the Holy Spirit; she will bear a son, and you shall call his name Jesus, for he will save his people from their sins." All this took place to fulfil what the Lord had spoken by the prophet: "Behold, a virgin shall conceive and bear a son, and his name shall be called Emman'u-el" (which means, God with us). When Joseph woke from sleep, he did as the angel of the Lord commanded him; he took his wife, but knew her not until she had borne a son; and he called his name Jesus.

December 29

Psalm 18:1-20 [page 602] ❖ *Psalm 18:21-50* [page 604]*

A Reading (Lesson) from the Book of Isaiah [12:1-6]

You will say in that day: "I will give thanks to thee, O Lord, for though thou wast angry with me, thy anger turned away, and thou didst comfort me. Behold, God is my salvation; I will trust, and will not be afraid; for the Lord God is my strength and my song, and he has become my salvation." With joy you will draw water from the wells of salvation. And you will say in that day: "Give thanks to the Lord, call upon his name; make known his deeds among the nations, proclaim that his name is exalted. Sing praises to the Lord, for he has done gloriously; let this be known in all the earth. Shout, and sing for joy, O inhabitant of Zion, for great in your midst is the Holy One of Israel."

A Reading (Lesson) from the Revelation to John [1:1-8]

The Revelation of Jesus Christ, which God gave him to show to his servants what must soon take place; and he made it known by sending his angel to his servant John, who bore witness to the word of God and to the testimony of Jesus Christ, even to all that he saw. Blessed is he who reads aloud the words of the prophecy, and blessed are

**If today is Saturday, use Psalms 23 [page 612] and 27 [page 617] at Evening Prayer.*

those who hear, and who keep what is written therein; for the time is near. John to the seven churches that are in Asia: Grace to you and peace from him who is and who was and who is to come, and from the seven spirits who are before his throne, and from Jesus Christ the faithful witness, the first-born of the dead, and the ruler of the kings on earth. To him who loves us and has freed us from our sins by his blood and made us a kingdom, priests to his God and Father, to him be glory and dominion for ever and ever. Amen. Behold, he is coming with the clouds, and every eye will see him, every one who pierced him; and all tribes of the earth will wail on account of him. Even so. Amen. "I am the Alpha and the Omega," says the Lord God, who is and who was and who is to come, the Almighty.

A Reading (Lesson) from the Gospel according to John
[7:37-52]

On the last day of the feast of Tabernacles, the great day, Jesus stood up and proclaimed, "If any one thirst, let him come to me and drink. He who believes in me, as the scripture has said, 'Out of his heart shall flow rivers of living water.'" Now this he said about the Spirit, which those who believed in him were to receive; for as yet the Spirit had not been given, because Jesus was not yet glorified. When they heard these words, some of the people said, "This is really the prophet." Others said, "This is the Christ." But some said, "Is the Christ to come from Galilee? Has not the scripture said that the Christ is descended from David, and comes from Bethlehem, the village where David was?" So there was a division among the people over him. Some of them wanted to arrest him, but no one laid hands on him. The officers then went back to the chief priests and Pharisees, who said to them, "Why did you not bring him?" The officers answered, "No man ever spoke like this man!" The Pharisees answered them,

"Are you led astray, you also? Have any of the authorities or of the Pharisees believed in him? But this crowd, who do not know the law, are accursed." Nicode'mus, who had gone to him before, and who was one of them, said to them, "Does our law judge a man without first giving him a hearing and learning what he does?" They replied, "Are you from Galilee too? Search and you will see that no prophet is to rise from Galilee."

December 30

Psalm 20 [page 608], *Psalm 21:1-7(8-14)* [page 608] ❖
Psalm 23 [page 612], *Psalm 27* [page 617]

A Reading (Lesson) from the Book of Isaiah [25:1-9]

O Lord, thou art my God; I will exalt thee, I will praise thy name; for thou hast done wonderful things, plans formed of old, faithful and sure. For thou hast made the city a heap, the fortified city a ruin; the palace of aliens is a city no more, it will never be rebuilt. Therefore strong peoples will glorify thee; cities of ruthless nations will fear thee. For thou hast been a stronghold to the poor, a stronghold to the needy in his distress, a shelter from the storm and a shade from the heat; for the blast of the ruthless is like a storm against a wall, like heat in a dry place. Thou dost subdue the noise of the aliens; as heat by the shade of a cloud, so the song of the ruthless is stilled. On this mountain the Lord of hosts will make for all peoples a feast of fat things, a feast of wine on the lees, of fat things full of marrow, of wine on the lees well refined. And he will destroy on this mountain the covering that is cast over all peoples, the veil that is spread over all nations. He will swallow up death for ever, and the Lord God will wipe away tears from all faces, and the reproach of his people he will take away from all the earth; for the Lord has spoken. It will be said on that day, "Lo, this is our God; we have waited for him, that he might save us. This is the Lord; we have waited for him; let us be glad and rejoice in his salvation."

A Reading (Lesson) from the Revelation to John [1:9-20]

I John, your brother, who share with you in Jesus the tribulation and the kingdom and the patient endurance, was on the island called Patmos on account of the word of God and the testimony of Jesus. I was in the Spirit on the Lord's day, and I heard behind me a loud voice like a trumpet saying, "Write what you see in a book and send it to the seven churches, to Ephesus and to Smyrna and to Per'gamum and to Thyati'ra and to Sardis and to Philadelphia and to La-odice'a." Then I turned to see the voice that was speaking to me, and on turning I saw seven golden lampstands, and in the midst of the lampstands one like a son of man, clothed with a long robe and with a golden girdle round his breast; his head and his hair were white as white wool, white as snow; his eyes were like a flame of fire, his feet were like burnished bronze, refined as in a furnace, and his voice was like the sound of many waters; in his right hand he held seven stars, from his mouth issued a sharp two-edged sword, and his face was like the sun shining in full strength. When I saw him, I fell at his feet as though dead. But he laid his right hand upon me, saying, "Fear not, I am the first and the last, and the living one; I died, and behold I am alive for evermore, and I have the keys of Death and Hades. Now write what you see, what is and what is to take place hereafter. As for the mystery of the seven stars which you saw in my right hand, and the seven golden lampstands, the seven stars are the angels of the seven churches and the seven lampstands are the seven churches."

John 7:53—8:11   [page 27 above]

December 31

(Morning Prayer)   *Psalm 46* [page 649],   *Psalm 48* [page 651]

A Reading (Lesson) from the Book of Isaiah [26:1-9]

In that day this song will be sung in the land of Judah: "We have a strong city; he sets up salvation as walls and bulwarks. Open the gates, that the righteous nation which keeps faith may enter in. Thou dost keep him in perfect peace, whose mind is stayed on thee, because he trusts in thee. Trust in the Lord for ever, for the Lord God is an everlasting rock. For he has brought low the inhabitants of the height, the lofty city. He lays it low, lays it low to the ground, casts it to the dust. The foot tramples it, the feet of the poor, the steps of the needy." The way of the righteous is level; thou dost make smooth the path of the righteous. In the path of thy judgments, O Lord, we wait for thee; thy memorial name is the desire of our soul. My soul yearns for thee in the night, my spirit within me earnestly seeks thee. For when thy judgments are in the earth, the inhabitants of the world learn righteousness.

A Reading (Lesson) from the Second Letter of Paul to the Corinthians [5:16—6:2]

From now on we regard no one from a human point of view; even though we once regarded Christ from a human point of view, we regard him thus no longer. Therefore, if any one is in Christ, he is a new creation; the old has passed away, behold, the new has come. All this is from God, who through Christ reconciled us to himself and gave us the ministry of reconciliation; that is, in Christ God was reconciling the world to himself, not counting their trespasses against them, and entrusting to us the message of reconciliation. So we are ambassadors for Christ, God making his appeal through us. We beseech you on behalf of Christ, be reconciled to God. For our sake he made him to be sin who knew no sin, so that in him we might become the righteousness of God. Working together with him, then, we entreat you not to accept the grace of God in vain. For he says, "At the acceptable time I have listened to you, and helped you on the day of salvation." Behold, now is the acceptable time; behold, now is the day of salvation.

A Reading (Lesson) from the Gospel according to John [8:12-19]

Jesus spoke to the scribes and Pharisees, saying, "I am the light of the world; he who follows me will not walk in darkness, but will have the light of life." The Pharisees then said to him, "You are bearing witness to yourself; your testimony is not true." Jesus answered, "Even if I do bear witness to myself, my testimony is true, for I know whence I have come and whither I am going, but you do not know whence I come or whither I am going. You judge according to the flesh, I judge no one. Yet even if I do judge, my judgment is true, for it is not I alone that judge, but I and he who sent me. In your law it is written that the testimony of two men is true; I bear witness to myself, and the Father who sent me bears witness to me." They said to him therefore, "Where is your Father?" Jesus answered, "You know neither me nor my Father; if you knew me, you would know my Father also."

Eve of Holy Name

(Evening Prayer)   *Psalm 90* [page 717]

A Reading (Lesson) from the Book of Isaiah [65:15b-25]

Thus says the Lord God: "The Lord God will call his servants by a different name. So that he who blesses himself in the land shall bless himself by the God of truth, and he who takes an oath in the land shall swear by the God of truth; because the former troubles are forgotten and are hid from my eyes. For behold, I create new heavens and a new earth; and the former things shall not be remembered or come into mind. But be glad and rejoice for ever in that which I create; for behold, I create Jerusalem a rejoicing, and her people a joy. I will rejoice in Jerusalem, and be glad in my people; no more shall be heard in it the sound of weeping and the cry of distress. No more shall there be in it an infant that lives but a few days, or an old man who does not fill out his days, for the child shall die a hundred years old, and the sinner a hundred years old shall be accursed. They shall build houses and inhabit them; they shall plant vineyards and eat their fruit. They shall not build and another inhabit; they shall not plant and another eat; for like the days of a tree shall the days of my people be, and my chosen shall long enjoy the work of their hands. They shall not labor in vain, or bear children for calamity; for they shall be the offspring of the blessed of the Lord, and their children with them. Before they call I will answer, while they are yet speaking I will hear. The wolf and the lamb shall feed together, the lion shall eat straw like the ox; and dust shall be the serpent's food. They shall not hurt or destroy in all my holy mountain, says the Lord."

A Reading (Lesson) from the Revelation to John [21:1-6]

I saw a new heaven and a new earth; for the first heaven and the first earth had passed away, and the sea was no more. And I saw the holy city, new Jerusalem, coming down out of heaven from God, prepared as a bride adorned for her husband; and I heard a loud voice from the throne saying, "Behold, the dwelling of God is with men. He will dwell with them, and they shall be his people, and God himself will be with them; he will wipe away every tear from their eyes, and death shall be no more, neither shall there be mourning nor crying nor pain any more, for the former things have passed away." And he who sat upon the throne said, "Behold, I make all things new." Also he said, "Write this, for these words are trustworthy and true." And he said to me, "It is done! I am the Alpha and the Omega, the beginning and the end. To the thirsty I will give from the fountain of the water of life without payment."

Holy Name

Psalm 103 [page 733]   ❖   *Psalm 148* [page 805]

A Reading (Lesson) from the Book of Genesis
[17:1-12a,15-16]

When Abram was ninety-nine years old the Lord appeared to Abram, and said to him, "I am God Almighty; walk before me, and be blameless. And I will make my covenant between me and you, and will multiply you exceedingly." Then Abram fell on his face; and God said to him, "Behold, my covenant is with you, and you shall be the father of a multitude of nations. No longer shall your name be Abram, but your name shall be Abraham; for I have made you the father of a multitude of nations. I will make you exceedingly fruitful; and I will make nations of you, and kings shall come forth from you. And I will establish my covenant between me and you and your descendants after you throughout their generations for an everlasting covenant, to be God to you and to your descendants after you. And I will give to you, and to your descendants after you, the land of your sojournings, all the land of Canaan, for an everlasting possession; and I will be their God." And God said to Abraham, "As for you, you shall keep my covenant, you and your descendants after you throughout their generations. This is my covenant, which you shall keep, between me and you and your descendants after you: Every male among you shall be circumcised. You shall be circumcised in the flesh of your foreskins, and it shall be a sign of the covenant between me and you. He that is eight days old shall be circumcised."

And God said to Abraham, "As for Sar'ai your wife, you shall not call her name Sar'ai, but Sarah shall be her name. I will bless her, and moreover I will give you a son by her; I will bless her, and she shall be a mother of nations; kings of people shall come from her."

A Reading (Lesson) from the Letter of Paul to the Colossians [2:6-12]

As therefore you received Christ Jesus the Lord, so live in him, rooted and built up in him and established in the faith, just as you were taught, abounding in thanksgiving. See to it that no one makes a prey of you by philosophy and empty deceit, according to human tradition, according to the elemental spirits of the universe, and not according to Christ. For in him the whole fulness of deity dwells bodily, and you have come to fulness of life in him, who is the head of all rule and authority. In him also you were circumcised with a circumcision made without hands, by putting off the body of flesh in the circumcision of Christ; and you were buried with him in baptism, in which you were also raised with him through faith in the working of God, who raised him from the dead.

A Reading (Lesson) from the Gospel according to John [16:23b-30]

Jesus said to the disciples, "Truly, truly, I say to you, if you ask anything of the Father, he will give it to you in my name. Hitherto you have asked nothing in my name; ask, and you will receive, that your joy may be full. I have said this to you in figures; the hour is coming when I shall no longer speak to you in figures but tell you plainly of the Father. In that day you will ask in my name; and I do not say to you that I shall pray the Father for you; for the Father himself loves you, because you have loved me and have believed that I came from the Father. I came from the Father and have come into the world; again, I am leaving the world and going to the Father." His disciples said, "Ah, now you are speaking plainly, not in any figure! Now we know that you know all things, and need none to question you; by this we believe that you came from God."

Second Sunday after Christmas

Psalm 66 [page 673],   *Psalm 67* [page 675]   ❖
Psalm 145 [page 801]

A Reading (Lesson) from the Book of Ecclesiasticus
[3:3-9,14-17]

Whoever honors his father atones for sins, and whoever glorifies his mother is like one who lays up treasure. Whoever honors his father will be gladdened by his own children, and when he prays he will be heard. Whoever glorifies his father will have long life, and whoever obeys the Lord will refresh his mother; he will serve his parents as his masters. Honor your father by word and deed, that a blessing from him may come upon you. For a father's blessing strengthens the houses of the children, but a mother's curse uproots their foundations. For kindness to a father will not be forgotten, and against your sins it will be credited to you; in the day of your affliction it will be remembered in your favor; as frost in fair weather, your sins will melt away. Whoever forsakes his father is like a blasphemer, and whoever angers his mother is cursed by the Lord. My son, perform your tasks in meekness; then you will be loved by those whom God accepts.

A Reading (Lesson) from the First Letter of John [2:12-17]

I am writing to you, little children, because your sins are forgiven for his sake. I am writing to you, fathers, because you know him who is from the beginning. I am writing to you, young men, because you have overcome the evil one. I write to you, children, because you know the Father. I write to you, fathers, because you know him who is from the beginning. I write to you, young men, because you are strong, and the word of God abides in you, and you have overcome the evil one. Do not love the world or the things in the world. If any one loves the world, love for the Father is not in him. For all that is in the world, the lust of the flesh and the lust of the eyes and the pride of life, is not of the Father but is of the world. And the world passes away, and the lust of it; but he who does the will of God abides for ever.

A Reading (Lesson) from the Gospel according to John [6:41-47]

The Jews murmured at Jesus, because he said, "I am the bread which came down from heaven." They said, "Is not this Jesus, the son of Joseph, whose father and mother we know? How does he now say, 'I have come down from heaven'?" Jesus answered them, "Do not murmur among yourselves. No one can come to me unless the Father who sent me draws him; and I will raise him up at the last day. It is written in the prophets, 'And they shall all be taught by God.' Every one who has heard and learned from the Father comes to me. Not that any one has seen the Father except him who is from God; he has seen the Father. Truly truly, I say to you, he who believes has eternal life."

January 2

Psalm 34 [page 627]   ❖   *Psalm 33* [page 626]

A Reading (Lesson) from the Book of Genesis [12:1-7]

The Lord said to Abram, "Go from your country and your kindred and your father's house to the land that I will show you. And I will make of you a great nation, and I will bless you, and make your name great, so that you will be a blessing. I will bless those who bless you, and him who curses you I will curse; and by you all the families of the earth shall bless themselves." So Abram went, as the Lord had told him; and Lot went with him. Abram was seventy-five years old when he departed from Haran. And Abram took Sar'ai his wife, and Lot his brother's son, and all their possessions which they had gathered, and the persons that they had gotten in Haran; and they set forth to go to the land of Canaan. When they had come to the land of Canaan, Abram passed through the land to the place at Shechem, to the oak of Moreh. At that time the Canaanites were in the land. Then the Lord appeared to Abram, and said, "To your descendants I will give this land." So he built there an altar to the Lord, who had appeared to him.

A Reading (Lesson) from the Letter to the Hebrews
[11:1-12]

Faith is the assurance of things hoped for, the conviction of things not seen. For by it the men of old received divine approval. By faith we understand that the world was created by the word of God, so that what is seen was made out of things which do not appear. By faith Abel offered to God a more acceptable sacrifice than Cain, through which he received approval as righteous, God bearing witness by accepting his gifts; he died, but through his faith he is still speaking. By faith Enoch was taken up so that he should not see death; and he was not found, because God had taken him. Now before he was taken he was attested as having pleased God. And without faith it is impossible to please him. For whoever would draw near to God must believe that he exists and that he rewards those who seek him. By faith Noah, being warned by God concerning events as yet unseen, took heed and constructed an ark for the saving of his household; by this he condemned the world and became an heir of the righteousness which comes by faith. By faith Abraham obeyed when he was called to go out to a place which he was to receive as an inheritance; and he went out, not knowing where he was to go. By faith he sojourned in the land of promise, as in a foreign land, living in tents with Isaac and Jacob, heirs with him of the same promise. For he looked forward to the city which has foundations, whose builder and maker is God. By faith Sarah herself received power to conceive, even when she was past the age, since she considered him faithful who had promised. Therefore from one man, and him as good as dead, were born descendants as many as the stars of heaven and as the innumerable grains of sand by the seashore.

A Reading (Lesson) from the Gospel according to John
[6:35-42,48-51]

Jesus said to the Jews, "I am the bread of life; he who comes to me shall not hunger, and he who believes in me shall never thirst. But I said to you that you have seen me and yet do not believe. All that the Father gives me will come to me; and him who comes to me I will not cast out. For I have come down from heaven, not to do my own will, but the will of him who sent me; and this is the will of him who sent me, that I should lose nothing of all that he has given me, but raise it up at the last day. For this is the will of my Father, that every one who sees the Son and believes in him should have eternal life; and I will raise him up at the last day." The Jews then murmured at him, because he said; "I am the bread which came down from heaven." They said, "Is not this Jesus, the son of Joseph, whose father and mother we know? How does he now say 'I have come down from heaven'?" Jesus answered them, "I am the bread of life. Your fathers ate the manna in the wilderness, and they died. This is the bread which comes down from heaven, that a man may eat of it and not die. I am the living bread which came down from heaven; if any one eats of this bread, he will live for ever; and the bread which I shall give for the life of the world is my flesh."

January 3

Psalm 68 [page 676] ❖ *Psalm 72* [page 685]*

A Reading (Lesson) from the Book of Genesis [28:10-22]

Jacob left Beer-sheba, and went toward Haran. And he came to a certain place, and stayed there that night, because the sun had set. Taking one of the stones of the place, he put it under his head and lay down in that place to sleep. And he dreamed that there was a ladder set up on the earth, and the top of it reached to heaven; and behold, the angels of God were ascending and descending on it! And behold, the Lord stood above it and said, "I am the Lord, the God of Abraham your father and the God of Isaac; the land on which you lie I will give to you and to your descendants; and your descendants shall be like the dust of the earth, and you shall spread abroad to the west and to the east and to the north and to the south; and by you and your descendants shall all the families of the earth bless themselves. Behold, I am with you and will keep you wherever you go, and will bring you back to this land; for I will not leave you until I have done that of which I have spoken to you." Then Jacob awoke from his sleep and said, "Surely the Lord is in this place; and I did not know it." And he was afraid, and said, "How awesome is this place! This is none other than the house of God, and this is the gate of heaven." So Jacob rose early in the morning, and he took the stone which he had put under his head and set it up for a pillar and poured oil on the top of it. He called the name of that place Bethel; but the name of the city was Luz at the first. Then Jacob made a vow, saying, "If God will be with me, and will keep me in this way that I go, and will give me bread to eat and clothing to wear, so that I come again to my father's house in peace, then the

If today is Saturday, use Psalm 136 [page 789] at Evening Prayer

Lord shall be my God, and this stone, which I have set up for a pillar, shall be God's house; and of all that thou givest me I will give the tenth to thee."

A Reading (Lesson) from the Letter to the Hebrews
[11:13-22]

These all died in faith, not having received what was promised, but having seen it and greeted it from afar, and having acknowledged that they were strangers and exiles on the earth. For people who speak thus make it clear that they are seeking a homeland. If they had been thinking of that land from which they had gone out, they would have had opportunity to return. But as it is, they desire a better country, that is a heavenly one. Therefore God is not ashamed to be called their God, for he has prepared for them a city. By faith Abraham, when he was tested, offered up Isaac, and he who had received the promises was ready to offer up his only son, of whom it was said, "Through Isaac shall your descendants be named." He considered that God was able to raise men even from the dead; hence figuratively speaking, he did receive him back. By faith Isaac invoked future blessings on Jacob and Esau. By faith Jacob, when dying, blessed each of the sons of Joseph, bowing in worship over the head of his staff. By faith Joseph, at the end of his life, made mention on the exodus of the Israelites and gave directions concerning his burial.

A Reading (Lesson) from the Gospel according to John
[10:7-17]

Jesus said to the Pharisees, "Truly, truly, I say to you, I am the door of the sheep. All who came before me are thieves and robbers; but the sheep did not heed them. I am the door; if any one enters by me, he will be saved, and will go in and out and find pasture. The thief comes only to steal and kill and destroy; I came that they may have life, and have it abundantly. I am the good shepherd. The good shepherd lays down his life for the sheep. He who is a hireling and not a shepherd, whose own the sheep are not, sees the wolf coming and leaves the sheep and flees; and the wolf snatches them and scatters them. He flees because he is a hireling and cares nothing for the sheep. I am the good shepherd; I know my own and my own know me, as the Father knows me and I know the Father; and I lay down my life for the sheep. And I have other sheep, that are not of this fold; I must bring them also, and they will heed my voice. So there shall be one flock, one shepherd. For this reason the Father loves me, because I lay down my life, that I may take it again."

January 4

Psalm 85 [page 708], *Psalm 87* [page 711] ❖
Psalm 89:1-29 [page 713]*

A Reading (Lesson) from the Book of Exodus [3:1-12]

Moses was keeping the flock of his father-in-law, Jethro, the priest of Midian; and he led his flock to the west side of the wilderness, and came to Horeb, the mountain of God. And the angel of the Lord appeared to him in a flame of fire out of the midst of a bush; and he looked, and lo, the bush was burning, yet it was not consumed. And Moses said, "I will turn aside and see this great sight, why the bush is not burnt." When the Lord saw that he turned aside to see, God called to him out of the bush, "Moses, Moses!" And he said, "Here am I." Then he said, "Do not come near; put off your shoes from your feet, for the place on which you are standing is holy ground." And he said, "I am the God of your father, the God of Abraham, the God of Isaac, and the God of Jacob." And Moses hid his face, for he was afraid to look at God. Then the Lord said, "I have seen the affliction of my people who are in Egypt, and have heard their cry because of their taskmasters; I know

**If today is Saturday, use Psalm 136 [page 789] at Evening Prayer*

their sufferings, and I have come down to deliver them out of the hand of the Egyptians, and to bring them up out of that land to a good and broad land, a land flowing with milk and honey, to the place of the Canaanites, the Hittites, the Amorites, the Per'izzites, the Hivites, and the Jeb'usites. And now, behold, the cry of the people of Israel has come to me, and I have seen the oppression with which the Egyptians oppress them. Come, I will send you to Pharoah that you may bring forth my people, the sons of Israel, out of Egypt." But Moses said to God, "Who am I that I should go to Pharaoh, and bring the sons of Israel out of Egypt?" He said, "But I will be with you; and this shall be the sign for you, that I have sent you: when you have brought forth the people out of Egypt, you shall serv God upon this mountain."

A Reading (Lesson) from the Letter to the Hebrews
[11:23-31]

By faith Moses, when he was born, was hid for three months by his parents, because they saw that the child was beautiful; and they were not afraid of the king's edict. By faith Moses, when he was grown up, refused to be called the son of Pharaoh's daughter, choosing rather to share ill-treatment with the people of God than to enjoy the fleeting pleasures of sin. He considered abuse suffered for the Christ greater wealth than the treasures of Egypt, for he looked to the reward. By faith he left Egypt, not being afraid of the anger of the king; for he endured as seeing him who is invisible. By faith he kept the Passover and sprinkled the blood, so that the Destroyer of the first-born might not touch them. By faith the people crossed the Red Sea as if on dry land; but the Egyptians, when they attempted to do the same, were drowned. By faith the walls of Jericho fell down after they had been encircled for seven days. By faith Rahab the harlot did not perish with those who were disobedient, because she had given friendly welcome to the spies.

A Reading (Lesson) from the Gospel according to John
[14:6-14]

Jesus said to Thomas, "I am the way, and the truth, and the life; no one comes to the Father, but by me. If you had known me, you would have known my Father also; henceforth you know him and have seen him." Philip said to him, "Lord, show us the Father, and we shall be satisfied." Jesus said to him, "Have I been with you so long, and yet you do not know me, Philip? He who has seen me has seen the Father; how can you say, 'Show us the Father'? Do you not believe that I am in the Father and the Father in me? The words that I say to you I do not speak on my own authority; but the Father who dwells in me does his works. Believe me that I am in the Father and the Father in me; or else believe me for the sake of the works themselves. Truly, truly, I say to you, he who believes in me will also do the works that I do; and greater works than these will he do, because I go to the Father. Whatever you ask in my name, I will do it, that the Father may be glorified in the Son; if you ask anything in my name, I will do it."

January 5

(Morning Prayer)

Psalm 2 [page 586], *Psalm 110:1-5(6-7)* [page 753]

A Reading (Lesson) from the Book of Joshua [1:1-9]

After the death of Moses the servant of the Lord, the Lord said to Joshua the son of Nun, Moses' minister, "Moses my servant is dead; now therefore arise, go over this Jordan, you and all this people, into the land which I am giving to them, to the people of Israel. Every place that the sole of your foot will tread upon I have given to you, as I promised to Moses. From the wilderness and this Lebanon as far as the great river, the river Eu-phra'tes, all the land of the Hittites to the Great Sea toward the going own of the sun shall be your territory. No man shall be able to stand before you all the days of your life; as I was with Moses, so I will be with you; I will not fail you or forsake you. Be strong and of good courage; for you shall cause this people to inherit the land which I swore to their fathers to give them. Only be strong and very courageous, being careful to do according to all the law which Moses my servant commmanded you; turn not from it to the right hand or to the left, that you may have good success wherever you go. This book of the law shall not depart out of your mouth, but you shall meditate on it day and night, that you may be careful to do according to all that is written in it; for then you shall make your way prosperous, and then you shall have good success. Have I not commanded you? Be strong and of good courage; be not frightened, neither be dismayed; for the Lord your God is with you wherever you go."

A Reading (Lesson) from the Letter to the Hebrews
[11:32—12:2]

What more shall I say? For time would fail me to tell of Gideon, Barak, Samson, Jephthah, of David and Samuel and the prophets—who through faith conquered kingdoms, enforced justice, received promises, stopped the mouths of lions, quenched raging fire, escaped the edge of the sword, won strength out of weakness, became mighty in war, put foreign armies to flight. Women received their dead by resurrection. Some were tortured, refusing to accept release, that they might rise again to a better life. Others suffered mocking and scourging, and even chains and imprisonment. They were stoned, they were sawn in two, they were killed with the sword; they went about in skins of sheep and goats, destitute, afflicted, ill-treated—of whom the world was not worthy—wandering over deserts and mountains, and in dens and caves of the earth. And all these, though well attested by their faith, did not receive what was promised, since God had foreseen something better for us, that apart from us they should not be made perfect. Therefore, since we are surrounded by so great a cloud of witnesses, let us also lay aside every weight, and sin which clings so closely, and let us run with perseverance the race that is set before us, looking to Jesus the pioneer and perfecter of our faith, who for the joy that was set before him endured the cross, despising the shame, and is seated at the right hand of the throne of God.

A Reading (Lesson) from the Gospel according to John [15:1-16]

Jesus said to the disciples, "I am the true vine, and my Father is the vinedresser. Every branch of mine that bears no fruit, he takes away, and every branch that does bear fruit he prunes, that it may bear more fruit. You are already made clean by the word which I have spoken to you. Abide in me, and I in you. As the branch cannot bear fruit by itself, unless it abides in the vine, neither can you, unless you abide in me. I am the vine, you are the branches. He who abides in me, and I in him, he it is that bears much fruit, for apart from me you can do nothing. If a man does not abide in me, he is cast forth as a branch and withers; and the branches are gathered, thrown into the fire and burned. If you abide in me, and my words abide in you, ask whatever you will, and it shall be done for you. By this my Father is glorified, that you bear much fruit, and so prove to be my disciples. As the Father has loved me, so have I loved you; abide in my love. If you keep my commandments, you will abide in my love, just as I have kept my Father's commandments and abide in his love. These things I have spoken to you, that my joy may be in you, and that your joy may be full. This is my commandment, that you love one another as I have loved you. Greater love has no man than this, that a man lay down his life for his friends. You are my friends if you do what I command you. No longer do I call you servants, for the servant does not know what his master is doing; but I have called you friends, for all that I have heard from my Father I have made known to you. You did not choose me, but I chose you and appointed you that you should go and bear fruit and that your fruit should abide; so that whatever you ask the Father in my name, he may give it to you."

Eve of Epiphany

(Evening Prayer)   *Psalm 29* [page 620],   *Psalm 98* [page 727]

A Reading (Lesson) from the Book of Isaiah [66:18-23]

Thus says the Lord: "For I know their works and their thoughts, and I am coming to gather all nations and tongues; and they shall come and shall see my glory, and I will set a sign among them. And from them I will send survivors to the nations, to Tarshish, Put, and Lud, who draw the bow, to Tubal and Javan, to the coastlands afar off, that have not heard my fame or seen my glory; and they shall declare my glory among the nations. And they shall bring all your brethren from all the nations as an offering to the Lord, upon horses, and in chariots, and in litters, and upon mules, and upon dromedaries, to my holy mountain Jerusalem, says the Lord, just as the Israelites bring their cereal offering in a clean vessel to the house of the Lord. And some of them also I will take for priests and for Levites, says the Lord. For as the new heavens and the new earth which I will make shall remain before me, says the Lord; so shall your descendants and your name remain. From new moon to new moon, and from sabbath to sabbath, all flesh shall come to worship before me, says the Lord."

*A Reading (Lesson) from the Letter of Paul
to the Romans* [15:7-13]

Welcome one another, therefore, as Christ has welcomed
you, for the glory of God. For I tell you that Christ became
a servant to the circumcised to show God's truthfulness, in
order to confirm the promises given to the patriarchs, and
in order that the Gentiles might glorify God for his mercy.
As it is written, "Therefore I will praise thee among the
Gentiles, and sing to thy name"; and again it is said,
"Rejoice, O Gentiles, with his people"; and again, "Praise
the Lord, all Gentiles, and let all the peoples praise him";
and further Isaiah says, "The root of Jesse shall come, he
who rises to rule the Gentiles; in him shall the Gentiles
hope." May the God of hope fill you with all joy and peace
in believing, so that by the power of the Holy spirit you
may abound in hope.

The Epiphany and Following

Epiphany

Psalm 46 [page 649],   *Psalm 97* [page 726]   ❖
Psalm 96 [page 725],   *Psalm 100* [page 729]

A Reading (Lesson) from the Book of Isaiah [52:7-10]

How beautiful upon the mountains are the feet of him who
brings good tidings, who publishes peace, who brings good
tidings of good, who publishes salvation, who says to
Zion, "Your God reigns." Hark, your watchmen lift up
their voice, together they sing for joy; for eye to eye they
see the return of the Lord to Zion. Break forth together
into singing, you waste places of Jerusalem; for the Lord
has comforted his people, he has redeemed Jerusalem. The
Lord has bared his holy arm before the eyes of all the
nations; and all the ends of the earth shall see the salvation
of our God.

A Reading (Lesson) from the Revelation to John [21:22-27]

I saw no temple in the city, for its temple is the Lord God
the Almighty and the Lamb. And the city has no need of
sun or moon to shine upon it, for the glory of God is its
light, and its lamp is the Lamb. By its light shall the nations
walk; and the kings of the earth shall bring their glory into
it, and its gates shall never be shut by day—and there shall
be no night there; they shall bring into it the glory and the
honor of the nations. But nothing unclean shall enter it,
nor any one who practices abomination or falsehood, but
only those who are written in the Lamb's book of life.

A Reading (Lesson) from the Gospel according to Matthew
[12:14-21]

The Pharisees went out from the synagogue and took
counsel against Jesus, how to destroy him. Jesus, aware of
this, withdrew from there. And many followed him, and he
healed them all, and ordered them not to make him
known. This was to fulfil what was spoken by the prophet
Isaiah: "Behold, my servant whom I have chosen, my
beloved with whom my soul is well pleased. I will put my
Spirit upon him, and he shall proclaim justice to the
Gentiles. he will not wrangle or cry aloud, nor will any one
hear his voice in the streets; he will not break a bruised
reed or quench a smoldering wick, till he brings justice to
victory; and in his name will the Gentiles hope."

January 7*

Psalm 103 [page 733]   ❖   *Psalm 114* [page 756],
Psalm 115 [page 757]

**The Psalms and Readings for the dated days after the Epiphany are
used only until the following Saturday evening.*

A Reading (Lesson) from the Book of Isaiah [52:3-6]

Thus says the Lord: "You were sold for nothing, and you shall be redeemed without money. For thus says the Lord God: My people went down at the first into Egypt to sojourn there, and the Assyrian oppressed them for nothing. Now therefore what have I here, says the Lord, seeing that my people are taken away for nothing? Their rulers wail, says the Lord, and continually all the day my name is despised. Therefore my people shall know my name; therefore in that day they shall know that it is I who speak; here am I."

A Reading (Lesson) from the Revelation to John [2:1-7]

One like a son of man said to me, "To the angel of the church in Ephesus write: 'The words of him who holds the seven stars in his right hand, who walks among the seven golden lampstands. I know your works, your toil and your patient endurance, and how you cannot bear evil men but have tested those who call themselves apostles but are not, and found them to be false; I know you are enduring patiently and bearing up for my name's sake, and you have not grown weary. But I have this against you, that you have abandoned the love you had at first. Remember then from what you have fallen, repent and do the works you did at first. If not, I will come to you and remove your lampstand from its place, unless you repent. Yet this you have, you hate the works of the Nicola'itans, which I also hate. He who has an ear, let him hear what the Spirit says to the churches. To him who conquers I will grant to eat of the tree of life, which is in the paradise of God.'"

A Reading (Lesson) from the Gospel according to John
[2:1-11]

On the third day there was a marriage at Cana in Galilee, and the mother of Jesus was there; Jesus also was invited to the marriage, with his disciples. When the wine gave out, the mother of Jesus said to him, "They have no wine."

And Jesus said to her, "O woman, what have you to do with me? My hour has not yet come." His mother said to the servants, "Do whatever he tells you." Now six stone jars were standing there, for the Jewish rites of purification, each holding twenty or thirty gallons. Jesus said to them, "Fill the jars with water." And they filled them up to the brim. He said to them, "Now draw some out, and take it to the steward of the feast." So they took it. When the steward of the feast tasted the water now become wine, and did not know where it came from (though the servants who had drawn the water knew), the steward of the feast called the bridegroom and said to him, "Every man serves the good wine first; and when men have drunk freely, then the poor wine; but you have kept the good wine until now." This, the first of his signs, Jesus did at Cana in Galilee, and manifested his glory; and his disciples believed in him.

January 8

Psalm 117 [page 760], *Psalm 118* [page 760] ❖
Psalm 112 [page 755], *Psalm 113* [page 756]

A Reading (Lesson) from the Book of Isaiah [59:15-21]

Truth is lacking, and he who departs from evil makes himself a prey. The Lord saw it, and it displeased him that there was no justice. He saw that there was no man, and wondered that there was no one to intervene; then his own arm brought him victory, and his righteousness upheld him. He put on righteousness as a breastplate, and a helmet of salvation upon his head; he put on garments of vengeance for clothing, and wrapped himself in fury as a mantle. According to their deeds, so will he repay, wrath to his adversaries, requital to his enemies; to the coastlands he will render requital. So they shall fear the name of the Lord from the west, and his glory from the rising of the sun; for he will come like a rushing stream, which the wind of the Lord drives. "And he will come to Zion as Redeemer, to those in Jacob who turn from transgression, says the Lord. And as for me, this is my covenant with them, says the Lord: my spirit which is upon you, and my words which I have put in your mouth, shall not depart out of your mouth, or out of the mouth of your children, or out of the mouth of your children's children, says the Lord, from this time forth and for evermore."

A Reading (Lesson) from the Revelation to John [2:8-17]

One like a son of man said to me, "To the angel of the church in Smyrna write: 'The words of the first and the last, who died and came to life. I know your tribulation and your poverty (but you are rich) and the slander of those who say that they are Jews and are not, but are a synagogue of Satan. Do not fear what you are about to suffer. Behold, the devil is about to throw some of you into prison, that you may be tested, and for ten days you will have tribulation. Be faithful unto death, and I will give you the crown of life. He who has an ear, let him hear what the Spirit says to the churches. He who conquers shall not be hurt by the second death.' And to the angel of the church in Per'gamum write: 'The words of him who has the sharp two-edged sword. I know where you dwell, where Satan's throne is; you hold fast my name and you did not deny my faith even in the days of An'tipas my witness, my faithful one, who was killed among you, where Satan dwells. But I have a few things against you: you have some there who hold the teaching of Balaam, who taught Balak to put a stumbling block before the sons of Israel, that they might eat food sacrificed to idols and practice immorality. So you also have some who hold the teaching of the Nicola'itans. Repent then. If not, I will come to you soon and war against them with the sword of my mouth. He who has an ear, let him hear what the Spirit says to the churches. To him who conquers I will give some of the hidden manna, and I will give him a white stone, with a new name written on the stone which no one knows except him who receives it.'"

A Reading (Lesson) from the Gospel according to John
[4:46-54]

Jesus came again to Cana in Galilee, where he had made the water wine. And at Caper'na-um there was an official whose son was ill. When he heard that Jesus had come from Judea to Galilee, he went and begged him to come down and heal his son, for he was at the point of death. Jesus therefore said to him, "Unless you see signs and wonders you will not believe." The official said to him, "Sir, come down before my child dies." Jesus said to him, "Go; your son will live." The man believed the word that Jesus spoke to him and went his way. As he was going down, his servants met him and told him that his son was living. So he asked them the hour when he began to mend, and they said to him, "Yesterday at the seventh hour the fever left him." The father knew that was the hour when Jesus had said to him, "Your son will live"; and he himself believed, and all his household. This was now the second sign that Jesus did when he had come from Judea to Galilee.

January 9

Psalm 121 [page 779],   *Psalm 122* [page 779],
Psalm 123 [page 780]   ❖   *Psalm 131* [page 785],
Psalm 132 [page 785]

A Reading (Lesson) from the Book of Isaiah [63:1-5]

Who is this that comes from Edom, in crimsoned garments from Bozrah, he that is glorious in his apparel, marching in the greatness of his strength? "It is I, announcing vindication, mighty to save." Why is thy apparel red, and thy garments like his that treads in the wine press? "I have trodden the wine press alone, and from the peoples no one was with me; I trod them in my anger and trampled them in my wrath; their lifeblood is sprinkled upon my garments, and I have stained all my raiment. For the day of vengeance was in my heart, and my year of redemption has come. I looked, but there was no one to help; I was appalled, but there was no one to uphold; so my own arm brought me victory, and my wrath upheld me."

A Reading (Lesson) from the Revelation to John [2:18-29]

One like a son of man said to me, "To the angel of the church in Thyati'ra write: 'The words of the Son of God, who has eyes like a flame of fire, and whose feet are like burnished bronze. I know your works, your love and faith and service and patient endurance, and that your latter works exceed the first. But I have this against you, that you tolerate the woman Jez'ebel, who calls herself a prophetess and is teaching and beguiling my servants to practice immorality and to eat food sacrificed to idols. I gave her time to repent, but she refuses to repent of her immorality. Behold, I will throw her on a sickbed, and those who commit adultery with her I will throw into great tribulation, unless they repent of her doings; and I will strike her children dead. And all the churches shall know that I am he who searches mind and heart, and I will give to each of you as your works deserve. But to the rest of you in Thyati'ra, who do not hold this teaching, who have not learned what some call the deep things of Satan, to you I say, I do not lay upon you any other burden; only hold fast what you have, until I come. He who conquers and who keeps my works until the end, I will give him power over the nations, and he shall rule them with a rod of iron, as when earthen pots are broken in pieces, even as I myself have received power from my Father; and I will give him the morning star. He who has an ear, let him hear what the Spirit says to the churches.'"

A Reading (Lesson) from the Gospel according to John [5:1-15]

There was a feast of the Jews, and Jesus went up to

Jerusalem. Now there is in Jerusalem by the Sheep Gate a pool, in Hebrew called Beth-za'tha, which has five porticoes. In these lay a multitude of invalids, blind, lame, paralyzed. One man was there, who had been ill for thirty-eight years. When Jesus saw him and knew that he had been lying there a long time, he said to him, "Do you want to be healed?" The sick man answered him, "Sir, I have no man to put me into the pool when the water is troubled, and while I am going another steps down before me." Jesus said to him, "Rise, take up your pallet, and walk." And at once the man was healed, and he took up his pallet and walked. Now that day was the sabbath. So the Jews said to the man who was cured, "It is the sabbath, it is not lawful for you to carry your pallet." But he answered them, "The man who healed me said to me, 'Take up your pallet, and walk.'" They asked him, "Who is the man who said to you, 'Take up your pallet, and walk'?" Now the man who had been healed did not know who it was, for Jesus had withdrawn, as there was a crowd in the place. Afterward, Jesus found him in the temple, and said to him, "See, you are well! Sin no more, that nothing worse befall you." The man went away and told the Jews that it was Jesus who had healed him.

January 10

Psalm 138 [page 793],
Psalm 139:1-17 (18-23) [page 794]   ❖
Psalm 147 [page 804]

A Reading (Lesson) from the Book of Isaiah [65:1-9]

I was ready to be sought by those who did not ask for me; was ready to be found by those who did not seek me. I said, "Here am I, here am I," to a nation that did not call on my name. I spread out my hands all the day to a rebellious people, who walk in a way that is not good, following their own devices; a people who provoke me to my face continually, sacrificing in gardens and burning incense upon bricks; who sit in tombs, and spend the night in secret places; who eat swine's flesh, and broth of abominable things is in their vessels; who say, "Keep to yourself, do not come near me, for I am set apart from you." These are a smoke in my nostrils, a fire that burns all the day. Behold, it is written before me: "I will not keep silent, but I will repay, yea, I will repay into their bosom their iniquities and their fathers' iniquities together, says the Lord; because they burned incense upon the mountains and reviled me upon the hills, I will measure into their bosom payment for their former doings." Thus says the Lord: "As the wine is found in the cluster, and they say, 'Do not destroy it, for there is a blessing in it,' so I will do for my servants' sake, and not destroy them all. I will bring forth descendants from Jacob, and from Judah inheritors of my mountains; my chosen shall inherit it, and my servants shall dwell there."

A Reading (Lesson) from the Revelation to John [3:1-6]

One like a son of man said to me, "To the angel of the church in Sardis write: 'The words of him who has the seven spirits of God and the seven stars. I know your works; you have the name of being alive, and you are dead. Awake, and strengthen what remains and is on the point of death, for I have not found your works perfect in the sight of my God. Remember then what you received and heard; keep that, and repent. If you will not awake, I will come like a thief, and you will not know at what hour I will come upon you. Yet you have still a few names in Sardis, people who have not soiled their garments; and they shall walk with me in white, for they are worthy. He who conquers shall be clad thus in white garments, and I will not blot his name out of the book of life; I will confess his name before my Father and before his angels. He who has an ear, let him hear what the Spirit says to the churches.'"

A Reading (Lesson) from the Gospel according to John
[6:1-14]

Jesus went to the other side of the Sea of Galilee, which is the Sea of Tibe'ri-as. And a multitude followed him, because they saw the signs which he did on those who were diseased. Jesus went up on the mountain, and there sat down with his disciples. Now the Passover, the feast of the Jews, was at hand. Lifting up his eyes, then, and seeing that a multitude was coming to him, Jesus said to Philip, "How are we to buy bread, so that these people may eat?" This he said to test him, for he himself knew what he would do. Philip answered him, "Two hundred denarii would not buy enough bread for each of them to get a little." One of his disciples, Andrew, Simon Peter's brother, said to him, "There is a lad here who has five barley loaves and two fish; but what are they among so many?" Jesus said, "Make the people sit down." Now there was much grass in the place; so the men sat down, in number about five thousand. Jesus then took the loaves, and when he had given thanks, he distributed them to those who were seated; so also the fish, as much as they wanted. And when they had eaten their fill, he told his disciples, "Gather up the fragments left over, that nothing may be lost." So they gathered them up and filled twelve baskets with fragments from the five barley loaves, left by those who had eaten. When the people saw the sign which he had done, they said, "This is indeed the prophet who is to come into the world!"

January 11

Psalm 148 [page 805], *Psalm 150* [page 807] ❖
Psalm 91 [page 719], *Psalm 92* [page 720]

A Reading (Lesson) from the Book of Isaiah [65:13-16]

Thus says the Lord God: "Behold, my servants shall eat, but you shall be hungry; behold, my servants shall drink, but you shall be thirsty; behold, my servants shall rejoice, but you shall be put to shame; behold, my servants shall sing for gladness of heart, but you shall cry out for pain of heart, and shall wail for anguish of spirit. You shall leave your name to my chosen for a curse, and the Lord God will slay you; but his servants he will call by a different name. So that he who blesses himself in the land shall bless himself by the God of truth, and he who takes an oath in the land shall swear by the God of truth; because the former troubles are forgotten and are hid from my eyes."

A Reading (Lesson) from the Revelation to John [3:7-13]

One like a son of man said to me, "To the angel of the church in Philadelphia write: 'The words of the holy one, the true one, who has the key of David, who opens and no one shall shut, who shuts and no one opens. I know your works. Behold, I have set before you an open door, which no one is able to shut; I know that you have but little power, and yet you have kept my word and have not denied my name. Behold, I will make those of the synagogue of Satan who say that they are Jews and are not, but lie — behold, I will make them come and bow down before your feet, and learn that I have loved you. Because you have kept my word of patient endurance, I will keep you from the hour of trial which is coming on the whole world, to try those who dwell upon the earth. I am coming soon; hold fast what you have, so that no one may seize your crown. He who conquers, I will make him a pillar in the temple of my God; never shall he go out of it, and I will write on him the name of my God, and the name of the city of my God, the new Jerusalem which comes down from my God out of heaven, and my own new name. He who has an ear, let him hear what the Spirit says to the churches.'"

A Reading (Lesson) from the Gospel according to John
[6:15-27]

Perceiving that the people were about to come and take him by force to make him king, Jesus withdrew again to the mountain by himself. When evening came, his disciples went down to the sea, got into a boat, and started across the sea to Caper'na-um. It was now dark, and Jesus had not yet come to them. The sea rose because a strong wind was blowing. When they had rowed about three or four miles, they saw Jesus walking on the sea and drawing near to the boat. They were frightened, but he said to them, "It is I; do not be afraid." Then they were glad to take him into the boat, and immediately the boat was at the land to which they were going. On the next day the people who remained on the other side of the sea saw that there had been only one boat there, and that Jesus had not entered the boat with his disciples, but that his disciples had gone away alone. However, boats from Tibe'ri-as came near the place where they ate the bread after the Lord had given thanks. So when the people saw that Jesus was not there, nor his disciples, they themselves got into the boats and went to Caper'na-um, seeking Jesus. When they found him on the other side of the sea, they said to him, "Rabbi, when did you come here?" Jesus answered them, "Truly, truly, I say to you, you seek me, not because you saw signs, but because you ate your fill of the loaves. Do not labor for the food which perishes, but for the food which endures to eternal life, which the Son of Man will give to you; for on him has God the Father set his seal."

January 12

(Morning Prayer) *Psalm 98* [page 727], *Psalm 99* [page 728], *(Psalm 100* [page 729])

A Reading (Lesson) from the Book of Isaiah [66:1-2, 22-23]

Thus says the Lord: "Heaven is my throne and the earth is
my footstool; what is the house which you would build for
me, and what is the place of my rest? All these things my
hand has made, and so all these things are mine, says the
Lord. But this is the man to whom I will look, he that is
humble and contrite in spirit, and trembles at my word.
For as the new heavens and the new earth which I will
make shall remain before me, says the Lord; so shall your
descendants and your name remain. From new moon to
new moon, and from sabbath to sabbath, all flesh shall
come to worship before me, says the Lord."

A Reading (Lesson) from the Revelation to John [3:14-22]

One like a son of man said to me, "To the angel of the
church in La-odice′a write: 'The words of the Amen, the
faithful and true witness, the beginning of God's creation.
I know your works: you are neither cold nor hot. Would
that you were cold or hot! So, because you are lukewarm,
and neither cold nor hot, I will spew you out of my mouth.
For you say, I am rich, I have prospered, and I need
nothing; not knowing that you are wretched, pitiable,
poor, blind, and naked. Therefore I counsel you to buy
from me gold refined by fire, that you may be rich, and
white garments to clothe you and to keep the shame of
your nakedness from being seen, and salve to annoint your
eyes, that you may see. Those whom I love, I reprove and
chasten; so be zealous and repent. Behold, I stand at the
door and knock; if any one hears my voice and opens the
door, I will come in to him and eat with him, and he with
me. He who conquers, I will grant him to sit with me on
my throne, as I myself conquered and sat down with my
Father on his throne. He who has an ear, let him hear what
the Spirit says to the churches.'"

A Reading (Lesson) from the Gospel according to John
[9:1-12, 35-38]

As Jesus passed by, he saw a man blind from his birth. And his disciples asked him, "Rabbi, who sinned, this man or his parents, that he was born blind?" Jesus answered, "It was not that this man sinned, or his parents, but that the works of God might be made manifest in him. We must work the works of him who sent me, while it is day; night comes, when no one can work. As long as I am in the world, I am the light of the world." As he said this, he spat on the ground and made clay of the spittle and anointed the man's eyes with the clay, saying to him, "Go, wash in the pool of Silo'am" (which means Sent). So he went and washed and came back, seeing. The neighbors and those who had seen him before as a beggar, said, "Is not this the man who used to sit and beg?" Some said, "It is he"; others said, "No, but he is like him." He said, "I am the man." They said to him, "Then how were your eyes opened?" He answered, "The man called Jesus made clay and anointed my eyes and said to me, 'Go to Silo'am and wash'; so I went and washed and received my sight. They said to him, "Where is he?" He said, "I do not know." Jesus heard that they had cast him out, and having found him he said, "Do you believe in the Son of man?" He answered, "And who is he, sir, that I may believe in him?" Jesus said to him, "You have seen him, and it is he who speaks to you." He said, "Lord, I believe"; and he worshiped him.

Eve of 1 Epiphany

(Evening Prayer)   *Psalm 104* [page 735]

A Reading (Lesson) from the Book of Isaiah [61:1-91]

The Spirit of the Lord God is upon me, because the Lord has anointed me to bring good tidings to the afflicted; he has sent me to bind up the brokenhearted, to proclaim liberty to the captives, and the opening of the prison to those who are bound; to proclaim the year of the Lord's favor, and the day of vengeance of our God; to comfort all who mourn; to grant to those who mourn in Zion—to give them a garland instead of ashes, the oil of gladness instead of mourning, the mantle of praise instead of a faint spirit; that they may be called oaks of righteousness, the planting of the Lord, that he may be glorified. They shall build up the ancient ruins, they shall raise up the former devastations; they shall repair the ruined cities, the devastations of many generations. Aliens shall stand and feed your flocks, foreigners shall be your plowmen and vinedressers; but you shall be called the priests of the Lord, men shall speak of you as the ministers of our God; you shall eat the wealth of the nations, and in their riches you shall glory. Instead of your shame you shall have a double portion, instead of dishonor you shall rejoice in your lot; therefore in your land you shall possess a double portion; yours shall be everlasting joy. For I the Lord love justice, I hate robbery and wrong; I will faithfully give them their recompense, and I will make an everlasting covenant with them. Their descendants shall be known among the nations, and their offspring in the midst of the peoples; all who see them shall acknowledge them, that they are a people whom the Lord has blessed.

A Reading (Lesson) from the Letter of Paul to the Galatians [3:23-29; 4:4-7]

Before faith came, we were confined under the law, kept under restraint until faith should be revealed. So that the law was our custodian until Christ came, that we might be justified by faith. But now that faith has come, we are no longer under a custodian; for in Christ Jesus you are all sons of God, through faith. For as many of you as were baptized into Christ have put on Christ. There is neither Jew nor Greek, there is neither slave nor free, there is neither male nor female; for you are all one in Christ Jesus. And if you are Christ's, then you are Abraham's offspring, heirs according to promise. But when the time had fully come, God sent forth his Son, born of woman, born under the law, to redeem those who were under the law, so that we might receive adoption as sons. And because you are sons, God has sent the Spirit of his Son into our hearts, crying, "Abba! Father!" So through God you are no longer a slave but a son, and if a son then an heir.

Week of 1 Epiphany

Sunday

Psalm 146 [page 803], *Psalm 147* [page 804] ❖
Psalm 111 [page 754], *Psalm 112* [page 755],
Psalm 113 [page 756]

A Reading from the Book of Isaiah [40:1-11]

Comfort, comfort my people, says your God. Speak tenderly to Jerusalem, and cry to her that her warfare is ended, that her iniquity is pardoned, that she has received from the Lord's hand double for all her sins. A voice cries: "In the wilderness prepare the way of the Lord, make straight in the desert a highway for our God. Every valley shall be lifted up, and every mountain and hill be made low; the uneven ground shall become level, and the rough places a plain. And the glory of the Lord shall be revealed, and all flesh shall see it together, for the mouth of the Lord has spoken." A voice says, "Cry!" And I said, "What shall I cry?" All flesh is grass, and all its beauty is like the flower of the field. The grass withers, the flower fades, when the breath of the Lord blows upon it; surely the people is grass. The grass withers, the flower fades; but the word of our God will stand for ever. Get you up to a high mountain, O Zion, herald of good tidings; lift up your voice with strength, O Jerusalem, herald of good tidings, lift it up, fear not; say to the cities of Judah, "Behold your God!" Behold, the Lord God comes with might, and his arm rules for him; behold, his reward is with him, and his recompense before him. He will feed his flock like a shepherd, he will gather the lambs in his arms, he will carry them in his bosom, and gently lead those that are with young.

A Reading (Lesson) from the Letter to the Hebrews
[1:1-12]

In many and various ways God spoke of old to our fathers by the prophets; but in these last days he has spoken to us by a Son, whom he appointed the heir of all things, through whom also he created the world. He reflects the glory of God and bears the very stamp of his nature, upholding the universe by his word of power. When he had made purification for sins, he sat down at the right hand of the Majesty on high, having become as much superior to angels as the name he has obtained is more excellent than theirs. For to what angel did God ever say, "Thou art my Son, today I have begotten thee"? Or again, "I will be to him a father, and he shall be to me a son"? And again, when he brings the first-born into the world, he says, "Let all God's angels worship him." Of the angels he says, "Who makes his angels winds, and his servants flames of fire." But of the Son he says, "Thy throne, O God, is for ever and ever, the righteous scepter is the scepter of thy kingdom. Thou hast loved righteousness and hated lawlessness; therefore God, thy God, has anointed thee with the oil of gladness beyond thy comrades." And, "Thou, Lord, didst found the earth in the beginning, and the heavens are the work of thy hands; they will perish, but thou remainest; they will all grow old like a garment, like a mantle thou wilt roll them up, and they will be changed. But thou art the same, and thy years will never end."

A Reading (Lesson) from the Gospel according to John
[1:1-7,19-20,29-34]

In the beginning was the Word, and the Word was with
God, and the Word was God. He was in the beginning
with God; all things were made through him, and without
him was not anything made that was made. In him was
life, and the life was the light of men. The light shines in
the darkness, and the darkness has not overcome it. There
was a man sent from God, whose name was John. He came
for testimony, to bear witness to the light, that all might
believe through him. And this is the testimony of John,
when the Jews sent priests and Levites from Jerusalem to
ask him, "Who are you?" He confessed, he did not deny,
but confessed, "I am not the Christ." The next day he saw
Jesus coming toward him, and said, "Behold, the Lamb of
God, who takes away the sin of the world! This is he of
whom I said, 'After me comes a man who ranks before me,
for he was before me.' I myself did not know him; but for
this I came baptizing with water, that he might be revealed
to Israel." And John bore witness, "I saw the Spirit descend
as a dove from heaven, and it remained on him. I myself
did not know him; but he who sent me to baptize with
water said to me, 'He on whom you see the Spirit descend
and remain, this is he who baptizes with the Holy Spirit.'
And I have seen and have borne witness that this is the Son
of God."

Monday

Psalm 1 [page 585],   *Psalm 2* [page 586],   *Psalm 3* [page 587]
❖   *Psalm 4* [Page 587],   *Psalm 7* [page 590]

A Reading (Lesson) from the Book of Isaiah   [40:12-23]

Who has measured the waters in the hollow of his hand
and marked off the heavens with a span, enclosed the dust
of the earth in a measure and weighed the mountains in

scales and the hills in a balance? Who has directed the Spirit of the Lord, or as his counselor has instructed him? Whom did he consult for his enlightenment and who taught him the path of justice, and taught him knowledge, and showed him the way of understanding? Behold, the nations are like a drop from a bucket, and are accounted as the dust on the scales; behold, he takes up the isles like fine dust. Lebanon would not suffice for fuel, nor are its beasts enough for a burnt offering. All the nations are as nothing before him, they are accounted by him as less than nothing and emptiness. To whom then will you liken God, or what likeness compare with him? The idol! a workman casts it, and a goldsmith overlays it with gold, and casts for it silver chains. He who is impoverished chooses for an offering wood that will not rot; he seeks out a skilful craftsman to set up an image that will not move. Have you not known? Have you not heard? Has it not been told you from the beginning? Have you not understood from the foundations of the earth? It is he who sits above the circle of the earth, and its inhabitants are like grasshoppers; who stretches out the heavens like a curtain, and spreads them like a tent to dwell in; who brings princes to nought, and makes the rulers of the earth as nothing.

A Reading (Lesson) from the Letter of Paul to the Ephesians [1:1-14]

Paul, an apostle of Christ Jesus by the will of God, To the saints who are also faithful in Christ Jesus: Grace to you and peace from God our Father and the Lord Jesus Christ. Blessed be the God and Father of our Lord Jesus Christ, who has blessed us in Christ with every spiritual blessing in the heavenly places, even as he chose us in him before the foundation of the world, that we should be holy and blameless before him. He destined us in love to be his sons through Jesus Christ, according to the purpose of his will, to the praise of his glorious grace which he freely bestowed on us in the Beloved. In him we have redemption through his blood, the forgiveness of our trespasses, according to the riches of his grace which he lavished upon us. For he has made known to us in all wisdom and insight the mystery of his will, according to his purpose which he set forth in Christ as a plan for the fulness of time, to unite all things in him, things in heaven and things on earth. In him, according to the purpose of him who accomplishes all things according to the counsel of his will, we who first hoped in Christ have been destined and appointed to live for the praise of his glory. In him you also, who have heard the word of truth, the gospel of your salvation, and have believed in him, were sealed with the promised Holy Spirit, which is the guarantee of our inheritance until we acquire possession of it, to the praise of his glory.

A Reading (Lesson) from the Gospel according to Mark [1:1-13]

The beginning of the gospel of Jesus Christ, the Son of God. As it is written in Isaiah the prophet, "Behold, I send my messenger before thy face, who shall prepare thy way; the voice of one crying in the wilderness: Prepare the way of the Lord, make his paths straight—" John the baptizer appeared in the wilderness, preaching a baptism of repentance for the forgiveness of sins. And there went out to him all the country of Judea, and all the people of Jerusalem; and they were baptized by him in the river Jordan, confessing their sins. Now John was clothed with camel's hair, and had a leather girdle around his waist and ate locusts and wild honey. And he preached, saying, "After me comes he who is mightier than I, the thong of whose sandals I am not worthy to stoop down and untie. I have baptized you with water; but he will baptize you with the Holy Spirit." In those days Jesus came from Nazareth of Galilee and was baptized by John in the Jordan. And when he came up out of the water, immediately he saw the heavens opened and the Spirit descending upon him like a dove; and a voice came from heaven, "Thou art my beloved Son; with thee I am well pleased." The Spirit immediately drove him out into the wilderness. And he was in the wilderness forty days, tempted by Satan; and he was with the wild beasts; and the angels ministered to him.

Tuesday

Psalm 5 [page 588],   *Psalm 6* [page 589]   ❖
Psalm 10 [page 594],   *Psalm 11* [page 596]

A Reading (Lesson) from the Book of Isaiah [40:25-31]

To whom then will you compare me, that I should be like him? says the Holy One. Lift up your eyes on high and see: who created these? He who brings out their host by number, calling them all by name; by the greatness of his might, and because he is strong in power not one is missing. Why do you say, O Jacob, and speak, O Israel, "My way is hid from the Lord, and my right is disregarded by my God"? Have you not known? Have you not heard? The Lord is the everlasting God, the Creator of the ends of the earth. He does not faint or grow weary, his understanding is unsearchable. He gives power to the faint, and to him who has no might he increases strength. Even youths shall faint and be weary, and young men shall fall exhausted; but they who wait for the Lord shall renew their strength, they shall mount up with wings like eagles, they shall run and not be weary, they shall walk and not faint.

A Reading (Lesson) from the Letter of Paul to the Ephesians [1:15-23]

For this reason, because I have heard of your faith in the Lord Jesus and your love toward all the saints, I do not cease to give thanks for you, remembering you in my prayers, that the God of our Lord Jesus Christ, the Father of glory, may give you a spirit of wisdom and of revelation

in the knowledge of him, having the eyes of your hearts
enlightened, that you may know what is the hope to which
he has called you, what are the riches of his glorious
inheritance in the saints, and what is the immeasurable
greatness of his power in us who believe, according to the
working of his great might which he accomplished in
Christ when he raised him from the dead and made him sit
at his right hand in the heavenly places, far above all rule
and authority and power and dominion, and above every
name that is named, not only in this age but also in that
which is to come; and he has put all things under his feet
and has made him the head over all things for the church,
which is his body, the fulness of him who fills all in all.

A Reading (Lesson) from the Gospel according to Mark
[1:14-28]

After John was arrested, Jesus came into Galilee,
preaching the gospel of God, and saying, "The time is
fulfilled, and the kingdom of God is at hand; repent, and
believe in the gospel." And passing along by the Sea of
Galilee, he saw Simon and Andrew the brother of Simon
casting a net in the sea; for they were fishermen. And Jesus
said to them, "Follow me and I will make you become
fishers of men." And immediately they left their nets and
followed him. And going on a little farther, he saw James
the son of Zeb'edee and John his brother, who were in their
boat mending the nets. And immediately he called them;
and they left their father Zeb'edee in the boat with the
hired servants, and followed him. And they went into
Caper'na-um; and immediately on the sabbath he entered
the synagogue and taught. And they were astonished at his
teaching, for he taught them as one who had authority,
and not as the scribes. And immediately there was in their
synagogue a man with an unclean spirit; and he cried out,
"What have you to do with us, Jesus of Nazareth? Have you
come to destroy us? I know who you are, the Holy One of
God." But Jesus rebuked him, saying, "Be silent, and come

out of him!" And the unclean spirit, convulsing him and crying with a loud voice, came out of him. And they were all amazed, so that they questioned among themselves, saying, "What is this? A new teaching! With authority he commands even the unclean spirits, and they obey him." And at once his fame spread everywhere throughout all the surrounding region of Galilee.

Wednesday

Psalm 119:1-24 [page 763]   ❖   *Psalm 12* [page 597],
Psalm 13 [page 597],   *Psalm 14* [page 598]

A Reading (Lesson) from the Book of Isaiah [41:1-16]

Listen to me in silence, O coastlands; let the peoples renew their strength; let them approach, then let them speak; let us together draw near for judgment. Who stirred up one from the east whom victory meets at every step? He gives up nations before him, so that he tramples kings under foot; he makes them like dust with his sword, like driven stubble with his bow. He pursues them and passes on safely, by paths his feet have not trod. Who has performed and done this, calling the generations from the beginning? I, the Lord, the first, and with the last; I am He. The coastlands have seen and are afraid, the ends of the earth tremble; they have drawn near and come. Every one helps his neighbor, and says to his brother, "Take courage!" The craftsman encourages the goldsmith, and he who smooths with the hammer him who strikes the anvil, saying of the soldering, "It is good"; and they fasten it with nails so that it cannot be moved. But you, Israel, my servant, Jacob, whom I have chosen, the offspring of Abraham, my friend; you whom I took from the ends of the earth, and called from its farthest corners, saying to you, "You are my servant, I have chosen you and not cast you off"; fear not, for I am with you, be not dismayed, for I am your God; I will strengthen you, I will help you, I will uphold you with my victorious right hand. Behold, all who are incensed against you shall be put to shame and confounded; those who strive against you shall be as nothing and shall perish. You shall seek those who contend with you, but you shall not find them; those who war against you shall be as nothing at all. For I, the Lord your God, hold your right hand; it is I who say to you, "Fear not, I will help you." Fear not, you worm Jacob, you men of Israel! I will help you, says the Lord; your Redeemer is the Holy One of Israel. Behold, I will make of you a threshing sledge, new, sharp, and having teeth; you shall thresh the mountains and crush them, and you shall make the hills like chaff; you shall winnow them and the wind shall carry them away, and the tempest shall scatter them. And you shall rejoice in the Lord; in the Holy One of Israel you shall glory.

A Reading (Lesson) from the Letter of Paul to the Ephesians [2:1-10]

You he made alive, when you were dead through the trespasses and sins in which you once walked, following the course of this world, following the prince of the power of the air, the spirit that is now at work in the sons of disobedience. Among these we all once lived in the passions of our flesh, following the desires of body and mind, and so we were by nature children of wrath, like the rest of mankind. But God, who is rich in mercy, out of the great love with which he loved us, even when we were dead through our trespasses, made us alive together with Christ (by grace you have been saved), and raised us up with him, and made us sit with him in the heavenly places in Christ Jesus, that in the coming ages he might show the immeasurable riches of his grace in kindness toward us in Christ Jesus. For by grace you have been saved through faith; and this is not your own doing, it is the gift of God—not because of works, lest any man should boast.

For we are his workmanship, created in Christ Jesus for good works, which God prepared beforehand, that we should walk in them.

A Reading (Lesson) from the Gospel according to Mark
[1:29-45]

Immediately Jesus left the synagogue, and entered the house of Simon and Andrew, with James and John. Now Simon's mother-in-law lay sick with a fever, and immediately they told him of her. And he came and took her by the hand and lifted her up, and the fever left her; and she served them. That evening, at sundown, they brought to him all who were sick or possessed with demons. And the whole city was gathered together about the door. And he healed many who were sick with various diseases, and cast out many demons; and he would not permit the demons to speak, because they knew him. And in the morning, a great while before day, he rose and went out to a lonely place, and there he prayed. And Simon and those who were with him pursued him, and they found him and said to him, "Every one is searching for you." And he said to them, "Let us go on to the next towns, that I may preach there also; for that is why I came out." And he went throughout all Galilee, preaching in their synagogues and casting out demons. And a leper came to him beseeching him, and kneeling said to him, "If you will, you can make me clean." Moved with pity, he stretched out his hand and touched him, and said to him, "I will; be clean." And immediately the leprosy left him, and he was made clean. And he sternly charged him, and sent him away at once, and said to him, "See that you say nothing to any one; but go, show yourself to the priest, and offer for your cleansing what Moses commanded, for a proof to the people." But he went out and began to talk freely about it, and to spread the news, so that Jesus could no longer openly enter a town, but was out in the country; and people came to him from every quarter.

Thursday

Psalm 18:1-20 [page 602] ❖ *Psalm 18:21-50* [page 604]

A Reading (Lesson) from the Book of Isaiah [41:17-29]

When the poor and needy seek water, and there is none, and their tongue is parched with thirst, I the Lord will answer them, I the God of Israel will not forsake them. I will open rivers on the bare heights, and fountains in the midst of the valleys; I will make the wilderness a pool of water, and the dry land springs of water. I will put in the wilderness the cedar, the acacia, the myrtle, and the olive; I will set in the desert the cypress, the plane and the pine together; that men may see and know, may consider and understand together, that the hand of the Lord has done this, the Holy One of Israel has created it. Set forth your case, says the Lord; bring your proofs, says the King of Jacob. Let them bring them, and tell us what is to happen. Tell us the former things, what they are, that we may consider them, that we may know their outcome; or declare to us the things to come. Tell us what is to come hereafter, that we may know that you are gods; do good, or do harm, that we may be dismayed and terrified. Behold, you are nothing, and your work is nought; an abomination is he who chooses you. I stirred up one from the north, and he has come, from the rising of the sun, and he shall call on my name; he shall trample on rulers as on mortar, as the potter treads clay. Who declared it from the beginning, that we might know, and beforetime, that we might say, "He is right"? There was none who declared it, none who proclaimed, none who heard your words. I first have declared it to Zion, and I give to Jerusalem a herald of good tidings. But when I look there is no one; among these there is no counselor who, when I ask, gives an answer. Behold, they are all a delusion; their works are nothing; their molten images are empty wind.

*A Reading (Lesson) from the Letter of Paul
to the Ephesians* [2:11-22]

Remember that at one time you Gentiles in the flesh, called
the uncircumcision by what is called the circumcision,
which is made in the flesh by hands—remember that you
were at that time separated from Christ, alienated from the
commonwealth of Israel, and strangers to the covenants of
promise, having no home and without God in the world.
But now in Christ Jesus you who once were far off have
been brought near in the blood of Christ. For he is our
peace, who has made us both one, and has broken down
the dividing wall of hostility, by abolishing in his flesh the
law of commandments and ordinances, that he might
create in himself one new man in place of the two, so
making peace, and might reconcile us both to God in one
body through the cross, thereby bringing the hostility to an
end. And he came and preached peace to you who were far
off and peace to those who were near; for through him we
both have access in one Spirit to the Father. So then you
are no longer strangers and sojourners, but you are fellow
citizens with the saints and members of the household of
God, built upon the foundation of the apostles and
prophets, Christ Jesus himself being the cornerstone in
whom the whole structure is joined together and grows
into a holy temple in the Lord; in whom you also are built
into it for a dwelling place of God in the spirit.

A Reading (Lesson) from the Gospel according to Mark
[2:1-12]

When Jesus returned to Caper'na-um after some days, it
was reported that he was at home. And many were
gathered together, so that there was no longer room for
them, not even about the door; and he was preaching the
word to them. And they came, bringing to him a paralytic
carried by four men. And when they could not get near
him because of the crowd, they removed the roof above

him; and when they had made an opening, they let down the pallet on which the paralytic lay. And when Jesus saw their faith, he said to the paralytic, "My son, your sins are forgiven." Now some of the scribes were sitting there, questioning in their hearts, "Why does this man speak thus? It is blasphemy! Who can forgive sins but God alone?" And immediately Jesus, perceiving in his spirit that they thus questioned within themselves, said to them, "Why do you question thus in your hearts? Which is easier, to say to the paralytic, 'Your sins are forgiven,' or to say, 'Rise, take up your pallet and walk'? But that you may know that the Son of man has authority on earth to forgive sins"—he said to the paralytic—"I say to you, rise, take up your pallet and go home." And he rose, and immediately took up the pallet and went out before them all; so that they were all amazed and glorified God, saying, "We never saw anything like this!"

Friday

Psalm 16 [page 599],   *Psalm 17* [page 600]   ❖
Psalm 22 [page 610]

A Reading (Lesson) from the Book of Isaiah [42:(1-9)10-17]

Behold my servant, whom I uphold, my chosen, in whom my soul delights; I have put my Spirit upon him, he will bring forth justice to the nations. He will not cry or lift up his voice, or make it heard in the street; a bruised reed he will not break, and a dimly burning wick he will not quench; he will faithfully bring forth justice. He will not fail or be discouraged till he has established justice in the earth; and the coastlands wait for his law. Thus says God, the Lord, who created the heavens and stretched them out, who spread forth the earth and what comes from it, who gives breath to the people upon it and spirit to those who walk in it: "I am the Lord, I have called you in righteousness, I have taken you by the hand and kept you; I have given you as a covenant to the people, a light to the nations, to open the eyes that are blind, to bring out the prisoners from the dungeon, from the prison those who sit in darkness. I am the Lord, that is my name; my glory I give to no other, nor my praise to graven images. Behold, the former things have come to pass, and new things I now declare; before they spring forth I tell you of them."

Sing to the Lord a new song, his praise from the end of the earth! Let the sea roar and all that fills it, the coastlands and their inhabitants. Let the desert and its cities lift up their voice, the villages that Kedar inhabits; let the inhabitants of Sela sing for joy, let them shout from the top of the mountains. Let them give glory to the Lord, and declare his praise in the coastlands. The Lord goes forth like a mighty man, like a man of war he stirs up his fury; he cries out, he shouts aloud, he shows himself mighty against his foes. For a long time I have held my peace, I have kept still and restrained myself; now I will cry out like a woman in travail, I will gasp and pant. I will lay waste mountains and hills, and dry up all their herbage; I will turn the rivers into islands, and dry up the pools. And I will lead the blind in a way that they know not, in paths that they have not known I will guide them. I will turn the darkness before them into light, the rough places into level ground. These are the things I will do, and I will not forsake them. They shall be turned back and utterly put to shame, who trust in graven images, who say to molten images, "You are our gods."

A Reading (Lesson) from the Letter of Paul to the Ephesians [3:1-13]

For this reason I, Paul, a prisoner for Christ Jesus on behalf of you Gentiles—assuming that you have heard of the stewardship of God's grace that was given to me for you, how the mystery was made known to me by revelation, as

I have written briefly. When you read this you can perceive my insight into the mystery of Christ, which was not made known to the sons of men in other generations as it has now been revealed to his holy apostles and prophets by the Spirit; that is, how the Gentiles are fellow heirs, members of the same body, and partakers of the promise in Christ Jesus through the gospel. Of this gospel I was made a minister according to the gift of God's grace which was given me by the working of his power. To me, though I am the very least of all the saints, this grace was given, to preach to the Gentiles the unsearchable riches of Christ, and to make all men see what is the plan of the mystery hidden for ages in God who created all things; that through the church the manifold wisdom of God might now be made known to the principalities and powers in the heavenly places. This was according to the eternal purpose which he has realized in Christ Jesus our Lord, in whom we have boldness and confidence of access through our faith in him. So I ask you not to lose heart over what I am suffering for you, which is your glory.

A Reading (Lesson) from the Gospel according to Mark [2:13-22]

Jesus went out again beside the sea; and all the crowd gathered about him, and he taught them. And as he passed on, he saw Levi the son of Alphaeus sitting at the tax office, and he said to him, "Follow me." And he rose and followed him. And as he sat at table in his house, many tax collectors and sinners were sitting with Jesus and his disciples; for there were many who followed him. And the scribes of the Pharisees, when they saw that he was eating with sinners and tax collectors, said to his disciples, "Why does he eat with tax collectors and sinners?" And when Jesus heard it, he said to them, "Those who are well have no need of a physician, but those who are sick; I came not to call the righteous, but sinners." Now John's disciples and the Pharisees were fasting; and people came and said to him, "Why do John's disciples and the disciples of the Pharisees fast, but your disciples do not fast?" And Jesus said to them, "Can the wedding guests fast while the bridgeroom is with them? As long as they have the bridegroom with them, they cannot fast. The days will come, when the bridegroom is taken away from them, and then they will fast in that day. No one sews a piece of unshrunk cloth on an old garment; if he does, the patch tears away from it, the new from the old, and a worse tear is made. And no one puts new wine into old wineskins; if he does, the wine will burst the skins, and the wine is lost, and so are the skins; but new wine is for fresh skins."

Saturday

Psalm 20 [page 608], *Psalm 21:1-7(8-14)* [page 608]
❖ *Psalm 110:1-5(6-7)* [page 753],
Psalm 116 [page 759], *Psalm 117* [page 760]

A Reading (Lesson) from the Book of Isaiah [43:1-13]

Thus says the Lord, he who created you, O Jacob, he who formed you, O Israel: "Fear not, for I have redeemed you; I have called you by name, you are mine. When you pass through the waters I will be with you; and through the rivers, they shall not overwhelm you; when you walk through fire you shall not be burned, and the flame shall not consume you. For I am the Lord your God, the Holy One of Israel, your Savior. I give Egypt as your ransom, Ethiopia and Seba in exchange for you. Because you are precious in my eyes, and honored, and I love you, I give men in return for you, peoples in exchange for your life. Fear not, for I am with you; I will bring your offspring from the east, and from the west I will gather you; I will say to the north, give up, and to the south, Do not withhold; bring my sons from afar and my daughters from the end of the earth, every one who is called by my name, whom I created for my glory, whom I formed and made."

Bring forth the people who are blind, yet have eyes, who are deaf, yet have ears! Let all the nations gather together, and let the peoples assemble. Who among them can declare this, and show us the former things? Let them bring their witnesses to justify them, and let them hear and say, It is true. "You are my witnesses," says the Lord, "and my servant whom I have chosen, that you may know and believe me and understand that I am He. Before me no god was formed, nor shall there by any after me. I, I am the Lord, and besides me there is no savior. I declared and saved and proclaimed, when there was no strange god among you; and you are my witnesses," says the Lord. "I am God, and also henceforth I am He; there is none who can deliver from my hand; I work and who can hinder it?"

A Reading (Lesson) from the Letter of Paul to the Ephesians [3:14-21]

For this reason I bow my knees before the Father, from whom every family in heaven and on earth is named, that according to the riches of his glory he may grant you to be strengthened with might through his Spirit in the inner man, and that Christ may dwell in your hearts through faith; that you, being rooted and grounded in love, may have power to comprehend with all the saints what is the breadth and length and height and depth, and to know the love of Christ which surpasses knowledge, that you may be filled with all the fulness of God. Now to him who by the power at work within us is able to do far more abundantly than all that we ask or think, to him be glory in the church and in Christ Jesus to all generations, for ever and ever. Amen.

A Reading (Lesson) from the Gospel according to Mark [2:23—3:6I]

One sabbath Jesus was going through the grainfields; and as they made their way his disciples began to pluck heads of grain. And the Pharisees said to him, "Look, why are they doing what is not lawful on the sabbath?" And he said to them, "Have you never read what David did, when he was in need and was hungry, he and those who were with him: how he entered the house of God, when Abi'athar was high priest, and ate the bread of the Presence, which it is not lawful for any but the priests to eat, and also gave it to those who were with him?" And he said to them, "The sabbath was made for man, not man for the sabbath; so the Son of man is lord even of the sabbath." Again he entered the synagogue, and a man was there who had a withered hand. And they watched him, to see whether he would heal him on the sabbath, so that they might accuse him. And he said to the man who had the withered hand, "Come here." And he said to them, "Is it lawful on the sabbath to do good or to do harm, to save life or to kill?" But they were silent. And he looked around at them with anger, grieved at their hardness of heart, and said to the man, "Stretch out your hand." He stretched it out, and his hand was restored. The Pharisees went out, and immediately held counsel with the Hero'di-ans against him, how to destroy him.

Week of 2 Epiphany

Sunday

Psalm 148 [page 805],   *Psalm 149* [page 807],
Psalm 150 [page 807]   ❖   *Psalm 114* [page 756],
Psalm 115 [page 757]

A Reading (Lesson) from the Book of Isaiah [43:14—44:5]

Thus says the Lord, your Redeemer, the Holy One of Israel: "For your sake I will send to Babylon and break down all the bars, and the shouting of the Chalde'ans will be turned to lamentations. I am the Lord, your Holy One, the Creator of Israel, your King." Thus says the Lord, who makes a way in the sea, a path in the mighty waters, who brings forth chariot and horse, army and warrior; they lie down, they cannot rise, they are extinguished, quenched like a wick: "Remember not the former things, nor consider the things of old. Behold, I am doing a new thing; now it springs forth, do you not perceive it? I will make a way in the wilderness and rivers in the desert. The wild beasts will honor me, the jackals and the ostriches; for I give water in the wilderness, rivers in the desert, to give drink to my chosen people, the people whom I formed for myself that they might declare my praise. Yet you did not call upon me, O Jacob; but you have been weary of me, O Israel! You have not brought me your sheep for burnt offerings, or honored me with your sacrifices. I have not burdened you with offerings, or wearied you with frankincense. You have not bought me sweet cane with money, or satisfied me with the fat of your sacrifices. But you have burdened me with your sins, you have wearied me with your iniquities. I, I am He who blots out your transgressions for my own sake, and I will not remember your sins. Put me in remembrance, let us argue together; set forth your case, that you may be proved right. Your first father sinned, and your mediators transgressed against me. Therefore I profaned the princes of the sanctuary, I delivered Jacob to utter destruction and Israel to reviling. But now hear, O Jacob my servant, Israel whom I have chosen! Thus says the Lord who made you, who formed you from the womb and will help you: Fear not, O Jacob my servant, Jeshu'run whom I have chosen. For I will pour water on the thirsty land, and streams on the dry ground; I will pour my Spirit upon your descendants, and my blessing on your offspring. They shall spring up like grass amid waters, like willows by flowing streams. This one will say, 'I am the Lord's,' another will call himself by the name of Jacob, and another will write on his hand, 'The Lord's,' and surname himself by the name of Israel."

A Reading (Lesson) from the Letter to the Hebrews
[6:17—7:10]

When God desired to show more convincingly to the heirs of the promise the unchangeable character of his purpose, he interposed with an oath, so that through two unchangeable things, in which it is impossible that God should prove false, we who have fled for refuge might have strong encouragement to seize the hope set before us. We have this as a sure and steadfast anchor of the soul, a hope that enters into the inner shrine behind the curtain, where Jesus has gone as a forerunner on our behalf, having become a high priest for ever after the order of Melchizedek. For this Melchizedek, king of Salem, priest of the Most High God, met Abraham returning from the slaughter of the kings and blessed him; and to him Abraham apportioned a tenth part of everything. He is first, by translation of his name, king of righteousness, and then he is also king of Salem, that is, king of peace. He is without father or mother or geneaology, and has neither beginning of days nor end of life, but resembling the Son of God he continues a priest for ever. See how great he is! Abraham the patriarch gave him a tithe of the spoils. And those descendants of Levi who receive the priestly office have a commandment in the law to take tithes from the people, that is, from their brethren, though these also are descended from Abraham. But this man who has not their genealogy received tithes from Abraham and blessed him who had the promises. It is beyond dispute that the inferior is blessed by the superior. Here tithes are received by mortal men; there, by one of whom it is testified that he lives. One might even say that Levi himself, who receives tithes, paid tithes through Abraham, for he was still in the loins of his ancestor when Melchizedek met him.

A Reading (Lesson) from the Gospel according to John
[4:27-42]

Just then the disciples of Jesus came. They marveled that

he was talking with a woman, but none said, "What do you wish?" or, "Why are you talking with her?" So the woman left her water jar, and went away into the city, and said to the people, "Come, see a man who told me all that I ever did. Can this be the Christ?" They went out of the city and were coming to him. Meanwhile the disciples besought him, saying, "Rabbi, eat." But he said to them, "I have food to eat of which you do not know." So the disciples said to one another, "Has any one brought him food?" Jesus said to them, "My food is to do the will of him who sent me, and to accomplish his work. Do you not say, 'There are yet four months, then comes the harvest'? I tell you, lift up your eyes, and see how the fields are already white for harvest. He who reaps receives wages, and gathers fruit for eternal life, so that sower and reaper may rejoice together. For here the saying holds true, 'One sows and another reaps.' I sent you to reap that for which you did not labor; others have labored, and you have entered into their labor." Many Samaritans from that city believed in him because of the woman's testimony. "He told me all that I ever did." So when the Samaritans came to him, they asked him to stay with them; and he stayed there two days. And many more believed because of his word. They said to the woman, "It is no longer because of your words that we believe, for we have heard for ourselves, and we know that this is indeed the Savior of the world."

Monday

Psalm 25 [page 614] ❖ *Psalm 9* [page 593],
Psalm 15 [page 599]

A Reading (Lesson) from the Book of Isaiah [44:6-8,21-23]

Thus says the Lord, the King of Israel and his Redeemer, the Lord of hosts: "I am the first and I am the last; besides me there is no god. Who is like me? Let him proclaim it, let him declare and set it forth before me. Who has announced from of old the things to come? Let them tell us what is yet to be. Fear not, nor be afraid; have I not told you from of old and declared it? And you are my witnesses! Is there a God besides me? There is no Rock; I know not any." Remember these things, O Jacob, and Israel, for you are my servant; I formed you, you are my servant; O Israel, you will not be forgotten by me. I have swept away your transgressions like a cloud, and your sins like mist; return to me, for I have redeemed you. Sing, O heavens, for the Lord has done it; shout, O depths of the earth; break forth into singing, O mountains, O forest, and every tree in it! For the Lord has redeemed Jacob, and will be glorified in Israel.

A Reading (Lesson) from the Letter of Paul to the Ephesians [4:1-16]

I therefore, a prisoner for the Lord, beg you to lead a life worthy of the calling to which you have been called, with all lowliness and meekness, with patience, forbearing one another in love, eager to maintain the unity of the Spirit in the bond of peace. There is one body and one Spirit, just as you were called to the one hope that belongs to your call, one Lord, one faith, one baptism, on God and Father of us all, who is above all and through all and in all. But grace was given to each of us according to the measure of Christ's gift. Therefore it is said, "When he ascended on high he led a host of captives, and he gave gifts to men." (In saying, "He ascended," what does it mean but that he had also descended into the lower parts of the earth? He who descended is he who also ascended far above all the heavens, that he might fill all things.) And his gifts were that some should be apostles, some prophets, some evangelists, some pastors and teachers, to equip the saints for the work of ministry, for building up the body of Christ, until we all attain to the unity of the faith and of the knowledge of the Son of God, to mature manhood, to the measure of the stature of the fulness of Christ; so that we may no longer be children, tossed to and fro and carried about with every wind of doctrine, by the cunning of men, by their craftiness in deceitful wiles. Rather, speaking the truth in love, we are to grow up in every way into him who is the head, into Christ, from whom the whole body, joined and knit together by every joint with which it is supplied, when each part is working properly, makes bodily growth and upbuilds itself in love.

A Reading (Lesson) from the Gospel according to Mark
[3:7-19a]

Jesus withdrew with his disciples to the sea, and a great multitude from Galilee followed; also from Judea and Jerusalem and Idume'a and from beyond the Jordan and from about Tyre and Sidon a great multitude, hearing all that he did, came to him. And he told his disciples to have a boat ready for him because of the crowd, lest they should crush him; for he had healed many, so that all who had diseases pressed upon him to touch him. And whenever the unclean spirits beheld him, they fell down before him and cried out, "You are the Son of God." And he strictly ordered them not to make him known. And he went up on the mountain, and called to him those whom he desired; and they came to him. And he appointed twelve, to be with him, and to be sent out to preach and have authority to cast out demons: Simon whom he surnamed Peter; James the son of Zeb'edee and John the brother of James, whom he surnamed Bo-aner'ges, that is, sons of thunder; Andrew, and Philip, and Bartholomew, and Matthew, and Thomas, and James the son of Alphaeus, and Thaddaeus, and Simon the Cananaean, and Judas Iscariot, who betrayed him.

Tuesday

Psalm 26 [page 616],   *Psalm 28* [page 619] ❖
Psalm 36 [page 632],   *Psalm 39* [page 638]

A Reading (Lesson) from the Book of Isaiah [44:9-20]

All who make idols are nothing, and the things they delight in do not profit; their witnesses neither see nor know, that they may be put to shame. Who fashions a god or casts an image, that is profitable for nothing? Behold, all his fellows shall be put to shame, and the craftsmen are but men; let them all assemble, let them stand forth, they shall be terrified, they shall be put to shame together. The ironsmith fashions it and works it over the coals; he shapes it with hammers, and forges it with his strong arm; he becomes hungry and his strength fails, he drinks no water and is faint. The carpenter stretches a line, he marks it out with a pencil; he fashions it with planes, and marks it with a compass; he shapes it into the figure of a man, with the beauty of a man, to dwell in a house. He cuts down cedars; or he chooses a holm tree or an oak and lets it grow strong among the trees of the forest; he plants a cedar and the rain nourishes it. Then it becomes fuel for a man; he takes a part of it and warms himself, he kindles a fire and bakes bread; also he makes a god and worships it, he makes it a graven image and falls down before it. Half of it he burns in the fire; over the half he eats flesh, he roasts meat and is satisfied; also he warms himself and says, "Aha, I am warm, I have seen the fire!" And the rest of it he makes into a god, his idol; and falls down to it and worships it; he prays to it and says, "Deliver me, for thou art my god!" They know not, nor do they discern; for he has shut their eyes, so that they cannot see, and their minds, so they cannot understand. No one considers, nor is there knowledge or discernment to say, "Half of it I burned in the fire, I also baked bread on its coals, I roasted flesh and have eaten; and shall I make the residue of it an

abomination? Shall I fall down before a block of wood?"
He feeds on ashes; a deluded mind has led him astray, and
he cannot deliver himself or say, "Is there not a lie in my
right hand?"

*A Reading (Lesson) from the Letter of Paul
to the Ephesians* [4:17-32]

This I affirm and testify in the Lord, that you must no
longer live as the Gentiles do, in the futility of their minds;
they are darkened in their understanding, alienated from
the life of God because of the ignorance that is in them,
due to their hardness of heart; they have become callous
and have given themselves up to licentiousness, greedy to
practice every kind of uncleanness. You did not so learn
Christ!—assuming that you have heard about him and
were taught in him, as the truth is in Jesus. Put off your old
nature which belongs to your former manner of life and is
corrupt through deceitful lusts, and be renewed in the
spirit of your minds, and put on the new nature, created
after the likeness of God in true righteousness and
holiness. Therefore, putting away falsehood, let every one
speak the truth with his neighbor, for we are members one
of another. Be angry but do not sin; do not let the sun go
down on your anger, and give no opportunity to the devil.
Let the thief no longer steal, but rather let him labor, doing
honest work with his hands, so that he may be able to give
to those in need. Let no evil talk come out of your mouths,
but only such as is good for edifying, as fits the occasion,
that it may impart grace to those who hear. And do not
grieve the Holy Spirit of God, in whom you were sealed for
the day of redemption. Let all bitterness and wrath and
anger and clamor and slander be put away from you, with
all malice, and be kind to one another, tenderhearted,
forgiving one another, as God in Christ forgave you.

A Reading (Lesson) from the Gospel according to Mark
[3:19b-35]

Jesus went home; and the crowd came together again, so that they could not even eat. And when his family heard it, they went out to seize him, for people were saying, "He is beside himself." And the scribes who came down from Jerusalem said, "He is possessed by Be-el'zebul, and by the prince of demons he casts out the demons." And he called them to him, and said to them in parables, "How can Satan cast out Satan? If a kingdom is divided against itself, that kingdom cannot stand. And if a house is divided against itself, that house will not be able to stand. And if Satan has risen up against himself and is divided, he cannot stand, but is coming to an end. But no one can enter a strong man's house and plunder his goods, unless he first binds the strong man; then indeed he may plunder his house. Truly, I say to you, all sins will be forgiven the sons of men, and whatever blasphemies they utter; but whoever blasphemes against the Holy Spirit never has forgiveness, but is guilty of an eternal sin"—for they had said, "He has an unclean spirit." And his mother and his brothers came; and standing outside they sent to him and called him. And a crowd was sitting about him; and they said to him, "Your mother and your brothers are outside, asking for you." And he replied, "Who are my mother and my brothers?" And looking around on those who sat about him, he said, "Here are my mother and my brothers! Whoever does the will of God is my brother, sister, and mother."

Wednesday

Psalm 38 [page 636]   ❖   *Psalm 119:25-48* [page 765]

A Reading (Lesson) from the Book of Isaiah [44:24—45:7]

Thus says the Lord, your Redeemer, who formed you from the womb: "I am the Lord, who made all things, who stretched out the heavens alone, who spread out the earth—Who was with me?—who frustrates the omens of liars, and makes fools of diviners; who turns wise men back, and makes their knowledge foolish; who confirms the word of his servant, and performs the counsel of his messengers; who says of Jerusalem, 'She shall be inhabited,' and of the cities of Judah, 'They shall be built, and I will raise up their ruins'; who says to the deep, 'Be dry, I will dry up your rivers'; who says of Cyrus, 'He is my shepherd, and he shall fulfil all my purpose'; saying of Jerusalem, 'She shall be built,' and of the temple, 'Your foundations shall be laid.'" Thus says the Lord to his anointed, to Cyrus, whose right hand I have grasped, to subdue nations before him and ungird the loins of kings, to open doors before him that gates may not be closed: "I will go before you and level the mountains, I will break in pieces the doors of bronze and cut asunder the bars of iron, I will give you the treasures of darkness and the hoards in secret places, that you may know that it is I, the Lord, the God of Israel who call you by your name. For the sake of my servant Jacob, and Israel my chosen, I call you by your name, I surname you, though you do not know me. I am the Lord, and there is no other, besides me there is no God; I gird you, though you do not know me, that men may know, from the rising of the sun and from the west, that there is none besides me; I am the Lord, and there is no other. I form light and create darkness, I make weal and create woe, I am the Lord, who do all these things."

A Reading (Lesson) from the Letter of Paul to the Ephesians [5:1-14]

Be imitators of God, as beloved children. And walk in love, as Christ loved us and gave himself up for us, a fragrant offering and sacrifice to God. But fornication and all impurity or covetousness must not even be named among you, as is fitting among saints. Let there be no filthiness, nor silly talk, nor levity, which are not fitting;

but instead let there be thanksgiving. Be sure of this, that no fornicator or impure man, or one who is covetous (that is, an idolater), has any inheritance in the kingdom of Christ and of God. Let no one deceive you with empty words, for it is because of these things that the wrath of God comes upon the sons of disobedience. Therefore do not associate with them, for once you were darkness, but now you are light in the Lord; walk as children of light (for the fruit of light is found in all that is good and right and true), and try to learn what is pleasing to the Lord. Take no part in the unfruitful works of darkness, but instead expose them. For it is a shame even to speak of the things that they do in secret; but when anything is exposed by the light it becomes visible, for anything that becomes visible is light. Therefore it is said, "Awake, O sleeper, and arise from the dead, and Christ shall give you light."

A Reading (Lesson) from the Gospel according to Mark [4:1-20]

Again Jesus began to teach beside the sea. And a very large crowd gathered about him, so that he got into a boat and sat in it on the sea; and the whole crowd was beside the sea on the land. And he taught them many things in parables, and in his teaching he said to them: "Listen! A sower went out to sow. And as he sowed, some seed fell along the path, and the birds came and devoured it. Other seed fell on rocky ground, where it had not much soil, and immediately it sprang up, since it had no depth of soil; and when the sun rose it was scorched, and since it had no root it withered away. Other seed fell among thorns and the thorns grew up and choked it, and it yielded no grain. And other seeds fell into good soil and brought forth grain, growing up and increasing and yielding thirtyfold and sixtyfold and a hundredfold." And he said, "He who has ears to hear, let him hear." And when he was alone, those who were about him with the twelve asked him concerning the parables. And he said to them, "To you has been given the secret of the kingdom of God, but for those outside everything is in parables; so that they may indeed see but not perceive, and may indeed hear but not understand; lest they should turn again, and be forgiven." And he said to them, "Do you not understand this parable? How then will you understand all the parables? The sower sows the word. And these are the ones along the path, where the word is sown; when they hear, Satan immediately comes and takes away the word which is sown in them. And these in like manner are the ones sown upon rocky ground, who, when they hear the word, immediately receive it with joy; and they have no root in themselves, but endure for a while; then, when tribulation or persecution arises on account of the word, immediately they fall away. And others are the ones sown among thorns; they are those who hear the word, but the cares of the world, and the delight in riches, and the desire for other things, enter in and choke the word, and it proves unfruitful. But those that were sown upon the good soil are the ones who hear the word and accept it and bear fruit, thirtyfold and sixtyfold and a hundredfold."

Thursday

Psalm 37:1-18 [page 633] ❖ *Psalm 37:19-42* [page 634]

A Reading (Lesson) from the Book of Isaiah [45:5-17]

Thus says the Lord to his anointed, to Cyrus: "I am the Lord, and there is no other, besides me there is no God; I gird you, though you do not know me, that men may know, from the rising of the sun and from the west, that there is none beside me; I am the Lord, and there is no other. I form light and create darkness, I make weal and create woe, I am the Lord, who do all these things. Shower, O heavens, from above, and let the skies rain down righteousness; let the earth open, that salvation may sprout forth, and let it cause righteousness to spring up also; I the Lord have created it. Woe to him who strives with his Maker, an earthen vessel with the potter! Does the clay say to him who fashions it, 'What are you making'? or 'Your work has no handles'? Woe to him who says to a father, 'What are you begetting?' or to a woman, 'With what are you in travail?'" Thus says the Lord, the Holy One of Israel, and his Maker: "Will you question me about my children, or command me concerning the work of my hands? I made the earth, and created man upon it; it was my hands that stretched out the heavens, and I commanded all their host. I have aroused him in righteousness, and I will make straight all his ways; he shall build my city and set my exiles free, not for price or reward, says the Lord of hosts. Thus says the Lord: "The wealth of Egypt and the merchandise of Ethiopia, and the Sabe'ans, men of stature, shall come over to you and be yours, they shall follow you; they shall come over in chains and bow down to you. They will make supplication to you, saying: 'God is with you only, and there is no other, no god besides him.'" Truly, thou art a God who hidest thyself, O God of Israel, the Savior. All of them are put to shame and confounded, the makers of idols go in confusion together. But Israel is saved by the Lord with everlasting salvation; you shall not be put to shame or confounded to all eternity.

A Reading (Lesson) from the Letter of Paul to the Ephesians [5:15-33]

Look carefully then how you walk, not as unwise men but as wise, making the most of the time, because the days are evil. Therefore do not be foolish, but understand what the will of the Lord is. And do not get drunk with wine, for that is debauchery; but be filled with the Spirit, addressing one another in psalms and hymns and spiritual songs, singing and making melody to the Lord with all your heart, always and for everything giving thanks in the name of our Lord Jesus Christ to God the Father. Be subject to one another out of reverence for Christ. Wives, be subject to your husbands, as to the Lord. For the husband is the head of the wife as Christ is the head of the church, his body, and is himself its Savior. As the church is subject to Christ, so let wives also be subject in everything to their husbands. Husbands, love your wives, as Christ loved the church and gave himself up for her, that he might sanctify her, having cleansed her by the washing of water with the word, that he might present the church to himself in splendor, without spot or wrinkle or any such thing, that she might be holy and without blemish. Even so husbands should love their wives as their own bodies. He who loves his wife loves himself. For no man ever hates his own flesh, but nourishes and cherishes it, as Christ does the church, because we are members of his body. "For this reason a man shall leave his father and mother and be joined to his wife and the two shall become one flesh." This mystery is a profound one, and I am saying that it refers to Christ and the church; however, let each one of you love his wife as himself, and let the wife see that she respects her husband.

A Reading (Lesson) from the Gospel according to Mark
[4:21-34]

Jesus said to them, "Is a lamp brought in to be put under a bushel, or under a bed, and not on a stand? For there is nothing hid, except to be made manifest; nor is anything secret, except to come to light. If any man has ears to hear, let him hear." And he said to them, "Take heed what you hear; the measure you give will be the measure you get, and still more will be given you. For to him who has will more be given; and from him who has not, even what he has will be taken away." And he said, "The kingdom of God is as if a man should scatter seed upon the ground, and should sleep and rise night and day, and the seed should sprout and grow, he knows not how. The earth produces of itself, first the blade, then the ear, then the full grain in the ear. But when the grain is ripe, at once he puts in the sickle, because the harvest has come." And he said,

"With what can we compare the kingdom of God, or what parable shall we use for it? It is like a grain of mustard seed, which, when sown upon the ground, is the smallest of all the seeds on earth; yet when it is sown it grows up and becomes the greatest of all shrubs, and puts forth large branches, so that the birds of the air can make nests in its shade." With many such parables he spoke the word to them, as they were able to hear it; he did not speak to them without a parable, but privately to his own disciples he explained everything.

Friday

Psalm 31 [page 622] ❖ *Psalm 35* [page 629]

A Reading (Lesson) from the Book of Isaiah [45:18-25]

Thus says the Lord, who created the heavens (he is God!), who formed the earth and made it (he established it; he did not create it a chaos, he formed it to be inhabited!): "I am the Lord, and there is no other. I did not speak in secret, in a land of darkness; I did not say to the offspring of Jacob, 'Seek me in chaos.' I the Lord speak the truth, I declare what is right. Assemble yourselves and come, draw near together, you survivors of the nations! They have no knowledge who carry about their wooden idols, and keep on praying to a god that cannot save. Declare and present your case; let them take counsel together! Who told this long ago? Who declared it of old? Was it not I, the Lord? And there is no other god besides me, a righteous God and a Savior; there is none besides me. Turn to me and be saved, all the ends of the earth! For I am God, and there is no other. By myself I have sworn, from my mouth has gone forth in righteousness a word that shall not return: 'To me every knee shall bow, every tongue shall swear.' Only in the Lord it shall be said of me, are righteousness and strength; to him shall come and be ashamed, all who were incensed against him. In the Lord all the offspring of Israel shall triumph and glory."

*A Reading (Lesson) from the Letter of Paul
to the Ephesians* [6:1-9]

Children, obey your parents in the Lord, for this is right.
"Honor your father and mother" (this is the first
commandment with a promise), "that it may be well with
you and that you may live long on the earth." Fathers, do
not provoke your children to anger, but bring them up in
the discipline and instruction of the Lord. Slaves, be
obedient to those who are your earthly masters, with fear
and trembling, in singleness of heart, as to Christ; not in
the way of eye-service, as men-pleasers, but as servants of
Christ, doing the will of God from the heart, rendering
service with a good will as to the Lord and not to men,
knowing that whatever good any one does, he will receive
the same again from the Lord, whether he is a slave or free
Masters, do the same to them, and forbear threatening,
knowing that he who is both their Master and yours is in
heaven, and that there is no partiality with him.

A Reading (Lesson) from the Gospel according to Mark
[4:35-41]

On that day, when evening had come, Jesus said to the
disciples, "Let us go across to the other side." And leaving
the crowd, they took him with them in the boat, just as he
was. And other boats were with him. And a great storm of
wind arose, and the waves beat into the boat, so that the
boat was already filling. But he was in the stern, asleep on
the cushion; and they woke him and said to him, "Teacher
do you not care if we perish?" And he awoke and rebuked
the wind, and said to the sea, "Peace! Be still!" And the
wind ceased, and there was a great calm. He said to them,
"Why are you afraid? Have you no faith?" And they were
filled with awe, and said to one another, "Who then is this
that even wind and sea obey him?"

Saturday

Psalm 30 [page 621], *Psalm 32* [page 624] ❖
Psalm 42 [page 643], *Psalm 43* [page 644]

A Reading (Lesson) from the Book of Isaiah [46:1-13]

Bel bows down, Nebo stoops, their idols are on beasts and cattle; these things you carry are loaded as burdens on weary beasts. They stoop, they bow down together, they cannot save the burden, but themselves go into captivity. "Hearken to me, O house of Jacob, all the remnant of the house of Israel, who have been borne by me from your birth, carried from the womb; even to your old age I am He, and to gray hairs I will carry you. I have made, and I will bear; I will carry and will save. To whom will you liken me and make me equal, and compare me, that we may be alike? Those who lavish gold from the purse, and weigh out silver in the scales, hire a goldsmith, and he makes it into a god; then they fall down and worship! They lift it upon their shoulders, they carry it, they set it in its place, and it stands there; it cannot move from its place. If one cries to it, it does not answer or save him from his trouble. Remember this and consider, recall it to mind, you transgressors, remember the former things of old; for I am God, and there is no other; I am God, and there is none like me, declaring the end from the beginning and from ancient times things not yet done, saying, 'My counsel shall stand, and I will accomplish all my purpose,' calling a bird of prey from the east, the man of my counsel from a far country. I have spoken, and I will bring it to pass; I have purposed, and I will do it. Hearken to me, you stubborn of heart, you who are far from deliverance: I bring near my deliverance, it is not far off, and my salvation will not tarry; I will put salvation in Zion, for Israel my glory."

*A Reading (Lesson) from the Letter of Paul
to the Ephesians* [6:10-24]

Finally, be strong in the Lord and in the strength of his
might. Put on the whole armor of God, that you may be
able to stand against the wiles of the devil. For we are not
contending against flesh and blood, but against the
principalities, against the powers, against the world rulers
of this present darkness, against the spiritual hosts of
wickedness in the heavenly places. Therefore, take the
whole armor of God, that you may be able to withstand in
the evil day, and having done all, to stand. Stand therefore,
having girded your loins with truth, and having put on the
breastplate of righteousness, and having shod your feet
with the equipment of the gospel of peace; besides all
these, taking the shield of faith, with which you can
quench all the flaming darts of the evil one. And take the
helmet of salvation, and the sword of the Spirit, which is
the word of God. Pray at all times in the Spirit, with all
prayer and supplication. To that end keep alert with all
perseverance, making supplication for all the saints, and
also for me, that utterance may be given me in opening my
mouth boldly to proclaim the mystery of the gospel, for
which I am an ambassador in chains; that I may declare
boldly, as I ought to speak. Now that you also may know
how I am and what I am doing, Tych'icus the beloved
brother and faithful minister in the Lord will tell you
everything. I have sent him to you for this very purpose,
that you may know how we are, and that he may
encourage your hearts. Peace be to the brethren, and love
with faith, from God the Father and the Lord Jesus Christ.
Grace be with all who love our Lord Jesus Christ with love
undying.

A Reading (Lesson) from the Gospel according to Mark
[5:1-20]

Jesus and his disciples came to the other side of the sea, to the country of the Ger'asenes. And when he had come out of the boat, there met him out of the tombs a man with an unclean spirit, who lived among the tombs; and no one could bind him any more, even with a chain; for he had often been bound with fetters and chains, but the chains he wrenched apart, and the fetters he broke in pieces; and no one had the strength to subdue him. Night and day among the tombs and on the mountains he was always crying out, and bruising himself with stones. And when he saw Jesus from afar, he ran and worshiped him; and crying out with a loud voice, he said, "What have you to do with me, Jesus, Son of the Most High God? I adjure you by God, do not torment me." For he had said to him, "Come out of the man, you unclean spirit!" And Jesus asked him, "What is your name?" He replied, "My name is Legion; for we are many." And he begged him eagerly not to send them out of the country. Now a great herd of swine was feeding there on the hillside; and they begged him, "Send us to the swine, let us enter them." So he gave them leave. And the unclean spirits came out, and entered the swine; and the herd, numbering about two thousand, rushed down the steep bank into the sea, and were drowned in the sea. The herdsmen fled, and told it in the city and in the country. And people came to see what it was that had happened. And they came to Jesus, and saw the demoniac sitting there, clothed and in his right mind, the man who had had the legion; and they were afraid. And those who had seen it told what had happened to the demoniac and to the swine. And they began to beg Jesus to depart from their neighborhood. And as he was getting into the boat, the man who had been possessed with demons begged him that he might be with him. But he refused, and said to him, "Go home to your friends, and tell them how much the Lord has done for you, and how he has had mercy on you." And he went away and began to proclaim in the Decap'olis how much Jesus had done for him; and all men marveled.

Week of 3 Epiphany

Sunday

Psalm 63:1-8(9-11) [page 670],
Psalm 98 [page 727] ❖ *Psalm 103* [page 733]

A Reading (Lesson) from the Book of Isaiah [47:1-15]

Come down and sit in the dust, O virgin daughter of
Babylon; sit on the ground without a throne, O daughter
of the Chalde′ans! For you shall no more be called tender
and delicate. Take the millstones and grind meal, put off
your veil, strip off your robe, uncover your legs, pass
through the rivers. Your nakedness shall be uncovered,
and your shame shall be seen. I will take vengeance, and I
will spare no man. Our Redeemer—the Lord of hosts is his
name—is the Holy One of Israel. Sit in silence, and go into
darkness, O daughter of the Chalde′ans; for you shall no
more be called the mistress of kingdoms. I was angry with
my people, I profaned my heritage; I gave them into your
hand, you showed them no mercy; on the aged you made
your yoke exceedingly heavy. You said, "I shall be mistress
for ever," so that you did not lay these things to heart or
remember their end. Now therefore hear this, you lover of
pleasures, who sit securely, who say in your heart, "I am,
and there is no one besides me; I shall not sit as a widow or
know the loss of children": These two things shall come to
you in a moment, in one day; the loss of children and
widowhood shall come upon you in full measure, in spite
of your many sorceries and the great power of your
enchantments. You felt secure in your wickedness, you
said, "No one sees me"; your wisdom and your knowledge
led you astray, and you said in your heart, "I am, and there
is no one besides me." But evil shall come upon you, for
which you cannot atone; disaster shall fall upon you,
which you will not be able to expiate; and ruin shall come

on you suddenly, of which you know nothing. Stand fast in your enchantments and your many sorceries, with which you have labored from your youth; perhaps you may be able to succeed, perhaps you may inspire terror. You are wearied with your many counsels; let them stand forth and save you, those who divide the heavens, who gaze at the stars, who at the new moons predict what shall befall you. Behold, they are like stubble, the fire consumes them; they cannot deliver themselves from the power of the flame. No coal for warming oneself is this, no fire to sit before! Such to you are those with whom you have labored, who have trafficked with you from your youth; they wander about each in his own direction; there is no way to save you.

A Reading (Lesson) from the Letter to the Hebrews
[10:19-31]

Therefore, brethren, since we have confidence to enter the sanctuary by the blood of Jesus, by the new and living way which he opened for us through the curtain, that is, through his flesh, and since we have a great priest over the house of God, let us draw near with a true heart in full assurance of faith, with our hearts sprinkled clean from an evil conscience and our bodies washed with pure water. Let us hold fast the confession of our hope without wavering, for he who promised is faithful; and let us consider how to stir up one another to love and good works, not neglecting to meet together, as is the habit of some, but encouraging one another, and all the more as you see the Day drawing near. For if we sin deliberately after receiving the knowledge of the truth, there no longer remains a sacrifice for sins, but a fearful prospect of judgment, and a fury of fire which will consume the adversaries. A man who has violated the law of Moses dies without mercy at the testimony of two or three witnesses. How much worse punishment do you think will be deserved by the man who has spurned the Son of God, and profaned the blood of the covenant by which he was sanctified, and outraged the Spirit of grace? For we know him who said, "Vengeance is mine, I will repay." And again, "The Lord will judge his people." It is a fearful thing to fall into the hands of the living God.

A Reading (Lesson) from the Gospel according to John
[5:2-18]

Now there is in Jerusalem by the Sheep Gate a pool, in Hebrew called Beth-za'tha, which has five porticoes. In these lay a multitude of invalids, blind, lame, paralyzed. One man was there, who had been ill for thirty-eight years. When Jesus saw him and knew that he had been lying there a long time, he said to him, "Do you want to be healed?" The sick man answered him, "Sir, I have no man to put me into the pool when the water is troubled, and while I am going another steps down before me." Jesus said to him, "Rise, take up your pallet, and walk." And at once the man was healed, and he took up his pallet and walked. Now that day was the sabbath. So the Jews said to the man who was cured, "It is the sabbath, it is not lawful for you to carry your pallet." But he answered them, "The man who healed me said to me, 'Take up your pallet, and walk.'" They asked him, "Who is the man who said to you, 'Take up your pallet, and walk'?" Now the man who had been healed did not know who it was, for Jesus had withdrawn, as there was a crowd in the place. Afterward, Jesus found him in the temple, and said to him, "See, you are well! Sin no more, that nothing worse befall you." The man went away and told the Jews that it was Jesus who had healed him. And this was why the Jews persecuted Jesus, because he did this on the sabbath. But Jesus answered them, "My Father is working still, and I am working." This was why the Jews sought all the more to kill him, because he not only broke the sabbath but also called God his own Father, making himself equal with God.

Monday

Psalm 41 [page 641], *Psalm 52* [page 657]   ❖
Psalm 44 [page 645]

A Reading (Lesson) from the Book of Isaiah [48:1-11]

Hear this, O house of Jacob, who are called by the name of Israel, and who came forth from the loins of Judah; who swear by the name of the Lord, and confess the God of Israel, but not in truth or right. For they call themselves after the holy city, and stay themselves on the God of Israel; the Lord of hosts is his name. "The former things I declared of old, they went forth from my mouth and I made them known; then suddenly I did them and they came to pass. Because I know that you are obstinate, and your neck is an iron sinew and your forehead brass, I declared them to you from of old, before they came to pass I announced them to you, lest you should say, 'My idol did them, my graven image and my molten image commanded them.' You have heard; now see all this; and will you not declare it? From this time forth I make you hear new things, hidden things which you have not known. They are created now, not long ago; before today you have never heard of them, lest you should say, 'Behold, I knew them.' You have never heard, you have never known, from of old your ear has not been opened. For I knew that you would deal very treacherously, and that from birth you were called a rebel. For my name's sake I defer my anger, for the sake of praise I restrain it for you, that I may not cut you off. Behold, I have refined you, but not like silver; I have tried you in the furnace of affliction. For my own sake, for my own sake, I do it, for how should my name be profaned? My glory I will not give to another."

*A Reading (Lesson) from the Letter of Paul
to the Galatians* [1:1-17]

Paul an apostle—not from men nor through man, but
through Jesus Christ and God the Father, who raised him
from the dead—and all the brethren who are with me, To
the churches of Galatia: Grace to you and peace from God
the Father and our Lord Jesus Christ, who gave himself for
our sins to deliver us from the present evil age, according
to the will of our God and Father; to whom be the glory
for ever and ever. Amen. I am astonished that you are so
quickly deserting him who called you in the grace of Christ
and turning to a different gospel—not that there is another
gospel, but that there are some who trouble you and want
to pervert the gospel of Christ. But even if we, or an angel
from heaven, should preach to you a gospel contrary to
that which we preached to you, let him be accursed. As we
have said before, so now I say again, If any one is
preaching to you a gospel contrary to that which you
received, let him be accursed. Am I now seeking the favor
of men, or of God? Or am I trying to please men? If I were
still pleasing men, I should not be a servant of Christ. For I
would have you know, brethren, that the gospel which was
preached by me is not man's gospel. For I did not receive it
from man, nor was I taught it, but it came through a
revelation of Jesus Christ. For you have heard of my
former life in Judaism, how I persecuted the church of God
violently and tried to destroy it; and I advanced in Judaism
beyond many of my own age among my people, so
extremely zealous was I for the traditions of my fathers.
But when he who had set me apart before I was born, and
had called me through his grace, was pleased to reveal his
Son to me, in order that I might preach him among the
Gentiles, I did not confer with flesh and blood, nor did I go
up to Jerusalem to those who were apostles before me, but
I went away into Arabia; and again I returned to
Damascus.

A Reading (Lesson) from the Gospel according to Mark
[5:21-43]

When Jesus had crossed again in the boat to the other side,
a great crowd gathered about him; and he was beside the
sea. Then came one of the rulers of the synagogue, Ja'irus
by name; and seeing him, he fell at his feet, and besought
him, saying, "My little daughter is at the point of death.
Come and lay your hands on her, so that she may be made
well, and live." And he went with him. And a great crowd
followed him and thronged about him. And there was a
woman who had had a flow of blood for twelve years, and
who had suffered much under many physicians, and had
spent all that she had, and was no better but rather grew
worse. She had heard the reports about Jesus, and came up
behind him in the crowd and touched his garment. For she
said, "If I touch even his garments, I shall be made well."
And immediately the hemorrhage ceased; and she felt in
her body that she was healed of her disease. And Jesus,
perceiving in himself that power had gone forth from him,
immediately turned about in the crowd, and said, "Who
touched my garments?" And his disciples said to him,
"You see the crowd pressing around you, and yet you say,
'Who touched me?'" And he looked around to see who had
done it. But the woman, knowing what had been done to
her, came in fear and trembling and fell down before him,
and told him the whole truth. And he said to her,
"Daughter, your faith has made you well; go in peace, and
be healed of your disease." While he was still speaking,
there came from the ruler's house some who said, "Your
daughter is dead. Why trouble the Teacher any further?"
But ignoring what they said, Jesus said to the ruler of the
synagogue, "Do not fear, only believe." And he allowed no
one to follow him except Peter and James and John the
brother of James. When they came to the house of the ruler
of the synagogue, he saw a tumult, and people weeping
and wailing loudly. And when he had entered, he said to
them, "Why do you make a tumult and weep? The child is

not dead but sleeping." And they laughed at him. But he put them all outside, and took the child's father and mother and those who were with him, and went in where the child was. Taking her by the hand he said to her, "Tal'itha cu'mi"; which means, "Little girl, I say to you, arise." And immediately the girl got up and walked (she was twelve years of age), and they were immediately overcome with amazement. And he strictly charged them that no one should know this, and told them to give her something to eat.

Tuesday

Psalm 45 [page 647]   ❖   *Psalm 47* [page 650], *Psalm 48* [page 651]

A Reading (Lesson) from the Book of Isaiah [48:12-21]

"Hearken to me, O Jacob, and Israel, whom I called! I am He, I am the first, and I am the last. My hand laid the foundation of the earth, and my right hand spread out the heavens; when I call to them, they stand forth together. Assemble, all of you, and hear! Who among them has declared these things? The Lord loves him; he shall perform his purpose on Babylon, and his arm shall be against the Chalde'ans. I, even I, have spoken and called him, I have brought him, and he will prosper in his way. Draw near to me, hear this: from the beginning I have not spoken in secret, from the time it came to be I have been there." And now the Lord God has sent me and his Spirit. Thus says the Lord, your Redeemer, the Holy One of Israel: "I am the Lord your God, who teaches you to profit, who leads you in the way you should go. O that you had hearkened to my commandments! Then your peace would have been like a river, and your righteousness like the waves of the sea; your offspring would have been like the sand, and your descendants like its grains; their name would never be cut off or destroyed from before me." Go forth from Babylon, flee from Chalde'a, declare this with a shout of joy, proclaim it, send it forth to the end of the earth; say, "The Lord has redeemed his servant Jacob!" They thirsted not when he led them through the deserts; he made water flow for them from the rock; he cleft the rock and the water gushed out.

A Reading (Lesson) from the Letter of Paul to the Galatians [1:18—2:10]

After three years I went up to Jerusalem to visit Cephas, and remained with him fifteen days. But I saw none of the other apostles except James the Lord's brother. (In what I am writing to you, before God, I do not lie!) Then I went into the regions of Syria and Cili'cia. And I was still not known by sight to the churches of Christ in Judea; they only heard it said, "He who once persecuted us is now preaching the faith he once tried to destroy." And they glorified God because of me. Then after fourteen years I went up again to Jerusalem with Barnabas, taking Titus along with me. I went up by revelation; and I laid before them (but privately before those who were of repute) the gospel which I preach among the Gentiles, lest somehow I should be running or had run in vain. But even Titus, who was with me, was not compelled to be circumcised, though he was a Greek. But because of false brethren secretely brought in, who slipped in to spy out our freedom which we have in Christ Jesus, that they might bring us into bondage—to them we did not yield submission even for a moment, that the truth of the gospel might be preserved for you. And from those who were reputed to be something (what they were makes no difference to me; God shows no partiality)—those, I say, who were of repute added nothing to me; but on the contrary, when they saw that I had been entrusted with the gospel to the uncircumcised, just as Peter had been entrusted with the gospel to the circumcised (for he who worked through

Peter for the mission to the circumcised worked through me also for the Gentiles), and when they perceived the grace that was given to me, James and Cephas and John, who were reputed to be pillars, gave to me and Barnabas the right hand of fellowship, that we should go to the Gentiles and they to the circumcised; only they would have us remember the poor, which very thing I was eager to do.

A Reading (Lesson) from the Gospel according to Mark [6:1-13]

Jesus went away from there and came to his own country; and his disciples followed him. And on the sabbath he began to teach in the synagogue; and many who heard him were astonished, saying, "Where did this man get all this? What is the wisdom given to him? What mighty works are wrought by his hands! Is not this the carpenter, the son of Mary and brother of James and Joses and Judas and Simon, and are not his sisters here with us?" And they took offense at him. And Jesus said to them, "A prophet is not without honor, except in his own country, and among his own kin, and in his own house." And he could do no mighty work there, except that he laid his hands upon a few sick people and healed them. And he marveled because of their unbelief. And he went about among the villages teaching. And he called to him the twelve, and began to send them out two by two, and gave them authority over the unclean spirits. He charged them to take nothing for their journey except a staff; no bread, no bag, no money in their belts; but to wear sandals and not put on two tunics. And he said to them, "Where you enter a house, stay there until you leave the place. And if any place will not receive you and they refuse to hear you, when you leave, shake off the dust that is on your feet for a testimony against them." So they went out and preached that men should repent. And they cast out many demons, and anointed with oil many that were sick and healed them.

Wednesday

Psalm 119:49-72 [page 767] ❖
Psalm 49 [page 652], *(Psalm 53* [page 658])

A Reading (Lesson) from the Book of Isaiah [49:1-12]

Listen to me, O coastlands, and hearken, you peoples from
afar. The Lord called me from the womb, from the body of
my mother he named my name. He made my mouth like a
sharp sword, in the shadow of his hand he hid me; he
made me a polished arrow, in his quiver he hid me away.
And he said to me, "You are my servant, Israel, in whom I
will be glorified." But I said, "I have labored in vain, I have
spent my strength for nothing and vanity; yet surely my
right is with the Lord, and my recompense with my God."
And now the Lord says, who formed me from the womb to
be his servant, to bring Jacob back to him, and that Israel
might be gathered to him, for I am honored in the eyes of
the Lord, and my God has become my strength—he says:
"It is too light a thing that you should be my servant to raise
up the tribes of Jacob and to restore the preserved of Israel;
I will give you as a light to the nations, that my salvation
may reach to the end of the earth." Thus says the Lord, the
Redeemer of Israel and his Holy One, to one deeply
despised, abhorred by the nations, the servant of rulers:
"Kings shall see and arise; princes, and they shall prostrate
themselves; because of the Lord, who is faithful, the Holy
One of Israel, who has chosen you." Thus says the Lord:
"In a time of favor I have answered you, in a day of
salvation I have helped you; I have kept you and given you
as a covenant to the people, to establish the land, to
apportion the desolate heritages; saying to the prisoners,
'Come forth,' to those who are in darkness, 'Appear.' They
shall feed along the ways, on all bare heights shall be their
pasture; they shall not hunger or thirst, neither scorching
wind nor sun shall smite them, for he who has pity on
them will lead them. And I will make all my mountains a

way, and my highways shall be raised up. Lo, these shall come from afar, and lo, these from the north and from the west, and these from the land of Syene."

A Reading (Lesson) from the Letter of Paul to the Galatians [2:11-21]

When Cephas came to Antioch I opposed him to his face, because he stood condemned. For before certain men came from James, he ate with the Gentiles; but when they came he drew back and separated himself, fearing the circumcision party. And with him the rest of the Jews acted insincerely, so that even Barnabas was carried away by their insincerity. But when I saw that they were not straightforward about the truth of the gospel, I said to Cephas before them all, "If you, though a Jew, live like a Gentile and not like Jew, how can you compel the Gentile to live like Jews?" We ourselves, who are Jews by birth and not Gentile sinners, yet who know that a man is not justified by works of the law but through faith in Jesus Christ, even we have believed in Christ Jesus, in order to be justified by faith in Christ, and not by works of the law because by works of the law shall no one be justified. But if, in our endeavor to be justified in Christ, we ourselves were found to be sinners, is Christ then an agent of sin? Certainly not! But if I build up again those things which I tore down, then I prove myself a transgressor. For I through the law died to the law, that I might live to God. have been crucified with Christ; it is no longer I who live, but Christ who lives in me; and the life I now live in the flesh I live by faith in the Son of God, who loved me and gave himself for me. I do not nullify the grace of God; for justification were through the law, then Christ died to no purpose.

A Reading (Lesson) from the Gospel according to Mark
[6:13-29]

The disciples cast out many demons, and anointed with oil many that were sick and healed them. King Herod heard of it; for Jesus' name had become known. Some said, "John the baptizer has been raised from the dead; that is why these powers are at work in him." But others said, "It is Eli'jah." And others said, "It is a prophet, like one of the prophets of old." But when Herod heard of it he said, "John, whom I beheaded, has been raised." For Herod had sent and seized John, and bound him in prison for the sake of Hero'di-as, his brother Philip's wife; because he had married her. For John said to Herod, "It is not lawful for you to have your brother's wife." And Hero'di-as had a grudge against him, and wanted to kill him. But she could not, for Herod feared John, knowing that he was a righteous and holy man, and kept him safe. When he heard him, he was much perplexed; and yet he heard him gladly. But an opportunity came when Herod on his birthday gave a banquet for his courtiers and officers and the leading men of Galilee. For when Hero'di-as' daughter came in and danced, she pleased Herod and his guests; and the king said to the girl, "Ask me for whatever you wish, and I will grant it." And he vowed to her, "Whatever you ask me, I will give you, even half of my kingdom." And she went out, and said to her mother, "What shall I ask?" And she said, "The head of John the baptizer." And she came in immediately with haste to the king, and asked, saying, "I want you to give me at once the head of John the Baptist on a platter." And the king was exceedingly sorry; but because of his oaths and his guests he did not want to break his word to her. And immediately the king sent a soldier of the guard and gave orders to bring his head. He went and beheaded him in the prison, and brought his head on a platter, and gave it to the girl; and the girl gave it to her mother. When his disciples heard of it, they came and took his body, and laid it in a tomb.

Thursday

Psalm 50 [page 654] ❖ *(Psalm 59* [page 665],
Psalm 60 [page 667]) *or* *Psalm 118* [page 760]

A Reading (Lesson) from the Book of Isaiah [49:13-23]

Sing for joy, O heavens, and exult, O earth; break forth, C
mountains, into singing! For the Lord has comforted his
people, and will have compassion on his afflicted. But Zio
said, "The Lord has forsaken me, my Lord has forgotten
me." "Can a woman forget her sucking child, that she
should have no compassion on the son of her womb? Eve
these may forget, yet I will not forget you. Behold, I have
graven you on the palms of my hands; your walls are
continually before me. Your builders outstrip your
destroyers, and those who laid you waste go forth from
you. Lift up your eyes round about and see; they all gathe
they come to you. As I live, says the Lord, you shall put
them all on as an ornament, you shall bind them on as a
bride does. Surely your waste and your desolate places an
your devastated land—surely now you will be too narrow
for your inhabitants, and those who swallowed you up wi
be far away. The children born in the time of your
bereavement will yet say in your ears: 'The place is too
narrow for me; make room for me to dwell in.' Then you
will say in your heart: 'Who has borne me these? I was
bereaved and barren, exiled and put away, but who has
brought up these? Behold, I was left alone; whence then
have these come?'" Thus says the Lord God: "Behold, I
will lift up my hand to the nations, and raise my signal to
the peoples; and they shall bring your sons in their bosom
and your daughters shall be carried on their shoulders.
Kings shall be your foster fathers, and their queens your
nursing mothers. With their faces to the ground they shall
bow down to you, and lick the dust of your feet. Then you
will know that I am the Lord; those who wait for me shall
not be put to shame."

*A Reading (Lesson) from the Letter of Paul
to the Galatians* [3:1-14]

O foolish Galatians! Who has bewitched you, before
whose eyes Jesus Christ was publicly portrayed as
crucified? Let me ask you only this: Did you receive the
Spirit by works of the law, or by hearing with faith? Are
you so foolish? Having begun with the Spirit, are you now
ending with the flesh? Did you experience so many things
in vain?—if it really is in vain. Does he who supplies the
Spirit to you and works miracles among you do so by
works of the law, or by hearing with faith? Thus Abraham
"believed God, and it was reckoned to him as
righteousness." So you see that it is men of faith who are
the sons of Abraham. And the scripture, foreseeing that
God would justify the Gentiles by faith, preached the
gospel beforehand to Abraham, saying, "In you shall all
the nations be blessed." So then, those who are men of
faith are blessed with Abraham who had faith. For all who
rely on works of the law are under a curse; for it is written,
"Cursed be every one who does not abide by all things
written in the book of the law, and do them." Now it is
evident that no man is justified before God by the law; for
"He who through faith is righteous shall live"; but the law
does not rest on faith, for "He who does them shall live by
them." Christ redeemed us from the curse of the law,
having become a curse for us—for it is written, "Cursed be
every one who hangs on a tree"—that in Christ Jesus the
blessing of Abraham might come upon the Gentiles, that
we might receive the promise of the Spirit through faith.

A Reading (Lesson) from the Gospel according to Mark
[6:30-46]

The apostles returned to Jesus, and told him all that they
had done and taught. And he said to them, "Come away
by yourselves to a lonely place, and rest a while." For
many were coming and going, and they had no leisure even

to eat. And they went away in the boat to a lonely place by
themselves. Now many saw them going, and knew them,
and they ran there on foot from all the towns, and got
there ahead of them. As he went ashore he saw a great
throng, and he had compassion on them, because they
were like sheep without a shepherd; and he began to teach
them many things. And when it grew late, his disciples
came to him and said, "This is a lonely place, and the hour
is now late; send them away, to go into the country and
villages round about and buy themselves something to
eat." But he answered them, "You give them something to
eat." And they said to him, "Shall we go and buy two
hundred denarii worth of bread, and give it to them to
eat?" And he said to them, "How many loaves have you?
Go and see." And when they had found out, they said,
"Five, and two fish." Then he commanded them all to sit
down by companies upon the green grass. So they sat
down in groups, by hundreds and by fifties. And taking the
five loaves and the two fish he looked up to heaven, and
blessed, and broke the loaves, and gave them to the
disciples to set before the people; and he divided the two
fish among them all. And they all ate and were satisfied.
And they took up twelve baskets full of broken pieces and
of the fish. And those who ate the loaves were five
thousand men. Immediately he made his disciples get into
the boat and go before him to the other side, to Beth-sa'ida
while he dismissed the crowd. And after he had taken leave
of them, he went up on the mountain to pray.

Friday

Psalm 40 [page 640],   *Psalm 54* [page 659]   ❖
Psalm 51 [page 656]

A Reading (Lesson) from the Book of Isaiah [50:1-11]

Thus says the Lord: "Where is your mother's bill of
divorce, with which I put her away? Or which of my

creditors is it to whom I have sold you? Behold, for your iniquities you were sold, and for your transgressions your mother was put away. Why, when I came, was there no man? When I called, was there no one to answer? Is my hand shortened, that it cannot redeem? Or have I no power to deliver? Behold, by my rebuke I dry up the sea, I make the rivers a desert; their fish stink for lack of water, and die of thirst. I clothe the heavens with blackness, and make sackcloth their covering." The Lord God has given me the tongue of those who are taught, that I may know how to sustain with a word him that is weary. Morning by morning he wakens, he wakens my ear to hear as those who are taught. The Lord God has opened my ear, and I was not rebellious, I turned not backward. I gave my back to the smiters, and my cheeks to those who pulled out the beard; I hid not my face from shame and spitting. For the Lord God helps me; therefore I have not been confounded; therefore I have set my face like a flint, and I know that I shall not be put to shame; he who vindicates me is near. Who will contend with me? Let us stand up together. Who is my adversary? Let him come near to me. Behold, the Lord God helps me; who will declare me guilty? Behold, all of them will wear out like a garment; the moth will eat them up. Who among you fears the Lord and obeys the voice of his servant, who walks in darkness and has no light, yet trusts in the name of the Lord and relies upon his God? Behold, all you who kindle a fire, who set brands alight! Walk by the light of your fire, and by the brands which you have kindled! This shall you have from my hand: you shall lie down in torment.

A Reading (Lesson) from the Letter of Paul to the Galatians [3:15-22]

To give a human example, brethren: no one annuls even a man's will, or adds to it, once it has been ratified. Now the promises were made to Abraham and to his offspring. It does not say, "And to offsprings," referring to many; but, referring to one, "And to your offspring," which is Christ. This is what I mean: the law, which came four hundred and thirty years afterward, does not annul a covenant previously ratified by God, so as to make the promise void. For if the inheritance is by the law, it is no longer by promise; but God gave it to Abraham by a promise. Why then the law? It was added because of transgressions, till the offspring should come to whom the promise had been made; and it was ordained by angels through an intermediary. Now an intermediary implies more than one; but God is one. Is the law then against the promises of God? Certainly not; for if a law had been given which could make alive, then righteousness would indeed be by the law. But the scripture consigned all things to sin, that what was promised to faith in Jesus Christ might be given to those who believe.

A Reading (Lesson) from the Gospel according to Mark
[6:47-56]

When evening came, the boat was out on the sea, and Jesus was alone on the land. And he saw that they were making headway painfully, for the wind was against them. And about the fourth watch of the night he came to them, walking on the sea. He meant to pass by them, but when they saw him walking on the sea they thought it was a ghost, and cried out; for they all saw him, and were terrified. But immediately he spoke to them and said, "Take heart, it is I; have no fear." And he got into the boat with them and the wind ceased. And they were utterly astounded, for they did not understand about the loaves, but their hearts were hardened. And when they had crossed over, they came to land at Gennes'aret, and moored to the shore. And when they got out of the boat, immediately the people recognized him, and ran about the whole neighborhood and began to bring sick people on their pallets to any place where they heard he was. And wherever he came, in villages, cities, or country, they laid the sick in the market places, and besought him that they might touch even the fringe of his garment; and as many as touched it were made well.

Saturday

Psalm 55 [page 660] ❖ *Psalm 138* [page 793], *Psalm 139:1-17(18-23)* [page 794]

A Reading (Lesson) from the Book of Isaiah [51:1-8]

"Hearken to me, you who pursue deliverance, you who seek the Lord; look to the rock from which you were hewn, and to the quarry from which you were digged. Look to Abraham your father and to Sarah who bore you; for when he was but one I called him, and I blessed him and made him many. For the Lord will comfort Zion; he will comfort all her waste places, and will make her wilderness like Eden, her desert like the garden of the Lord; joy and gladness will be found in her, thanksgiving and the voice of song. Listen to me, my people, and give ear to me, my nation; for a law will go forth from me, and my justice for a light to the peoples. My deliverance draws near speedily, my salvation has gone forth, and my arms will rule the peoples; the coastlands will wait for me, and for my arm they hope. Lift up your eyes to the heavens, and look to the earth beneath; for the heavens will vanish like smoke, the earth will wear out like a garment, and they who dwell in it will die like gnats; but my salvation will be for ever, and my deliverance will never be ended. Hearken to me, you who know righteousness, the people in whose heart is my law; fear not the reproach of men, and be not dismayed at their revilings. For the moth will eat them up like a garment, and the worm will eat them like wool; but my deliverance will be for ever, and my salvation to all generations."

*A Reading (Lesson) from the Letter of Paul
to the Galatians* [3:23-29]

Now before faith came, we were confined under the law,
kept under restraint until faith should be revealed. So that
the law was our custodian until Christ came, that we might
be justified by faith. But now that faith has come, we are
no longer under a custodian; for in Christ Jesus you are all
sons of God, through faith. For as many of you as were
baptized into Christ have put on Christ. There is neither
Jew nor Greek, there is neither slave nor free, there is
neither male nor female; for you are all one in Christ Jesus.
And if you are Christ's, then you are Abraham's offspring,
heirs according to promise.

A Reading (Lesson) from the Gospel according to Mark
[7:1-23]

When the Pharisees gathered together to Jesus, with some
of the scribes, who had come from Jerusalem, they saw
that some of his disciples ate with hands defiled, that is,
unwashed. (For the Pharisees, and all the Jews, do not eat
unless they wash their hands, observing the tradition of the
elders; and when they come from the market place, they do
not eat unless they purify themselves; and there are many
other traditions which they observe, the washing of cups
and pots and vessels of bronze.) And the Pharisees and the
scribes asked him, "Why do your disciples not live
according to the tradition of the elders, but eat with hands
defiled?" And he said to them, "Well did Isaiah prophesy
of you hypocrites, as it is written, 'This people honors me
with their lips, but their heart is far from me; in vain do
they worship me, teaching as doctrines the precepts of
men.' You leave the commandment of God, and hold fast
the tradition of men." And he said to them, "You have a
fine way of rejecting the commandment of God, in order to
keep your tradition! For Moses said, 'Honor your father
and your mother'; and, 'He who speaks evil of father or

mother, let him surely die'; but you say, 'If a man tells his father or his mother, What you would have gained from me is Corban' (that is, given to God)—then you no longer permit him to do anything for his father or mother, thus making void the word of God through your tradition which you hand on. And many such things you do." And he called the people to him again, and said to them, "Hear me, all of you, and understand: there is nothing outside a man which by going into him can defile him; but the things which come out of a man are what defile him." And when he had entered the house, and left the people, his disciples asked him about the parable. And he said to them, "Then are you also without understanding? Do you not see that whatever goes into a man from outside cannot defile him, since it enters, not his heart but his stomach, and so passes on? (Thus he declared all foods clean.) And he said, "What comes out of a man is what defiles a man. For from within, out of the heart of man, come evil thoughts, fornication, theft, murder, adultery, coveting, wickedness, deceit, licentiousness, envy, slander, pride, foolishness. All these evil things come from within, and they defile a man."

Week of 4 Epiphany

Sunday

Psalm 24 [page 613],   *Psalm 29* [page 620]   ❖
Psalm 8 [page 592],   *Psalm 84* [page 707]

A Reading (Lesson) from the Book of Isaiah [51:9-16]

Awake, awake, put on strength, O arm of the Lord; awake as in days of old, the generations of long ago. Was it not thou that didst cut Rahab in pieces, that didst pierce the dragon? Was it not thou that didst dry up the sea, the waters of the great deep; that didst make the depths of the sea a way for the redeemed to pass over? And the ransomed of the Lord shall return, and come to Zion with singing; everlasting joy shall be upon their heads; they shall obtain joy and gladness, and sorrow and sighing shall flee away. "I, I am he that comforts you; who are you that you are afraid of man who dies, of the son of man who is made like grass, and have forgotten the Lord, your Maker, who stretched out the heavens and laid the foundations of the earth, and fear continually all the day because of the fury of the oppressor, when he sets himself to destroy? And where is the fury of the oppressor? He who is bowed down shall speedily be released; he shall not die and go down to the Pit, neither shall his bread fail. For I am the Lord your God, who stirs up the sea so that its waves roar—the Lord of hosts is his name. And I have put my words in your mouth, and hid you in the shadow of my hand, stretching out the heavens and laying the foundations of the earth, and saying to Zion, 'You are my people.'"

A Reading (Lesson) from the Letter to the Hebrews
[11:8-16]

By faith Abraham obeyed when he was called to go out to a place which he was to receive as an inheritance; and he went out, not knowing where he was to go. By faith he sojourned in the land of promise, as in a foreign land, living in tents with Isaac and Jacob, heirs with him of the same promise. For he looked forward to the city which has foundations, whose builder and maker is God. By faith Sarah herself received power to conceive, even when she was past the age, since she considered him faithful who had promised. Therefore from one man, and him as good as dead, were born descendants as many as the stars of heaven and as the innumerable grains of sand by the seashore. These all died in faith, not having received what was promised, but having seen it and greeted it from afar, and having acknowledged that they were strangers and exiles on the earth. For people who speak thus make it clear that they are seeking a homeland. If they had been thinking of that land from which they had gone out, they would have had opportunity to return. But as it is, they desire a better country, that is, a heavenly one. Therefore God is not ashamed to be called their God, for he has prepared for them a city.

A Reading (Lesson) from the Gospel according to John [7:14-31]

About the middle of the feast of Tabernacles Jesus went up into the temple and taught. The Jews marveled at it, saying, "How is it that this man has learning, when he has never studied?" So Jesus answered them, "My teaching is not mine, but his who sent me; if any man's will is to do his will, he shall know whether the teaching is from God or whether I am speaking on my own authority. He who speaks on his own authority seeks his own glory; but he who seeks the glory of him who sent him is true, and in him there is no falsehood. Did not Moses give you the law? Yet none of you keeps the law. Why do you seek to kill me?" The people answered, "You have a demon! Who is seeking to kill you?" Jesus answered them, "I did one deed, and you all marvel at it. Moses gave you circumcision (not that it is from Moses, but from the fathers), and you circumcise a man upon the sabbath. If on the sabbath a man receives circumcision, so that the law of Moses may not be broken, are you angry with me because on the sabbath I made a man's whole body well? Do not judge by appearances, but judge with right judgment." Some of the people of Jerusalem therefore said, "Is not this the man whom they seek to kill? And here he is, speaking openly, and they say nothing to him! Can it be that the authorities really know that this is the Christ? Yet we know where this man comes from; and when the Christ appears, no one will know where he comes from." So Jesus proclaimed, as he taught in the temple, "You know me, and you know where I come from? But I have not come of my own accord; he who sent me is true, and him you do not know. I know him, for I come from him, and he sent me." So they sought to arrest him; but no one laid hands on him, because his hour had not yet come. Yet many of the people believed in him; they said, "When the Christ appears, will he do more signs than this man has done?"

Monday

Psalm 56 [page 662], *Psalm 57* [page 663],
(Psalm 58 [page 664]) ❖ *Psalm 64* [page 671],
Psalm 65 [page 672]

A Reading (Lesson) from the Book of Isaiah [51:17-23]

Rouse yourself, rouse yourself, stand up, O Jerusalem, you who have drunk at the hand of the Lord the cup of his wrath, who have drunk to the dregs the bowl of staggering. There is none to guide her among all the sons she has borne; there is none to take her by the hand among all the sons she has brought up. These two things have befallen you—who will condole with you?—devastation and destruction, famine and sword; who will comfort you? Your sons have fainted, they lie at the head of every street like an antelope in a net; they are full of the wrath of the Lord, the rebuke of your God. Therefore hear this, you who are afflicted, who are drunk, but not with wine; Thus says your Lord, the Lord, your God who pleads the cause of his people: "Behold, I have taken from your hand the cup of staggering; the bow of my wrath you shall drink no more; and I will put it into the hand of your tormentors, who have said to you, 'Bow down, that we may pass over'; and you have made your back like the ground and like the street for them to pass over."

*A Reading (Lesson) from the Letter of Paul
to the Galatians* [4:1-11]

I mean that the heir, as long as he is a child, is no better than a slave, though he is owner of all the estate; but he is under guardians and trustees until the date set by the father. So with us; when we were children, we were slaves to the elemental spirits of the universe. But when the time had fully come, God sent forth his Son, born of woman, born under the law, to redeem those who were under the law, so that we might receive adoption as sons. And because you are sons, God has sent the Spirit of his Son into our hearts, crying, "Abba! Father!" So through God you are no longer a slave but a son, and if a son then an heir. Formerly, when you did not know God, you were in bondage to beings that by nature are no gods; but now that you have come to know God, or rather to be known by God, how can you turn back again to the weak and beggarly elemental spirits, whose slaves you want to be once more? You observe days, and months, and seasons, and years! I am afraid I have labored over you in vain.

A Reading (Lesson) from the Gospel according to Mark
[7:24-37]

From there Jesus arose and went away to the region of Tyre and Sidon. And he entered a house, and would not have any one know it; yet he could not be hid. But immediately a woman, whose little daughter was possessed by an unclean spirit, heard of him, and came and fell down at his feet. Now the woman was a Greek, a Syrophoeni'cian by birth. And she begged him to cast the demon out of her daughter. And he said to her, "Let the children first be fed, for it is not right to take the children's bread and throw it to the dogs." But she answered him, "Yes, Lord; yet even the dogs under the table eat the children's crumbs." And he said to her, "For this saying you may go your way; the demon has left your daughter." And she went home, and found the child lying in bed, and the demon gone. Then he returned from the region of Tyre, and went through Sidon to the Sea of Galilee, through the region of the Decap'olis. And they brought to him a man

who was deaf and had an impediment in his speech; and
they besought him to lay his hand upon him. And taking
him aside from the multitude privately, he put his fingers
into his ears, and he spat and touched his tongue; and
looking up to heaven, he sighed, and said to him,
"Eph'phatha," that is, "Be opened." And his ears were
opened, his tongue was released, and he spoke plainly. And
he charged them to tell no one; but the more he charged
them, the more zealously they proclaimed it. And they
were astonished beyond measure, saying, "He has done all
things well; he even makes the deaf hear and the dumb
speak."

Tuesday

Psalm 61 [page 668], *Psalm 62* [page 669] ❖
Psalm 68:1-20(21-23)24-36 [page 676]

A Reading (Lesson) from the Book of Isaiah [52:1-12]

Awake, awake, put on your strength, O Zion; put on your
beautiful garments, O Jersualem, the holy city; for there
shall no more come into you the uncircumcised and the
unclean. Shake yourself from the dust, arise, O captive
Jerusalem; loose the bonds from your neck, O captive
daughter of Zion. For thus says the Lord: "You were sold
for nothing, and you shall be redeemed without money.
For thus says the Lord God: My people went down at the
first into Egypt to sojourn there, and the Assyrian
oppressed them for nothing. Now therefore what have I
here, says the Lord, seeing that my people are taken away
for nothing? Their rulers wail, says the Lord, and
continually all the day my name is despised. Therefore my
people shall know my name; therefore in that day they
shall know that it is I who speak; here am I." How
beautiful upon the mountains are the feet of him who
brings good tidings, who publishes peace, who brings good

tidings of good, who publishes salvation, who says to Zion, "Your God reigns." Hark, your watchmen lift up their voice, together they sing for joy; for eye to eye they see the return of the Lord to Zion. Break forth together into singing, you waste places of Jersualem; for the Lord has comforted his people, he has redeemed Jerusalem. The Lord has bared his holy arm before the eyes of all the nations; and all the ends of the earth shall see the salvation of our God. Depart, depart, go out thence, touch no unclean thing; go out from the midst of her, purify yourselves, you who bear the vessels of the Lord. For you shall not go out in haste, and you shall not go in flight, for the Lord will go before you, and the God of Israel will be your rear guard.

A Reading (Lesson) from the Letter of Paul to the Galatians [4:12-20]

Brethren, I beseech you, become as I am, for I also have become as you are. You did me no wrong; you know it was because of a bodily ailment that I preached the gospel to you at first; and though my condition was a trial to you, you did not scorn or despise me, but received me as an angel of God, as Christ Jesus. What has become of the satisfaction you felt? For I bear you witness that, if possible, you would have plucked out your eyes and given them to me. Have I then become your enemy by telling you the truth? They make much of you, but for no good purpose; they want to shut you out, that you may make much of them. For a good purpose it is always good to be made much of, and not only when I am present with you. My little children, with whom I am again in travail until Christ be formed in you! I could wish to be present with you now and to change my tone, for I am perplexed about you.

A Reading (Lesson) from the Gospel according to Mark
[8:1-10]

In those days, when again a great crowd had gathered, and they had nothing to eat, Jesus called his disciples to him, and said to them, "I have compassion on the crowd, because they have been with me now three days, and have nothing to eat; and if I send them away hungry to their homes, they will faint on the way; and some of them have come a long way." And his disciples answered him, "How can one feed these men with bread here in the desert?" And he asked them, "How many loaves have you?" They said, "Seven." And he commanded the crowd to sit down on the ground; and he took the seven loaves, and having given thanks he broke them and gave them to his disciples to set before the people; and they set them before the crowd. And they had a few small fish; and having blessed them, he commanded that these also should be set before them. And they ate, and were satisfied; and they took up the broken pieces left over, seven baskets full. And there were about four thousand people. And he sent them away; and immediately he got into the boat with his disciples, and went to the district of Dalmanu'tha.

Wednesday

Psalm 72 [page 685]   ❖   *Psalm 119:73-96* [page 769]

A Reading (Lesson) from the Book of Isaiah
[54:1-10(11-17)]

"Sing, O barren one, who did not bear; break forth into singing and cry aloud, you who have not been in travail! For the children of the desolate one will be more than the children of her that is married, says the Lord. Enlarge the place of your tent, and let the curtains of your habitations be stretched out; hold not back, lengthen your cords and strengthen your stakes. For you will spread abroad to the right and to the left, and your descendants will possess the nations and will people the desolate cities. Fear not, for you will not be ashamed; be not confounded, for you will not be put to shame; for you will forget the shame of your youth, and the reproach of your widowhood you will remember no more. For your Maker is your husband, the Lord of Hosts is his name; and the Holy One of Israel is your Redeemer, the God of the whole earth he is called. For the Lord has called you like a wife forsaken and grieved in spirit, like a wife of youth when she is cast off, says your God. For a brief moment I forsook you, but with great compassion I will gather you. In overflowing wrath for a moment I hid my face from you, but with everlasting love I will have compassion on you, says the Lord, your Redeemer. For this is like the days of Noah to me: as I swore that the waters of Noah should no more go over the earth, so I have sworn that I will not be angry with you and will not rebuke you. For the mountains may depart and the hills be removed, but my steadfast love shall not depart from you, and my covenant of peace shall not be removed, says the Lord, who has compassion on you."

"O afflicted one, storm-tossed, and not comforted, behold, I will set your stones in antimony, and lay your foundations with sapphires. I will make your pinnacles of agate, your gates of carbuncles, and all your wall of precious stones. All your sons shall be taught by the Lord, and great shall be the prosperity of your sons. In righteousness you shall be established; you shall not be far from oppression, for you shall not fear; and from terror, for it shall not come near you. If any one stirs up strife, it is not from me; whoever stirs up strife with you shall fall because of you. Behold, I have created the smith who blows the fire of coals, and produces a weapon for its purpose. I have also created the ravager to destroy; no weapon that is fashioned against you shall prosper, and you shall confute every tongue that rises against you in judgment. This is the heritage of the servants of the Lord and their vindication from me, says the Lord."

*A Reading (Lesson) from the Letter of Paul
to the Galatians* [4:21-31]

Tell me, you who desire to be under law, do you not hear
the law? For it is written that Abraham had two sons, one
by a slave and one by a free woman. But the son of the
slave was born according to the flesh, the son of the free
woman through promise. Now this is an allegory: these
women are two covenants. One is from Mount Sinai,
bearing children for slavery; she is Hagar. Now Hagar is
Mount Sinai in Arabia; she corresponds to the present
Jerusalem, for she is in slavery with her children. But the
Jerusalem above is free, and she is our mother. For it is
written, "Rejoice, O barren one who does not bear; break
forth and shout, you who are not in travail; for the
children of the desolate one are many more than the
children of her that is married." Now we, brethren, like
Isaac, are children of promise. But as at that time he who
was born according to the flesh persecuted him who was
born according to the Spirit, so it is now. But what does
the scripture say? "Cast out the slave and her son; for the
son of the slave shall not inherit with the son of the free
woman." So, brethren, we are not children of the slave but
of the free woman.

A Reading (Lesson) from the Gospel according to Mark
[8:11-26]

The Pharisees came and began to argue with Jesus, seeking
from him a sign from heaven, to test him. And he sighed
deeply in his spirit, and said, "Why does this generation
seek a sign? Truly, I say to you, no sign shall be given to
this generation." And he left them, and getting into the
boat again he departed to the other side. Now they had
forgotten to bring bread; and they had only one loaf with
them in the boat. And he cautioned them, saying, "Take
heed, beware of the leaven of the Pharisees and the leaven
of Herod." And they discussed it with one another, saying,
"We have no bread." And being aware of it, Jesus said to

them, "Why do you discuss the fact that you have no bread? Do you not yet perceive or understand? Are your hearts hardened? Having eyes do you not see, and having ears do you not hear? And do you not remember? When I broke the five loaves for the five thousand, how many baskets full of broken pieces did you take up?" They said to him, "Twelve." "And the seven for the four thousand, how many baskets full of broken pieces did you take up?" And they said to him, "Seven." And he said to them, "Do you not yet understand?" And they came to Beth-sa'ida. And some people brought to him a blind man, and begged him to touch him. And he took the blind man by the hand, and led him out of the village; and when he had spit on his eyes and laid his hands upon him, he asked him, "Do you see anything?" And he looked up and said, "I see men; but they look like trees, walking." Then again he laid his hands upon his eyes; and he looked intently and was restored, and saw everything clearly. And he sent him away to his home, saying, "Do not even enter the village."

Thursday

(Psalm 70 [page 682]), *Psalm 71* [page 683] ❖
Psalm 74 [page 689]

A Reading (Lesson) from the Book of Isaiah [55:1-13]

"Ho, every one who thirsts, come to the waters; and he who has no money, come, buy and eat! Come, buy wine and milk without money and without price. Why do you spend your money for that which is not bread, and your labor for that which does not satisfy? Hearken diligently to me, and eat what is good, and delight yourselves in fatness. Incline your ear, and come to me; hear, that your soul may live; and I will make with you an everlasting covenant, my steadfast, sure love for David. Behold, I made him a witness to the peoples, a leader and commander for the peoples. Behold, you shall call nations that you know not, and nations that knew you not shall run to you, because of the Lord your God, and of the Holy One of Israel, for he has glorified you. Seek the Lord while he may be found, call upon him while he is near; let the wicked forsake his way, and the unrighteous man his thoughts; let him return to the Lord, that he may have mercy on him, and to our God, for he will abundantly pardon. For my thoughts are not your thoughts, neither are your ways my ways says the Lord. For as the heavens are higher than the earth, so are my ways higher than your ways and my thoughts than your thoughts. For as the rain and the snow come down from heaven, and return not thither but water the earth, making it bring forth and sprout, giving seed to the sower and bread to the eater, so shall my word be that goes forth from my mouth; it shall not return to me empty, but it shall accomplish that which I purpose, and prosper in the thing for which I sent it. For you shall go out in joy, and be led forth in peace; the mountains and the hills before you shall break forth into singing, and all the trees of the field shall clap their hands. Instead of the thorn shall come up the cypress; instead of the brier shall come up the myrtle; and it shall be to the Lord for a memorial, for an everlasting sign which shall not be cut off."

A Reading (Lesson) from the Letter of Paul to the Galatians [5:1-15]

For freedom Christ has set us free; stand fast therefore, and do not submit again to a yoke of slavery. Now I, Paul, say to you that if you receive circumcision, Christ will be of no advantage to you. I testify again to every man who receives circumcision that he is bound to keep the whole law. You are severed from Christ, you who would be justified by the law; you have fallen away from grace. For through the Spirit, by faith, we wait for the hope of righteousness. For in Christ Jesus neither circumcision nor uncircumcision is of any avail, but faith working through love. You were running well; who hindered you from obeying the truth? This persuasion is not from him who calls you. A little leaven leavens the whole lump. I have confidence in the Lord that you will take no other view than mine; and he who is troubling you will bear his judgment, whoever he is. But if I, brethren, still preach circumcision, why am I still persecuted? In that case the stumbling block of the cross has been removed. I wish those who unsettle you would mutilate themselves! For you were called to freedom, brethren; only do not use your freedom as an opportunity for the flesh, but through love be servants of one another. For the whole law is fulfilled in one word, "You shall love your neighbor as yourself." But if you bite and devour one another take heed that you are not consumed by one another.

A Reading (Lesson) from the Gospel according to Mark
[8:27—9:1]

Jesus went on with his disciples from Beth-sa'ida, to the villages of Caesare'a Philippi; and on the way he asked his disciples, "Who do men say that I am?" And they told him, "John the Baptist; and others say, Eli'jah; and others one of the prophets." And he asked them, "But who do you say that I am?" Peter answered him, "You are the Christ." And he charged them to tell no one about him. And he began to teach them that the Son of man must suffer many things, and be rejected by the elders and the chief priests and the scribes, and be killed, and after three days rise again. And he said this plainly. And Peter took him, and began to rebuke him. But turning and seeing his disciples, he rebuked Peter, and said, "Get behind me, Satan! For you are not on the side of God, but of men." And he called to him the multitude with his disciples, and said to them, "If any man would come after me, let him deny himself and take up his cross and follow me. For whoever would save his life will lose it; and whoever loses his life for my sake and the gospel's will save it. For what does it profit a man, to gain the whole world and forfeit his life? For what can a man give in return for his life? For whoever is ashamed of me and and of my words in this adulterous and sinful generation, of him will the Son of man also be ashamed, when he comes in the glory of his Father with the holy angels." And he said to them, "Truly, I say to you, there are some standing here who will not taste death before they see that the kingdom of God has come with power."

Friday

Psalm 69:1-23(24-30)31-38 [page 679] ❖
Psalm 73 [page 687]

A Reading (Lesson) from the Book of Isaiah [56:1-8]

Thus says the Lord: "Keep justice, and do righteousness, for soon my salvation will come, and my deliverance be revealed. Blessed is the man who does this, and the son of man who holds it fast, who keeps the sabbath, not profaning it, and keeps his hand from doing any evil." Let not the foreigner who has joined himself to the Lord say, "The Lord will surely separate me from his people"; and let not the eunuch say, "Behold, I am a dry tree." For thus says the Lord: "To the eunuchs who keep my sabbaths, who choose the things that please me and hold fast my covenant, I will give in my house and within my walls a monument and a name better than sons and daughters; I will give them an everlasting name which shall not be cut off. And the foreigners who join themselves to the Lord, to minister to him, to love the name of the Lord, and to be his servants, every one who keeps the sabbath, and does not profane it, and holds fast my covenant—these I will bring to my holy mountain, and make them joyful in my house of prayer; their burnt offerings and their sacrifices will be accepted on my altar; for my house shall be called a house of prayer for all peoples. Thus says the Lord God, who gathers the outcasts of Israel, I will gather yet others to him besides those already gathered."

*A Reading (Lesson) from the Letter of Paul
to the Galatians* [5:16-24]

But I say, walk by the Spirit, and do not gratify the desires
of the flesh. For the desires of the flesh are against the
Spirit, and the desires of the Spirit are against the flesh; for
these are opposed to each other, to prevent you from doing
what you would. But if you are led by the Spirit you are
not under the law. Now the works of the flesh are plain:
fornication, impurity, licentiousness, idolatry, sorcery,
enmity, strife, jealousy, anger, selfishness, dissension, party
strife, envy, drunkenness, carousing, and the like. I warn
you, as I warned you before, that those who do such things
shall not inherit the kingdom of God. But the fruit of the
Spirit is love, joy, peace, patience, kindness, goodness,
faithfulness, gentleness, self-control; against such there is
no law. And those who belong to Christ Jesus have
crucified the flesh with its passions and desires.

A Reading (Lesson) from the Gospel according to Mark
[9:2-13]

After six days Jesus took with him Peter and James and
John, and led them up a high mountain apart by
themselves; and he was transfigured before them, and his
garments became glistening, intensely white, as no fuller
on earth could bleach them. And there appeared to them
Eli'jah with Moses; and they were talking to Jesus. And
Peter said to Jesus, "Master, it is well that we are here; let
us make three booths, one for you and one for Moses and
one for Eli'jah." For he did not know what to say, for they
were exceedingly afraid. And a cloud overshadowed them,
and a voice came out of the cloud, "This is my beloved
Son; listen to him." And suddenly looking around they no
longer saw any one with them but Jesus only. And as they
were coming down the mountain, he charged them to tell
no one what they had seen, until the Son of man should
have risen from the dead. So they kept the matter to

themselves, questioning what the rising from the dead meant. And they asked him, "Why do the scribes say that first Eli'jah must come?" And he said to them, "Eli'jah does come first to restore all things; and how is it written of the Son of man, that he should suffer many things and be treated with contempt? But I tell you that Eli'jah has come, and they did to him whatever they pleased, as it is written of him."

Saturday

Psalm 75 [page 691], *Psalm 76* [page 692] ❖
Psalm 23 [page 612], *Psalm 27* [page 617]

A Reading (Lesson) from the Book of Isaiah [57:3-13]

Draw near hither, sons of the sorceress, offspring of the adulterer and the harlot. Of whom are you making sport? Against whom do you open your mouth wide and put out your tongue? Are you not children of transgression, the offspring of deceit, you who burn with lust among the oaks, under every green tree; who slay your children in the valleys, under the clefts of the rocks? Among the smooth stones of the valley is your portion; they, they, are your lot to them you have poured out a drink offering, you have brought a cereal offering. Shall I be appeased for these things? Upon a high and lofty mountain you have set your bed, and thither you went up to offer sacrifice. Behind the door and the doorpost you have set up your symbol; for, deserting me, you have uncovered your bed, you have gone up to it, you have made it wide; and you have made a bargain for yourself with them, you have loved their bed, you have looked on nakedness. You journeyed to Molech with oil and multiplied your perfumes; you sent your envoys far off, and sent down even to Sheol. You were wearied with the length of your way, but you did not say, "It is hopeless"; you found new life for your strength, and so you were not faint. Whom did you dread and fear, so that you lied, and did not remember me, did not give me a thought? Have I not held my peace, even for a long time, and so you do not fear me? I will tell of your righteousness and your doings, but they will not help you. When you cry out, let your collection of idols deliver you! The wind will carry them off, a breath will take them away. But he who takes refuge in me shall possess the land, and shall inherit my holy mountain.

A Reading (Lesson) from the Letter of Paul to the Galatians [5:25—6:10]

If we live by the Spirit, let us also walk by the Spirit. Let us have no self-conceit, no provoking of one another, no envy of one another. Brethren, if a man is overtaken in any trespass, you who are spiritual should restore him in a spirit of gentleness. Look to yourself, lest you too be tempted. Bear one another's burdens, and so fulfil the law of Christ. For if any one thinks he is something, when he is nothing, he deceives himself. But let each one test his own work, and then his reason to boast will be in himself alone and not in his neighbor. For each man will have to bear his own load. Let him who is taught the word share all good things with him who teaches. Do not be deceived; God is not mocked, for whatever a man sows, that he will also reap. For he who sows to his own flesh will from the flesh reap corruption; but he who sows to the Spirit will from the Spirit reap eternal life. And let us not grow weary in well-doing, for in due season we shall reap, if we do not lose heart. So then, as we have opportunity, let us do good to all men, and especially to those who are of the household of faith.

A Reading (Lesson) from the Gospel according to Mark [9:14-29]

When Jesus and Peter and James and John came to the disciples, they saw a great crowd about them, and scribes arguing with them. And immediately all the crowd, when they saw him, were greatly amazed, and ran up to him and greeted him. And they asked them, "What are you discussing with them?" And one of the crowd answered him, "Teacher, I brought my son to you, for he has a dumb spirit; and wherever it seizes him, it dashes him down; and he foams and grinds his teeth and becomes rigid; and I asked your disciples to cast it out, and they were not able." And he answered them, "O faithless generation, how long am I to be with you? How long am I to bear with you? Bring him to me." And they brought the boy to him; and when the spirit saw him, immediately it convulsed the boy, and he fell on the ground and rolled about, foaming at the mouth. And Jesus asked his father, "How long has he had this?" And he said, "From childhood. And it has often cast him into the fire and into the water, to destroy him; but if you can do anything, have pity on us and help us." And Jesus said to him, "If you can! All things are possible to him who believes." Immediately the father of the child cried out and said, "I believe; help my unbelief!" And when Jesus saw that a crowd came running together, he rebuked the unclean spirit, saying to it, "You dumb and deaf spirit, I command you, come out of him, and never enter him again." And after crying out and convulsing him terribly, it came out, and the boy was like a corpse; so that most of them said, "He is dead." But Jesus took him by the hand and lifted him up, and he arose. And when he had entered the house, his disciples asked him privately, "Why could we not cast it out?" And he said to them, "This kind cannot be driven out by anything but prayer."

Week of 5 Epiphany

Sunday

Psalm 93 [page 722],   *Psalm 96* [page 725]   ❖
Psalm 34 [page 627]

A Reading (Lesson) from the Book of Isaiah [57:14-21]

It shall be said, "Build up, build up, prepare the way, remove every obstruction from my people's way." For thus says the high and lofty One who inhabits eternity, whose name is Holy: "I dwell in the high and holy place, and also with him who is of a contrite and humble spirit, to revive the spirit of the humble, and to revive the heart of the contrite. For I will not contend for ever, nor will I always be angry; for from me proceeds the spirit, and I have made the breath of life. Because of the iniquity of his covetousness I was angry, I smote him, I hid my face and was angry; but he went on backsliding in the way of his own heart. I have seen his ways, but I will heal him; I will lead him and requite him with comfort, creating for his mourners the fruit of the lips. Peace, peace, to the far and to the near, says the Lord; and I will heal him. But the wicked are like the tossing sea; for it cannot rest, and its waters toss up mire and dirt. There is no peace, says my God, for the wicked."

A Reading (Lesson) from the Letter to the Hebrews [12:1-6]

Therefore, since we are surrounded by so great a cloud of witnesses, let us also lay aside every weight, and sin which clings so closely, and let us run with perseverance the race that is set before us, looking to Jesus the pioneer and perfecter of our faith, who for the joy that was set before him endured the cross, despising the shame, and is seated at the right hand of the throne of God. Consider him who endured from sinners such hostility against himself, so that you may not grow weary or faint-hearted. In your struggle against sin you have not yet resisted to the point of shedding your blood. And have you forgotten the exhortation which addresses you as sons?—"My son, do not regard lightly the discipline of the Lord, nor lose courage when you are punished by him. For the Lord disciplines him whom he loves, and chastises every son whom he receives."

A Reading (Lesson) from the Gospel according to John
[7:37-46]

On the last day of the feast of Tabernacles, the great day, Jesus stood up and proclaimed, "If any one thirst, let him come to me and drink. He who believes in me, as the scripture has said, 'Out of his heart shall flow rivers of living water.'" Now this he said about the Spirit, which those who believed in him were to receive; for as yet the Spirit had not been given, because Jesus was not yet glorified. When they heard these words, some of the people said, "This is really the prophet." Others said, "This is the Christ." But some said, "Is the Christ to come from Galilee? Has not the scripture said that the Christ is descended from David, and comes from Bethlehem, the village where David was?" So there was a division among the people over him. Some of them wanted to arrest him, but no one laid hands on him. The officers then went back to the chief priests and Pharisees, who said to them, "Why did you not bring him?" The officers answered, "No man ever spoke like this man!"

Monday

Psalm 80 [page 702] ❖ *Psalm 77* [page 693], *(Psalm 79* [page 701])

A Reading (Lesson) from the Book of Isaiah [58:1-12]

"Cry aloud, spare not, lift up your voice like a trumpet; declare to my people their transgression, to the house of Jacob, their sins. Yet they seek me daily, and delight to know my ways, as if they were a nation that did righteousness and did not forsake the ordinance of their God; they ask of me righteous judgments, they delight to draw near to God. 'Why have we fasted, and thou seest it not? Why have we humbled ourselves, and thou takest no knowledge of it?' Behold, in the day of your fast you seek your own pleasure, and oppress all your workers. Behold, you fast only to quarrel and to fight and to hit with wicked fist. Fasting like yours this day will not make your voice to be heard on high. Is such the fast that I choose, a day for a man to humble himself? Is it to bow down his head like a rush, and to spread sackcloth and ashes under him? Will you call this a fast, and a day acceptable to the Lord? Is not this the fast that I choose: to loose the bonds of wickedness, to undo the thongs of the yoke, to let the oppressed go free, and to break every yoke? Is it not to share your bread with the hungry, and bring the homeless poor into your house; when you see the naked, to cover him, and not to hide yourself from your own flesh? Then shall your light break forth like the dawn, and your healing shall spring up speedily; your righteousness shall go before you, the glory of the Lord shall be your rear guard. Then you shall call, and the Lord will answer; you shall cry, and he will say, Here I am. If you take away from the midst of you the yoke, the pointing of the finger, and speaking wickedness, if you pour yourself out for the hungry and satisfy the desire of the afflicted, then shall your light rise in the darkness and your gloom be as the noonday. And the Lord will guide you continually, and satisfy your desire with good things, and make your bones strong; and you shall be like a watered garden, like a spring of water, whose waters fail not. And your ancient ruins shall be rebuilt; you shall raise up the foundations of many generations; you shall be called the repairer of the breach, the restorer of streets to dwell in.

A Reading (Lesson) from the Letter of Paul to the Galatians [6:11-18]

See with what large letters I am writing to you with my own hand. It is those who want to make a good showing in the flesh that would compel you to be circumcised, and only in order that they may not be persecuted for the cross of Christ. For even those who receive circumcision do not themselves keep the law, but they desire to have you circumcised that they may glory in your flesh. But far be it from me to glory except in the cross of your Lord Jesus Christ, by which the world has been crucified to me, and I to the world. For neither circumcision counts for anything nor uncircumcision, but a new creation. Peace and mercy be upon all who walk by this rule, upon the Israel of God. Henceforth let no man trouble me; for I bear on my body the marks of Jesus. The grace of our Lord Jesus Christ be with your spirit, brethren. Amen.

A Reading (Lesson) from the Gospel according to Mark [9:30-41]

Jesus and his disciples went on from there and passed through Galilee. And he would not have any one know it; for he was teaching his disciples, saying to them, "The Son of man will be delivered into the hands of men, and they will kill him; and when he is killed, after three days he will rise." But they did not understand the saying, and they were afraid to ask him. And they came to Caper'na-um; and when he was in the house he asked them, "What were you discussing on the way?" But they were silent; for on the way they had discussed with one another who was the greatest. And he sat down and called the twelve; and he said to them, "If any one would be first, he must be last of all and servant of all." And he took a child, and put him in the midst of them; and taking him in his arms, he said to them, "Whoever receives one such child in my name receives me; and whoever receives me, receives not me but him who sent me." John said to him, "Teacher, we saw a man casting out demons in your name, and we forbade him, because he was not following us." But Jesus said, "Do not forbid him; for no one who does a mighty work in my name will be able soon after to speak evil of me. For he that is not against us is for us. For truly, I say to you, whoever gives you a cup of water to drink because you bear the name of Christ, will by no means lose his reward.

Tuesday

Psalm 78:1-39 [page 694] ❖ *Psalm 78:40-72* [page 698]

A Reading (Lesson) from the Book of Isaiah [59:1-15a]

Behold, the Lord's hand is not shortened, that it cannot save, or his ear dull, that it cannot hear; but your iniquities have made a separation between you and your God, and your sins have hid his face from you so that he does not hear. For your hands are defiled with blood and your fingers with iniquity; your lips have spoken lies, your tongue mutters wickedness. No one enters suit justly, no one goes to law honestly; they rely on empty pleas, they speak lies, they conceive mischief and bring forth iniquity. They hatch adders' eggs, they weave the spider's web; he who eats their eggs dies, and from one which is crushed a viper is hatched. Their webs will not serve as clothing; men will not cover themselves with what they make. Their works are works of iniquity, and deeds of violence are in their hands. Their feet run to evil, and they make haste to shed innocent blood; their thoughts are thoughts of iniquity, desolation and destruction are in their highways. The way of peace they know not, and there is no justice in their paths; they have made their roads crooked, no one who goes in them knows peace. Therefore justice is far from us, and righteousness does not overtake us; we look for light, and behold, darkness, and for brightness, but we walk in gloom. We grope for the wall like the blind, we grope like those who have no eyes; we stumble at noon as in the twilight, among those in full vigor we are like dead men. We all growl like bears, we moan and moan like doves; we look for justice, but there is none; for salvation, but it is far from us. For our transgressions are multiplied before thee, and our sins testify against us; for our transgressions are with us, and we know our iniquities: transgressing, and denying the Lord, and turning away from following our God, speaking oppression and revolt,

conceiving and uttering from the heart lying words. Justic
is turned back, and righteousness stands afar off; for truth
has fallen in the public squares, and uprightness cannot
enter. Truth is lacking, and he who departs from evil
makes himself a prey.

*A Reading (Lesson) from the Second Letter of Paul
to Timothy* [1:1-14]

Paul, an apostle of Christ Jesus by the will of God
according to the promise of the life which is in Christ
Jesus, To Timothy, my beloved child: Grace, mercy, and
peace from God the Father and Christ Jesus our Lord. I
thank God whom I serve with a clear conscience, as did m
fathers, when I remember you constantly in my prayers. A
I remember your tears, I long night and day to see you, tha
I may be filled with joy. I am reminded of your sincere
faith, a faith that dwelt first in your grandmother Lois anc
your mother Eunice and now, I am sure, dwells in you.
Hence I remind you to rekindle the gift of God that is
within you through the laying on of my hands; for God di
not give us a spirit of timidity but a spirit of power and
love and self-control. Do not be ashamed then of testifyin;
to our Lord, nor of me his prisoner, but share in suffering
for the gospel in the power of God, who saved us and
called us with a holy calling, not in virtue of our works bu
in virtue of his own purpose and the grace which he gave
us in Christ Jesus ages ago, and now has manifested
through the appearing of our Savior Christ Jesus, who
abolished death and brought life and immortality to light
through the gospel. For this gospel I was appointed a
preacher and apostle and teacher, and therefore I suffer as
I do. But I am not ashamed, for I know whom I have
believed, and I am sure that he is able to guard until that
Day what has been entrusted to me. Follow the pattern of
the sound words which you have heard from me, in the
faith and love which are in Christ Jesus; guard the truth
that has been entrusted to you by the Holy Spirit who
dwells within us.

A Reading (Lesson) from the Gospel according to Mark
[9:42-50]

Jesus said to his disciples, "Whoever causes one of these little ones who believe in me to sin, it would be better for him if a great millstone were hung around his neck and he were thrown into the sea. And if your hand causes you to sin, cut it off; it is better for you to enter life maimed than with two hands to go to hell, to the unquenchable fire. And if your foot causes you to sin, cut it off; it is better for you to enter life lame than with two feet to be thrown into hell. And if your eye causes you to sin, pluck it out; it is better for you to enter the kingdom of God with one eye than with two eyes to be thrown into hell, where their worm does not die, and the fire is not quenched. For every one will be salted with fire. Salt is good; but if the salt has lost its saltness, how will you season it? Have salt in yourselves, and be at peace with one another.

Wednesday

Psalm 119:97-120 [page 771]   ❖   *Psalm 81* [page 704],
Psalm 82 [page 705]

Isaiah 59:15b-21   [page 67 above]

A Reading (Lesson) from the Second Letter of Paul to Timothy [1:15—2:13]

You are aware that all who are in Asia turned away from me, and among them Phy'gelus and Hermog'enes. May the Lord grant mercy to the household of Onesiph'orus, for he often refreshed me; he was not ashamed of my chains, but when he arrived in Rome he searched for me eagerly and found me—may the Lord grant him to find mercy from the Lord on that Day—and you well know all the service he rendered at Ephesus. You then, my son, be strong in the grace that is in Christ Jesus, and what you have heard from me before many witnesses entrust to faithful men who will be able to teach others also. Share in suffering as a good soldier of Christ Jesus. No soldier on service gets entangled in civilian pursuits, since his aim is to satisfy the one who enlisted him. An athlete is not crowned unless he competes according to the rules. It is the hard-working farmer who ought to have the first share of the crops. Think over what I say, for the Lord will grant you understanding in everything. Remember Jesus Christ, risen from the dead, descended from David, as preached in my gospel, the gospel for which I am suffering and wearing fetters like a criminal. But the word of God is not fettered. Therefore I endure everything for the sake of the elect, that they also may obtain salvation in Christ Jesus with its eternal glory. The saying is sure: If we have died with him, we shall also live with him; if we endure, we shall also reign with him; if we deny him, he also will deny us; if we are faithless, he remains faithful—for he cannot deny himself.

A Reading (Lesson) from the Gospel according to Mark
[10:1-16]

Jesus left Caper'na-um and went to the region of Judea and beyond the Jordan, and crowds gathered to him again; and again, as his custom was, he taught them. And Pharisees came up and in order to test him asked, "Is it lawful for a man to divorce his wife?" He answered them, "What did Moses command you?" They said, "Moses allowed a man to write a certificate of divorce, and to put her away." But Jesus said to them, "For your hardness of heart he wrote you this commandment. But from the beginning of creation, 'God made them male and female.' 'For this reason a man shall leave his father and mother and be joined to his wife, and the two shall become one flesh.' So they are no longer two but one flesh. What therefore God has joined together, let not man put asunder." And in the house the disciples asked him again about this matter. And he said to them, "Whoever divorces his wife and marries another, commits adultery against her; and if she divorces

her husband and marries another, she commits adultery."
And they were bringing children to him that he might
touch them; and the disciples rebuked them. But when
Jesus saw it he was indignant, and said to them, "Let the
children come to me, do not hinder them; for to such
belongs the kingdom of God. Truly, I say to you, whoever
does not receive the kingdom of God like a child shall not
enter it." And he took them in his arms and blessed them,
laying his hands upon them.

Thursday

(Psalm 83 [page 706])   *or*   *Psalm 146* [page 803],
Psalm 147 [page 804]   ❖   *Psalm 85* [page 708],
Psalm 86 [page 709]

A Reading (Lesson) from the Book of Isaiah [60:1-17]

Arise, shine; for your light has come, and the glory of the
Lord has risen upon you. For behold, darkness shall cover
the earth, and thick darkness the peoples; but the Lord will
arise upon you, and his glory will be seen upon you. And
nations shall come to your light, and kings to the
brightness of your rising. Lift up your eyes round about,
and see; they all gather together, they come to you; your
sons shall come from far, and your daughters shall be
carried in the arms. Then you shall see and be radiant,
your heart shall thrill and rejoice; because the abundance
of the sea shall be turned to you, the wealth of the nations
shall come to you. A multitude of camels shall cover you,
the young camels of Mid'ian and Ephah; all those from
Sheba shall come. They shall bring gold and frankincense,
and shall proclaim the praise of the Lord. All the flocks of
Kedar shall be gathered to you, the rams of Nebai'oth shall
minister to you; they shall come up with acceptance on my
altar, and I will glorify my glorious house. Who are these
that fly like a cloud, and like doves to their windows? For
the coastlands shall wait for me, the ships of Tarshish first,

to bring your sons from far, their silver and gold with them, for the name of the Lord your God, and for the Holy One of Israel, because he has glorified you. Foreigners shall build up your walls, and their kings shall minister to you; for in my wrath I smote you, but in my favor I have had mercy on you. Your gates shall be open continually; day and night they shall not be shut; that men may bring to you the wealth of the nations, with their kings led in procession. For the nation and kingdom that will not serve you shall perish; those nations shall be utterly laid waste. The glory of Lebanon shall come to you, the cypress, the plane, and the pine, to beautify the place of my sanctuary; and I will make the place of my feet glorious. The sons of those who oppressed you shall come bending low to you; and all who despised you shall bow down at your feet; they shall call you the City of the Lord, the Zion of the Holy One of Israel. Whereas you have been forsaken and hated, with no one passing through, I will make you majestic for ever, a joy from age to age. You shall suck the milk of nations, you shall suck the breast of kings; and you shall know that I, the Lord, am your Savior and your Redeemer, the Mighty One of Jacob. Instead of bronze I will bring gold, and instead of iron I will bring silver; instead of wood, bronze, instead of stones, iron. I will make your overseers peace and your taskmasters righteousness.

A Reading (Lesson) from the Second Letter of Paul to Timothy [2:14-26]

Remind them of this, and charge them before the Lord to avoid disputing about words, which does no good, but only ruins the hearers. Do your best to present yourself to God as one approved, a workman who has no need to be ashamed, rightly handling the word of truth. Avoid such godless chatter, for it will lead people into more and more ungodliness, and their talk will eat its way like gangrene. Among them are Hymenae'us and Phile'tus, who have swerved from the truth by holding that the resurrection is past already. They are upsetting the faith of some. But God's firm foundation stands, bearing this seal: "The Lord knows those who are his," and "Let every one who names the name of the Lord depart from iniquity." In a great house there are not only vessels of gold and silver but also of wood and earthenware, and some for noble use, some for ignoble. If any one purifies himself from what is ignoble, then he will be a vessel for noble use, consecrated and useful to the master of the house, ready for any good work. So shun youthful passions and aim at righteousness, faith, love, and peace, along with those who call upon the Lord from a pure heart. Have nothing to do with stupid, senseless controversies; you know that they breed quarrels. And the Lord's servant must not be quarrelsome but kindly to every one, an apt teacher, forbearing, correcting his opponents with gentleness. God may perhaps grant that they will repent and come to know the truth, and they may escape from the snare of the devil, after being captured by him to do his will.

A Reading (Lesson) from the Gospel according to Mark
[10:17-31]

As Jesus was setting out on his journey, a man ran up and knelt before him, and asked him, "Good Teacher, what must I do to inherit eternal life?" And Jesus said to him, "Why do you call me good? No one is good but God alone. You know the commandments: 'Do not kill, Do not commit adultery, Do not steal, Do not bear false witness, Do not defraud, Honor your father and mother.'" And he said to him, "Teacher, all these I have observed from my youth." And Jesus looking upon him loved him, and said to him, "You lack one thing; go, sell what you have, and give to the poor, and you will have treasure in heaven; and come, follow me." At that saying his countenance fell, and he went away sorrowful; for he had great possessions. And Jesus looked around and said to his disciples, "How hard it will be for those who have riches to enter the kingdom of God!" And the disciples were amazed at his words. But Jesus said to them again, "Children, how hard it is to enter the kingdom of God! It is easier for a camel to go through the eye of a needle than for a rich man to enter the kingdom of God." And they were exceedingly astonished, and said to him, "Then who can be saved?" Jesus looked at them and said, "With men it is impossible, but not with God; for all things are possible with God." Peter began to say to him, "Lo, we have left everything and followed you." Jesus said, "Truly, I say to you, there is no one who has left house or brothers or sisters or mother or father or children or lands, for my sake and for the gospel, who will not receive a hundredfold now in this time, houses and brothers and sisters and mothers and children and lands, with persecutions, and in the age to come eternal life. But many that are first will be last, and the last first."

Friday

Psalm 88 [page 712]   ❖   *Psalm 91* [page 719],
Psalm 92 [page 720]

Isaiah 61:1-9   [page 106 above]

A Reading (Lesson) from the Second Letter of Paul to Timothy [3:1-17]

Understand this, that in the last days there will come times of stress. For men will be lovers of self, lovers of money, proud, arrogant, abusive, disobedient to their parents, ungrateful, unholy, inhuman, implacable, slanderers, profligates, reckless, swollen with conceit, lovers of pleasure rather than lovers of God, holding the form of religion but denying the power of it. Avoid such people. For among them are those who make their way into households and capture weak women, burdened with sins and swayed by various impulses, who will listen to anybody and can never arrive at a knowledge of the truth. As Jannes and Jambres opposed Moses, so these men also oppose the truth, men of corrupt mind and counterfeit faith; but they will not get very far, for their folly will be plain to all, as was that of those two men. Now you have observed my teaching, my conduct, my aim in life, my faith, my patience, my love, my steadfastness, my persecutions, my sufferings, what befell me at Antioch, at Ico'nium, and at Lystra, what persecutions I endured; yet from them all the Lord rescued me. Indeed all who desire to live a godly life in Christ Jesus will be persecuted, while evil men and impostors will go on from bad to worse, deceivers and deceived. But as for you, continue in what you have learned and have firmly believed, knowing from whom you learned it and how from childhood you have been acquainted with the sacred writings which are able to instruct you for salvation through faith in Christ Jesus. All scripture is inspired by God and profitable for teaching, for reproof, for correction, and for training in righteousness, that the man of God may be complete, equipped for every good work.

A Reading (Lesson) from the Gospel according to Mark
[10:32-45]

Jesus and his disciples were on the road, going up to Jerusalem, and Jesus was walking ahead of them; and they were amazed, and those who followed were afraid. And taking the twelve again, he began to tell them what was to happen to him, saying, "Behold, we are going up to Jerusalem; and the Son of man will be delivered to the chief priests and the scribes, and they will condemn him to death, and deliver him to the Gentiles; and they will mock him, and spit upon him, and scourge him, and kill him; and after three days he will rise." And James and John, the sons of Zeb'edee, came forward to him, and said to him, "Teacher, we want you to do for us whatever we ask of you." And he said to them, "What do you want me to do for you?" And they said to him, "Grant us to sit, one at your right hand and one at your left, in your glory." But Jesus said to them, "You do not know what you are asking. Are you able to drink the cup that I drink, or to be baptized with the baptism with which I am baptized?" And they said to him, "We are able." And Jesus said to them, "The cup that I drink you will drink; and with the baptism with which I am baptized, you will be baptized; but to sit at my right hand or at my left is not mine to grant, but it is for those for whom it has been prepared." And when the ten heard it, they began to be indignant at James and John. And Jesus called them to him and said to them, "You know that those who are supposed to rule over the Gentiles lord it over them, and their great men exercise authority over them. But it shall not be so among you; but whoever would be great among you must be your servant, and whoever would be first among you must be slave of all. For the Son of man also came not to be served but to serve, and to give his life as a ransom for many."

Saturday

Psalm 87 [page 711], *Psalm 90* [page 717] ❖
Psalm 136 [page 789]

A Reading (Lesson) from the Book of Isaiah [61:10—62:5]

I will greatly rejoice in the Lord, my soul shall exult in my God; for he has clothed me with the garments of salvation, he has covered me with the robe of righteousness, as the bridegroom decks himself with a garland, and as a bride adorns herself with her jewels. For as the earth brings forth its shoots, and as a garden causes what is sown in it to spring up, so the Lord God will cause righteousness and praise to spring forth before all the nations. For Zion's sake I will not keep silent, and for Jerusalem's sake I will not rest, until her vindication goes forth as brightness, and her salvation as a burning torch. The nations shall see you vindication, and all the kings your glory; and you shall be called by a new name which the mouth of the Lord will give. You shall be a crown of beauty in the hand of the Lord, and a royal diadem in the hand of your God. You shall no more be termed Forsaken, and your land shall no more be termed Desolate; but you shall be called My delight is in her, and your land Married; for the Lord delights in you, and your land shall be married. For as a young man marries a virgin, so shall your sons marry you, and as the bridegroom rejoices over the bride, so shall your God rejoice over you.

A Reading (Lesson) from the Second Letter of Paul to Timothy [4:1-8]

I charge you in the presence of God and of Christ Jesus who is to judge the living and the dead, and by his appearing and his kingdom: preach the word, be urgent in season and out of season, convince, rebuke, and exhort, be unfailing in patience and in teaching. For the time is coming when people will not endure sound teaching, but having itching ears they will accumulate for themselves teachers to suit their own likings, and will turn away from listening to the truth and wander into myths. As for you, always be steady, endure suffering, do the work of an evangelist, fulfil your ministry. For I am already on the point of being sacrificed; the time of my departure has come. I have fought the good fight, I have finished the race, I have kept the faith. Henceforth there is laid up for me the crown of righteousness, which the Lord, the righteous judge, will award to me on that Day, and not only to me but also to all who have loved his appearing.

A Reading (Lesson) from the Gospel according to Mark [10:46-52]

Jesus and his disciples came to Jericho; and as he was leaving Jericho with his disciples and a great multitude, Bartimae'us, a blind beggar, the son of Timae'us, was sitting by the roadside. And when he heard that it was Jesus of Nazareth, he began to cry out and say, "Jesus, Son of David, have mercy on me!" And many rebuked him, telling him to be silent; but he cried out all the more, "Son of David, have mercy on me!" And Jesus stopped and said, "Call him." And they called the blind man, saying to him, "Take heart; rise, he is calling you." And throwing off his mantle he sprang up and came to Jesus. And Jesus said to him, "What do you want me to do for you?" And the blind man said to him. "Master, let me receive my sight." And Jesus said to him, "Go your way; your faith has made you well." And immediately he received his sight and followed him on the way.

Week of 6 Epiphany

Sunday

Psalm 66 [page 673],   *Psalm 67* [page 675]   ❖
Psalm 19 [page 606],   *Psalm 46* [page 649]

A Reading (Lesson) from the Book of Isaiah   [62:6-12]

Upon your walls, O Jerusalem, I have set watchmen; all the day and all the night they shall never be silent. You who put the Lord in remembrance, take no rest, and give him no rest until he establishes Jerusalem and makes it a praise in the earth. The Lord has sworn by his right hand and by his mighty arm: "I will not again give your grain to be food for your enemies, and foreigners shall not drink your wine for which you have labored; but those who garner it shall eat it and praise the Lord, and those who gather it shall drink it in the courts of my sanctuary." Go through, go through the gates, prepare the way for the people; build up, build up the highway, clear it of stones, lift up an ensign over the peoples. Behold, the Lord has proclaimed to the end of the earth: Say to the daughter of

Zion, "Behold, your salvation comes; behold, his reward is with him, and his recompense before him." And they shall be called The holy people, The redeemed of the Lord; and you shall be called Sought out, a city not forsaken.

A Reading (Lesson) from the First Letter of John [2:3-11]

By this we may be sure that we know him, if we keep his commandments. He who says "I know him" but disobeys his commandments is a liar, and the truth is not in him; but whoever keeps his word, in him truly love for God is perfected. By this we may be sure that we are in him: he who says he abides in him ought to walk in the same way in which he walked. Beloved, I am writing you no new commandment, but an old commandment which you had from the beginning; the old commandment is the word which you have heard. Yet I am writing you a new commandment, which is true in him and in you, because the darkness is passing away and the true light is already shining. He who says he is in the light and hates his brother is in the darkness still. He who loves his brother abides in the light, and in it there is no cause for stumbling. But he who hates his bother is in the darkness and walks in the darkness, and does not know where he is going, because the darkness has blinded his eyes.

John 8:12-19   [page 77 above]

Monday

Psalm 89:1-18 [page 713]   ❖   *Psalm 89:19-52* [page 715]

A Reading (Lesson) from the Book of Isaiah [63:1-6]

Who is this that comes from Edom, in crimsoned garments from Bozrah, he that is glorious in his apparel, marching in the greatness of his strength? "It is I, announcing the vindication, mighty to save." Why is thy apparel red, and thy garments like his that treads in the wine press? "I have trodden the wine press alone, and from the peoples no one was with me; I trod them in my anger and trampled them in my wrath; their lifeblood is sprinkled upon my garments, and I have stained all my raiment. For the day of vengeance was in my heart, and my year of redemption has come. I looked, but there was no one to help; I was appalled, but there was no one to uphold; so my own arm brought me victory, and my wrath upheld me. I trod down the peoples in my anger, I made them drunk in my wrath, and I poured out their lifeblood on the earth."

A Reading (Lesson) from the First Letter of Paul to Timothy [1:1-17]

Paul, an apostle of Christ Jesus by command of God our Savior and of Christ Jesus our hope, To Timothy, my true child in the faith: Grace, mercy and peace from God the Father and Christ Jesus our Lord. As I urged you when I was going to Macedo'nia, remain at Ephesus that you may charge certain persons not to teach any different doctrine, nor to occupy themselves with myths and endless genealogies which promote speculations rather than the divine training that is in faith; whereas the aim of our charge is love that issues from a pure heart and a good conscience and sincere faith. Certain persons by swerving from these have wandered away into vain discussion, desiring to be teachers of the law, without understanding either what they are saying or the things about which they make assertions. Now we know that the law is good, if anyone uses it lawfully, understanding this, that the law is not laid down for the just but for the lawless and disobedient, for the ungodly and sinners, for the unholy and profane, for murderers of fathers and murderers of mothers, for manslayers, immoral persons, sodomites, kidnapers, liars, perjurers, and whatever else is contrary to sound doctrine, in accordance with the glorious gospel of the blessed God with which I have been entrusted. I thank him who has given me strength for this, Christ Jesus our

Lord, because he judged me faithful by appointing me to his service, though I formerly blasphemed and persecuted and insulted him; but I received mercy because I had acted ignorantly in unbelief, and the grace of our Lord overflowed for me with the faith and love that are in Christ Jesus. The saying is sure and worthy of full acceptance, that Christ Jesus came into the world to save sinners. And I am the foremost of sinners; but I received mercy for this reason, that in me, as the foremost, Jesus Christ might display his perfect patience for an example to those who were to believe in him for eternal life. To the King of ages, immortal, invisible, the only God, be honor and glory for ever and ever. Amen.

A Reading (Lesson) from the Gospel according to Mark
[11:1-11]

When they drew near to Jerusalem, to Beth'phage and Bethany, at the Mount of Olives, Jesus sent two of his disciples, and said to them, "Go into the village opposite you, and immediately as you enter it you will find a colt tied, on which no one has ever sat; untie it and bring it. If any one says to you, 'Why are you doing this?' say, 'The Lord has need of it and will send it back here immediately.'" And they went away, and found a colt tied at the door out in the open street; and they untied it. And those who stood there said to them, "What are you doing, untying the colt?" And they told them what Jesus had said; and they let them go. And they brought the colt to Jesus, and threw their garments on it; and he sat upon it. And many spread their garments on the road, and others spread leafy branches which they had cut from the fields. And those who went before and those who followed cried out, "Hosanna! Blessed is he who comes in the name of the Lord! Blessed is the kingdom of our father David that is coming! Hosanna in the highest!" And he entered Jerusalem, and went into the temple; and when he had looked round at everything, as it was already late, he went out to Bethany with the twelve.

Tuesday

Psalm 97 [page 726],   *Psalm 99* [page 728],
(Psalm 100 [page 729]) ❖ *Psalm 94* [page 722],
(Psalm 95 [page 724])

A Reading (Lesson) from the Book of Isaiah [63:7-14]

I will recount the steadfast love of the Lord, the praises of
the Lord, according to all that the Lord has granted us, and
the great goodness to the house of Israel which he has
granted them according to his mercy, according to the
abundance of his steadfast love. For he said, Surely they
are my people, sons who will not deal falsely; and he
became their Savior. In all their affliction he was afflicted,
and the angel of his presence saved them; in his love and in
his pity he redeemed them; he lifted them up and carried
them all the days of old. But they rebelled and grieved his
holy Spirit; therefore he turned to be their enemy, and
himself fought against them. Then he remembered the days
of old, of Moses his servant. Where is he who brought up
out of the sea the shepherds of his flock? Where is he who
put in the midst of them his holy Spirit, who caused his
glorious arm to go at the right hand of Moses, who divided
the waters before them to make for himself an everlasting
name, who led them through the depths? Like a horse in
the desert, they did not stumble. Like cattle that go down
into the valley, the Spirit of the Lord gave them rest. So
thou didst lead thy people, to make for thyself a glorious
name.

*A Reading (Lesson) from the First Letter of Paul
to Timothy* [1:18—2:8]

This charge I commit to you, Timothy, my son, in
accordance with the prophetic utterances which pointed to
you, that inspired by them you may wage the good
warfare, holding faith and a good conscience. By rejecting

conscience, certain persons have made shipwreck of their faith, among them Hymenae'us and Alexander, whom I have delivered to Satan that they may learn not to blaspheme. First of all, then, I urge that supplications, prayers, intercessions, and thanksgivings be made for all men, for kings and all who are in high positions, that we may lead a quiet and peaceable life, godly and respectful in every way. This is good, and it is acceptable in the sight of God our Savior, who desires all men to be saved and to come to the knowledge of the truth. For there is one God, and there is one mediator between God and men, the man Christ Jesus, who gave himself as a ransom for all, the testimony to which was borne at the proper time. For this I was appointed a preacher and apostle (I am telling the truth, I am not lying), a teacher of the Gentiles in faith and truth. I desire then that in every place the men should pray, lifting holy hands without anger or quarreling.

A Reading (Lesson) from the Gospel according to Mark [11:12-26]

On the following day, when they came from Bethany, Jesus was hungry. And seeing in the distance a fig tree in leaf, he went to see if he could find anything on it. When he came to it, he found nothing but leaves, for it was not the season for figs. And he said to it, "May no one ever eat fruit from you again." And his disciples heard it. And they came to Jerusalem. And he entered the temple and began to drive out those who sold and those who bought in the temple, and he overturned the tables of the money-changers and the seats of those who sold pigeons; and he would not allow any one to carry anything through the temple. And he taught, and said to them, "Is it not written, 'My house shall be called a house of prayer for all the nations'? But you have made it a den of robbers." And the chief priests and the scribes heard it and sought a way to destroy him; for they feared him, because all the multitude was astonished at his teaching. And when evening came they went out of the city. As they passed by in the morning, they saw the fig tree withered away to its roots. And Peter remembered and said to him, "Master, look! The fig tree which you cursed has withered." And Jesus answered them, "Have faith in God. Truly, I say to you, whoever says to this mountain, 'Be taken up and cast into the sea,' and does not doubt in his heart, but believes that what he says will come to pass, it will be done for him. Therefore I tell you, whatever you ask in prayer, believe that you have received it, and it will be yours. And whenever you stand praying, forgive, if you have anything against any one; so that your Father also who is in heaven may forgive you your trespasses."

Wednesday

Psalm 101 [page 730], *Psalm 109:1-4(5-19)20-30* [page 750]
❖ *Psalm 119:121-144* [page 733]

A Reading (Lesson) from the Book of Isaiah [63:15—64:9]

Look down from heaven and see, from thy holy and glorious habitation. Where are thy zeal and thy might? The yearning of thy heart and thy compassion are withheld from me. For thou art our Father, though Abraham does not know us and Isreal does not acknowledge us; thou, O Lord, art our Father, our Redeemer from of old is thy name. O Lord, why dost thou make us err from thy ways and harden our heart, so that we fear thee not? Return for the sake of thy servants, the tribes of thy heritage. Thy holy people possessed thy sanctuary a little while; our adversaries have trodden it down. We have become like those over whom thou hast never ruled, like those who are not called by thy name. O that thou wouldst rend the heavens and come down, that the mountains might quake at thy presence—as when fire kindles brushwood and the fire causes water to boil—to make thy name known to thy adversaries, and that the nations might tremble at thy presence! When thou didst terrible things which we looked not for, thou camest down, the mountains quaked at thy presence. From of old no one has heard or perceived by the ear, no eye has seen a God besides thee, who works for those who wait for him. Thou meetest him that joyfully works righteousness, those that remember thee in thy ways. Behold, thou wast angry, and we sinned; in our sins we have been a long time, and shall we be saved? We have all become like one who is unclean, and all our righteous deeds are like a polluted garment. We all fade like a leaf, and our iniquities, like the wind, take us away. There is no one that calls upon thy name, that bestirs himself to take hold of thee; for thou hast hid thy face from us, and hast delivered us into the hand of our iniquities. Yet, O Lord, thou art our Father; we are the clay, and thou art our potter; we are all the work of thy hand. Be not exceedingly angry, O Lord, and remember not iniquity for ever. Behold, consider, we are all thy people.

A Reading (Lesson) from the First Letter of Paul to Timothy [3:1-16]

The saying is sure: If any one aspires to the office of bishop, he desires a noble task. Now a bishop must be above reproach, the husband of one wife, temperate, sensible, dignified, hospitable, an apt teacher, no drunkard, not violent but gentle, not quarrelsome, and no lover of money. He must manage his own household well, keeping his children submissive and respectful in every way; for if a man does not know how to manage his own household, how can he care for God's church? He must not be a recent convert, or he may be puffed up with conceit and fall into the condemnation of the devil; moreover he must be well thought of by outsiders, or he may fall into reproach and the snare of the devil. Deacons likewise must be serious, not double-tongued, not addicted to much wine, not greedy for gain; they must hold the mystery of the faith with a clear conscience. And let them also be tested first; then if they prove themselves blameless let them serve as deacons. The women likewise must be serious, no slanderers, but temperate, faithful in all things. Let deacons be the husband of one wife, and let them manage their children and their households well; for those who serve well as deacons gain a good standing for themselves and also great confidence in the faith which is in Christ Jesus. I hope to come to you soon, but I am writing these instructions to you so that, if I am delayed, you may know how one ought to behave in the household of God, which is the church of the living God, the pillar and bulwark of the truth. Great indeed, we confess, is the mystery of our religion: He was manifested in the flesh, vindicated in the Spirit, seen by angels, preached among the nations, believed on in the world, taken up in glory.

A Reading (Lesson) from the Gospel according to Mark
[11:27—12:12]

Jesus and his disciples came again to Jerusalem. And as he was walking in the temple, the chief priests and the scribes and the elders came to him, and they said to him, "By what authority are you doing these things, or who gave you this authority to do them." Jesus said to them, "I will ask you a question; answer me, and I will tell you by what authority I do these things. Was the baptism of John from heaven or from men? Answer me." And they argued with one another, "If we say, 'From heaven,' he will say, 'Why then did you not believe him?' But shall we say 'From men'?"—they were afraid of the people, for all held that John was a real prophet. So they answered Jesus, "We do not know." And Jesus said to them, "Neither will I tell you by what authority I do these things." And he began to speak to them in parables. "A man planted a vineyard, and set a hedge around it, and dug a pit for the wine press, and built a tower, and let it out to tenants, and went into another country. When the time came, he sent a servant to the tenants, to get from them some of the fruit of the vineyard. And they took him and beat him, and sent him away empty-handed. Again he sent to them another servant, and they wounded him in the head, and treated him shamefully. And he sent another, and him they killed; and so with many others, some they beat and some they killed. He had still one other, a beloved son; finally he sent him to them, saying, 'They will respect my son.' But those tenants said to one another, 'This is the heir; come, let us kill him, and the inheritance will be ours.' And they took him and killed him, and cast him out of the vineyard. What will the owner of the vineyard do? He will come and destroy the tenants, and give the vineyard to others. Have you not read this scripture: 'The very stone which the builders rejected has become the head of the corner; this was the Lord's doing, and it is marvelous in our eyes'?" And they tried to arrest him, but feared the multitude, for they perceived that he had told the parable against them; so they left him and went away.

Thursday

Psalm 105:1-22 [page 738] ❖ *Psalm 105:23-45* [page 739]

A Reading (Lesson) from the Book of Isaiah [65:1-12]

I was ready to be sought by those who did not ask for me; I was ready to be found by those who did not seek me. I said, "Here am I, here am I," to a nation that did not call on my name. I spread out my hands all the day to a rebellious people, who walk in a way that is not good, following their own devices; a people who provoke me to my face continually, sacrificing in gardens and burning incense upon bricks; who sit in tombs, and spend the night in secret places; who eat swine's flesh, and broth of abominable things is in their vessels; who say "Keep to yourself, do not come near me, for I am set apart from you." These are a smoke in my nostrils, a fire that burns all the day. Behold it is written before me: "I will not keep silent, but I will repay, yea, I will repay into their bosom their iniquities and their fathers' iniquities together, says the Lord; because they burned incense upon the mountains and reviled me upon the hills, I will measure into their bosom payment for their former doings." Thus says the Lord: "As the wine is found in the cluster, and they say, 'Do not destroy it, for there is a blessing in it,' so I will do for my servants' sake, and not destroy them all. I will bring forth descendants from Jacob, and from Judah inheritors of my mountains; my chosen shall inherit it, and my servants shall dwell there. Sharon shall become a pasture for flocks, and the Valley of Achor a place for herds to lie down, for my people who have sought me. But you who forsake the Lord, who forget my holy mountain, who set a table for Fortune and fill cups of mixed wine for Destiny; I will destine you to the sword, and all of you shall bow down to the slaughter; because, when I called, you did not answer, when I spoke, you did not listen, but you did what was evil in my eyes, and chose what I did not delight in."

A Reading (Lesson) from the First Letter of Paul to Timothy [4:1-16]

The Spirit expressly says that in later times some will depart from the faith by giving heed to deceitful spirits and doctrines of demons, through the pretensions of liars whose consciences are seared, who forbid marriage and enjoin abstinence from foods which God created to be received with thanksgiving by those who believe and know the truth. For everything created by God is good, and nothing is to be rejected if it is received with thanksgiving; for then it is consecrated by the word of God and prayer. If you put these instructions before the brethren, you will be a good minister of Christ Jesus, nourished on the words of the faith and of the good doctrine which you have followed. Have nothing to do with godless and silly myths. Train yourself in godliness; for while bodily training is of some value, godliness is of value in every way, as it holds promise for the present life and also for the life to come. The saying is sure and worthy of full acceptance. For to this end we toil and strive, because we have our hope set on the living God, who is the Savior of all men, especially of those who believe. Command and teach these things. Let no one despise your youth, but set the believers an example in speech and conduct, in love, in faith, in purity. Till I come, attend to the public reading of scripture, to preaching, to teaching. Do not neglect the gift you have, which was given you by prophetic utterance when the council of elders laid their hands upon you. Practise these duties, devote yourself to them, so that all may see your progress. Take heed to yourself and to your teaching; hold to that, for by so doing you will save both yourself and your hearers.

A Reading (Lesson) from the Gospel according to Mark [12:13-27]

The chief priests and the scribes and the elders sent to Jesus some of the Pharisees and some of the Hero'di-ans, to entrap him in his talk. And they came and said to him, "Teacher, we know that you are true, and care for no man; for you do not regard the position of men, but truly teach the way of God. Is it lawful to pay taxes to Caesar, or not? Should we pay them, or should we not?" But knowing their hypocrisy, he said to them, "Why put me to the test? Bring me a coin, and let me look at it." And they brought one. And he said to them, "Whose likeness and inscription is this?" They said to him, "Caesar's." Jesus said to them, "Render to Caesar the things that are Caesar's, and to God the things that are God's." And they were amazed at him. And Sad'ducees came to him, who say there is no resurrection; and they asked him a question, saying, "Teacher, Moses wrote for us that if a man's brother dies and leaves a wife, but leaves no child, the man must take the wife, and raise up children for his brother. There were seven brothers; the first took a wife, and when he died left no children; and the second took her, and died, leaving no children; and the third likewise; and the seven left no children. Last of all the woman also died. In the resurrection whose wife will she be? For the seven had her as wife." Jesus said to them, "Is not this why you are wrong, that you know neither the scriptures nor the power of God? For when they rise from the dead, they neither marry nor are given in marriage, but are like angels in heaven. And as for the dead being raised, have you not read in the book of Moses, in the passage about the bush, how God said to him, "I am the God of Abraham, and the God of Isaac, and the God of Jacob'? He is not God of the dead, but of the living; you are quite wrong."

Friday

Psalm 102 [page 731] ❖ *Psalm 107:1-32* [page 746]

A Reading (Lesson) from the Book of Isaiah [65:17-25]

Therefore thus says the Lord God: "Behold, I create new heavens and a new earth; and the former things shall not be remembered or come into mind. But be glad and rejoice for ever in that which I create; for behold, I create Jerusalem a rejoicing, and her people a joy. I will rejoice in Jerusalem, and be glad in my people; no more shall be heard in it the sound of weeping and the cry of distress. No more shall there be in it an infant that lives but a few days, or an old man who does not fill out his days, for the child shall die a hundred years old, and the sinner a hundred years old shall be accursed. They shall build houses and inhabit them; they shall plant vineyards and eat their fruit. They shall not build and another inhabit; they shall not plant and another eat; for like the days of a tree shall the days of my people be, and my chosen shall long enjoy the work of their hands. They shall not labor in vain, or bear children for calamity; for they shall be the offspring of the blessed of the Lord, and their children with them. Before they call I will answer, while they are yet speaking I will hear. The wolf and the lamb shall feed together, the lion shall eat straw like the ox; and dust shall be the serpent's food. They shall not hurt or destroy in all my holy mountain, says the Lord."

A Reading (Lesson) from the First Letter of Paul to Timothy [5:17-22(23-25)]

Let the elders who rule well be considered worthy of double honor, especially those who labor in preaching and teaching; for the scripture says, "You shall not muzzle an ox when it is treading out the grain," and, "The laborer deserves his wages." Never admit any charge against an elder except on the evidence of two or three witnesses. As for those who persist in sin, rebuke them in the presence of all, so that the rest may stand in fear. In the presence of God and of Christ Jesus and of the elect angels I charge you to keep these rules without favor, doing nothing from partiality. Do not be hasty in the laying on of hands, nor participate in another man's sins; keep yourself pure.

> No longer drink only water, but use a little wine for the sake of your stomach and your frequent ailments. The sins of some men are conspicuous, pointing to judgment, but the sins of others appear later. So also good deeds are conspicuous; and even when they are not, they cannot remain hidden.

A Reading (Lesson) from the Gospel according to Mark [12:28-34]

One of the scribes came up and heard them disputing with one another, and seeing that Jesus answered them well asked him, "Which commandment is the first of all?" Jesus answered, "The first is, 'Hear, O Israel: The Lord our God, the Lord is one; and you shall love the Lord your God with all your heart, and with all your soul, and with all your mind, and with all your strength.' The second is this, 'You shall love your neighbor as yourself.' There is no other commandment greater than these." And the scribe said to him, "You are right, Teacher; you have truly said that he is one, and there is no other but he; and to love him with all the heart, and with all the understanding, and with all the strength, and to love one's neighbor as oneself, is much more than all the whole burnt offerings and sacrifices." And when Jesus saw that he answered wisely, he said to him, "You are not far from the kingdom of God." And after that no one dared to ask him any question.

Saturday

Psalm 107:33-43 [page 749],
Psalm 108:1-6(7-13) [page 749]   ❖   *Psalm 33* [page 626]

A Reading (Lesson) from the Book of Isaiah [66:1-6]

Thus says the Lord: "Heaven is my throne and the earth is my footstool; what is the house which you would build for me, and what is the place of my rest? All these things my hand has made, and so all these things are mine, says the Lord. But this is the man to whom I will look, he that is humble and contrite in spirit, and trembles at my word. He who slaughters an ox is like him who kills a man; he who sacrifices a lamb, like him who breaks a dog's neck; he who presents a cereal offering, like him who offers swine's blood; he who makes a memorial offering of frankincense, like him who blesses an idol. These have chosen their own ways, and their soul delights in their abominations; I also will choose affliction for them, and bring their fears upon them; because, when I called, no one answered, when I spoke they did not listen; but they did what was evil in my eyes, and chose that in which I did not delight." Hear the word of the Lord, you who tremble at his word: "Your brethren who hate you and cast you out for my name's sake have said, 'Let the Lord be glorified, that we may see your joy'; but it is they who shall be put to shame. Hark, an uproar from the city! A voice from the temple! The voice of the Lord, rendering recompense to his enemies!"

A Reading (Lesson) from the First Letter of Paul to Timothy [6:6-21]

There is great gain in godliness with contentment; for we brought nothing into the world, and we cannot take anything out of the world; but if we have food and clothing, with these we shall be content. But those who desire to be rich fall into temptation, into a snare, into many senseless and hurtful desires that plunge men into ruin and destruction. For the love of money is the root of all evils; it is through this craving that some have wandered away from the faith and pierced their hearts with many pangs. But as for you, man of God, shun all this; aim at righteousness, godliness, faith, love, steadfastness, gentleness. Fight the good fight of the faith; take hold of the eternal life to which you were called when you made the good confession in the presence of many witnesses. In the presence of God who gives life to all things, and of Christ Jesus who in his testimony before Pontius Pilate made the good confession, I charge you to keep the commandment unstained and free from reproach until the appearing of our Lord Jesus Christ; and this will be made manifest at the proper time by the blessed and only Sovereign, the King of kings and Lord of lords, who alone has immortality and dwells in unapproachable light, whom no man has ever seen or can see. To him be honor and eternal dominion. Amen. As for the rich in the world, charge them not to be haughty, nor to set their hopes on uncertain riches but on God who richly furnishes us with everything to enjoy. They are to do good, to be rich in good deeds, liberal and generous, thus laying up for themselves a good foundation for the future, so that they may take hold of the life which is life indeed. O Timothy, guard what has been entrusted to you. Avoid the godless chatter and contradictions of what is falsely called knowledge, for by professing it some have missed the mark as regards the faith. Grace be with you.

A Reading (Lesson) from the Gospel according to Mark
[12:35-44]

As Jesus taught in the temple, he said, "How can the scribes say that the Christ is the son of David? David himself, inspired by the Holy Spirit, declared, 'The Lord said to my Lord, Sit at my right hand, till I put thy enemies under thy feet.' David himself calls him Lord; so how is he his son?" And the great throng heard him gladly. And in his teaching he said, "Beware of the scribes, who like to go about in long robes, and to have salutations in the market places and the best seats in the synagogues and the places of honor at feasts, who devour widows' houses and for a pretense make long prayers. They will receive the greater condemnation." And he sat down opposite the treasury and watched the multitude putting money into the treasury. Many rich people put in large sums. And a poor widow came, and put in two copper coins, which make a penny. And he called his disciples to him, and said to them, "Truly, I say to you, this poor widow has put in more than all those who are contributing to the treasury. For they all contributed out of their abundance; but she out of her poverty has put in everything she had, her whole living."

Week of 7 Epiphany

Sunday

Psalm 118 [page 760] ❖ *Psalm 145* [page 80]

A Reading (Lesson) from the Book of Isaiah [66:7-14]

Thus says the Lord: "Before she was in labor she gave birth; before her pain came upon her she was delivered of son. Who has heard such a thing? Who has seen such things? Shall a land be born in one day? Shall a nation be brought forth in one moment? For as soon as Zion was in labor she brought forth her sons. Shall I bring to the birth and not cause to bring forth? says the Lord; shall I, who cause to bring forth, shut the womb? says your God. Rejoice with Jerusalem, and be glad for her, all you who love her; rejoice with her in joy, all you who mourn over her; that you may suck and be satisfied with her consoling breasts; that you may drink deeply with delight from the abundance of her glory." For thus says the Lord: "Behold, I will extend prosperity to her like a river, and the wealth of the nations like an overflowing stream; and you shall suck, you shall be carried upon her hip, and dandled upon her knees. As one whom his mother comforts, so I will comfort you; you shall be comforted in Jerusalem. You shall see, and your heart shall rejoice; your bones shall flourish like the grass; and it shall be known that the hand of the Lord is with his servants, and his indignation is against his enemies."

A Reading (Lesson) from the First Letter of John [3:4-10]

Every one who commits sin is guilty of lawlessness; sin is lawlessness. You know that he appeared to take away sins, and in him there is no sin. No one who abides in him sins; no one who sins has either seen him or known him. Little children, let no one deceive you. He who does right is righteous, as he is righteous. He who commits sin is of the devil; for the devil has sinned from the beginning. The reason the Son of God appeared was to destroy the works of the devil. No one born of God commits sin; for God's nature abides in him, and he cannot sin because he is born of God. By this is may be seen who are the children of God, and who are the children of the devil: whoever does not do right is not of God, nor he who does not love his brother.

A Reading (Lesson) from the Gospel according to John [10:7-16]

Jesus again said to the Pharisees, "Truly, truly, I say to you, I am the door of the sheep. All who came before me are thieves and robbers; but the sheep did not heed them. I am the door; if any one enters by me, he will be saved, and will go in and out and find pasture. The thief comes only to steal and kill and destroy; I came that they may have life, and have it abundantly. I am the good shepherd. The good shepherd lays down his life for the sheep. He who is a hireling and not a shepherd, whose own the sheep are not, sees the wolf coming and leaves the sheep and flees; and the wolf snatches them and scatters them. He flees because he is a hireling and cares nothing for the sheep. I am the good shepherd; I know my own and my own know me, as the Father knows me and I know the Father; and I lay down my life for the sheep. And I have other sheep, that are not of this fold; I must bring them also, and they will heed my voice. So there shall be one flock, one shepherd.

Monday

Psalm 106:1-18 [page 741] ❖ *Psalm 106:19-48* [page 743]

A Reading (Lesson) from the Book of Ruth [1:1-14]

In the days when the judges ruled there was a famine in the land, and a certain man of Bethlehem in Judah went to sojourn in the country of Moab, he and his wife and his two sons. The name of the man was Elim'elech and the name of his wife Na'omi, and the names of his two sons were Mahlon and Chil'ion; they were Eph'rathites from Bethlehem in Judah. They went into the country of Moab and remained there. But Elim'elech, the husband of Na'omi, died, and she was left with her two sons. These took Moabite wives; the name of one was Orpah and the name of the other Ruth. They lived there about ten years; and both Mahlon and Chil'ion died, so that the woman was bereft of her two sons and her husband. Then she started with her daughters-in-law to return from the country of Moab, for she had heard in the country of Moab that the Lord had visited his people and given them food. So she set out from the place where she was, with her two daughers-in-law, and they went on the way to return to the land of Judah. But Na'omi said to her two daughters-in-law, "Go, return each of you to her mother's house. May the Lord deal kindly with you, as you have dealt with the dead and with me. The Lord grant that you may find a home, each of you in the house of her husband!" Then she kissed them, and they lifted up their voices and wept. And they said to her, "No, we will return with you to your people." But Na'omi said, "Turn back, my daughters, why will you go with me? Have I yet sons in my womb that they may become your husbands? Turn back, my daughters, go your way, for I am too old to have a husband. If I should say I have hope, even if I should have a husband this night and should bear sons, would you therefore wait till they were grown? Would you therefore refrain from marrying? No, my daughters, for it is exceedingly bitter to me for your sake that the hand of the Lord has gone forth against me." Then they lifted up their voices and wept again; and Orpah kissed her mother-in-law, but Ruth clung to her.

A Reading (Lesson) from the Second Letter of Paul to the Corinthians [1:1-11]

Paul, an apostle of Christ Jesus by the will of God, and Timothy our brother. To the church of God which is at Corinth, with all the saints who are in the whole of Acha'ia: Grace to you and peace from God our Father and the Lord Jesus Christ. Blessed be the God and Father of our Lord Jesus Christ, the Father of mercies and God of all comfort, who comforts us in all our affliction, so that we may be able to comfort those who are in any affliction, with the comfort with which we ourselves are comforted by God. For as we share abundantly in Christ's sufferings, so through Christ we share abundantly in comfort too. If we are afflicted, it is for your comfort and salvation; and if we are comforted, it is for your comfort, which you experience when you patiently endure the same sufferings that we suffer. Our hope for you is unshaken; for we know that as you share in our sufferings, you will also share in our comfort. For we do not want you to be ignorant, brethren, of the affliction we experienced in Asia; for we were so utterly, unbearably crushed that we despaired of life itself. Why, we felt that we had received the sentence of death; but that was to make us rely not on ourselves but on God who raises the dead; he delivered us from so deadly a peril, and he will deliver us; on him we have set our hope that he will deliver us again. You also must help us by prayer, so that many will give thanks on our behalf for the blessing granted us in answer to many prayers.

A Reading (Lesson) from the Gospel according to Matthew [5:1-12]

Seeing the crowds, Jesus went up on the mountain, and when he sat down his disciples came to him. And he opened his mouth and taught them, saying: "Blessed are the poor in spirit, for theirs is the kingdom of heaven. Blessed are those who mourn, for they shall be comforted. Blessed are the meek, for they shall inherit the earth. Blessed are those who hunger and thirst for righteousness, for they shall be satisfied. Blessed are the merciful, for they shall obtain mercy. Blessed are the pure in heart, for they shall see God. Blessed are the peacemakers, for they shall be called sons of God. Blessed are those who are persecuted for righteousness' sake, for theirs is the kingdom of heaven. Blessed are you when men revile you and persecute you and utter all kinds of evil against you falsely on my account. Rejoice and be glad, for your reward is great in heaven, for so men persecuted the prophets who were before you."

Tuesday

(Psalm 120 [page 778]), *Psalm 121* [page 779],
Psalm 122 [page 779], *Psalm 123* [page 780] ❖
Psalm 124 [page 781], *Psalm 125* [page 781],
Psalm 126 [page 782], *(Psalm 127* [page 782])

A Reading (Lesson) from the Book of Ruth [1:15-22]

Na'omi said to Ruth, "See, your sister-in-law has gone
back to her people and to her gods; return after your
sister-in-law." But Ruth said, "Entreat me not to leave you
or return from following you; for where you go I will go,
and where you lodge I will lodge; your people shall be my
people, and your God my God; where you die I will die,
and there will I be buried. May the Lord do so to me and
more also if even death parts me from you." And when
Na'omi saw that she was determined to go with her, she
said no more. So the two of them went on until they came
to Bethlehem. And when they came to Bethlehem, the
whole town was stirred because of them; and the women
said, "Is this Na'omi?" She said to them, "Do not call me
Na'omi, call me Mara, for the Almighty has dealt very
bitterly with me. I went away full, and the Lord has
brought me back empty. Why call me Na'omi, when the
Lord has afflicted me and the Almighty has brought
calamity upon me?" So Na'omi returned, and Ruth the
Moabitess her daughter-in-law with her, who returned
from the country of Moab. And they came to Bethlehem at
the beginning of barley harvest.

A Reading (Lesson) from the Second Letter of Paul to the Corinthians [1:12-22]

Our boast is this, the testimony of our conscience that we
have behaved in the world, and still more toward you,
with holiness and godly sincerity, not by earthly wisdom
but by the grace of God. For we write you nothing but

what you can read and understand; I hope you will understand fully, as you have understood in part, that you can be proud of us as we can be of you, on the day of the Lord Jesus. Because I was sure of this, I wanted to come to you first, so that you might have a double pleasure; I wanted to visit you on my way to Macedo'nia, and to come back to you from Macedo'nia and have you send me on my way to Judea. Was I vacillating when I wanted to do this? Do I make my plans like a worldly man, ready to say Yes and No at once? As surely as God is faithful, our word to you has not been Yes and No. For the Son of God, Jesus Christ, whom we preached among you, Silva'nus and Timothy and I, was not Yes and No; but in him it is always Yes. For all the promises of God find their Yes in him. That is why we utter the Amen through him, to the glory of God. But it is God who establishes us with you in Christ, and has commissioned us; he has put his seal upon us and given us his Spirit in our hearts as a guarantee.

A Reading (Lesson) from the Gospel according to Matthew

[5:13-20]

Jesus opened his mouth and taught his disciples, saying, "You are the salt of the earth; but if salt has lost its taste, how shall its saltness be restored? It is no longer good for anything except to be thrown out and trodden under foot by men. You are the light of the world. A city set on a hill cannot be hid. Nor do men light a lamp and put it under a bushel, but on a stand, and it gives light to all in the house. Let your light so shine before men, that they may see your good works and give glory to your Father who is in heaven. Think not that I have come to abolish the law and the prophets; I have come not to abolish them but to fulfil them. For truly, I say to you, till heaven and earth pass away, not an iota, not a dot, will pass from the law until all is accomplished. Whoever then relaxes one of the least of these commandments and teaches men so, shall be called least in the kingdom of heaven; but he who does them and teaches them shall be called great in the kingdom of heaven. For I tell you, unless your righteousness exceeds that of the scribes and Pharisees, you will never enter the kingdom of heaven."

Wednesday

Psalm 119:145-176 [page 775] ❖ *Psalm 128* [page 783], *Psalm 129* [page 784], *Psalm 130* [page 784]

A Reading (Lesson) from the Book of Ruth [2:1-13]

Na'omi had a kinsman of her husband's, a man of wealth, of the family of Elim'elech, whose name was Bo'az. And Ruth the Moabitess said to Na'omi, "Let me go to the field, and glean among the ears of grain after him in whose sight I shall find favor." And she said to her, "Go, my daughter." So she set forth and went and gleaned in the field after the reapers; and she happened to come to the part of the field belonging to Bo'az, who was of the family of Elim'elech. And behold, Bo'az came from Bethlehem; and he said to the reapers, "The Lord be with you!" And they answered, "The Lord bless you." Then Bo'az said to his servant who was in charge of the reapers, "Whose maiden is this?" And the servant who was in charge of the reapers answered, "It is the Moabite maiden, who came back with Na'omi from the country of Moab. She said, 'Pray, let me glean and gather among the sheaves after the reapers.' So she came, and she has continued from early morning until now, without resting even for a moment." Then Bo'az said to Ruth, "Now, listen, my daughter, do not go to glean in another field or leave this one, but keep close to my maidens. Let your eyes be upon the field which they are reaping, and go after them. Have I not charged the young men not to molest you? And when you are thirsty, go to the vessels and drink what the young men have drawn." Then she fell on her face, bowing to the ground, and said to him, "Why have I found favor in your eyes, that you should take notice of me, when I am a foreigner?" But Bo'az answered her, "All that you have done for your mother-in-law since the death of her husband has been fully told me, and how you left your father and mother an your native land and came to a people that you did not know before. The Lord recompense you for what you hav done, and a full reward be given you by the Lord, the God of Israel, under whose wings you have come to take refuge!" Then she said, "You are most gracious to me, my lord, for you have comforted me and spoken kindly to your maidservant, though I am not one of your maidservants."

A Reading (Lesson) from the Second Letter of Paul to the Corinthians [1:23—2:17]

I call God to witness against me—it was to spare you that refrained from coming to Corinth. Not that we lord it ove your faith; we work with you for your joy, for you stand firm in your faith. For I made up my mind not to make yo another painful visit. For if I cause you pain, who is there to make me glad but the one whom I have pained? And I wrote as I did, so that when I came I might not suffer pain from those who should have made me rejoice, for I felt sure of all of you, that my joy would be the joy of you all. For I wrote you out of much affliction and anguish of hear and with many tears, not to cause you pain but to let you know the abundant love that I have for you. But if any on has caused pain, he has caused it not to me, but in some measure—not to put it too severely—to you all. For such one this punishment by the majority is enough; so you should rather turn to forgive and comfort him, or he may be overwhelmed by excessive sorrow. So I beg you to reaffirm your love for him. For this is why I wrote, that I might test you and know whether you are obedient in everything. Any one whom you forgive, I also forgive. What I have forgiven, if I have forgiven anything, has beer for your sake in the presence of Christ, to keep Satan from gaining the advantage over us; for we are not ignorant of his designs. When I came to Tro'as to preach the gospel of Christ, a door was opened for me in the Lord; but my mind could not rest because I did not find my brother Titus there. So I took leave of them and went on to Macedo'nia. But thanks be to God, who in Christ always leads us in triumph, and through us spreads the fragrance of the knowledge of him everywhere. For we are the aroma of Christ to God among those who are being saved and among those who are perishing, to one a fragrance from death to death, to the other a fragrance from life to life. Who is sufficient for these things? For we are not, like so many, peddlers of God's word; but as men of sincerity, as commissioned by God, in the sight of God we speak in Christ.

A Reading (Lesson) from the Gospel according to Matthew
[5:21-26]

Jesus opened his mouth and taught his disciples, saying: "You have heard that it was said to the men of old, 'You shall not kill; and whoever kills shall be liable to judgment.' But I say to you that every one who is angry with his brother shall be liable to judgment; whoever insults his brother shall be liable to the council, and whoever says, 'You fool!' shall be liable to the hell of fire. So if you are offering your gift at the altar, and there remember that your brother has something against you, leave your gift there before the altar and go; first be reconciled to your brother, and then come and offer your gift. Make friends quickly with your accuser, while you are going with him to court, lest your accuser hand you over to the judge, and the judge to the guard, and you be put in prison; truly, I say to you, you will never get out till you have paid the last penny."

Thursday

Psalm 131 [page 758],   *Psalm 132* [page 785],
(Psalm 133 [page 787])   ❖   *Psalm 134* [page 787],
Psalm 135 [page 788]

A Reading (Lesson) from the Book of Ruth [2:14-23]

At mealtime Bo'az said to Ruth, "Come here, and eat some bread, and dip your morsel in the wine." So she sat beside the reapers, and he passed to her parched grain; and she ate until she was satisfied, and she had some left over. When she rose to glean, Bo'az instructed his young men, saying "Let her glean even among the sheaves, and do not reproach her. And also pull out some from the bundles for her, and leave it for her to glean, and do not rebuke her." So she gleaned in the field until evening; then she beat out what she had gleaned, and it was about an ephah of barley. And she took it up and went into the city; she showed her mother-in-law what she had gleaned, and she also brought out and gave her what food she had left over after being satisfied. And her mother-in-law said to her, "Where did you glean today? And where have you worked? Blessed be the man who took notice of you." So she told her mother-in-law with whom she had worked, and said, "The man's name with whom I worked today is Bo'az." And Na'omi said to her daughter-in-law, "Blessed be he by the Lord, whose kindness has not forsaken the living or the dead!" Na'omi also said to her, "The man is a relative of ours, one of our nearest kin." And Ruth the Moabitess said, "Besides, he said to me, 'You shall keep close by my servants, till they have finished all my harvest.'" And Na'omi said to Ruth, her daughter-in-law, "It is well, my daughter, that you go out with his maidens, lest in another field you be molested." So she kept close to the maidens of Bo'az, gleaning until the end of the barley and wheat harvests; and she lived with her mother-in-law.

*A Reading (Lesson) from the Second Letter of Paul
to the Corinthians* [3:1-18]

Are we beginning to commend ourselves again? Or do we
need, as some do, letters of recommendation to you, or
from you? You yourselves are our letter of
recommendation, written on your hearts, to be known and
read by all men; and you show that you are a letter from
Christ delivered by us, written not with ink but with the
Spirit of the living God, not on tablets of stone but on
tablets of human hearts. Such is the confidence that we
have through Christ toward God. Not that we are
competent of ourselves to claim anything as coming from
us; our competence is from God, who has made us
competent to be ministers of a new covenant, not in a
written code but in the Spirit; for the written code kills, but
the Spirit gives life. Now if the dispensation of death,
carved in letters on stone, came with such splendor that the
Israelites could not look at Moses' face because of its
brightness, fading as this was, will not the dispensation of
the Spirit be attended with greater splendor? For if there
was splendor in the dispensation of condemnation, the
dispensation of righteousness must far exceed it in
splendor. Indeed, in this case, what once had splendor has
come to have no splendor at all, because of the splendor
that surpasses it. For if what faded away came with
splendor, what is permanent must have much more
splendor. Since we have such a hope, we are very bold, not
like Moses, who put a veil over his face so that the
Israelites might not see the end of the fading splendor. But
their minds were hardened; for to this day, when they read
the old covenant, that same veil remains unlifted, because
only through Christ is it taken away. Yes, to this day
whenever Moses is read a veil lies over their minds; but
when a man turns to the Lord the veil is removed. Now the
Lord is the Spirit, and where the Spirit of the Lord is, there
is freedom. And we all, with unveiled face, beholding the
glory of the Lord, are being changed into his likeness from

one degree of glory to another; for this comes from the Lord who is the Spirit.

A Reading (Lesson) from the Gospel according to Matthew [5:27-37]

Jesus opened his mouth and taught his disciples, saying: "You have heard that it was said, 'You shall not commit adultery.' But I say to you that every one who looks at a woman lustfully has already committed adultery with her in his heart. If your right eye causes you to sin, pluck it out and throw it away; it is better that you lose one of your members than that your whole body go into hell. And if your right hand causes you to sin, cut it off and throw it away; it is better that you lose one of your members than that your whole body go into hell. It was also said, 'Whoever divorces his wife, let him give her a certificate of divorce.' But I say to you that every one who divorces his wife, except on the ground of unchastity, makes her an adulteress; and whoever marries a divorced woman commits adultery. Again you have heard that it was said to the men of old, 'You shall not swear falsely, but shall perform to the Lord what you have sworn.' But I say to you, Do not swear at all, either by heaven, for it is the throne of God, or by the earth, for it is his footstool, or by Jerusalem, for it is the city of the great King. And do not swear by your head, for you cannot make one hair white or black. Let what you say be simply 'Yes' or 'No'; anything more than this comes from evil."

Friday

Psalm 140 [page 796], *Psalm 142* [page 798] ❖
Psalm 141 [page 797], *Psalm 143:1-11(12)* [page 798]

A Reading (Lesson) from the Book of Ruth [3:1-18]

Na'omi her mother-in-law said to Ruth, "My daughter,

should I not seek a home for you, that it may be well with you? Now is not Bo'az our kinsman, with whose maidens you were? See, he is winnowing barley tonight at the threshing floor. Wash therefore and anoint yourself, and put on your best clothes and go down to the threshing floor; but do not make yourself known to the man until he has finished eating and drinking. But when he lies down, observe the place where he lies; then, go and uncover his feet and lie down; and he will tell you what to do." And she replied, "All that you say I will do." So she went down to the threshing floor and did just as her mother-in-law had told her. And when Bo'az had eaten and drunk, and his heart was merry, he went to lie down at the end of the heap of grain. Then she came, softly, and uncovered his feet, and lay down. At midnight the man was startled, and turned over, and behold, a woman lay at his feet! He said, "Who are you?" And she answered, "I am Ruth, your maidservant; spread your skirt over your maidservant, for you are next of kin." And he said, "May you be blessed by the Lord, my daughter; you have made this last kindness greater than the first, in that you have not gone after young men, whether poor or rich. And now, my daughter, do not fear, I will do for you all that you ask, for all my fellow townsmen know that you are a woman of worth. And now it is true that I am a near kinsman, yet there is a kinsman nearer than I. Remain this night, and in the morning, if he will do the part of the next of kin for you, well; let him do it; but if he is not willing to do the part of the next of kin for you, then, as the Lord lives, I will do the part of the next of kin for you. Lie down until the morning." So she lay at his feet until the morning, but arose before one could recognize another; and he said, "Let it not be known that the woman came to the threshing floor." And he said, "Bring the mantle you are wearing and hold it out." So she held it, and he measured out six measures of barley, and laid it upon her; then she went into the city. And when she came to her mother-in-law, she said, "How did you fare, my daughter?" The she told her all that the man had done for her, saying, "These six measures of barley he gave to me, for he said, 'You must not go back empty-handed to your mother-in-law.'" She replied, "Wait, my daughter, until you learn how the matter turns out, for the man will not rest, but will settle the matter today."

A Reading (Lesson) from the Second Letter of Paul to the Corinthians [4:1-12]

Having this ministry by the mercy of God, we do not lose heart. We have renounced disgraceful, underhanded ways; we refuse to practice cunning or to tamper with God's word, but by the open statement of the truth we would commend ourselves to every man's conscience in the sight of God. And even if our gospel is veiled, it is veiled only to those who are perishing. In their case the god of this world has blinded the minds of the unbelievers, to keep them from seeing the light of the gospel of the glory of Christ, who is the likeness of God. For what we preach is not ourselves, but Jesus Christ as Lord, with ourselves as your servants for Jesus' sake. For it is the God who said, "Let light shine out of darkness," who has shown in our hearts to give the light of the knowledge of the glory of God in the face of Christ. But we have this treasure in earthen vessels, to show that the transcendent power belongs to God and not to us. We are afflicted in every way, but not crushed; perplexed, but not driven to despair; persecuted, but not forsaken; struck down, but not destroyed; always carrying in the body the death of Jesus, so that the life of Jesus may also be manifested in our bodies. For while we live we are always being given up to death for Jesus' sake, so that the life of Jesus may be manifested in our mortal flesh. So death is at work in us, but life in you.

A Reading (Lesson) from the Gospel according to Matthew
[5:38-48]

Jesus opened his mouth and taught his disciples, saying:
"You have heard that it was said, 'An eye for an eye and a
tooth for a tooth.' But I say to you, Do not resist one who
is evil. But if any one strikes you on the right cheek, turn to
him the other also; and if any one would sue you and take
your coat, let him have your cloak as well; and if any one
forces you to go one mile, go with him two miles. Give to
him who begs from you, and do not refuse him who would
borrow from you. You have heard that it was said, 'You
shall love your neighbor and hate your enemy.' But I say to
you, Love your enemies and pray for those who persecute
you, so that you may be sons of your Father who is in
heaven; for he makes his sun rise on the evil and on the
good, and sends rain on the just and on the unjust. For if
you love those who love you, what reward have you? Do
not even the tax collectors do the same? And if you salute
only your brethren, what more are you doing than others?
Do not even the Gentiles do the same? You, therefore,
must be perfect, as your heavenly Father is perfect."

Saturday

Psalm 137:1-6(7-9) [page 792],
Psalm 144 [page 801]   ❖   *Psalm 104* [page 735]

A Reading (Lesson) from the Book of Ruth [4:1-17]

Bo'az went up to the gate and sat down there; and behold,
the next of kin, of whom Bo'az had spoken, came by. So
Bo'az said, "Turn aside, friend; sit down here"; and he
turned aside and sat down. And he took ten men of the
elders of the city, and said, "Sit down here"; so they sat
down. Then he said to the next of kin, "Na'omi, who has
come back from the country of Moab, is selling the parcel
of land which belonged to our kinsman Elim'elech. So I

thought I would tell you of it, and say, Buy it in the presence of those sitting here, and in the presence of the elders of my people. If you will redeem it, redeem it; but if you will not, tell me, that I may know, for there is no one besides you to redeem it, and I come after you." And he said, "I will redeem it." Then Bo'az said, "The day you buy the field from the hand of Na'omi, you are also buying Ruth the Moabitess, the widow of the dead, in order to restore the name of the dead to his inheritance." Then the next of kin said, "I cannot redeem it for myself, lest I impair my own inheritance. Take my right of redemption yourself, for I cannot redeem it." Now this was the custom in former times in Israel concerning redeeming and exchanging: to confirm a transaction, the one drew off his sandal and gave it to the other, and this was the manner of attesting in Israel. So when the next of kin said to Bo'az, "Buy it for yourself," he drew off his sandal. Then Bo'az said to the elders and all the people, "You are witnesses this day that I have bought from the hand of Na'omi all that belonged to Elim'elech and all that belonged to Chil'ion and to Mahlon. Also Ruth the Moabitess, the widow of Mahlon, I have bought to be my wife, to perpetuate the name of the dead in his inheritance, that the name of the dead may not be cut off from among his brethren and from the gate of his native place; you are witnesses this day." Then all the people who were at the gate, and the elders, said, "We are witnesses. May the Lord make the woman, who is coming into your house, like Rachel and Leah, who together built up the house of Israel. May you prosper in Eph'rathah and be renowned in Bethlehem; and may your house be like the house of Perez, whom Tamar bore to Judah, because of the children that the Lord will give you by the young woman." So Bo'az took Ruth and she became his wife; and he went in to her, and the Lord gave her conception, and she bore a son. Then the women said to Na'omi, "Blessed be the Lord, who has not left you this day without next of kin; and may his name be renowned in

Israel! He shall be to you a restorer of life and a nourisher of your old age; for your daughter-in-law who loves you, who is more to you than seven sons, has borne him." Then Na'omi took the child and laid him in her bosom, and became his nurse. And the women of the neighborhood gave him a name, saying, "A son has been born to Na'omi." They named him Obed; he was the father of Jesse, the father of David.

A Reading (Lesson) from the Second Letter of Paul to the Corinthians [4:13—5:10]

Since we have the same spirit of faith as he had who wrote, "I believed, and so I spoke," we too believe, and so we speak, knowing that he who raised the Lord Jesus will raise us also with Jesus and bring us with you into his presence. For it is all for your sake, so that as grace extends to more and more people it may increase thanksgiving, to the glory of God. So we do not lose heart. Though our outer nature is wasting away, our inner nature is being renewed every day. For this slight momentary affliction is preparing for us an eternal weight of glory beyond all comparison, because we look not to the things that are seen but to the things that are unseen; for the things that are seen are transient, but the things that are unseen are eternal. For we know that if the earthly tent we live in is destroyed, we have a building from God, a house not made with hands, eternal in the heavens. Here indeed we groan, and long to put on our heavenly dwelling, so that by putting it on we may not be found naked. For while we are still in this tent, we sigh with anxiety; not that we would be unclothed, but that we would be further clothed, so that what is mortal may be swallowed up by life. He who has prepared us for this very thing is God, who has given us the Spirit as a guarantee. So we are always of good courage; we know that while we are at home in the body we are away from the Lord, for we walk by faith, not by sight. We are of good courage, and we would rather be away from the body and at home with the Lord. So whether we are at home or away, we make it our aim to please him. For we must all appear before the judgment seat of Christ, so that each one may receive good or evil, according to what he has done in the body.

A Reading (Lesson) from the Gospel according to Matthew [6:1-6]

Jesus opened his mouth and taught his disciples, saying: "Beware of practicing your piety before men in order to be seen by them; for then you will have no reward from your Father who is in heaven. Thus, when you give alms, sound no trumpet before you, as the hypocrites do in the synagogues and in the streets, that they may be praised by men. Truly, I say to you, they have received their reward. But when you give alms, do not let your left hand know what your right hand is doing, so that your alms may be in secret; and your Father who sees in secret will reward you. And when you pray, you must not be like the hypocrites; for they love to stand and pray in the synagogues and at the street corners, that they may be seen by men. Truly, I say to you, they have received their reward. But when you pray, go into your room and shut the door and pray to your Father who is in secret; and your Father who sees in secret will reward you."

Week of 8 Epiphany

Sunday

Psalm 146 [page 803], *Psalm 147* [page 804] ❖
Psalm 111 [page 754], *Psalm 112* [page 755],
Psalm 113 [page 756]

A Reading (Lesson) from the Book of Deuteronomy
[4:1-9]

Moses undertook to explain the law, saying, "And now, O Israel, give heed to the statutes and the ordinances which I teach you, and do them; that you may live, and go in and take possession of the land which the Lord, the God of your fathers, gives you. You shall not add to the word which I command you, not take from it; that you may keep the commandments of the Lord your God which I command you. Your eyes have seen what the Lord did at Ba'al-pe'or; for the Lord your God destroyed from among you all the men who followed the Ba'al of Pe'or; but you who held fast to the Lord your God are all alive this day. Behold, I have taught you statutes and ordinances, as the Lord my God commanded me, that you should do them in the land which you are entering to take possession of it. Keep them and do them; for that will be your wisdom and your understanding in the sight of the peoples, who, when they hear all these statutes, will say, 'Surely this great nation is a wise and understanding people.' For what great nation is there that has a god so near to it as the Lord our God is to us, whenever we call upon him? And what great nation is there, that has statutes and ordinances so righteous as all this law which I set before you this day? Only take heed and keep your soul diligently, lest you forget the things which your eyes have seen, and lest they depart from your heart all the days of your life; make them known to your children and your children's children."

2 Timothy 4:1-8   [page 195 above]

A Reading (Lesson) from the Gospel according to John
[12:1-8]

Six days before the Passover, Jesus came to Bethany, where Laz'arus was, whom Jesus had raised from the dead. There they made him a supper; Martha served, and Laz'arus was one of those at table with him. Mary took a pound of costly ointment of pure nard and anointed the feet of Jesus and wiped his feet with her hair; and the house was filled with the fragrance of the ointment. But Judas Iscariot, one of his disciples (he who was to betray him), said, "Why was this ointment not sold for three hundred denarii and given to the poor?" This he said, not that he cared for the poor but because he was a thief, and as he had the money box he used to take what was put into it. Jesus said, "Let her alone, let her keep it for the day of my burial. The poor you always have with you, but you do not always have me."

Monday

Psalm 1 [page 585],   *Psalm 2* [page 586],
Psalm 3 [page 587]   ❖   *Psalm 4* [page 587],
Psalm 7 [page 590]

A Reading (Lesson) from the Book of Deuteronomy
[4:9-14]

Moses undertook to explain the law, saying, "Take heed, and keep your soul diligently, lest you forget the things which your eyes have seen, and lest they depart from your heart all the days of your life; make them known to your children and your children's children—how on the day that you stood before the Lord your God at Horeb, the Lord said to me, 'Gather the people to me, that I may let them hear my words, so that they may learn to fear me all the days that they live upon the earth, and that they may teach their children so.' And you came near and stood at the foot of the mountain, while the mountain burned with fire to the heart of heaven, wrapped in darkness, cloud, and gloom. Then the Lord spoke to you out of the midst of the fire; you heard the sound of words, but saw no form; there was only a voice. And he declared to you his covenant, which he commanded you to perform, that is, the ten commandments; and he wrote them upon two tables of stone. And the Lord commanded me at that time to teach you statutes and ordinances, that you might do them in the land which you are going over to possess."

A Reading (Lesson) from the Second Letter of Paul to the Corinthians [10:1-18]

I, Paul, myself entreat you, by the meekness and gentleness of Christ—I who am humble when face to face with you, but bold to you when I am away!—I beg of you that when I am present I may not have to show boldness with such confidence as I count on showing against some who suspect us of acting in worldly fashion. For though we live in the world we are not carrying on a worldly war, for the weapons of our warfare are not worldly but have divine power to destroy strongholds. We destroy arguments and every proud obstacle to the knowledge of God, and take every thought captive to obey Christ, being ready to punish every disobedience, when your obedience is complete. Look at what is before your eyes. If any one is confident that he is Christ's, let him remind himself that as he is Christ's, so are we. For even if I boast a little too much of our authority, which the Lord gave for building you up and not for destroying you, I shall not be put to shame. I would not seem to be frightening you with letters. For they say, "His letters are weighty and strong, but his bodily presence is weak, and his speech of no account." Let such people understand that what we say by letter when absent, we do when present. Not that we venture to class or compare ourselves with some of those who commend themselves. But when they measure themselves by one another, and compare themselves with one another, they are without understanding. But we will not boast beyond limit, but will keep to the limits God has apportioned us, to reach even to you. For we are not overextending ourselves, as though we did not reach you; we were the first to come all the way to you with the gospel of Christ. We do not boast beyond limit, in other men's labors; but our hope is that as your faith increases, our field among you may be greatly enlarged, so that we may preach the gospel in lands beyond you, without boasting of work already done in another's field. "Let him who boasts, boast of the Lord." For it is not the man who commends himself that is accepted, but the man whom the Lord commends.

A Reading (Lesson) from the Gospel according to Matthew [6:7-15]

Jesus opened his mouth and taught his disciples, saying: "In praying do not heap up empty phrases as the Gentiles do; for they think that they will be heard for their many words. Do not be like them, for your Father knows what you need before you ask him. Pray then like this: Our Father who art in heaven, Hallowed be thy name. Thy kingdom come, Thy will be done, On earth as it is in heaven. Give us this day our daily bread; and forgive us our debts, As we also have forgiven our debtors; And lead us not into temptation, But deliver us from evil. For if you forgive men their trespasses, your heavenly Father also will forgive you; but if you do not forgive men their trespasses, neither will your Father forgive your trespasses."

Tuesday

Psalm 5 [page 588],   *Psalm 6* [page 589]   ❖
Psalm 10 [page 594],   *Psalm 11* [page 596]

A Reading (Lesson) from the Book of Deuteronomy [4:15-24]

Moses undertook to explain the law, saying, "Take good heed to yourselves. Since you saw no form on the day that the Lord spoke to you at Horeb out of the midst of the fire, beware lest you act corruptly by making a graven image for yourselves, in the form of any figure, the likeness of male or female, the likeness of any beast that is on the earth, the likeness of any winged bird that flies in the air, the likeness of anything that creeps on the ground, the likeness of any fish that is in the water under the earth. And beware lest you lift up your eyes to heaven, and when you see the sun and the moon and the stars, all the host of heaven, you be drawn away and worship them and serve them, things which the Lord your God has allotted to all the peoples under the whole heaven. But the Lord has taken you, and brought you forth out of the iron furnace, out of Egypt, to be a people of his own possession, as at this day. Furthermore the Lord was angry with me on your account, and he swore that I should not cross the Jordan, and that I should not enter the good land which the Lord your God gives you for an inheritance. For I must die in this land, I must not go over the Jordan; but you shall go over and take possession of that good land. Take heed to yourselves, lest you forget the covenant of the Lord your God, which he made with you, and make a graven image in the form of anything which the Lord your God has forbidden you. For the Lord your God is a devouring fire, a jealous God.

A Reading (Lesson) from the Second Letter of Paul to the Corinthians [11:1-21a]

I wish you would bear with me in a little foolishness. Do bear with me! I feel a divine jealousy for you, for I betrothed you to Christ to present you as a pure bride to her one husband. But I am afraid that as the serpent deceived Eve by his cunning, your thoughts will be led astray from a sincere and pure devotion to Christ. For if some one comes and preaches another Jesus than the one we preached, or if you receive a different spirit from the one you received, or if you accept a different gospel from the one you accepted, you submit to it readily enough. I think that I am not in the least inferior to these superlative apostles. Even if I am unskilled in speaking, I am not in knowledge; in every way we have made this plain to you in all things. Did I commit a sin in abasing myself so that you might be exalted, because I preached God's gospel without cost to you? I robbed other churches by accepting support from them in order to serve you. And when I was with you and was in want, I did not burden any one, for my needs were supplied by the brethren who came from Macedo'nia. So I refrained and will refrain from burdening you in any way. As the truth of Christ is in me, this boast of mine shall not be silenced in the regions of Acha'ia. And why? Because I do not love you? God knows I do! And what I do I will continue to do, in order to undermine the claim of those who would like to claim that in their boasted mission they work on the same terms as we do. For such men are false apostles, deceitful workmen, disguising themselves as apostles of Christ. And no wonder, for even Satan disguises himself as an angel of light. So it is not strange if his servants also disguise themselves as servants of righteousness. Their end will correspond to their deeds. I repeat, let no one think me foolish; but even if you do, accept me as a fool, so that I too may boast a little. (What I am saying I say not with the Lord's authority but as a fool, in this boastful confidence; since many boast of worldly things, I too will boast.) For you gladly bear with fools, being wise yourselves! For you bear it if a man makes slaves of you, or preys upon you, or takes advantage of you, or puts on airs, or strikes you in the face. To my shame, I must say, we were too weak for that!

A Reading (Lesson) from the Gospel according to Matthew [6:16-23]

Jesus opened his mouth and taught his disciples, saying: "When you fast, do not look dismal, like the hypocrites, for they disfigure their faces that their fasting may be seen by men. Truly, I say to you, they have received their reward. But when you fast, anoint your head and wash your face, that your fasting may not be seen by men but by your Father who is in secret; and your Father who sees in secret will reward you. Do not lay up for yourselves treasures on earth, where moth and rust consume and where thieves break in and steal, but lay up for yourselves treasure in heaven, where neither moth nor rust consumes and where thieves do not break in and steal. For where your treasure is, there will your heart be also. The eye is the lamp of the body. So, if your eye is sound, your whole body will be full of light; but if your eye is not sound, your whole body will be full of darkness. If then the light in you is darkness, how great is the darkness!"

Wednesday

Psalm 119:1-24 [page 763] ❖ *Psalm 12* [page 597], *Psalm 13* [page 597], *Psalm 14* [page 598]

A Reading (Lesson) from the Book of Deuteronomy [4:25-31]

Moses undertook to explain the law, saying, "When you beget children and children's children, and have grown old in the land, if you act corruptly by making a graven image in the form of anything, and by doing what is evil in the sight of the Lord your God, so as to provoke him to anger, I call heaven and earth to witness against you this day, that you will soon utterly perish from the land which you are going over the Jordan to possess; you will not live long upon it, but will be utterly destroyed. And the Lord will scatter you among the peoples, and you will be left few in number among the nations where the Lord will drive you. And there you will serve gods of wood and stone, the work of men's hands, that neither see, nor hear, nor eat, nor smell. But from there you will seek the Lord your God, and you will find him, if you search after him with all your heart and with all your soul. When you are in tribulation, and all these things come upon you in the latter days, you will return to the Lord your God and obey his voice, for the Lord your God is a merciful God; he will not fail you or destroy you or forget the covenant with your fathers which he swore to them."

A Reading (Lesson) from the Second Letter of Paul to the Corinthians [11:21b-33]

Whatever any one dares to boast of—I am speaking as a fool—I also dare to boast of that. Are they Hebrews? So am I. Are they Israelites? So am I. Are they descendants of Abraham? So am I. Are they servants of Christ? I am a better one—I am talking like a madman—with far greater labors, far more imprisonments, with countless beatings, and often near death. Five times I have received at the hands of the Jews the forty lashes less one. Three times I have been beaten with rods; once I was stoned. Three times I have been shipwrecked; a night and a day I have been adrift at sea; on frequent journeys, in danger from rivers, danger from robbers, danger from my own people, danger from Gentiles, danger in the city, danger in the wilderness, danger at sea, danger from false brethren; in toil and hardship, through many a sleepless night, in hunger and thirst, often without food, in cold and exposure. And, apart from other things, there is the daily pressure upon me of my anxiety for all the churches. Who is weak, and I am not weak? Who is made to fall, and I am not indignant? If I must boast, I will boast of the things that show my weakness. The God and Father of the Lord Jesus, he who is blessed for ever, knows that I do not lie. At Damascus, the governor under King Ar'etas guarded the city of Damascus in order to seize me, but I was let down in a basket through a window in the wall, and escaped his hands.

A Reading (Lesson) from the Gospel according to Matthew
[6:24-34]

Jesus opened his mouth and taught his disciples, saying: "No one can serve two masters; for either he will hate the one and love the other, or he will be devoted to the one and despise the other. You cannot serve God and mammon. Therefore I tell you, do not be anxious about your life, what you shall eat or what you shall drink, nor about your body, what you shall put on. Is not life more than food, and the body more than clothing? Look at the birds of the air: they neither sow nor reap nor gather into barns, and yet your heavenly Father feeds them. Are you not of more value than they? And which of you by being anxious can add one cubit to his span of life? And why are you anxious about clothing? Consider the lilies of the field, how they grow; they neither toil nor spin; yet I tell you, even Solomon in all his glory was not arrayed like one of these. But if God so clothes the grass of the field, which today is alive and tomorrow is thrown into the oven, will he not much more clothe you, O men of little faith? Therefore do not be anxious, saying 'What shall we eat?' or 'What shall we drink?' or 'What shall we wear?' For the Gentiles seek all these things; and your heavenly Father knows that you need them all. But seek first his kingdom and his righteousness, and all these things shall be yours as well. Therefore do not be anxious about tomorrow, for tomorrow will be anxious for itself. Let the day's own trouble be sufficient for the day."

Thursday

Psalm 18:1-20 [page 602] ❖ *Psalm 18:21-50* [page 604]

A Reading (Lesson) from the Book of Deuteronomy [4:32-40]

Moses undertook to explain the law, saying, "Ask now of

the days that are past, which were before you, since the day that God created man upon the earth, and ask from one end of heaven to the other, whether such a great thing as this has ever happened or was ever heard of. Did any people hear the voice of a god speaking out of the midst of the fire, as you have heard, and still live? Or has any god ever attempted to go and take a nation for himself from the midst of another nation, by trials, by signs, by wonders, and by war, by a mighty hand and an outstretched arm, and by great terrors, according to all that the Lord your God did for you in Egypt before your eyes? To you it was shown, that you might know that the Lord is God; there is no other besides him. Out of heaven he let you hear his voice, that he might discipline you; and on earth he let you see his great fire, and you heard his words out of the midst of the fire. And because he loved your fathers and chose their descendants after them, and brought you out of Egypt with his own presence, by his great power, driving out before you nations greater and mightier than yourselves, to bring you in, to give you their land for an inheritance, as at this day; know therefore this day, and lay it to your heart, that the Lord is God in heaven above and on the earth beneath; there is no other. Therefore you shall keep his statutes and his commandments, which I command you this day, that it may go well with you, and with your children after you, and that you may prolong your days in the land which the Lord your God gives you for ever."

A Reading (Lesson) from the Second Letter of Paul to the Corinthians [12:1-10]

I must boast; there is nothing to be gained by it, but I will go on to visions and revelations of the Lord. I know a man in Christ who fourteen years ago was caught up to the third heaven—whether in the body or out of the body I do not know, God knows. And I know that this man was caught up into Paradise—whether in the body or out of the body I do not know, God knows—and he heard things that cannot be told, which man may not utter. On behalf of this man I will boast, but on my own behalf I will not boast, except of my weaknesses. Though if I wish to boast, I shall not be a fool, for I shall be speaking the truth. But I refrain from it, so that no one may think more of me than he sees in me or hears from me. And to keep me from being too elated by the abundance of revelations, a thorn was given me in the flesh, a messenger of Satan, to harass me, to keep me from being too elated. Three times I besought the Lord about this, that it should leave me; but he said to me, "My grace is sufficient for you, for my power is made perfect in weakness." I will all the more gladly boast of my weaknesses, that the power of Christ may rest upon me. For the sake of Christ, then, I am content with weaknesses, insults, hardships, persecutions, and calamities; for when I am weak, then I am strong.

A Reading (Lesson) from the Gospel according to Matthew
[7:1-12]

Jesus opened his mouth and taught his disciples, saying: "Judge not, that you be not judged. For with the judgment you pronounce you will be judged, and the measure you give will be the measure you get. Why do you see the speck that is in your brother's eye, but do not notice the log that is in your own eye? Or how can you say to your brother, 'Let me take the speck out of your eye,' when there is the log in your own eye? You hypocrite, first take the log out of your own eye, and then you will see clearly to take the speck out of your brother's eye. Do not give dogs what is holy; and do not throw your pearls before swine, lest they trample them under foot and turn to attack you. Ask, and it will be given you; seek, and you will find; knock, and it will be opened to you. For every one who asks receives, and he who seeks finds, and to him who knocks it will be opened. Or what man of you, if his son asks him for bread, will give him a stone? Or if he asks for a fish, will give him a serpent? If you then, who are evil, know how to give good gifts to your children, how much more will your Father who is in heaven give good things to those who ask him! So whatever you wish that men would do to you, do so to them; for this is the law and the prophets."

Friday

Psalm 16 [page 599], *Psalm 17* [page 600] ❖
Psalm 22 [page 610]

A Reading (Lesson) from the Book of Deuteronomy
[5:1-22]

Moses summoned all Israel, and said to them, "Hear, O Israel, the statutes and the ordinances which I speak in your hearing this day, and you shall learn them and be careful to do them. The Lord our God made a covenant with us in Horeb. Not with our fathers did the Lord make this covenant, but with us, who are all of us here alive this day. The Lord spoke with you face to·face at the mountain out of the midst of the fire, while I stood between the Lord and you at that time, to declare to you the word of the Lord; for you were afraid because of the fire, and you did not go up into the mountain. He said: 'I am the Lord your God, who brought you out of the land of Egypt, out of the house of bondage. You shall have no other gods before me. You shall not make for yourself a graven image, or any likeness of anything that is in heaven above, or that is on the earth beneath, or that is in the water under the earth; you shall not bow down to them or serve them; for I the Lord your God am a jealous God, visiting the iniquity of the fathers upon the children to the third and fourth generation of those who hate me, but showing steadfast love to thousands of those who love me and keep my commandments. You shall not take the name of the Lord your God in vain: for the Lord will not hold him guiltless who takes his name in vain. Observe the sabbath day, to keep it holy, as the Lord your God commanded you. Six days you shall labor, and do all your work; but the seventh day is a sabbath to the Lord your God; in it you shall not do any work, you, or your son, or your daughter, or your manservant, or your maidservant, or your ox, or your ass, or any of your cattle, or the sojourner who is within your gates, that your manservant and your maidservant may rest as well as you. You shall remember that you were a servant in the land of Egypt, and the Lord your God brought you out thence with a mighty hand and an outstretched arm; therefore the Lord your God commanded you to keep the sabbath day. Honor your father and your mother, as the Lord your God commanded you; that your days may be prolonged, and that it may go well with you, in the land which the Lord your God gives you. You shall not kill. Neither shall you commit adultery. Neither shall you steal. Neither shall you bear false witness against your neighbor. Neither shall you covet your neighbor's wife; and you shall not desire your neighbor's house, his field, or his manservant, or his maidservant, his ox, or his ass, or anything that is your neighbor's.' These words the Lord spoke to all your assembly at the mountain out of the midst of the fire, the cloud, and the thick darkness, with a loud voice; and he added no more. And he wrote them upon two tables of stone, and gave them to me."

A Reading (Lesson) from the Second Letter of Paul to the Corinthians [12:11-21]

I have been a fool! You forced me to it, for I ought to have been commended by you. For I was not at all inferior to these superlative apostles, even though I am nothing. The signs of a true apostle were performed among you in all patience, with signs and wonders and mighty works. For in what were you less favored than the rest of the churches, except that I myself did not burden you? Forgive me this wrong! Here for the third time I am ready to come to you. And I will not be a burden, for I seek not what is yours but you; for children ought not to lay up for their parents, but parents for their children. I will most gladly spend and be spent for your souls. If I love you the more, am I to be loved the less? But granting that I myself did not burden you, I was crafty, you say, and got the better of you by guile. Did I take advantage of you through any of those whom I sent to you? I urged Titus to go, and sent the brother with him. Did Titus take advantage of you? Did we not act in the same spirit? Did we not take the same steps? Have you been thinking all along that we have been defending ourselves before you? It is in the sight of God that we have been speaking in Christ, and all for your upbuilding, beloved. For I fear that perhaps I may come and find you not what I wish, and that you may find me not what you wish; that perhaps there may be quarreling, jealousy, anger, selfishness, slander, gossip, conceit, and disorder. I fear that when I come again my God may humble me before you, and I may have to mourn over many of those who sinned before and have not repented of the impurity, immorality, and licentiousness which they have practiced.

A Reading (Lesson) from the Gospel according to Matthew [7:13-21]

Jesus opened his mouth and taught his disciples, saying: "Enter by the narrow gate; for the gate is wide and the way is easy, that leads to destruction, and those who enter by it are many. For the gate is narrow and the way is hard, that leads to life, and those who find it are few. Beware of false prophets, who come to you in sheep's clothing but inwardly are ravenous wolves. You will know them by their fruits. Are grapes gathered from thorns, or figs from thistles? So, every sound tree bears good fruit, but the bad tree bears evil fruit. A sound tree cannot bear evil fruit, nor can a bad tree bear good fruit. Every tree that does not bear good fruit is cut down and thrown into the fire. Thus you will know them by their fruits. Not every one who says to me, 'Lord, Lord,' shall enter the kingdom of heaven, but he who does the will of my Father who is in heaven."

Saturday

Psalm 20 [page 608],   *Psalm 21:1-7(8-13)* [page 608]   ❖
Psalm 110:1-5(6-7) [page 753],   *Psalm 116* [page 759],
Psalm 117 [page 760]

A Reading (Lesson) from the Book of Deuteronomy
[5:22-33]

Moses summoned all Israel, and said to them, "These words the Lord spoke to all your assembly at the mountain out of the midst of the fire, the cloud, and the thick darkness, with a loud voice; and he added no more. And he wrote them upon two tables of stone, and gave them to me. And when you heard the voice out of the midst of the darkness, while the mountain was burning with fire, you came near to me, all the heads of your tribes, and your elders; and you said, 'Behold, the Lord our God has shown us his glory and greatness, and we have heard his voice out of the midst of the fire; we have this day seen God speak with man and man still live. Now therefore why should we die? For this great fire will consume us; if we hear the voice of the Lord our God any more, we shall die. For who is there of all flesh, that has heard the voice of the living God speaking out of the midst of fire, as we have, and has still lived? Go near, and hear all that the Lord our God will say; and speak to us all that the Lord our God will speak to you; and we will hear and do it.' And the Lord heard your words, when you spoke to me; and the Lord said to me, 'I have heard the words of this people, which they have spoken to you; they have rightly said all that they have spoken. Oh that they had such a mind as this always, to fear me and to keep all my commandments, that it might go well with them and with their children for ever! Go and say to them, "Return to your tents." But you, stand here by me, and I will tell you all the commandment and the statutes and the ordinances which you shall teach them, that they may do them in the land which I give them to possess.' You shall be careful to do therefore as the Lord your God has commanded you; you shall not turn aside to the right hand or to the left. You shall walk in all the way which the Lord your God has commanded you, that you may live, and that it may go well with you, and that you may live long in the land which you shall possess."

A Reading (Lesson) from the Second Letter of Paul to the Corinthians [13:1-14]

This is the third time I am coming to you. Any charge must be sustained by the evidence of two or three witnesses. I warned those who sinned before and all the others, and I warn them now while absent, as I did when present on my second visit, that if I come again I will not spare them— since you desire proof that Christ is speaking in me. He is not weak in dealing with you, but is powerful in you. For he was crucified in weakness, but lives by the power of God. For we are weak in him, but in dealing with you we shall live with him by the power of God. Examine yourselves, to see whether you are holding to your faith. Test yourselves. Do you not realize that Jesus Christ is in you?—unless indeed you fail to meet the test! I hope you will find out that we have not failed. But we pray God that you may not do wrong—not that we may appear to have met the test, but that you may do what is right, though we may seem to have failed. For we cannot do anything against the truth, but only for the truth. For we are glad when we are weak and you are strong. What we pray for is your improvement. I write this while I am away from you, in order than when I come I may not have to be severe in my use of the authority which the Lord has given me for building up and not for tearing down. Finally, brethren, farewell. Mend your ways, heed my appeal, agree with one another, live in peace, and the God of love and peace will be with you. Greet one another with a holy kiss. All the saints greet you. The grace of the Lord Jesus Christ and the love of God and the fellowship of the Holy Spirit be with you all.

A Reading (Lesson) from the Gospel according to Matthew [7:22-29]

Jesus opened his mouth and taught his disciples, saying: "On that day many will say to me, 'Lord, Lord, did we not prophesy in your name, and cast out demons in your name, and do many mighty works in your name?' And then will I declare to them, 'I never knew you; depart from me, you evildoers.' Every one then who hears these words of mine and does them will be like a wise man who built his house upon the rock; and the rain fell, and the floods came, and the winds blew and beat upon that house, but it did not fall, because it had been founded on the rock. And every one who hears these words of mine and does not do them will be like a foolish man who built his house upon the sand; and the rain fell, and the floods came, and the winds blew and beat against that house, and it fell; and great was the fall of it." And when Jesus finished these sayings, the crowds were astonished at his teaching, for he taught them as one who had authority, and not as their scribes.

Week of Last Epiphany

Sunday

Psalm 148 [page 805],   *Psalm 149* [page 807],
Psalm 150 [page 807]   ❖   *Psalm 114* [page 756],
Psalm 115 [page 757]

A Reading (Lesson) from the Book of Deuteronomy
[6:1-9]

Moses summoned all Israel, and said to them, "This is the commandment, the statutes and the ordinances which the Lord your God commanded me to teach you, that you may do them in the land to which you are going over, to possess it; that you may fear the Lord your God, you and your son and your son's son, by keeping all his statutes and his commandments, which I command you, all the days of your life; and that your days may be prolonged. Hear therefore, O Israel, and be careful to do them; that it may go well with you, and that you may multiply greatly, as the Lord, the God of your fathers, has promised you, in a land flowing with milk and honey. Hear, O Israel: The Lord our God is one Lord; and you shall love the Lord your God with all your heart, and with all your soul, and with all your might. And these words which I command you this day shall be upon your heart; and you shall teach them diligently to your children, and shall talk of them when you sit in your house, and when you walk by the way, and when you lie down and when you rise. And you shall bind them as a sign upon your hand, and they shall be as frontlets between your eyes. And you shall write them on the doorposts of your house and on your gates."

Hebrews 12:18-29   [page 36 above]

A Reading (Lesson) from the Gospel according to John
[12:24-32]

Jesus answered Andrew and Philip, "Truly, truly, I say to you, unless a grain of wheat falls into the earth and dies, it remains alone; but if it dies, it bears much fruit. He who loves his life loses it, and he who hates his life in this world will keep it for eternal life. If any one serves me, he must follow me; and where I am, there shall my servant be also; if any one serves me, the Father will honor him. Now is my soul troubled. And what shall I say? 'Father, save me from this hour'? No, for this purpose I have come to this hour. Father, glorify thy name." Then a voice came from heaven, "I have glorified it, and I will glorify it again." The crowd standing by heard it and said that it had thundered. Others said, "An angel has spoken to him." Jesus answered, "This voice has come for your sake, not for mine. Now is the judgment of this world, now shall the ruler of this world be cast out; and I, when I am lifted up from the earth, will draw all men to myself."

Monday

Psalm 25 [page 614] ❖ *Psalm 9* [page 593],
Psalm 15 [page 599]

A Reading (Lesson) from the Book of Deuteronomy
[6:10-15]

Moses summoned all Israel, and said to them, "When the Lord your God brings you into the land which he swore to your fathers, to Abraham, to Isaac, and to Jacob, to give you, with great and goodly cities, which you did not build, and houses full of all good things, which you did not fill, and cisterns hewn out, which you did not hew, and vineyards and olive trees, which you did not plant, and when you eat and are full, then take heed lest you forget the Lord, who brought you out of the land of Egypt, out of the house of bondage. You shall fear the Lord your God;

you shall serve him, and swear by his name. You shall not
go after other gods, of the gods of the peoples who are
round about you; for the Lord your God in the midst of
you is a jealous God; lest the anger of the Lord your God
be kindled against you, and he destroy you from off the
face of the earth.

A Reading (Lesson) from the Letter to the Hebrews [1:1-

In many and various ways God spoke of old to our father
by the prophets; but in these last days he has spoken to us
by a Son, whom he appointed the heir of all things,
through whom he also created the world. He reflects the
glory of God and bears the very stamp of his nature,
upholding the universe by his word of power. When he
had made purification for sins, he sat down at the right
hand of the Majesty on high, having become as much
superior to angels as the name he has obtained is more
excellent than theirs. For to what angel did God ever say,
"Thou art my Son, today I have begotten thee"? Or again,
"I will be to him a father, and he shall be to me a son"? And
again, when he brings the firstborn into the world, he says
"Let all God's angels worship him." Of the angels he says,
"Who makes his angels winds, and his servants flames of
fire." But of the Son he says, "Thy throne, O God, is for
ever and ever, the righteous scepter is the scepter of thy
kingdom. Thou hast loved righteousness and hated
lawlessness; therefore God, thy God, has anointed thee
with the oil of gladness beyond thy comrades." And,
"Thou, Lord, didst found the earth in the beginning, and the
heavens are the work of thy hands; they will perish, but
thou remainest; they will all grow old like a garment, like
mantle thou wilt roll them up, and they will be changed.
But thou art the same, and thy years will never end." But
what angel has he ever said, "Sit at my right hand, till I
make thy enemies a stool for thy feet"? Are they not all
ministering spirits sent forth to serve, for the sake of those
who are to obtain salvation?

A Reading (Lesson) from the Gospel according to John
[1:1-18]

In the beginning was the Word, and the Word was with God, and the Word was God. He was in the beginning with God; all things were made through him, and without him was not anything made that was made. In him was life, and the life was the light of men. The light shines in the darkness, and the darkness has not overcome it. There was a man sent from God, whose name was John. He came for testimony, to bear witness to the light, that all might believe through him. He was not the light, but came to bear witness to the light. The true light that enlightens every man was coming into the world. He was in the world, and the world was made through him, yet the world knew him not. He came to his own home, and his own people received him not. But to all who received him, who believed in his name, he gave power to become children of God; who were born, not of blood nor of the will of the flesh nor of the will of man, but of God. And the Word became flesh and dwelt among us, full of grace and truth; we have beheld his glory, glory as of the only Son from the Father. (John bore witness to him, and cried, "This was he of whom I said, 'He who comes after me ranks before me, for he was before me.'") And from his fulness have we all received, grace upon grace. For the law was given through Moses; grace and truth came through Jesus Christ. No one has ever seen God; the only Son, who is in the bosom of the Father, he has made him known.

Tuesday

Psalm 26 [page 616], *Psalm 28* [page 619] ❖
Psalm 36 [page 632], *Psalm 39* [page 738]

A Reading (Lesson) from the Book of Deuteronomy
[6:16-25]

Moses summoned all Israel and said to them, "You shall not put the Lord your God to the test, as you tested him at Massah. You shall diligently keep the commandments of the Lord your God, and his testimonies, and his statutes, which he has commanded you. And you shall do what is right and good in the sight of the Lord, that it may go well with you, and that you may go in and take possession of the good land which the Lord swore to give to your fathers by thrusting out all your enemies from before you, as the Lord has promised. When your son asks you in time to come, 'What is the meaning of the testimonies and the statutes and the ordinances which the Lord our God has commanded you?' then you shall say to your son, 'We were Pharaoh's slaves in Egypt; and the Lord brought us out of Egypt with a mighty hand; and the Lord showed signs and wonders, great and grievous, against Egypt and against Pharaoh and all his household, before our eyes; and he brought us out from there, that he might bring us in and give us the land which he swore to give to our fathers. And the Lord commanded us to do all these statutes, to fear the Lord our God, for our good always, that he might preserve us alive, as at this day. And it will be righteousness for us, if we are careful to do all this commandment before the Lord our God, as he has commanded us.'"

A Reading (Lesson) from the Letter to the Hebrews [2:1-1

We must pay the closer attention to what we have heard, lest we drift away from it. For if the message declared by angels was valid and every transgression or disobedience received a just retribution, how shall we escape if we neglect such a great salvation? It was declared at first by the Lord, and it was attested to us by those who heard him while God also bore witness by signs and wonders and various miracles and by gifts of the Holy Spirit distributed according to his own will. For it was not to angels that God subjected the world to come, of which we are speaking. It has been testified somewhere, "What is man that thou art mindful of him, or the son of man, that thou carest for him? Thou didst make him for a little while lower than the angels, thou has crowned him with glory and honor, putting everything in subjection under his feet." Now in putting everything in subjection to him, he left nothing outside his control. As it is, we do not yet see everything in subjection to him. But we see Jesus, who for a little while was made lower than the angels, crowned with glory and honor because of the suffering of death, so that by the grace of God he might taste death for every one. For it was fitting that he, for whom and by whom all things exist, in bringing many sons to glory, should make the pioneer of their salvation perfect through suffering.

A Reading (Lesson) from the Gospel according to John
[1:19-28]

This is the testimony of John, when the Jews sent priests and Levites from Jerusalem to ask him, "Who are you?" He confessed, he did not deny, but confessed, "I am not the Christ." And they asked him, "What then? Are you Eli'jah?" He said, "I am not." "Are you the prophet?" And he answered, "No." They said to him then, "Who are you? Let us have an answer for those who sent us. What do you say about yourself?" He said, "I am the voice of one crying in the wilderness, 'Make straight the way of the Lord,' as the prophet Isaiah said." Now they had been sent from the Pharisees. They asked him, "Then why are you baptizing, if you are neither the Christ, nor Eli'jah, nor the prophet?" John answered them, "I baptize with water; but among you stands one whom you do not know, even he who comes after me, the thong of whose sandal I am not worthy to untie." This took place in Bethany beyond the Jordan, where John was baptizing.

Ash Wednesday

Psalm 95* [page 724] & Psalm 32 [page 624],
Psalm 143 [page 798] ❖ *Psalm 102* [page 731],
Psalm 130 [page 784]

A Reading (Lesson) from the Book of Jonah [3:1—4:11]

The word of the Lord came to Jonah the second time,
saying, "Arise, go to Nin'eveh, that great city, and
proclaim to it the message that I tell you." So Jonah arose
and went to Nin'eveh, according to the word of the Lord.
Now Nin'eveh was an exceedingly great city, three days'
journey in breadth. Jonah began to go into the city, going a
day's journey. And he cried, "Yet forty days, and Nin'eveh
shall be overthrown!" And the people of Nin'eveh believed
God; they proclaimed a fast, and put on sackcloth, from
the greatest of them to the least of them. Then tidings
reached the king of Nin'eveh, and he arose from his
throne, removed his robe, and covered himself with
sackcloth, and sat in ashes. And he made proclamation
and published through Nin'eveh, "By the decree of the
king and his nobles: Let neither man nor beast, herd nor
flock, taste anything; let them not feed, or drink water, but
let man and beast be covered with sackcloth, and let them
cry mightily to God; yea, let every one turn from his evil
way and from the violence which is in his hands. Who
knows, God may yet repent and turn from his fierce anger,
so that we perish not?" When God saw what they did, how
they turned from their evil way, God repented of the evil
which he had said he would do to them; and he did not do
it. But it displeased Jonah exceedingly, and he was angry.
And he prayed to the Lord and said, "I pray thee, Lord, is
not this what I said when I was yet in my country? That is
why I made haste to flee to Tarshish; for I knew that thou

* For the Invitatory

art a gracious God and merciful, slow to anger, and abounding in steadfast love, and repentest of evil. Therefore now, O Lord, take my life from me, I beseech thee, for it is better for me to die than to live." And the Lord said, "Do you do well to be angry?" Then Jonah went out of the city and sat to the east of the city, and made a booth for himself there. He sat under it in the shade, till he should see what would become of the city. And the Lord God appointed a plant, and made it come up over Jonah, that it might be a shade over his head, to save him from his discomfort. So Jonah was exceedingly glad because of the plant. But when dawn came up the next day, God appointed a worm which attacked the plant, so that it withered. When the sun rose, God appointed a sultry east wind, and the sun beat upon the head of Jonah so that he was faint; and he asked that he might die, and said, "It is better for me to die than to live." But God said to Jonah, "Do you do well to be angry for the plant?" And he said, "I do well to be angry, angry enough to die." And the Lord said, "You pity the plant, for which you did not labor, nor did you make it grow, which came into being in a night and perished in a night. And should not I pity Nin'eveh, that great city, in which there are more than a hundred and twenty thousand persons who do not know their right hand from their left, and also much cattle?"

A Reading (Lesson) from the Letter to the Hebrews
[12:1-14]

Therefore, since we are surrounded by so great a cloud of witnesses, let us also lay aside every weight, and sin which clings so closely, and let us run with perseverance the race that is set before us, looking to Jesus the pioneer and perfecter of our faith, who for the joy that was set before him endured the cross, despising the shame, and is seated at the right hand of the throne of God. Consider him who endured from sinners such hostility against himself, so that you may not grow weary or fainthearted. In your struggle against sin you have not yet resisted to the point of shedding your blood. And have you forgotten the exhortation which addresses you as sons?—"My son, do not regard lightly the discipline of the Lord, nor lose courage when you are punished by him. For the Lord disciplines him whom he loves, and chastises every son whom he receives." It is for discipline that you have to endure. God is treating you as sons; for what son is there whom his father does not discipline? If you are left without discipline, in which all have participated, then you are illegitimate children and not sons. Besides this, we have had earthly fathers to discipline us and we respected them. Shall we not much more be subject to the Father of spirits and live? For they disciplined us for a short time at their pleasure, but he disciplines us for our good, that we may share his holiness. For the moment all discipline seems painful rather than pleasant; later it yields the peaceful fruit of righteousness to those who have been trained by it. Therefore, lift your drooping hands and strengthen your weak knees, and make straight paths for your feet, so that what is lame may not be put out of joint but rather be healed. Strive for peace with all men, and for the holiness without which no one will see the Lord.

A Reading (Lesson) from the Gospel according to Luke [18:9-14]

Jesus told this parable to some who trusted in themselves that they were righteous and despised others: "Two men went up into the temple to pray, one a Pharisee and the other a tax collector. The Pharisee stood and prayed thus with himself, 'God, I thank thee that I am not like other men, extortioners, unjust, adulterers, or even like this tax collector. I fast twice a week, I give tithes of all that I get.' But the tax collector, standing far off, would not even lift up his eyes to heaven, but beat his breast, saying, 'God, be merciful to me a sinner!' I tell you, this man went down to his house justified rather than the other; for every one who exalts himself will be humbled, but he who humbles himself will be exalted."

Thursday

Psalm 37:1-18 [page 633] ❖ *Psalm 37:19-42* [page 634]

A Reading (Lesson) from the Book of Deuteronomy
[7:6-11]

Moses summoned all Israel, and said to them, "You are a people holy to the Lord your God; the Lord your God has chosen you to be a people for his own possession, out of all the peoples that are on the face of the earth. It was not because you were more in number than any other people that the Lord set his love upon you and chose you, for you were the fewest of all peoples; but it is because the Lord loves you, and is keeping the oath which he swore to your fathers, that the Lord has brought you out with a mighty hand, and redeemed you from the house of bondage, from the hand of Pharaoh king of Egypt. Know therefore that the Lord your God is God, the faithful God who keeps covenant and steadfast love with those who love him and keep his commandments, to a thousand generations, and requites to their face those who hate him, by destroying them; he will not be slack with him who hates him, he will requite him to his face. You shall therefore be careful to do the commandment, and the statutes, and the ordinances, which I command you this day."

A Reading (Lesson) from the Letter of Paul to Titus [1:1-16]

Paul, a servant of God and an apostle of Jesus Christ, to further the faith of God's elect and their knowledge of the truth which accords with godliness, in hope of eternal life which God, who never lies, promised ages ago and at the proper time manifested in his word through the preaching with which I have been entrusted by command of God our Savior; To Titus, my true child in a common faith: Grace and peace from God the Father and Christ Jesus our Savior. This is why I left you in Crete, that you might amend what was defective, and appoint elders in every town as I directed you, if any man is blameless, the husband of one wife, and his children are believers and not open to the charge of being profligate or insubordinate. For a bishop, as God's steward, must be blameless; he must not be arrogant or quick-tempered or a drunkard or violent or greedy for gain, but hospitable, a lover of goodness, master of himself, upright, holy, and self-controlled; he must hold firm to the sure word as taught, so that he may be able to give instruction in sound doctrine an also to confute those who contradict it. For there are many insubordinate men, empty talkers and deceivers, especially the circumcision party; they must be silenced, since they are upsetting whole families by teaching for base gain what they have no right to teach. One of themselves, a prophet of their own, said, "Cretans are always liars, evil beasts, lazy gluttons." This testimony is true. Therefore rebuke them sharply, that they may be sound in the faith, instead of giving heed to Jewish myths or to commands of men who reject the truth. To the pure all things are pure, but to the corrupt and unbelieving nothing is pure; their very minds and consciences are corrupted. They profess to know God, but they deny him by their deeds; they are detestable, disobedient, unfit for any good deed.

A Reading (Lesson) from the Gospel according to John
[1:29-34]

The next day John saw Jesus coming toward him, and said "Behold, the Lamb of God, who takes away the sin of the world! This is he of whom I said, 'After me comes a man who ranks before me, for he was before me.' I myself did not know him; but for this I came baptizing with water, that he might be revealed to Israel." And John bore witness, "I saw the Spirit descend as a dove from heaven, and it remained on him. I myself did not know him; but he who sent me to baptize with water said to me, 'He on whom you see the Spirit descend and remain, this is he who baptizes with the Holy Spirit.' And I have seen and borne witness that this is the Son of God."

Friday

*Psalm 95** [page 724]   &   *Psalm 31* [page 622]   ❖
Psalm 35 [page 629]

A Reading (Lesson) from the Book of Deuteronomy
[7:12-16]

Moses summoned all Israel, and said to them, "Because you hearken to these ordinances, and keep and do them, the Lord your God will keep with you the covenant and the steadfast love which he swore to your fathers to keep; he will love you, bless you, and multiply you; he will also bless the fruit of your body and the fruit of your ground, your grain and your wine and your oil, and increase of your cattle and the young of your flock, in the land which he swore to your fathers to give you. You shall be blessed above all peoples; there shall not be male or female barren among you, or among your cattle. And the Lord will take away from you all sickness; and none of the evil diseases of Egypt, which you knew, will he inflict upon you, but he will lay them upon all who hate you. And you shall destroy all the peoples that the Lord your God will give over to you, your eye shall not pity them; neither shall you serve their gods, for that would be a snare to you.

*For the Invitatory

*A Reading (Lesson) from the Letter of Paul
to Titus* [2:1-15]

As for you, teach what befits sound doctrine. Bid the older
men be temperate, serious, sensible, sound in faith, in love,
and in steadfastness. Bid the older women likewise to be
reverent in behavior, not to be slanderers or slaves to
drink; they are to teach what is good, and so train the
young women to love their husbands and children, to be
sensible, chaste, domestic, kind, and submissive to their
husbands, that the word of God may not be discredited.
Likewise urge the younger men to control themselves.
Show yourself in all respects a model of good deeds, and in
your teaching show integrity, gravity, and sound speech
that cannot be censured, so that an opponent may be put
to shame, having nothing evil to say of us. Bid slaves to be
submissive to their masters and to give satisfaction in every
respect; they are not to be refractory, nor to pilfer, but to
show entire and true fidelity, so that in everything they
may adorn the doctrine of God our Savior. For the grace of
God has appeared for the salvation of all men, training us
to renounce irreligion and worldly passions, and to live
sober, upright and godly lives in this world, awaiting our
blessed hope, the appearing of the glory of our great God
and Savior Jesus Christ, who gave himself for us to redeem
us from all iniquity and to purify for himself a people of
his own who are zealous for good deeds. Declare these
things; exhort and reprove with authority. Let no one
disregard you.

A Reading (Lesson) from the Gospel according to John
[1:35-42]

The next day again John was standing with two of his
disciples; and he looked at Jesus as he walked, and said,
"Behold, the Lamb of God!" The two disciples heard him
say this, and they followed Jesus. Jesus turned, and saw

them following, and said to them, "What do you seek?" And they said to him, "Rabbi" (which means Teacher), "where are you staying?" He said to them, "Come and see." They came and saw where he was staying; and they stayed with him that day, for it was about the tenth hour. One of the two who heard John speak, and followed him, was Andrew, Simon Peter's brother. He first found his brother Simon, and said to him, "We have found the Messiah" (which means Christ). He brought him to Jesus. Jesus looked at him, and said, "So you are Simon the son of John? You shall be called Cephas" (which means Peter).

Saturday

Psalm 30 [page 621], *Psalm 32* [page 624] ❖
Psalm 42 [page 643], *Psalm 43* [page 644]

A Reading (Lesson) from the Book of Deuteronomy [7:17-26]

Moses summoned all Israel, and said to them, "If you say in your heart, 'These nations are greater than I; how can I dispossess them?' you shall not be afraid of them, but you shall remember what the Lord your God did to Pharaoh and to all Egypt, the great trials which your eyes saw, the signs, the wonders, the mighty hand, and the outstretched arm, by which the Lord your God brought you out; so will the Lord your God do to all the peoples of whom you are afraid. Moreover the Lord your God will send hornets among them, until those who are left and hide themselves from you are destroyed. You shall not be in dread of them; for the Lord your God is in the midst of you, a great and terrible God. The Lord your God will clear away these nations before you little by little; you may not make an end of them at once, lest the wild beasts grow too numerous for you. But the Lord your God will give them over to you, and throw them into great confusion, until they are destroyed. And he will give their kings into your hand, and you shall make their name perish from under heaven; not a man shall be able to stand against you, until you have destroyed them. The graven images of their gods you shall burn with fire; you shall not covet the silver or the gold that is on them, or take it for yourselves, lest you be ensnared by it; for it is an abomination to the Lord your God. And you shall not bring an abominable thing into your house, and become accursed like it; you shall utterly detest and abhor it; for it is an accursed thing.

A Reading (Lesson) from the Letter of Paul to Titus [3:1-15]

Remind them to be submissive to rulers and authorities, to be obedient, to be ready for any honest work, to speak evil of no one, to avoid quarreling, to be gentle, and to show perfect courtesy toward all men. For we ourselves were once foolish, disobedient, led astray, slaves to various passions and pleasures, passing our days in malice and envy, hated by men and hating one another; but when the goodness and loving kindness of God our Savior appeared, he saved us, not because of deeds done by us in righteousness, but in virtue of his own mercy, by the washing of regeneration and renewal in the Holy Spirit, which he poured out upon us richly through Jesus Christ our Savior, so that we might be justified by his grace and become heirs in hope of eternal life. The saying is sure. I desire you to insist on these things, so that those who have believed in God may be careful to apply themselves to good deeds; these are excellent and profitable to men. But avoid stupid controversies, genealogies, dissensions, and quarrels over the law, for they are unprofitable and futile. As for a man who is factious, after admonishing him once or twice, have nothing more to do with him, knowing that such a person is perverted and sinful; he is self-condemned. When I send Artemas or Tych'icus to you, do your best to come to me at Nicop'olis, for I have decided to spend the winter there. Do your best to speed Zenas the lawyer and Apol'los on their way; see that they lack nothing. And let our people learn to apply themselves to good deeds, so as to help cases of urgent need, and not to be unfruitful. All who are with me send greetings to you. Greet those who love us in the faith. Grace be with you all.

A Reading (Lesson) from the Gospel according to John
[1:43-51]

The next day Jesus decided to go to Galilee. And he found Philip and said to him, "Follow me." Now Philip was from Beth-sa'ida, the city of Andrew and Peter. Philip found Nathan'a-el, and said to him, "We have found him of whom Moses in the law and also the prophets wrote, Jesus of Nazareth, the son of Joseph." Nathan'a-el said to him, "Can anything good come out of Nazareth?" Philip said to him, "Come and see." Jesus saw Nathan'a-el coming to him, and said of him, "Behold, an Israelite indeed, in whom is no guile!" Nathan'a-el said to him, "How do you know me?" Jesus answered him, "Before Philip called you, when you were under the fig tree, I saw you." Nathan'a-el answered him, "Rabbi, you are the Son of God! You are the King of Israel!" Jesus answered him, "Because I said to you, I saw you under the fig tree, do you believe? You shall see greater things than these." And he said to him, "Truly, truly, I say to you, you will see the heaven opened, and the angels of God ascending and descending upon the Son of man."

Week of 1 Lent

Sunday

Psalm 63:1-8(9-11) [page 670],
Psalm 98 [page 727] ❖ *Psalm 103* [page 733]

A Reading (Lesson) from the Book of Deuteronomy
[8:1-10]

Moses summoned all Israel, and said to them, "All the commandment which I command you this day you shall be careful to do, that you may live and multiply, and go in and possess the land which the Lord swore to give to your fathers. And you shall remember all the way which the Lord your God has led you these forty years in the wilderness, that he might humble you, testing you to know what was in your heart, whether you would keep his commandments, or not. And he humbled you and let you hunger and fed you with manna, which you did not know, nor did your fathers know; that he might make you know that man does not live by bread alone, but that man lives by everything that proceeds out of the mouth of the Lord. Your clothing did not wear out upon you, and your foot did not swell, these forty years. Know then in your heart that, as a man disciplines his son, the Lord your God disciplines you. So you shall keep the commandments of the Lord your God, by walking in his ways and by fearing him. For the Lord your God is bringing you into a good land, a land of brooks of water, of fountains and springs, flowing forth in valleys and hills, a land of wheat and barley, of vines and fig trees and pomegranates, a land of olive trees and honey, a land in which you will eat bread without scarcity, in which you will lack nothing, a land whose stones are iron, and out of whose hills you can dig copper. And you shall eat and be full, and you shall bless the Lord your God for the good land he has given you."

*A Reading (Lesson) from the First Letter of Paul
to the Corinthians* [1:17-31]

Christ did not send me to baptize but to preach the gospel, and not with eloquent wisdom, lest the cross of Christ be emptied of its power. For the word of the cross is folly to those who are perishing, but to us who are being saved it is the power of God. For it is written, "I will destroy the wisdom of the wise, and the cleverness of the clever I will thwart." Where is the wise man? Where is the scribe? Where is the debater of this age? Has not God made foolish the wisdom of the world? For since, in the wisdom of God, the world did not know God through wisdom, it pleased God through the folly of what we preach to save those who believe. For Jews demand signs and Greeks seek wisdom, but we preach Christ crucified, a stumbling block to Jews and folly to Gentiles, but to those who are called, both Jews and Greeks, Christ the power of God and the wisdom of God. For the foolishness of God is wiser than men, and the weakness of God is stronger than men. For consider your call, brethren; not many of you were wise according to worldly standards, not many were powerful, not many were of noble birth; but God chose what is foolish in the world to shame the wise, God chose what is weak in the world to shame the strong, God chose what is low and despised in the world, even things that are not, to bring to nothing things that are, so that no human being might boast in the presence of God. He is the source of your life in Christ Jesus, whom God made our wisdom, our righteousness and sanctification and redemption; therefore, as it is written, "Let him who boasts, boast of the Lord."

A Reading (Lesson) from the Gospel according to Mark
[2:18-22]

John's disciples and the Pharisees were fasting; and people came and said to Jesus, "Why do John's disciples and the disciples of the Pharisees fast, but your disciples do not fast?" And Jesus said to them, "Can the wedding guests fast while the bridgegroom is with them? As long as they have the bridegroom with them, they cannot fast. The days will come, when the bridegroom is taken away from them, and then they will fast in that day. No one sews a piece of unshrunk cloth on an old garment; if he does, the patch tears away from it, the new from the old, and a worse tear is made. And no one puts new wine into old wineskins; if he does, the wine will burst the skins, and the wine is lost, and so are the skins; but new wine is for fresh skins."

Monday

Psalm 41 [page 641], *Psalm 52* [page 657] ❖
Psalm 44 [page 645]

A Reading (Lesson) from the Book of Deuteronomy
[8:11-20]

Moses summoned all Israel, and said to them, "Take heed lest you forget the Lord your God, by not keeping his commandments and his ordinances and his statutes, which I command you this day: lest, when you have eaten and are full, and have built goodly houses and live in them, and when your herds and flocks multiply, and your silver and gold is multiplied, and all that you have is multiplied, then your heart be lifted up, and you forget the Lord your God, who brought you out of the land of Egypt, out of the house of bondage, who led you through the great and terrible wilderness, with its fiery serpents and scorpions and thirsty ground where there was no water, who brought you water out of the flinty rock, who fed you in the wilderness with manna which your fathers did not know, that he might humble you and test you, to do you good in the end. Beware lest you say in your heart, 'My power and the might of my hand have gotten me this wealth.' You shall remember the Lord your God, for it is he who gives you power to get wealth; that he may confirm his covenant which he swore to your fathers, as at this day. And if you forget the Lord your God and go after other gods and serve them and worship them, I solemnly warn you this day that you shall surely perish. Like the nations that the Lord makes to perish before you, so shall you perish, because you would not obey the voice of the Lord your God."

A Reading (Lesson) from the Letter to the Hebrews
[2:11-18]

He who sanctifies and those who are sanctified have all one origin. That is why he is not ashamed to call them brethren, saying, "I will proclaim thy name to my brethren, in the midst of the congregation I will praise thee." And again, "I will put my trust in him." And again, "Here am I, and the children God has given me." Since therefore the children share in flesh and blood, he himself partook of the same nature, that through death he might destroy him who has the power of death, that is, the devil, and deliver all those who through fear of death were subject to lifelong bondage. For surely it is not with angels that he is concerned but with the descendants of Abraham. Therefore he had to be made like his brethren in every respect, so that he might become a merciful and faithful high priest in the service of God, to make expiation for the sins of the people. For because he himself has suffered and been tempted, he is able to help those who are tempted.

A Reading (Lesson) from the Gospel according to John
[2:1-12]

On the third day there was a marriage at Cana in Galilee, and the mother of Jesus was there; Jesus also was invited to the marriage, with his disciples. When the wine gave out, the mother of Jesus said to him, "They have no wine." And Jesus said to her, "O woman, what have you to do with me? My hour has not yet come." His mother said to the servants, "Do whatever he tells you." Now six stone jars were standing there, for the Jewish rites of purification, each holding twenty or thirty gallons. Jesus said to them, "Fill the jars with water." And they filled them up to the brim. He said to them, "Now draw some out, and take it to the steward of the feast." So they took it. When the steward of the feast tasted the water now become wine, and did not know where it came from (though the servants who had drawn the water knew), the steward of the feast called the bridegroom and said to him, "Every man serves the good wine first; and when men have drunk freely, then the poor wine; but you have kept the good wine until now." This, the first of his signs, Jesus did at Cana in Galilee, and manifested his glory; and his disciples believed in him. After this he went down to Caper'na-um, with his mother and his brothers and his disciples; and there they stayed for a few days.

Tuesday

Psalm 45 [page 647] ❖ *Psalm 47* [page 650],
Psalm 48 [page 651]

A Reading (Lesson) from the Book of Deuteronomy
[9:4-12]

Moses summoned all Israel, and said to them, "Do not say in your heart, after the Lord your God has thrust them out before you, 'It is because of my righteousness that the Lord has brought me in to possess this land'; whereas it is because of the wickedness of these nations that the Lord is driving them out before you. Not because of your righteousness or the uprightness of your heart are you going in to possess their land; but because of the wickedness of these nations the Lord your God is driving them out from before you, and that he may confirm the word which the Lord swore to your fathers, to Abraham, to Isaac, and to Jacob. Know therefore, that the Lord your God is not giving you this good land to possess because of your righteousness; for you are a stubborn people. Remember and do not forget how you provoked the Lord your God to wrath in the wilderness; from the day you came out of the land of Egypt, until you came to this place, you have been rebellious against the Lord. Even at Horeb you provoked the Lord to wrath, and the Lord was so angry with you that he was ready to destroy you. When I went up the mountain to receive the tables of stone, the tables of the covenant which the Lord made with you, I remained on the mountain forty days and forty nights; I neither ate bread nor drank water. And the Lord gave me the two tables of stone written with the finger of God; and on them were all the words which the Lord had spoken with you on the mountain out of the midst of the fire on the day of the assembly. And at the end of forty days and forty nights the Lord gave me the two tables of stone, the tables of the covenant. Then the Lord said to me, 'Arise, go down quickly from here; for your people whom you have brought from Egypt have acted corruptly; they have turned aside quickly out of the way which I commanded them; they have made themselves a molten image.'"

A Reading (Lesson) from the Letter to the Hebrews
[3:1-11]

Holy brethren, who share in a heavenly call, consider Jesus, the apostle and high priest of our confession. He was faithful to him who appointed him, just as Moses also was faithful in God's house. Yet Jesus has been counted worthy of as much more glory than Moses as the builder of a house has more honor than the house. (For every house is built by some one, but the builder of all things is God.) Now Moses was faithful in all God's house as a servant, to testify to the things that were to be spoken later, but Christ was faithful over God's house as a son. And we are his house if we hold fast our confidence and pride in our hope.

Therefore, as the Holy Spirit says, "Today, when you hear his voice, do not harden your hearts as in the rebellion, on the day of testing in the wilderness, where your fathers put me to the test and saw my works for forty years. Therefore I was provoked with that generation, and said, 'They always go astray in their hearts; they have not known my ways.' As I swore in my wrath, 'They shall never enter my rest.'"

A Reading (Lesson) from the Gospel according to John
[2:13-22]

The Passover of the Jews was at hand, and Jesus went up to Jerusalem. In the temple he found those who were selling oxen and sheep and pigeons, and the money-changers at their business. And making a whip of cords, he drove them all, with the sheep and oxen, out of the temple; and he poured out the coins of the money-changers and overturned their tables. And he told those who sold the pigeons, "Take these things away; you shall not make my Father's house a house of trade." His disciples remembered that it was written, "Zeal for thy house will consume me." The Jews then said to him, "What sign have you to show us for doing this?" Jesus answered them, "Destroy this temple, and in three days I will raise it up." The Jews then said, "It has taken forty-six years to build this temple, and will you raise it up in three days?" But he spoke of the temple of his body. When therefore he was raised from the dead, his disciples remembered that he had said this; and they believed the scripture and the word which Jesus had spoken.

Wednesday

Psalm 119:49-72 [page 767]   ❖   *Psalm 49* [page 652],
(Psalm 53 [page 658])

A Reading (Lesson) from the Book of Deuteronomy
[9:13-21]

Moses summoned all Israel, and said to them,
"Furthermore the Lord said to me, 'I have seen this people,
and behold, it is a stubborn people; let me alone, that I
may destroy them and blot out their name from under
heaven; and I will make of you a nation mightier and
greater than they.' So I turned and came down from the
mountain, and the mountain was burning with fire;
the two tables of the covenant were in my two hands. And
I looked, and behold, you had sinned against the Lord
your God; you had made yourselves a molten calf; you had
turned aside quickly from the way which the Lord had
commanded you. So I took hold of the two tables, and cast
them out of my two hands, and broke them before your
eyes. Then I lay prostrate before the Lord as before, forty
days and forty nights; I neither ate bread nor drank water,
because of all the sin which you had committed, in doing
what was evil in the sight of the Lord, to provoke him to
anger. For I was afraid of the anger and hot displeasure
which the Lord bore against you, so that he was ready to
destroy you. But the Lord hearkened to me that time also.
And the Lord was so angry with Aaron that he was ready
to destroy him; and I prayed for Aaron also at the same
time. Then I took the sinful thing, the calf which you had
made, and burned it with fire and crushed it, grinding it
very small, until it was as fine as dust; and I threw the dust
of it into the brook that descended out of the mountain."

A Reading (Lesson) from the Letter to the Hebrews
[3:12-19]

Take care, brethren, lest there be in any of you an evil,
unbelieving heart, leading you to fall away from the living
God. But exhort one another every day, as long as it is
called "today," that none of you may be hardened by the
deceitfulness of sin. For we share in Christ, if only we hold

our first confidence firm to the end, while it is said, "Today, when you hear his voice, do not harden your hearts as in the rebellion." Who were they that heard and yet were rebellious? Was it not all those who left Egypt under the leadership of Moses? And with whom was he provoked forty years? Was it not with those who sinned, whose bodies fell in the wilderness? And to whom did he swear that they should never enter his rest, but to those who were disobedient? So we see that they were unable to enter because of unbelief.

A Reading (Lesson) from the Gospel according to John
[2:23—3:15]

When Jesus was in Jerusalem at the Passover feast, many believed in his name when they saw the signs which he did; but Jesus did not trust himself to them, because he knew all men and needed no one to bear witness of man; for he himself knew what was in man. Now there was a man of the Pharisees, named Nicode′mus, a ruler of the Jews. This man came to Jesus by night and said to him, "Rabbi, we know that you are a teacher come from God; for no one can do these signs that you do, unless God is with him." Jesus answered him, "Truly, truly, I say to you, unless one is born anew, he cannot see the kingdom of God." Nicode′mus said to him, "How can a man be born when he is old? Can he enter a second time into his mother's womb and be born?" Jesus answered, "Truly, truly, I say to you, unless one is born of water and the Spirit, he cannot enter the kingdom of God. That which is born of the flesh is flesh, and that which is born of the Spirit is spirit. Do not marvel that I said to you, 'You must be born anew.' The wind blows where it wills, and you hear the sound of it, but you do not know whence it comes or whither it goes; so it is with every one who is born of the Spirit." Nicode′mus said to him, "How can this be?" Jesus answered him, "Are you a teacher of Israel, and yet you do not understand this? Truly, truly, I say to you, we speak of what we know, and bear witness to what we have seen; but you do not receive our testimony. If I have told you earthly things and you do not believe, how can you believe if I tell you heavenly things? No one has ascended into heaven but he who descended from heaven, the Son of man. And as Moses lifted up the serpent in the wilderness, so must the Son of man be lifted up, that whoever believes in him may have eternal life."

Thursday

Psalm 50 [page 654] ❖ *(Psalm 59* [page 665],
Psalm 60 [page 667]) *or* *Psalm 19* [page 606],
Psalm 46 [page 649]

A Reading (Lesson) from the Book of Deuteronomy [9:23—10:5]

Moses summoned all Israel, and said to them, "When the Lord sent you from Ka'desh-bar'nea, saying, 'Go up and take possession of the land which I have given you,' then you rebelled against the commandment of the Lord your God, and did not believe him or obey his voice. You have been rebellious against the Lord from the day that I knew you. So I lay prostrate before the Lord for these forty days and forty nights, because the Lord had said he would destroy you. And I prayed to the Lord, 'O Lord God, destroy not thy people and thy heritage, whom thou hast redeemed through thy greatness, whom thou hast brought out of Egypt with a mighty hand. Remember thy servants, Abraham, Isaac, and Jacob; do not regard the stubbornness of this people, or their wickedness, or their sin, lest the land from which thou didst bring us say, "Because the Lord was not able to bring them into the land which he promised them, and because he hated them, he has brought them out to slay them in the wilderness." For they are thy people and thy heritage, whom thou didst bring out by thy great power and by thy outstretched arm.' At that time the Lord said to me, 'Hew two tables of stone like the first, and come up to me on the mountain, and make an ark of wood. And I will write on the tables the words that were on the first tables which you broke, and you shall put them in the ark.' So I made an ark of acacia wood, and hewed two tables of stone like the first, and went up the mountain with the two tables in my hand. And he wrote on the tables, as at the first writing, the ten commandments which the Lord has spoken to you on the mountain out of the midst of the fire on the day of the assembly; and the Lord gave them to me. Then I turned and came down from the mountain, and put the tables in the ark which I had made; and there they are, as the Lord commanded me."

A Reading (Lesson) from the Letter to the Hebrews
[4:1-10]

While the promise of entering his rest remains, let us fear lest any of you be judged to have failed to reach it. For good news came to us just as to them; but the message which they heard did not benefit them, because it did not meet with faith in the hearers. For we who have believed enter that rest, as he has said, "As I swore in my wrath, 'They shall never enter my rest,'" although his works were finished from the foundation of the world. For he has somewhere spoken of the seventh day in this way, "And God rested on the seventh day from all his works." And again in this place he said, "They shall never enter my rest." Since therefore it remains for some to enter it, and those who formerly received the good news failed to enter because of disobedience, again he sets a certain day, "Today," saying through David so long afterward, in the words already quoted, "Today, when you hear his voice, do not harden your hearts." For if Joshua had given them rest, God would not speak later of another day. So then, there remains a sabbath rest for the people of God; for whoever enters God's rest also ceases from his labors as God did from his.

John 3:16-21   [page 52 above]

Friday

*Psalm 95** [page 724]   &   *Psalm 40* [page 640],
Psalm 54 [page 659]   ❖   *Psalm 51* [page 656]

A Reading (Lesson) from the Book of Deuteronomy
[10:12-22]

Moses summoned all Israel, and said to them, "And now, Israel, what does the Lord your God require of you, but to fear the Lord your God, to walk in all his ways, to love him, to serve the Lord your God with all your heart and with all your soul, and to keep the commandments and statutes of the Lord, which I command you this day for your good? Behold, to the Lord your God belong heaven and the heaven of heavens, the earth with all that is in it; yet the Lord set his heart in love upon your fathers and chose their descendants after them, you above all peoples, as at this day. Circumcise therefore the foreskin of your heart, and be no longer stubborn. For the Lord your God is God of gods and Lord of lords, the great, the mighty, and the terrible God, who is not partial and takes no bribe. He executes justice for the fatherless and the widow, and loves the sojourner, giving him food and clothing. Love the sojourner therefore; for you were sojourners in the land of Egypt. You shall fear the Lord your God; you shall serve him and cleave to him, and by his name you shall swear. He is your praise; he is your God, who has done for you these great and terrible things which your eyes have seen.

*For the Invitatory

Your fathers went down to Egypt seventy persons; and now the Lord, our God has made you as the stars of heaven for multitude."

A Reading (Lesson) from the Letter to the Hebrews
[4:11-16]

Let us strive to enter that rest, that no one fall by the same sort of disobedience. For the word of God is living and active, sharper than any two-edged sword, piercing to the division of soul and spirit, of joints and marrow, and discerning the thoughts and intentions of the heart. And before him no creature is hidden, but all are open and laid bare to the eyes of him with whom we have to do. Since then we have a great high priest who has passed through the heavens, Jesus, the Son of God, let us hold fast our confession. For we have not a high priest who is unable to sympathize with our weaknesses, but one who in every respect has been tempted as we are, yet without sin. Let us then with confidence draw near to the throne of grace, that we may receive mercy and find grace to help in time of need.

A Reading (Lesson) from the Gospel according to John
[3:22-36]

Jesus and his disciples went into the land of Judea; there he remained with them and baptized. John also was baptizing at Aenon near Salim, because there was much water there and people came and were baptized. For John had not yet been put in prison. Now a discussion arose between John's disciples and a Jew over purifying. And they came to John and said to him, "Rabbi, he who was with you beyond the Jordan, to whom you bore witness, here he is, baptizing, and all are going to him." John answered, "No one can receive anything except what is given him from heaven. You yourselves bear me witness, that I said, I am not the Christ, but I have been sent before him. He who has the bride is the bridegroom; the friend of the bridegroom, who stands and hears him, rejoices greatly at the bridegroom's voice; therefore this joy of mine is now full. He must increase, but I must decrease." He who comes from above is above all; he who is of earth belongs to the earth, and of the earth he speaks; he who comes from heaven is above all. He bears witness to what he has seen and heard, yet no one receives his testimony; he who receives his testimony sets his seal to this, that God is true. For he whom God has sent utters the words of God, for it is not by measure that he gives the Spirit; the Father loves the Son, and has given all things into his hand. He who believes in the Son has eternal life; he who does not obey the Son shall not see life, but the wrath of God rests upon him.

Saturday

Psalm 55 [page 660]   ❖   *Psalm 138* [page 793], *Psalm 139:1-17(18-23)* [page 794]

A Reading (Lesson) from the Book of Deuteronomy
[11:18-28]

Moses summoned all Israel, and said to them, "You shall lay up these words of mine in your heart and in your soul; and you shall bind them as a sign upon your hand, and they shall be as frontlets between your eyes. And you shall teach them to your children, talking of them when you are sitting in your house, and when you are walking by the way, and when you lie down, and when you rise. And you shall write them upon the doorposts of your house and upon your gates, that your days and the days of your children may be multiplied in the land which the Lord swore to your fathers to give them, as long as the heavens are above the earth. For if you will be careful to do all this commandment which I command you to do, loving the Lord your God, walking in all his ways, and cleaving to him, then the Lord will drive out all these nations before you and you will dispossess nations greater and mightier than yourselves. Every place on which the sole of your foot treads shall be yours; your territory shall be from the wilderness and Lebanon and from the River, the river Eu-phra'tes, to the western sea. No man shall be able to stand against you; the Lord your God will lay the fear of you and the dread of you upon all the land that you shall tread, as he promised you. Behold, I set before you this day a blessing and a curse: the blessing, if you obey the commandments of the Lord your God, which I command you this day, and the curse, if you do not obey the commandments of the Lord your God, but turn aside from the way which I command you this day, to go after other gods which you have not known."

A Reading (Lesson) from the Letter to the Hebrews
[5:1-10]

Every high priest chosen from among men is appointed to act on behalf of men in relation to God, to offer gifts and sacrifices for sin. He can deal gently with the ignorant and wayward, since he himself is beset with weakness. Because of this he is bound to offer sacrifice for his own sins as well as those of the people. And one does not take the honor upon himself, but he is called by God, just as Aaron was. So also Christ did not exalt himself to be made a high priest, but was appointed by him who said to him, "Thou art my Son, today I have begotten thee"; as he says also in another place, "Thou art a priest for ever, after the order of Melchiz'edek." In the days of his flesh, Jesus offered up prayers and supplications, with loud cries and tears, to him who was able to save him from death, and he was heard for his godly fear. Although he was a Son, he learned obedience through what he suffered; and being made perfect he became the source of eternal salvation to all who obey him, being designated by God a high priest after the order of Melchiz'edek.

A Reading (Lesson) from the Gospel according to John
[4:1-26]

When the Lord knew that the Pharisees had heard that
Jesus was making and baptizing more disciples than John
(although Jesus himself did not baptize, but only his
disciples), he left Judea and departed again to Galilee. He
had to pass through Samar'ia. So he came to a city of
Samar'ia, called Sy'char, near the field that Jacob gave to
his son Joseph. Jacob's well was there, and so Jesus,
wearied as he was with his journey, sat down beside the
well. It was about the sixth hour. There came a woman of
Samar'ia to draw water. Jesus said to her, "Give me a
drink." For his disciples had gone into the city to buy food.
The Samaritan woman said to him, "How is it that you, a
Jew, ask a drink of me, a woman of Samar'ia?" For Jews
have no dealings with Samaritans. Jesus answered her, "If
you knew the gift of God, and who it is that is saying to
you, 'Give me a drink,' you would have asked him, and he
would have given you living water." The woman said to
him, "Sir, you have nothing to draw with, and the well is
deep; where do you get that living water? Are you greater
than our father Jacob, who gave us this well, and drank
from it himself, and his sons, and his cattle?" Jesus said to
her, "Everyone who drinks of this water will thirst again,
but whoever drinks of the water that I shall give him will
never thirst; the water that I shall give him will become in
him a spring of water welling up to eternal life." The
woman said to him, "Sir, give me this water, that I may not
thirst, nor come here to draw." Jesus said to her, "Go, call
your husband and come here." The woman answered him,
"I have no husband." Jesus said to her, "You are right in
saying, 'I have no husband'; for you have had five
husbands, and he whom you now have is not your
husband; this you said truly." The woman said to him, 'Sir,
I perceive that you are a prophet. Our fathers worshiped
on this mountain; and you say that in Jerusalem is the
place where men ought to worship." Jesus said to her,

"Woman, believe me, the hour is coming when neither on this mountain nor in Jerusalem will you worship the Father. You worship what you do not know; we worship what we know, for salvation is from the Jews. But the hour is coming, and now is, when the true worshipers will worship the Father in spirit and truth, for such the Father seeks to worship him. God is spirit, and those who worship him must worship in spirit and truth." The woman said to him, "I know that Messiah is coming (he who is called Christ); when he comes, he will show us all things." Jesus said to her, "I who speak to you am he."

Week of 2 Lent

Sunday

Psalm 24 [page 613], *Psalm 29* [page 620] ❖
Psalm 8 [page 592], *Psalm 84* [page 707]

A Reading (Lesson) from the Book of Jeremiah [1:1-10]

The words of Jeremiah, the son of Hilki'ah, of the priests who were in An'athoth in the land of Benjamin, to whom the word of the Lord came in the days of Josi'ah the son of Amon, king of Judah, in the thirteenth year of his reign. It came also in the days of Jehoi'akim the son of Josi'ah, king of Judah, and until the end of the eleventh year of Zedeki'ah, the son of Josi'ah, king of Judah, until the captivity of Jerusalem in the fifth month. Now the word of the Lord came to me saying, "Before I formed you in the womb I knew you, and before you were born I consecrated you; I appointed you a prophet to the nations." Then I said, "Ah, Lord God! Behold, I do not know how to speak for I am only a youth." But the Lord said to me, "Do not say, 'I am only a youth'; for to all to whom I send you you shall go, and whatever I command you you shall speak. Be not afraid of them, for I am with you to deliver you, says the Lord." Then the Lord put forth his hand and touched my mouth; and the Lord said to me, "Behold, I have put my words in your mouth. See, I have set you this day over nations and over kingdoms, to pluck up and to break down, to destroy and to overthrow, to build and to plant."

A Reading (Lesson) from the First Letter of Paul to the Corinthians [3:11-23]

No other foundation can any one lay than that which is laid, which is Jesus Christ. Now if any one builds on the foundation with gold, silver, precious stones, wood, hay, straw—each man's work will become manifest; for the Day will disclose it, because it will be revealed with fire, and the fire will test what sort of work each one has done. If the work which any man has built on the foundation survives, he will receive a reward. If any man's work is burned up, he will suffer loss, though he himself will be saved, but only as through fire. Do you not know that you are God's temple and that God's Spirit dwells in you? If any one destroys God's temple, God will destroy him. For God's temple is holy, and that temple you are. Let no one deceive himself. If any one among you thinks that he is wise in this age, let him become a fool that he may become wise. For the wisdom of this world is folly with God. For it is written, "He catches the wise in their craftiness," and again, "The Lord knows that the thoughts of the wise are futile." So let no one boast of men. For all things are yours, whether Paul or Apol′los or Cephas or the world or life or death or the present or the future, all are yours; and you are Christ's; and Christ is God's.

A Reading (Lesson) from the Gospel according to Mark [3:31—4:9]

Jesus' mother and his brothers came; and standing outside they sent to him and called him. And a crowd was sitting about him; and they said to him, "Your mother and your brothers are outside, asking for you." And he replied, "Who are my mother and my brothers?" And looking around on those who sat about him, he said, "Here are my mother and my brothers! Whoever does the will of God is my brother, and sister, and mother." Again he began to teach beside the sea. And a very large crowd gathered about him, so that he got into a boat and sat in it on the sea; and the whole crowd was beside the sea on the land. And he taught them many things in parables, and in his teaching he said to them: "Listen! A sower went out to sow. And as he sowed, some seed fell along the path, and the birds came and devoured it. Other seed fell on rocky ground, where it had not much soil, and immediately it sprang up, since it had no depth of soil; and when the sun rose it was scorched, and since it had no root it withered away. Other seed fell among thorns and the thorns grew up and choked it, and it yielded no grain. And other seeds fell into the good soil and brought forth grain, growing up and increasing and yielding thirtyfold and sixtyfold and a hundredfold." And he said, "He who has ears to hear, let him hear."

Monday

Psalm 56 [page 662], *Psalm 57* [page 663], *(Psalm 58* [page 664]) ❖ *Psalm 64* [page 671], *Psalm 65* [page 672]

A Reading (Lesson) from the Book of Jeremiah [1:11-19]

The word of the Lord came to me, saying, "Jeremiah, what do you see?" And I said, "I see a rod of almond." Then the Lord said to me, "You have seen well, for I am watching over my word to perform it." The word of the Lord came to me a second time, saying, "What do you see?" And I said, "I see a boiling pot, facing away from the north."

Then the Lord said to me, "Out of the north evil shall break forth upon all the inhabitants of the land. For, lo, I am calling all the tribes of the kingdoms of the north, says the Lord; and they shall come and every one shall set his throne at the entrance of the gates of Jerusalem, against all its walls round about, and against all the cities of Judah. And I will utter my judgments against them, for all their wickedness in forsaking me; they have burned incense to other gods, and worshiped the works of their own hands. But you, gird up your loins; arise, and say to them everything that I command you. Do not be dismayed by them, lest I dismay you before them. And I, behold, I make you this day a fortified city, an iron pillar, and bronze walls, against the whole land, against the kings of Judah, its princes, its priests, and the people of the land. They will fight against you; but they shall not prevail against you, for I am with you, says the Lord, to deliver you."

A Reading (Lesson) from the Letter of Paul to the Romans [1:1-15]

Paul, a servant of Jesus Christ, called to be an apostle, set apart for the gospel of God which he promised beforehand through his prophets in the holy scriptures, the gospel concerning his Son, who was descended from David according to the flesh and designated Son of God in power according to the Spirit of holiness by his resurrection from the dead, Jesus Christ our Lord, through whom we have received grace and apostleship to bring about the obedience of faith for the sake of his name among all the nations, including yourselves who are called to belong to Jesus Christ; To all God's beloved in Rome, who are called to be saints: Grace to you and peace from God our Father and the Lord Jesus Christ. First, I thank my God through Jesus Christ for all of you, because your faith is proclaimed in all the world. For God is my witness, whom I serve with my spirit in the gospel of his Son, that without ceasing I mention you always in my prayers, asking that somehow by God's will I may now at last succeed in coming to you. For I long to see you, that I may impart to you some spiritual gift to strengthen you, that is, that we may be mutually encouraged by each other's faith, both yours and mine. I want you to know, brethren, that I have often intended to come to you (but thus far have been prevented), in order that I may reap some harvest among you as well as among the rest of the Gentiles. I am under obligation both to Greeks and to barbarians, both to the wise and to the foolish: so I am eager to preach the gospel to you also who are in Rome.

John 4:27-42   [page 127 above]

Tuesday

Psalm 61 [page 668],   *Psalm 62* [page 669]   ❖
Psalm 68:1-20(21-23)24-36 [page 676]

A Reading (Lesson) from the Book of Jeremiah   [2:1-13]

The word of the Lord came to me, saying, "Go and proclaim in the hearing of Jerusalem, Thus says the Lord, remember the devotion of your youth, your love as a bride how you followed me in the wilderness, in a land not sown. Israel was holy to the Lord, the first fruits of his harvest. All who ate of it became guilty; evil came upon them, says the Lord." Hear the word of the Lord, O house of Jacob, and all the families of the house of Israel. Thus says the Lord: "What wrong did your fathers find in me that they went far from me, and went after worthlessness, and became worthless? They did not say, 'Where is the Lord who brought us up from the land of Egypt, who led us in the wilderness, in a land of deserts and pits, in a land of drought and deep darkness, in a land that none passes through, where no man dwells?' And I brought you into a plentiful land to enjoy its fruits and its good things. But when you came in you defiled my land, and made my heritage an abomination. The priests did not say, 'Where is the Lord?' Those who handle the law did not know me; the rulers transgressed against me; the prophets prophesied by Ba'al, and went after things that do not profit. Therefore I still contend with you, says the Lord, and with your children's children I will contend. For cross to the coasts of Cyrpus and see, or send to Kedar and examine with care; see if there has been such a thing. Has a nation changed its gods, even though they are no gods? But my people have changed their glory for that which does not profit. Be appalled, O Heavens, at this, be shocked, be utterly desolate, says the Lord, for my people have committed two evils: they have forsaken me, the fountain of living waters, and hewed out cisterns for themselves, broken cisterns, that can hold no water."

A Reading (Lesson) from the Letter of Paul to the Romans [1:16-25]

I am not ashamed of the gospel: it is the power of God for salvation to every one who has faith, to the Jew first and also to the Greek. For in it the righteousness of God is revealed through faith for faith; as it is written, "He who through faith is righteous shall live." For the wrath of God is revealed from heaven against all ungodliness and wickedness of men who by their wickedness suppress the truth. For what can be known about God is plain to them, because God has shown it to them. Ever since the creation of the world his invisible nature, namely, his eternal power and deity, has been clearly perceived in the things that have been made. So they are without excuse; for although they knew God they did not honor him as God or give thanks to him, but they became futile in their thinking and their senseless minds were darkened. Claiming to be wise, they became fools, and exchanged the glory of the immortal God for images resembling mortal man or birds or animals or reptiles. Therefore God gave them up in the lusts of their hearts to impurity, to the dishonoring of their bodies among themselves, because they exchanged the truth about God for a lie and worshiped and served the creature rather than the Creator, who is blessed for ever! Amen.

A Reading (Lesson) from the Gospel according to John [4:43-54]

After two days in Samar′ia Jesus departed to Galilee. For Jesus himself testified that a prophet has no honor in his own country. So when he came to Galilee, the Galileans welcomed him, having seen all that he had done in Jerusalem at the feast, for they too had gone to the feast. So he came again to Cana in Galilee, where he had made the water wine. And at Caper′na-um there was an official whose son was ill. When he heard that Jesus had come from Judea to Galilee, he went and begged him to come down and heal his son, for he was at the point of death. Jesus therefore said to him, "Unless you see signs and wonders you will not believe." The official said to him, "Sir, come down before my child dies." Jesus said to him, "Go, your son will live." The man believed the word that Jesus spoke to him and went his way. As he was going down, his servants met him and told him that his son was living. So he asked them the hour when he began to mend, and they said to him, "Yesterday at the seventh hour the fever left him." The father knew that was the hour when Jesus had said to him, "Your son will live"; and he himself believed, and all his household. This was now the second sign that Jesus did when he had come from Judea to Galilee.

Wednesday

Psalm 72 [page 685]   ❖   *Psalm 119:73-96* [page 769]

A Reading (Lesson) from the Book of Jeremiah [3:6-18]

The Lord said to me in the days of King Josi'ah: "Have
you seen what she did, that faithless one, Israel, how she
went up on every high hill and under every green tree, and
there played the harlot? And I thought, 'After she has done
all this she will return to me'; but she did not return, and
her false sister Judah saw it. She saw that for all the
adulteries of that faithless one, Israel, I had sent her away
with a decree of divorce; yet her false sister Judah did not
fear, but she too went and played the harlot. Because
harlotry was so light to her, she polluted the land,
committing adultery with stone and tree. Yet for all this
her false sister Judah did not return to me with her whole
heart, but in pretense, says the Lord." And the Lord said to
me, "Faithless Israel has shown herself less guilty than
false Judah. Go, and proclaim these words toward the
north, and say, 'Return, faithless Israel, says the Lord. I
will not look on you in anger, for I am merciful, says the
Lord; I will not be angry for ever. Only acknowledge your
guilt, that you rebelled against the Lord your God and
scattered your favors among strangers under every green
tree, and that you have not obeyed my voice, says the
Lord. Return, O faithless children, says the Lord; for I am
your master; I will take you, one from a city and two from
a family, and I will bring you to Zion. And I will give you
shepherds after my own heart, who will feed you with
knowledge and understanding. And when you have
multiplied and increased in the land, in those days, says the
Lord, they shall no more say, "The ark of the covenant of
the Lord." It shall not come to mind, or be remembered or
missed; it shall not be made again. At that time Jerusalem
shall be called the throne of the Lord, and all nations shall
gather to it, to the presence of the Lord in Jerusalem, and
they shall no more stubbornly follow their own evil heart.
In those days the house of Judah shall join the house of
Israel, and together they shall come from the land of the
north to the land that I gave your fathers for a heritage.'"

*A Reading (Lesson) from the Letter of Paul
to the Romans* [1:28—2:11]

Since they did not see fit to acknowledge God, God gave
them up to a base mind and to improper conduct. They
were filled with all manner of wickedness, evil,
covetousness, malice. Full of envy, murder, strife, deceit,
malignity, they are gossips, slanderers, haters of God,
insolent, haughty, boastful, inventors of evil, disobedient
to parents, foolish, faithless, heartless, ruthless. Though
they know God's decree that those who do such things
deserve to die, they not only do them but approve those
who practice them. Therefore you have no excuse, O man,
whoever you are, when you judge another; for in passing
judgment upon him you condemn yourself, because you,
the judge, are doing the very same things. We know that
the judgment of God rightly falls upon those who do such
things. Do you suppose, O man, that when you judge those
who do such things and yet do them yourself, you will
escape the judgment of God? Or do you presume upon the
riches of his kindness and forbearance and patience? Do
you not know that God's kindness is meant to lead you to
repentance? But by your hard and impenitent heart you are
storing up wrath for yourself on the day of wrath when
God's righteous judgment will be revealed. For he will
render to every man according to his works: to those who
by patience in well-doing seek for glory and honor and
immortality, he will give eternal life; but for those who are
factious and do not obey the truth, but obey wickedness,
there will be wrath and fury. There will be tribulation and
distress for every human being who does evil, the Jew first
and also the Greek, but glory and honor and peace for
every one who does good, the Jew first and also the Greek.
For God shows no partiality.

A Reading (Lesson) from the Gospel according to John
[5:1-18]

After the second sign in Cana there was a feast of the Jews, and Jesus went up to Jerusalem. Now there is in Jerusalem by the Sheep Gate a pool, in Hebrew called Beth-za'tha, which has five porticoes. In these lay a multitude of invalids, blind, lame, paralyzed. One man was there, who had been ill for thirty-eight years. When Jesus saw him and knew that he had been lying there a long time, he said to him, "Do you want to be healed?" The sick man answered him, "Sir, I have no man to put me into the pool when the water is troubled, and while I am going another steps down before me." Jesus said to him, "Rise, take up your pallet and walk." And at once the man was healed, and he took up his pallet and walked. Now that day was the sabbath. So the Jews said to the man who was cured, "It is the sabbath, it is not lawful for you to carry your pallet." But he answered him, "The man who healed me said to me, 'Take up your pallet and walk.'" They asked him, "Who is the man who said to you, 'Take up your pallet, and walk'?" Now the man who had been healed did not know who it was, for Jesus had withdrawn, as there was a crowd in the place. Afterward, Jesus found him in the temple, and said to him, "See, you are well! Sin no more, that nothing worse befall you." The man went away and told the Jews that it was Jesus who had healed him. And this was why the Jews persecuted Jesus, because he did this on the sabbath. But Jesus answered them, "My Father is working still, and I am working." This was why the Jews sought all the more to kill him, because he not only broke the sabbath but also called God his own Father, making himself equal with God.

Thursday

(Psalm 70 [page 682]),   *Psalm 71* [page 683]   ❖
Psalm 74 [page 689]

A Reading (Lesson) from the Book of Jeremiah
[4:9-10,19-28]

"In that day, says the Lord, courage shall fail both king and
princes; the priests shall be appalled and the prophets
astounded." Then I said, "Ah, Lord God, surely thou hast
utterly deceived this people and Jerusalem, saying 'It shall
be well with you'; whereas the sword has reached their
very life." My anguish, my anguish! I writhe in pain! Oh,
the walls of my heart! My heart is beating wildly; I cannot
keep silent; for I hear the sound of the trumpet, the alarm
of war. Disaster follows hard on disaster, the whole land is
laid waste. Suddenly my tents are destroyed, my curtains
in a moment. How long must I see the standard, and hear
the sound of the trumpet? "For my people are foolish, they
know me not; they are stupid children, they have no
understanding. They are skilled in doing evil, but how to
do good they know not." I looked on the earth, and lo, it
was waste and void; and to the heavens, and they had no
light. I looked on the mountains, and lo, they were
quaking, and all the hills moved to and fro. I looked, and
lo, there was no man, and all the birds of the air had fled.
I looked, and lo, the fruitful land was a desert, and all its
cities were laid in ruins before the Lord, before his fierce
anger. For thus says the Lord, "The whole land shall be a
desolation; yet I will not make a full end. For this the earth
shall mourn, and the heavens above be black; for I have
spoken, I have purposed; I have not relented nor will I turn
back."

*A Reading (Lesson) from the Letter of Paul
to the Romans* [2:12-24]

All who have sinned without the law will also perish
without the law, and all who have sinned under the law
will be judged by the law. For it is not the hearers of the
law who are righteous before God, but the doers of the law
who will be justified. When Gentiles who have not the law

do by nature what the law requires, they are a law to themselves, even though they do not have the law. They show that what the law requires is written on their hearts, while their conscience also bears witness and their conflicting thoughts accuse or perhaps excuse them on that day when, according to my gospel, God judges the secrets of men by Christ Jesus. But if you call yourself a Jew and rely upon the law and boast of your relation to God and know his will and approve what is excellent, because you are instructed in the law, and if you are sure that you are a guide to the blind, a light to those who are in darkness, a corrector of the foolish, a teacher of children, having in the law the embodiment of knowledge and truth—you then who teach others, will you not teach yourself? While you preach against stealing, do you steal? You who say that one must not commit adultery, do you commit adultery? You who abhor idols, do you rob temples? You who boast in the law, do you dishonor God by breaking the law? For, as it is written, "The name of God is blasphemed among the Gentiles because of you."

A Reading (Lesson) from the Gospel according to John
[5:19-29]

Jesus said to the Jews, "Truly, truly, I say to you, the Son can do nothing of his own accord, but only what he sees the Father doing; for whatever he does, that the Son does likewise. For the Father loves the Son, and shows him all that he himself is doing; and greater works than these will he show him, that you may marvel. For as the Father raises the dead and gives them life, so also the Son gives life to whom he will. The Father judges no one, but has given all judgment to the Son, that all may honor the Son, even as they honor the Father. He who does not honor the Son does not honor the Father who sent him. Truly, truly, I say to you, he who hears my word and believes him who sent me, has eternal life; he does not come into judgment, but has passed from death to life. Truly, truly, I say to you, the hour is coming, and now is, when the dead will hear the voice of the Son of God, and those who hear will live. For as the Father has life in himself, so he has granted the Son also to have life in himself, and has given him authority to execute judgment, because he is the Son of man. Do not marvel at this; for the hour is coming when all who are in the tombs will hear his voice and come forth, those who have done good, to the resurrection of life, and those who have done evil, to the resurrection of judgment."

Friday

*Psalm 95** [page 724]   &
Psalm 69:1-23(24-30)31-38 [page 679]   ❖
Psalm 73 [page 687]

A Reading (Lesson) from the Book of Jeremiah [5:1-9]

Run to and fro through the streets of Jerusalem, look and take note! Search her squares to see if you can find a man, one who does justice and seeks truth; that I may pardon her. Though they say, "As the Lord lives," yet they swear falsely. O Lord, do not thy eyes look for truth? Thou hast smitten them, but they felt no anguish; thou hast consumed them, but they refused to take correction. They have made their faces harder than rock; they have refused to repent. Then I said, These are only the poor, they have no sense; for they do not know the way of the Lord, the law of their God. I will go to the great, and will speak to them; for they know the way of the Lord, the law of their God." But they all alike had broken the yoke, they had burst the bonds. Therefore a lion from the forest shall slay them, a wolf from the desert shall destroy them. A leopard is watching against their cities, every one who goes out of them shall be torn in pieces; because their transgressions

For the Invitatory

are many, their apostasies are great. "How can I pardon you? Your children have forsaken me, and have sworn by those who are no gods. When I fed them to the full, they committed adultery and trooped to the houses of harlots. They were well-fed lusty stallions, each neighing for his neighbor's wife. Shall I not punish them for these things? says the Lord; and shall I not avenge myself on a nation such as this?"

A Reading (Lesson) from the Letter of Paul to the Romans [2:25—3:18]

Circumcision indeed is of value if you obey the law; but if you break the law, your circumcision becomes uncircumcision. So, if a man who is uncircumcised keeps the precepts of the law, will not his uncircumcision be regarded as circumcision? Then those who are physically uncircumcised but keep the law will condemn you who have the written code and circumcision but break the law. For he is not a real Jew who is one outwardly, nor is true circumcision something external and physical. He is a Jew who is one inwardly, and real circumcision is a matter of the heart, spiritual and not literal. His praise is not from men but from God. Then what advantage has the Jew? Or what is the value of circumcision? Much in every way. To begin with, the Jews are entrusted with the oracles of God. What if some were unfaithful? Does their faithlessness nullify the faithfulness of God? By no means! Let God be true though every man be false, as it is written, "That thou mayest be justified in thy words, and prevail when thou art judged." But if our wickedness serves to show the justice of God, what shall we say? That God is unjust to inflict wrath on us? (I speak in a human way.) By no means! For then how could God judge the world? But if through my falsehood God's truthfulness abounds to his glory, why am I still being condemned as a sinner? And why not do evil that good may come?—as some people slanderously charge us with saying. Their condemnation is just. What then? Are we Jews any better off? No, not at all; for I have already charged that all men, both Jews and Greeks, are under the power of sin, as it is written: "None is righteous, no, not one; no one understands, no one seeks for God. All have turned aside, together they have gone wrong; no one does good, not even one." "Their throat is an open grave, they use their tongues to deceive." "The venom of asps is under their lips." "Their mouth is full of curses and bitterness." "Their feet are swift to shed blood, in their paths are ruin and misery, and the way of peace they do not know." "There is no fear of God before their eyes."

John 5:30-47   [page 54 above]

Saturday

Psalm 75 [page 691],   *Psalm 76* [page 692]   ❖
Psalm 23 [page 612],   *Psalm 27* [page 617]

A Reading (Lesson) from the Book of Jeremiah   [5:20-31]

Declare this in the house of Jacob, proclaim it in Judah: "Hear this, O foolish and senseless people, who have eyes, but see not, who have ears, but hear not. Do you not fear me? says the Lord; Do you not tremble before me? I placed the sand as the bound for the sea, a perpetual barrier which it cannot pass; though the waves toss, they cannot prevail, though they roar, they cannot pass over it. But this people has a stubborn and rebellious heart; they have turned aside and gone away. They do not say in their hearts, 'Let us fear the Lord our God, who gives the rain in its season, the autumn rain and the spring rain, and keeps for us the weeks appointed for the harvest.' Your iniquities have turned these away, and your sins have kept good from you. For wicked men are found among my people; they lurk like fowlers lying in wait. They set a trap; they catch men. Like a basket full of birds, their houses are full of treachery; therefore they have become great and rich, they have grown fat and sleek. They know no bounds in deeds of wickedness; they judge not with justice the cause of the fatherless, to make it prosper, and they do not defend the rights of the needy. Shall I not punish them for these things? says the Lord, and shall I not avenge myself on a nation such as this?" An appalling and horrible thing has happened to the land: the prophets prophesy falsely, and the priests rule at their direction; my people love to have it so, but what will you do when the end comes?

A Reading (Lesson) from the Letter of Paul to the Romans [3:19-31]

We know that whatever the law says it speaks to those who are under the law, so that every mouth may be stopped, and the whole world may be held accountable to God. For no human being will be justified in his sight by works of the law, since through the law comes knowledge of sin. But now the righteousness of God has been manifested apart from law, although the law and the prophets bear witness to it, the righteousness of God through faith in Jesus Christ for all who believe. For there is no distinction; since all have sinned and fall short of the glory of God, they are justified by his grace as a gift, through the redemption which is in Christ Jesus, whom God put forward as an expiation by his blood, to be received by faith. This was to show God's righteousness, because in his divine forbearance he had passed over former sins; it was to prove at the present time that he himself is righteous and that he justifies him who has faith in Jesus. Now what becomes of our boasting? It is excluded. On what principle? On the principle of works? No, but on the principle of faith. For we hold that a man is justified by faith apart from works of law. Or is God the God of Jews only? Is he not the God of Gentiles also? Yes, of Gentiles also, since God is one; and he will justify the circumcised on the ground of their faith and the uncircumcised through their faith. Do we then overthrow the law by this faith? By no means! On the contrary, we uphold the law.

A Reading (Lesson) from the Gospel according to John [7:1-13]

Jesus went about in Galilee; he would not go about in Judea, because the Jews sought to kill him. Now the Jews' feast of Tabernacles was at hand. So his brothers said to him, "Leave here and go to Judea, that your disciples may see the works you are doing. For no man works in secret if he seeks to be known openly. If you do these things, show yourself to the world." For even his brothers did not believe in him. Jesus said to them, "My time has not yet come, but your time is always here. The world cannot hate you, but it hates me because I testify of it that its works are evil. Go to the feast yourselves; I am not going up to this feast, for my time has not yet fully come." So saying, he remained in Galilee. But after his brothers had gone up to the feast, then he also went up, not publicly but in private. The Jews were looking for him at the feast, and saying "Where is he?" And there was much muttering about him among the people. While some said, "He is a good man," others said, "No, he is leading the people astray." Yet for fear of the Jews no one spoke openly of him.

Week of 3 Lent

Sunday

Psalm 93 [page 722],   *Psalm 96* [page 725]   ❖
Psalm 34 [page 627]

A Reading (Lesson) from the Book of Jeremiah [6:9-15]

Thus says the Lord of hosts: "Glean thoroughly as a vine the remnant of Israel; like a grape-gatherer pass your hand again over its branches." To whom shall I speak and give warning, that they may hear? Behold, their ears are closed, they cannot listen; behold, the word of the Lord is to them an object of scorn, they take no pleasure in it. Therefore I am full of the wrath of the Lord; I am weary of holding it in. "Pour it out upon the children in the street, and upon the gatherings of young men, also; both husband and wife shall be taken, the old folk and the very aged. Their houses shall be turned over to others, their fields and wives together; for I will stretch out my hand against the inhabitants of the land," says the Lord. "For from the least to the greatest of them, every one is greedy for unjust gain; and from prophet to priest, every one deals falsely. They have healed the wound of my people lightly, saying 'Peace, peace,' when there is no peace. Were they ashamed when they committed abomination? No, they were not at all ashamed; they did not know how to blush. Therefore they shall fall among those who fall; at the time that I punish them, they shall be overthrown," says the Lord.

A Reading (Lesson) from the First Letter of Paul to the Corinthians [6:12-20]

"All things are lawful for me," but not all things are helpful. "All things are lawful for me," but I will not be enslaved by anything. "Food is meant for the stomach and the stomach for food"—and God will destroy both one and the other. The body is not meant for immorality, but for the Lord, and the Lord for the body. And God raised the Lord and will also raise us up by his power. Do you not know that your bodies are members of Christ? Shall I therefore take the members of Christ and make them members of a prostitute? Never! Do you not know that he who joins himself to a prostitute becomes one body with her? For, as

it is written, "The two shall become one flesh." But he who
is united to the Lord becomes one spirit with him. Shun
immorality. Every other sin which a man commits is
outside the body; but the immoral man sins against his
own body. Do you not know that your body is a temple of
the Holy Spirit within you, which you have from God?
You are not your own; you were bought with a price. So
glorify God in your body.

Mark 5:1-20 [page 142 above]

Monday

Psalm 80 [page 702] ❖ *Psalm 77* [page 693],
(Psalm 79 [page 701])

A Reading (Lesson) from the Book of Jeremiah [7:1-15]

The word that came to Jeremiah from the Lord: "Stand in
the gate of the Lord's house, and proclaim there this word,
and say, Hear the word of the Lord, all you men of Judah
who enter these gates to worship the Lord. Thus says the
Lord of hosts, the God of Israel, Amend your ways and
your doings, and I will let you dwell in this place. Do not
trust in these deceptive words: 'This is the temple of the
Lord, the temple of the Lord, the temple of the Lord.' For if
you truly amend your ways and your doings, if you truly
execute justice one with another, if you do not oppress the
alien, the fatherless or the widow, or shed innocent blood
in this place, and if you do not go after other gods to your
own hurt, then I will let you dwell in this place, in the land
that I gave of old to your fathers for ever. Behold, you trust
in deceptive words to no avail. Will you steal, murder,
commit adultery, swear falsely, burn incense to Ba'al, and
go after other gods that you have not known, and then
come and stand before me in this house, which is called by
my name, and say, 'We are delivered!'—only to go on

doing all these abominations? Has this house, which is called by my name, become a den of robbers in your eyes? Behold, I myself have seen it, says the Lord. Go now to my place that was in Shiloh, where I made my name dwell at first, and see what I did to it for the wickedness of my people Israel. And now, because you have done all these things, says the Lord, and when I spoke to you persistently you did not listen, and when I called you, you did not answer, therefore I will do to the house which is called by my name, and in which you trust, and to the place which I gave to you and to your fathers, as I did to Shiloh. And I will cast you out of my sight, as I cast out all your kinsmen, all the offspring of E'phraim.

A Reading (Lesson) from the Letter of Paul to the Romans [4:1-12]

What then shall we say about Abraham, our forefather according to the flesh? For if Abraham was justified by works, he has something to boast about, but not before God. For what does the scripture say? "Abraham believed God, and it was reckoned to him as righteousness." Now to one who works, his wages are not reckoned as a gift but as his due. And to one who does not work, but trusts him who justifies the ungodly, his faith is reckoned as righteousness. So also David pronounces a blessing upon the man to whom God reckons righteousness apart from works: "Blessed are those whose iniquities are forgiven, and whose sins are covered; blessed is the man against whom the Lord will not reckon his sin." Is this blessing pronounced only upon the circumcised, or also upon the uncircumcised? We say that faith was reckoned to Abraham as righteousness. How then was it reckoned to him? Was it before or after he had been circumcised? It was not after, but before he was circumcised. He received circumcision as a sign or seal of the righteousness which he had by faith while he was still uncircumcised. The purpose was to make him the father of all who believe without being circumcised and who thus have righteousness reckoned to them, and likewise the father of the circumcised who are not merely circumcised but also follow the example of the faith which our father Abraham had before he was circumcised.

A Reading (Lesson) from the Gospel according to John [7:14-36]

About the middle of the feast of Tabernacles Jesus went up into the temple and taught. The Jews marveled at it, saying, "How is it that this man has learning, when he has never studied?" So Jesus answered them, "My teaching is not mine, but his who sent me; if any man's will is to do his will, he shall know whether the teaching is from God or whether I am speaking on my own authority. He who speaks on his own authority seeks his own glory; but he who seeks the glory of him who sent him is true, and in him there is no falsehood. Did not Moses give you the law? Yet none of you keeps the law. Why do you seek to kill me? The people answered, "You have a demon! Who is seeking to kill you?" Jesus answered them, "I did one deed, and you all marvel at it. Moses gave you circumcision (not that it is from Moses, but from the fathers), and you circumcise a man upon the sabbath. If on the sabbath a man receives circumcision, so that the law of Moses may not be broken, are you angry with me because on the sabbath I made a man's whole body well? Do not judge by appearances, but judge with right judgment." Some of the people of Jerusalem therefore said, "Is not this the man whom they seek to kill? And here he is, speaking openly, and they say nothing to him! Can it be that the authorities really know that this is the Christ? Yet we know where this man comes from; and when the Christ appears, no one will know where he comes from." So Jesus proclaimed, as he taught in the temple, "You know me, and you know where I come from? But I have not come of my own accord; he who sent me is true, and him you do not know. I know him, for I come from him, and he sent me." So they sought to arrest him; but no one laid hands on him, because his hour had not yet come. Yet many of the people believed in him; they said, "When the Christ appears, will he do more signs than this man has done?" The Pharisees heard the crowd thus muttering about him, and the chief priests and Pharisees sent officers to arrest him. Jesus then said, "I shall be with you a little longer, and then I go to him who sent me; you will seek me and you will not find me; where I am you cannot come." The Jews said to one another, "Where does this man intend to go that we shall not find him? Does he intend to go to the Dispersion among the Greeks and teach the Greeks? What does he mean by saying, 'You will seek me and you will not find me,' and, 'Where I am going you cannot come'?"

Tuesday

Psalm 78:1-39 [page 694]   ❖   *Psalm 78:40-72* [page 698]

A Reading (Lesson) from the Book of Jeremiah [7:21-34]

Thus says the Lord of hosts, the God of Israel: "Add your burnt offerings to your sacrifices, and eat the flesh. For in the day that I brought them out of the land of Egypt, I did not speak to your fathers or command them concerning burnt offerings and sacrifices. But this command I gave them, 'Obey my voice, and I will be your God, and you shall be my people; and walk in all the way that I command you, that it may be well with you.' But they did not obey or incline their ear, but walked in their own counsels and the stubbornness of their evil hearts, and went backward and not forward. From the day that your fathers came out of the land of Egypt to this day, I have persistently sent all my servants the prophets to them, day after day; yet they did not listen to me, or incline their ear, but stiffened their neck. They did worse than their fathers.

So you shall speak all these words to them, but they will not listen to you. You shall call to them, but they will not answer you. And you shall say to them, 'This is the nation that did not obey the voice of the Lord their God, and did not accept discipline; truth has perished; it is cut off from their lips. Cut off your hair and cast it away; raise a lamentation on the bare heights, for the Lord has rejected and forsaken the generation of his wrath.' For the sons of Judah have done evil in my sight, says the Lord; they have set their abominations in the house which is called by my name, to defile it. And they have built the high place of Topheth, which is in the valley of the son of Hinnom, to burn their sons and their daughters in the fire; which I did not command, nor did it come into my mind. Therefore, behold, the days are coming, says the Lord, when it will no more be called Topheth, or the valley of the son of Hinnom, but the valley of Slaughter: for they will bury in Topheth, because there is no room elsewhere. And the dead bodies of this people will be food for the birds of the air, and for the beasts of the earth; and none will frighten them away. And I will make to cease from the cities of Judah and from the streets of Jerusalem the voice of mirth and the voice of gladness, the voice of the bridegroom and the voice of the bride; for the land shall become a waste."

A Reading (Lesson) from the Letter of Paul to the Romans [4:13-25]

The promise to Abraham and his descendants, that they should inherit the world, did not come through the law but through the righteousness of faith. If it is the adherents of the law who are to be the heirs, faith is null and the promise is void. For the law brings wrath, but where there is no law there is no transgression. That is why it depends on faith, in order that the promise may rest on grace and be guaranteed to all his descendants—not only to the adherents of the law but also to those who share the faith of Abraham, for he is the father of us all, as it is written,

"I have made you the father of many nations"—in the presence of the God in whom he believed, who gives life to the dead and calls into existence the things that do not exist. In hope he believed against hope, that he should become the father of many nations; as he had been told, "So shall your descendants be." He did not weaken in faith when he considered his own body, which was as good as dead because he was about a hundred years old, or when he considered the barrenness of Sarah's womb. No distrust made him waiver concerning the promise of God, but he grew strong in his faith as he gave glory to God, fully convinced that God was able to do what he had promised. That is why his faith was "reckoned to him as righteousness." But the words, "it was reckoned to him," were written not for his sake alone, but for ours also. It will be reckoned to us who believe in him that raised from the dead Jesus our Lord, who was put to death for our trespasses and raised for our justification.

John 7:37-52   [page 73 above]

Wednesday

Psalm 119:97-120 [page 771]   ❖   *Psalm 81* [page 704], *Psalm 82* [page 705]

A Reading (Lesson) from the Book of Jeremiah [8:18—9:6]

My grief is beyond healing, my heart is sick within me. Hark, the cry of the daughter of my people from the length and breadth of the land: "Is the Lord not in Zion? Is her King not in her?" "Why have they provoked me to anger with their graven images, and with their foreign idols?" "The harvest is past, the summer is ended, and we are not saved." For the wound of the daughter of my people is my heart wounded, I mourn and dismay has taken hold on me.

Is there no balm in Gilead? Is there no physician there? Why then has the health of the daughter of my people not been restored? O that my head were waters, and my eyes a fountain of tears, that I might weep day and night for the slain of the daughter of my people! O that I had in the desert a wayfarers' lodging place, that I might leave my people and go away from them! For they are all adulterers, a company of treacherous men. They bend their tongue like a bow; falsehood and not truth has grown strong in the land; for they proceed from evil to evil, and they do not know me, says the Lord. Let every one beware of his neighbor, and put no trust in any brother; for every brother is a supplanter, and every neighbor goes about as a slanderer. Every one deceives his neighbor, and no one speaks the truth; they have taught their tongue to speak lies; they commit iniquity and are too weary to repent. Heaping oppression upon oppression, and deceit upon deceit, they refuse to know me, says the Lord.

A Reading (Lesson) from the Letter of Paul to the Romans [5:1-11]

Since we are justified by faith we have peace with God through our Lord Jesus Christ. Through him we have obtained access to this grace in which we stand, and we rejoice in our hope of sharing the glory of God. More than that, we rejoice in our sufferings, knowing that suffering produces endurance, and endurance produces character, and character produces hope, and hope does not disappoint us, because God's love has been poured into our hearts through the Holy Spirit which has been given to us. While we were still weak, at the right time Christ died for the ungodly. Why, one will hardly die for a righteous man—though perhaps for a good man one will dare even to die. But God shows his love for us in that while we were yet sinners Christ died for us. Since, therefore, we are now justified by his blood, much more shall we be saved by him from the wrath of God. For if while we were enemies we were reconciled to God by the death of his Son, much more, now that we are reconciled, shall we be saved by his life. Not only so, but we also rejoice in God through our Lord Jesus Christ, through whom we have now received our reconciliation.

A Reading (Lesson) from the Gospel according to John
[8:12-20]

Again Jesus spoke to the scribes and Pharisees saying "I am the light of the world; he who follows me will not walk in darkness, but will have the light of life." The Pharisees then said to him, "You are bearing witness to yourself; your testimony is not true." Jesus answered, "Even if I do bear witness to myself, my testimony is true, for I know whence I have come and whither I am going, but you do not know whence I come or whither I am going. You judge according to the flesh, I judge no one. Yet even if I do judge, my judgment is true, for it is not I alone that judge, but I and he who sent me. In your law it is written that the testimony of two men is true; I bear witness to myself, and the Father who sent me bears witness to me." They said to him therefore, "Where is your Father?" Jesus answered, "You know neither me nor my Father; if you knew me, you would know my Father also." These words he spoke in the treasury, as he taught in the temple; but no one arrested him, because his hour had not yet come.

Thursday

(*Psalm 83* [page 706]) *or* *Psalm 42* [page 643],
Psalm 43 [page 644] ❖ *Psalm 85* [page 708],
Psalm 86 [page 709]

A Reading (Lesson) from the Book of Jeremiah [10:11-24]

Thus shall you say to them: "The gods who did not make the heavens and the earth shall perish from the earth and from under the heavens." It is he who made the earth by his power, who established the world by his wisdom, and by his understanding stretched out the heavens. When he utters his voice there is a tumult of waters in the heavens, and he makes the mist rise from the ends of the earth. He makes lightnings for the rain, and he brings forth the wind from his storehouses. Every man is stupid and without knowledge; every goldsmith is put to shame by his idols; for his images are false, and there is no breath in them. They are worthless, a work of delusion; at the time of their punishment they shall perish. Not like these is he who is the portion of Jacob, for he is the one who formed all things, and Israel is the tribe of his inheritance; the Lord of hosts is his name. Gather up your bundle from the ground, O you who dwell under siege! For thus says the Lord: "Behold, I am slinging out the inhabitants of the land at this time, and I will bring distress on them, that they may feel it." Woe is me because of my hurt! My wound is grievous. But I said, "Truly this is an affliction, and I must bear it." My tent is destroyed, and all my cords are broken; my children have gone from me, and they are not; there is no one to spread my tent again, and to set up my curtains. For the shepherds are stupid, and do not inquire of the Lord; therefore they have not prospered, and all their flock is scattered. Hark, a rumor! Behold, it comes!—a great commotion out of the north country to make the cities of Judah a desolation, a lair of jackals. I know, O Lord, that the way of man is not in himself, that it is not in man who walks to direct his steps. Correct me, O Lord, but in just measure; not in thy anger, lest thou bring me to nothing.

A Reading (Lesson) from the Letter of Paul to the Romans [5:12-21]

As sin came into the world through one man and death through sin, and so death spread to all men because all men sinned—sin indeed was in the world before the law was given, but sin is not counted where there is no law. Yet death reigned from Adam to Moses, even over those whose sins were not like the transgression of Adam, who was a type of the one who was to come. But the free gift is not like the trespass. For if many died through one man's trespass, much more have the grace of God and the free gift in the grace of that one man Jesus Christ abounded for many. And the free gift is not like the effect of that one man's sin. For the judgment following one trespass brought condemnation, but the free gift following many trespasses brings justification. If, because of one man's trespass, death reigned through that one man, much more will those who receive the abundance of grace and the free gift of righteousness reign in life through the one man Jesus Christ. Then as one man's trespass led to condemnation for all men, so one mans act of righteousness leads to acquittal and life for all men. For as by one man's disobedience many were made sinners, so by one man's obedience many will be made righteous. Law came in, to increase the trespass; but where sin increased, grace abounded all the more, so that, as sin reigned in death, grace also might reign through righteousness to eternal life through Jesus Christ our Lord.

A Reading (Lesson) from the Gospel according to John
[8:21-32]

Again Jesus said to the scribes and Pharisees, "I go away, and you will seek me and die in your sin; where I am going, you cannot come." Then said the Jews, "Will he kill himself, since he says, 'Where I am going you cannot come'?" He said to them, "You are from below, I am from above; you are of this world, I am not of this world. I told you that you would die in your sins, for you will die in your sins unless you believe that I am he." They said to him, "Who are you?" Jesus said to them, "Even what I have told you from the beginning. I have much to say about you and much to judge; but he who sent me is true, and I declare to the world what I have heard from him." They did not understand that he spoke to them of the Father. So Jesus said, "When you have lifted up the Son of man, then you will know that I am he, and that I do nothing on my own authority but speak thus as the Father taught me. And he who sent me is with me; he has not left me alone, for I always do what is pleasing to him." As he spoke thus, many believed in him. Jesus then said to the Jews who had believed in him, "If you continue in my word, you are truly my disciples, and you will know the truth and the truth will make you free."

Friday

*Psalm 95** [page 724] & *Psalm 88* [page 712] ❖
Psalm 91 [page 719], *Psalm 92* [page 720]

A Reading (Lesson) from the Book of Jeremiah
[11:1-8, 14-20]

The word that came to Jeremiah from the Lord: "Hear the words of this covenant, and speak to the men of Judah and the inhabitants of Jerusalem. You shall say to them, Thus says the Lord, the God of Israel: Cursed be the man who does not heed the words of this covenant which I commanded your fathers when I brought them out of the land of Egypt, from the iron furnace, saying, Listen to my voice, and do all that I command you. So shall you be my people, and I will be your God, that I may perform the oath which I swore to your fathers, to give them a land flowing with milk and honey, as at this day." Then I answered, "So be it, Lord." And the Lord said to me, "Proclaim all these words in the cities of Judah, and in the streets of Jerusalem: Hear the words of this covenant and

*For the Invitatory

do them. For I solemnly warned your fathers when I brought them up out of the land of Egypt, warning them persistently, even to this day, saying, Obey my voice. Yet they did not obey or incline their ear, but every one walked in the stubbornness of his evil heart. Therefore I brought upon them all the words of this covenant, which I commanded them to do, but they did not. Therefore do not pray for this people, or lift up a cry or prayer on their behalf, for I will not listen when they call to me in the time of their trouble. What right has my beloved in my house, when she has done vile deeds? Can vows and sacrificial flesh avert your doom? Can you then exult? The Lord once called you, 'A green olive tree, fair with goodly fruit'; but with the roar of a great tempest he will set fire to it, and its branches will be consumed. The Lord of hosts, who planted you, has pronounced evil against you, because of the evil which the house of Israel and the house of Judah have done, provoking me to anger by burning incense to Ba'al." The Lord made it known to me and I knew; then thou didst show me their evil deeds. But I was like a gentle lamb led to the slaughter. I did not know it was against me they devised schemes, saying, "Let us destroy the tree with its fruit, let us cut him off from the land of the living, that his name be remembered no more." But, O Lord of hosts, who judgest righteously, who triest the heart and the mind, let me see thy vengeance upon them, for to thee have I committed my cause.

A Reading (Lesson) from the Letter of Paul to the Romans [6:1-11]

What shall we say then? Are we to continue in sin that grace may abound? By no means! How can we who died to sin still live in it? Do you not know that all of us who have been baptized into Christ Jesus were baptized into his death? We were buried therefore with him by baptism into death, so that as Christ was raised from the dead by the glory of the Father, we too might walk in newness of life.

For if we have been united with him in a death like his, we shall certainly be united with him in a resurrection like his. We know that our old self was crucified with him so that the sinful body might be destroyed, and we might no longer be enslaved to sin. For he who has died is freed from sin. But if we have died with Christ, we believe that we shall also live with him. For we know that Christ being raised from the dead will never die again; death no longer has dominion over him. The death he died he died to sin, once for all, but the life his lives he lives to God. So you also must consider yourselves dead to sin and alive to God in Christ Jesus.

A Reading (Lesson) from the Gospel according to John [8:33-47]

The Jews answered Jesus, "We are descendants of Abraham, and have never been in bondage to any one. How is it that you say, 'You will be made free'?" Jesus answered them, "Truly, truly, I say to you, every one who commits sin is a slave to sin. The slave does not continue in the house for ever; the son continues for ever. So if the Son makes you free, you will be free indeed. I know that you are descendants of Abraham; yet you seek to kill me, because my word finds no place in you. I speak of what I have seen with my Father, and you do what you have heard from your father." They answered him, "Abraham is our father." Jesus said to them, "If you were Abraham's children, you would do what Abraham did, but now you seek to kill me, a man who has told you the truth which I heard from God; this is not what Abraham did. You do what your father did." They said to him, "We were not born of fornication; we have one Father, even God." Jesus said to them, "If God were your Father, you would love me, for I proceeded and came forth from God; I came not of my own accord, but he sent me. Why do you not understand what I say? It is because you cannot bear to hear my word. You are of your father the devil, and your will is to do your father's desires. He was a murderer from the beginning, and has nothing to do with the truth, because there is no truth in him. When he lies, he speaks according to his own nature, for he is a liar and the father of lies. But, because I tell the truth, you do not believe me. Which of you convicts me of sin? If I tell the truth, why do you not believe me? He who is of God hears the words of God; the reason why you do not hear them is that you are not of God."

Saturday

Psalm 87 [page 711], *Psalm 90* [page 717] ❖
Psalm 136 [page 789]

A Reading (Lesson) from the Book of Jeremiah [13:1-11]

Thus said the Lord to me, "Go and buy a linen waistcloth, and put in on your loins, and do not dip it in water." So I bought a waistcloth according to the word of the Lord, and put it on my loins. And the word of the Lord came to me a second time, "Take the waistcloth which you have bought, which is upon your loins, and arise, go to the Eu-phra'tes, and hide it there in a cleft of the rock." So I went, and hid it by the Eu-phra'tes, as the Lord commanded me. And after many days the Lord said to me, "Arise, go the the Eu-phra'tes, and take from there the waistcloth which I commanded you to hide there." Then I went to the Eu-phra'tes, and dug, and I took the waistcloth from the place where I had hidden it. And behold, the waistcloth was spoiled; it was good for nothing. Then the word of the Lord came to me: "Thus says the Lord: Even so will I spoil the pride of Judah and the great pride of Jerusalem. This evil people, who refuse to hear my words, who stubbornly follow their own heart and have gone after other gods to serve them and worship them, shall be like this waistcloth, which is good for nothing. For as the waistcloth clings to the loins of a man, so I made the whole house of Israel and the whole house of Judah cling to me, says the Lord, that they might be for me a people, a name, a praise, and a glory, but they would not listen."

A Reading (Lesson) from the Letter of Paul to the Romans [6:12-23]

Let not sin reign in your mortal bodies, to make you obey their passions. Do not yield your members to sin as instruments of wickedness, but yield yourselves to God as men who have been brought from death to life, and your members to God as instruments of righteousness. For sin will have no dominion over you, since you are not under law but under grace. What then? Are we to sin because we are not under law but under grace? By no means! Do you not know that if you yield yourselves to any one as obedient slaves, you are slaves of the one whom you obey, either of sin, which leads to death, or of obedience, which leads to righteousness? But thanks be to God, that you who were once slaves of sin have become obedient from the heart to the standard of teaching to which you were committed, and, having been set free from sin, have become slaves of righteousness. I am speaking in human terms, because of your natural limitations. For just as you once yielded your members to impurity and to greater and greater iniquity, so now yield your members to righteousness for santification. When you were slaves of sin, you were free in regard to righteousness. But then what return did you get from the things of which you are now ashamed? The end of those things is death. But now that you have been set free from sin and have become slaves of God, the return you get is sanctification and its end, eternal life. For the wages of sin is death, but the free gift of God is eternal life in Christ Jesus our Lord.

A Reading (Lesson) from the Gospel according to John
[8:47-59]

Jesus said to the Jews, "He who is of God hears the words of God; the reason why you do not hear them is that you are not of God." The Jews answered him, "Are we not right in saying that you are a Samaritan and have a demon?" Jesus answered, "I have not a demon; but I honor my Father, and you dishonor me. Yet I do not seek my own glory; there is One who seeks it and he will be the judge. Truly, truly, I say to you, if anyone keeps my word, he will never see death." The Jews said to him, "Now we know that you have a demon. Abraham died, as did the prophets; and you say, 'If any one keeps my word, he will never taste death.' Are you greater than our father Abraham, who died? And the prophets died! Who do you claim to be?" Jesus answered, "If I glorify myself, my glory is nothing; it is my Father who glorifies me, of whom you say that he is your God. But you have not known him; I know him. If I said, I do not know him, I should be a liar like you; but I do know him and I keep his word. Your father Abraham rejoiced that he was to see my day; he saw it and was glad." The Jews then said to him, "You are not yet fifty years old, and have you seeen Abraham?" Jesus said to them, "Truly, truly, I say to you, before Abraham was, I am." So they took up stones to throw at him; but Jesus hid himself, and went out of the temple.

Week of 4 Lent

Sunday

Psalm 66 [page 673],   *Psalm 67* [page 675]   ❖
Psalm 19 [page 606],   *Psalm 46* [page 649]

A Reading (Lesson) from the Book of Jeremiah
[14:1-9,17-22]

The word of the Lord which came to Jeremiah concerning the drought: "Judah mourns and her gates languish; her people lament on the ground, and the cry of Jerusalem goes up. Her nobles send their servants for water; they come to the cisterns, they find no water, they return with their vessels empty; they are ashamed and confounded and cover their heads. Because of the ground which is dismayed, since there is no rain on the land, the farmers are ashamed, they cover their heads. Even the hind in the field forsakes her newborn calf because there is no grass. The wild asses stand on the bare heights, they pant for air like jackals; their eyes fail because there is no herbage. Though our iniquities testify against us, act, O Lord, for thy name's sake; for our backslidings are many, we have sinned against thee. O thou hope of Israel, its savior in time of trouble, why shouldst thou be like a stranger in the land, like a wayfarer who turns aside to tarry for a night? Why shouldst thou be like a man confused, like a mighty man who cannot save? Yet thou, O Lord, art in the midst of us, and we are called by thy name; leave us not. You shall say to them this word: 'Let my eyes run down with tears night and day, and let them not cease, for the virgin daughter of my people is smitten with a great wound, with a very grievous blow. If I go out into the field, behold, those slain by the sword! And if I enter the city, behold the diseases of famine! For both prophet and priest ply their trade through the land, and have no knowledge.'" Hast thou utterly rejected Judah? Does thy soul loathe Zion? Why hast thou smitten us so that there is not healing for us? We looked for peace, but not good came; for a time of healing, but behold, terror. We acknowledge our wickedness, O Lord, and the iniquity of our fathers, for we have sinned against thee. Do not spurn us, for thy name's sake; do not dishonor thy glorious throne; remember and do not break thy covenant with us. Are there any among the false gods of the nations that can bring rain? Or can the heavens give showers? Art thou not he, O Lord our God? We set our hope on thee, for thou doest all these things.

A Reading (Lesson) from the Letter of Paul to the Galatians [4:21—5:1]

Tell me, you who desire to be under law, do you not hear the law? For it is written that Abraham had two sons, one by a slave and one by a free woman. But the son of the slave was born according to the flesh, the son of the free woman through promise. Now this is an allegory: these women are two covenants. One is from Mount Sinai, bearing children for slavery; she is Hagar. Now Hagar is Mount Sinai in Arabia; she corresponds to the present Jerusalem, for she is in slavery with her children. But the Jerusalem above is free, and she is our mother. For it is written, "Rejoice, O barren one who does not bear; break forth and shout, you who are not in travail; for the children of the desolate one are many more than the children of her that is married." Now we, brethren, like Isaac, are children of promise. But as at that time he who was born according to the flesh persecuted him who was born according to the Spirit, so it is now. But what does the scripture say? "Cast out the slave and her son; for the son of the slave shall not inherit with the son of the free woman." So, brethren, we are not children of the slave but of the free woman. For freedom Christ has set us free; stand fast therefore, and do not submit again to a yoke of slavery.

A Reading (Lesson) from the Gospel according to Mark [8:11-21]

The Pharisees came and began to argue with Jesus, seeking from him a sign from heaven, to test him. And he sighed deeply in his spirit, and said, "Why does this generation seek a sign? Truly, I say to you, no sign shall be given to this generation." And he left them, and getting into the boat again he departed to the other side. Now they had forgotten to bring bread; and they had only one loaf with them in the boat. And he cautioned them, saying, "Take heed, beware of the leaven of the Pharisees and the leaven of Herod." And they discussed it with one another, saying, "We have no bread." And being aware of it, Jesus said to them, "Why do you discuss the fact that you have no bread? Do you not yet perceive or understand? Are your hearts hardened? Having eyes do you not see, and having ears do you not hear? And do you not remember? When I broke the five loaves for the five thousand, how many baskets full of broken pieces did you take up?" They said to him, "Twelve." "And the seven for the four thousand, how many baskets full of broken pieces did you take up?" And they said to him, "Seven." And he said to them, "Do you not yet understand?"

Monday

Psalm 89:1-18 [page 713]   ❖   *Psalm 89:19-52* [page 715]

A Reading (Lesson) from the Book of Jeremiah [16:10-21]

The word of the Lord came to me: "When you tell this people all these words, and they say to you, 'Why has the Lord pronounced all this great evil against us? What is our iniquity? What is the sin that we have committed against the Lord our God?' then you shall say to them: 'Because your fathers have forsaken me, says the Lord, and have gone after other gods and have served and worshiped them, and have forsaken me and have not kept my law, and because you have done worse than your fathers, for behold, every one of you follows his stubborn evil will, refusing to listen to me; therefore I will hurl you out of this land into a land which neither you nor your fathers have known, and there you shall serve other gods day and night, or I will show you no favor.' Therefore, behold, the days are coming, says the Lord, when it shall no longer be said, 'As the Lord lives who brought up the people of Israel out of the Land of Egypt,' but 'As the Lord lives who brought up the people of Israel out of the north country and out of all the countries where he had driven them.' For I will bring them back to their own land which I gave to their fathers. Behold, I am sending for many fishers, says the Lord, and they shall catch them; and afterwards I will send for many hunters, and they shall hunt them from every mountain and every hill, and out of the clefts of the rocks. For my eyes are upon all their ways; they are not hid from me, nor is their iniquity concealed from my eyes. And I will doubly recompense their iniquity and their sin, because they have polluted my land with the carcasses of their detestable idols and have filled my inheritance with their abominations." O Lord, my strength and my stronghold, my refuge in the day of trouble, to thee shall the nations come from the ends of the earth and say: "Our fathers have inherited nought but lies, worthless things in which there is no profit. Can man make for himself gods? Such are no gods!" "Therefore, behold, I will make them know, this once I will make them know my power and my might, and they shall know that my name is the Lord."

A Reading (Lesson) from the Letter of Paul to the Romans [7:1-12]

Do you not know, brethren—for I am speaking to those who know the law—that the law is binding on a person only during his life? Thus a married woman is bound by law to her husband as long as he lives; but if her husband dies she is discharged from the law concerning the husband. Accordingly, she will be called an adulteress if she lives with another man while her husband is alive. But if her husband dies she is free from that law, and if she marries another man she is not an adulteress. Likewise, my brethren, you have died to the law through the body of

Christ, so that you may belong to another, to him who has been raised from the dead in order that we may bear fruit for God. While we were living in the flesh, our sinful passions, aroused by the law, were at work in our members to bear fruit for death. But now we are discharged from the law, dead to that which held us captive, so that we serve not under the old written code but in the new life of the Spirit. What then shall we say? That the law is sin? By no means! Yet, if it had not been for the law, I should not have known sin. I should not have known what it is to covet if the law had not said, "You shall not covet." But sin, finding opportunity in the commandment, wrought in me all kinds of covetousness. Apart from the law sin lies dead. I was once alive apart from the law, but when the commandment came, sin revived and I died; the very commandment which promised life proved to be death to me. For sin, finding opportunity in the commandment, deceived me and by it killed me. So the law is holy, and the commandment is holy and just and good.

A Reading (Lesson) from the Gospel according to John
[6:1-15]

Jesus went to the other side of the Sea of Galilee, which is the Sea of Tibe′ri-as. And a multitude followed him, because they saw the signs which he did on those who were diseased. Jesus went up on the mountain, and there sat down with his disciples. Now the Passover, the feast of the Jews, was at hand. Lifting up his eyes, then, and seeing that a multitude was coming to him, Jesus said to Philip, "How are we to buy bread, so that these people may eat?" This he said to test him, for he himself knew what he would do. Philip answered him, "Two hundred denarii would not buy enough bread for each of them to get a little." One of his disciples, Andrew, Simon Peter's brother, said to him, "There is a lad here who has five barley loaves and two fish; but what are they among so many?" Jesus said, "Make the people sit down." Now there was much grass in the place; so the men sat down, in number about five thousand. Jesus then took the loaves, and when he had given thanks, he distributed them to those who were seated; so also the fish, as much as they wanted. And when they had eaten their fill, he told his disciples, "Gather up the fragments left over, that nothing may be lost." So they gathered them up and filled twelve baskets with fragments from the five barley loaves, left by those who had eaten. When the people saw the sign which he had done, they said, "This is indeed the prophet who is to come into the world!" Perceiving then that they were about to come and take him by force to make him king, Jesus withdrew again to the mountain by himself.

Tuesday

Psalm 97 [page 726], *Psalm 99* [page 728],
(Psalm 100 [page 729])   ❖   *Psalm 94* [page 722],
(Psalm 95 [page 724])

A Reading (Lesson) from the Book of Jeremiah [17:19-27]

Thus said the Lord to me: "Go and stand in the Benjamin Gate, by which the kings of Judah enter and by which they go out, and in all the gates of Jerusalem, and say: 'Hear the word of the Lord, you kings of Judah, and all Judah, and all the inhabitants of Jerusalem, who enter by these gates. Thus says the Lord: Take heed for the sake of your lives, and do not bear a burden on the sabbath day or bring it in by the gates of Jerusalem. And do not carry a burden out of your houses on the sabbath or do any work, but keep the sabbath day holy, as I commanded your fathers. Yet they did not listen or incline their ear, but stiffened their neck, that they might not hear and receive instruction. But if you listen to me, says the Lord, and bring in no burden by the gates of this city on the sabbath day, but keep the sabbath day holy and do no work on it, then there shall enter by the gates of this city kings who sit on the throne of David, riding in chariots and on horses, they and their princes, the men of Judah and the inhabitants of Jerusalem; and this city shall be inhabited for ever. And people shall come from the cities of Judah and the places round about Jerusalem, from the land of Benjamin, from the Shephe'lah, from the hill country, and from the Negeb, bringing burnt offerings and sacrifices, cereal offerings and frankincense, and bringing thank offerings to the house of the Lord. But if you do not listen to me, to keep the sabbath day holy, and not to bear a burden and enter by the gates of Jerusalem on the sabbath day, then I will kindle a fire in its gates, and it shall devour the palaces of Jerusalem and shall not be quenched."

A Reading (Lesson) from the Letter of Paul to the Romans [7:13-25]

Did that which is good, then, bring death to me? By no means! It was sin, working death in me through what is good, in order that sin might be shown to be sin, and through the commandment might become sinful beyond measure. We know that the law is spiritual; but I am carnal, sold under sin. I do not understand my own actions. For I do not do what I want, but I do the very thing I hate. Now if I do what I do not want, I agree that the law is good. So then it is no longer I that do it, but sin which dwells within me. For I know that nothing good dwells within me, that is, in my flesh. I can will what is right, but I cannot do it. For I do not do the good I want, but the evil I do not want is what I do. Now if I do what I do not want, it is no longer I that do it, but sin which dwells within me. So I find it to be a law that when I want to do right, evil lies close at hand. For I delight in the law of God, in my inmost self, but I see in my members another law at war with the law of my mind and making me captive to the law of sin which dwells in my members.

Wretched man that I am! Who will deliver me from this body of death? Thanks be to God through Jesus Christ our Lord! So then, I of myself serve the law of God with my mind, but with my flesh I serve the law of sin.

John 6:15-27   [page 104 above]

Wednesday

Psalm 101 [page 730],
Psalm 109:1-4(5-19)20-30 [page 750]   ❖
Psalm 119:121-144 [page 773]

A Reading (Lesson) from the Book of Jeremiah [18:1-11]

The word that came to Jeremiah from the Lord: "Arise, and go down to the potter's house, and there I will let you hear my words." So I went down to the potter's house, and there he was working at his wheel. And the vessel he was making of clay was spoiled in the potter's hand, and he reworked it into another vessel, as it seemed good to the potter to do. Then the word of the Lord came to me: "O house of Israel, can I not do with you as this potter has done? says the Lord. Behold, like the clay in the potter's hand, so are you in my hand, O house of Israel. If at any time I declare concerning a nation or a kingdom, that I will pluck up and break down and destroy it, and if that nation, concerning which I have spoken, turns from its evil, I will repent of the evil that I intended to do to it. And if at any time I declare concerning a nation or a kingdom that I will build and plant it, and if it does evil in my sight, not listening to my voice, then I will repent of the good which I had intended to do to it. Now, therefore, say to the men of Judah and the inhabitants of Jerusalem: 'Thus says the Lord, Behold I am shaping evil against you. Return, every one from his evil way, and amend your ways and your doings.'"

*A Reading (Lesson) from the Letter of Paul
to the Romans* [8:1-11]

There is now no condemnation for those who are in Christ
Jesus. For the law of the Spirit of life in Christ Jesus has set
me free from the law of sin and death. For God has done
what the law, weakened by the flesh, could not do: sending
his own Son in the likeness of sinful flesh and for sin, he
condemned sin in the flesh, in order that the just
requirement of the law might be fulfilled in us, who walk
not according to the flesh but according to the Spirit. For
those who live according to the flesh set their minds on the
things of the flesh, but those who live according to the
Spirit set their minds on the things of the Spirit. To set the
mind on the flesh is death, but to set the mind on the Spirit
is life and peace. For the mind that is set on the flesh is
hostile to God; it does not submit to God's law, indeed it
cannot; and those who are in the flesh cannot please God.
But you are not in the flesh, you are in the Spirit, if in fact
the Spirit of God dwells in you. Any one who does not
have the Spirit of Christ does not belong to him. But if
Christ is in you, although your bodies are dead because of
sin, your spirits are alive because of righteousness. If the
Spirit of him who raised Jesus from the dead dwells in you,
he who raised Christ Jesus from the dead will give life to
your mortal bodies also through his Spirit which dwells in
you.

A Reading (Lesson) from the Gospel according to John
[6:27-40]

Jesus said to the people, "Do not labor for the food which
perishes, but for the food which endures to eternal life,
which the Son of man will give to you; for on him has God
the Father set his seal." Then they said to him, "What must
we do, to be doing the works of God?" Jesus answered
them, "This is the work of God, that you believe in him
whom he has sent." So they said to him, "Then what sign

do you do, that we may see, and believe you? What work do you perform? Our fathers ate manna in the wilderness; as it is written, 'He gave them bread from heaven to eat.'" Jesus then said to them, "Truly, truly, I say to you, it was not Moses who gave you the bread from heaven; my Father gives you the true bread from heaven. For the bread of God is that which comes down from heaven and gives life to the world." They said to him, "Lord, give us this bread always." Jesus said to them, "I am the bread of life; he who comes to me shall not hunger, and he who believes in me shall never thirst. But I said to you that you have seen me and yet do not believe. All that the Father gives me will come to me; and him who comes to me I will not cast out. For I have come down from heaven, not to do my own will, but the will of him who sent me; and this is the will of him who sent me, that I should lose nothing of all that he has given me, but raise it up at the last day. For this is the will of my Father, that every one who sees the Son and believes in him should have eternal life; and I will raise him up at the last day."

Thursday

Psalm 69:1-23(24-30)31-38 [page 679] ❖
Psalm 73 [page 687]

A Reading (Lesson) from the Book of Jeremiah [22:13-23]

"Woe to him who builds his house by unrighteousness, and his upper rooms by injustice; who makes his neighbor serve him for nothing, and does not give him his wages; who says, 'I will build myself a great house with spacious upper rooms,' and cuts out windows for it, paneling it with cedar, and painting it with vermilion. Do you think you are a king because you compete in cedar? Did not your father eat and drink and do justice and righteousness? Then it was well with him. He judged the cause of the poor and needy; then it was well. Is not this to know me? says the Lord. But you have eyes and heart only for your dishonest gain, for shedding innocent blood, and for practicing oppression and violence." Therefore thus says the Lord concerning Jehoi'akim the son of Josi'ah, king of Judah: "They shall not lament for him, saying, 'Ah my brother!' or 'Ah sister!' They shall not lament for him, saying, 'Ah lord!' or 'Ah his majesty!' With the burial of a ass he shall be buried, dragged and cast forth beyond the gates of Jerusalem." "Go up to Lebanon, and cry out, and lift up your voice in Bashan; cry from Ab'arim, for all you lovers are destroyed. I spoke to you in your prosperity, bu you said, 'I will not listen.' This has been your way from your youth, that you have not obeyed my voice. The wind shall shepherd all our shepherds, and your lovers shall go into captivity; then you will be ashamed and confounded because of all your wickedness. O inhabitant of Lebanon, nested among the cedars, how you will groan when pangs come upon you, pain as of a woman in travail!"

A Reading (Lesson) from the Letter of Paul to the Romans [8:12-27]

So then, brethren, we are debtors, not to the flesh, to live according to the flesh—for if you live according to the flesh you will die, but if by the Spirit you put to death the deeds of the body you will live. For all who are led by the Spirit of God are sons of God. For you did not receive the spirit of slavery to fall back into fear, but you have received the spirit of sonship. When we cry, "Abba! Father!" it is the Spirit himself bearing witness with our spirit that we are children of God, and if children, then heirs, heirs of God and fellow heirs with Christ, provided we suffer with him in order that we may also be glorified with him. I consider that the sufferings of this present time are not worth comparing with the glory that is to be revealed to us. For the creation waits with eager longing for the revealing of the sons of God; for the creation was subjected to futility, not of its own will but by the will of him who subjected it in hope; because the creation itself will be set free from its bondage to decay and obtain the glorious liberty of the children of God. We know that the whole creation has been groaning in travail together until now; and not only the creation, but we ourselves, who have the first fruits of the Spirit, groan inwardly as we wait for adoption as sons, the redemption of our bodies. For in this hope we were saved. Now hope that is seen is not hope. For who hopes for what he sees? But if we hope for what we do not see, we wait for it with patience. Likewise the Spirit helps us in our weakness; for we do not know how to pray as we ought, but the Spirit himself intercedes for us with sighs too deep for words. And he who searches the hearts of men knows what is the mind of the Spirit, because the Spirit intercedes for the saints according to the will of God.

A Reading (Lesson) from the Gospel according to John
[6:41-51]

The Jews murmured at Jesus, because he said, "I am the bread which came down from heaven." They said, "Is not this Jesus, the son of Joseph, whose father and mother we know? How does he now say, 'I have come down from heaven'?" Jesus answered them, "Do not murmur among yourselves. No one can come to me unless the Father who sent me draws him; and I will raise him up at the last day. It is written in the prophets, 'And they shall all be taught by God.' Every one who has heard and learned from the Father comes to me. Not that any one has seen the Father except him who is from God; he has seen the Father. Truly, truly, I say to you, he who believes has eternal life. I am the bread of life. Your fathers ate the manna in the wilderness, and they died. This is the bread which comes down from heaven, that a man may eat of it and not die. I am the living bread which came down from heaven; if any one eats of this bread, he will live for ever; and the bread which I shall give for the life of the world is my flesh."

Friday

Psalm 95* [page 724]   &   *Psalm 102* [page 731]   ❖
Psalm 107:1-32 [page 746]

A Reading (Lesson) from the Book of Jeremiah [23:1-8]

"Woe to the shepherds who destroy and scatter the sheep o
my pasture!" says the Lord. Therefore thus says the Lord,
the God of Israel, concerning the shepherds who care for
my people: "You have scattered my flock, and have driven
them away, and you have not attended to them. Behold, I
will attend to you for your evil doings, says the Lord. The
I will gather the remnant of my flock out of all the
countries where I have driven them, and I will bring them
back to their fold, and they shall be fruitful and multiply. I
will set shepherds over them who will care for them, and
they shall fear no more, nor be dismayed, neither shall any
be missing, says the Lord. Behold, the days are coming,
says the Lord, when I will raise up for David a righteous
Branch, and he shall reign as king and deal wisely, and
shall execute justice and righteousness in the land. In his
days Judah will be saved, and Israel will dwell securely.
And this is the name by which he will be called: 'The Lord
is our righteousness.' Therefore, behold, the days are
coming, says the Lord, when men shall no longer say, 'As
the Lord lives who brought up the people of Israel out of
the land of Egypt,' but 'As the Lord lives who brought up
and led the descendants of the house of Israel out of the
north country and out of all the countries where he had
driven them.' Then they shall dwell in their own land."

*For the Invitatory

*A Reading (Lesson) from the Letter of Paul
to the Romans* [8:28-39]

We know that in everything God works for good with
those who love him, who are called according to his
purpose. For those whom he foreknew he also predestined
to be conformed to the image of his Son, in order that he
might be the first-born among many brethren. And those
whom he predestined he also called; and those whom he
called he also justified; and those whom he justified he also
glorified. What then shall we say to this? If God is for us,
who is against us? He who did not spare his own Son but
gave him up for us all, will he not also give us all things
with him? Who shall bring any charge against God's elect?
It is God who justifies; who is to condemn? Is it Christ
Jesus, who died, yes, who was raised from the dead, who is
at the right hand of God, who indeed intercedes for us?
Who shall separate us from the love of Christ? Shall
tribulation, or distress, or persecution, or famine, or
nakedness, or peril, or sword? As it is written, "For thy
sake we are being killed all the day long; we are regarded
as sheep to be slaughtered." No, in all those things we are
more than conquerors through him who loved us. For I am
sure that neither death, nor life, nor angels, nor
principalities, nor things present, nor things to come, nor
powers, nor height, nor depth, nor anything else in all
creation will be able to separate us from the love of God in
Christ Jesus our Lord.

A Reading (Lesson) from the Gospel according to John
[6:52-59]

The Jews disputed among themselves, saying, "How can
this man give us his flesh to eat?" So Jesus said to them,
"Truly, truly, I say to you, unless you eat the flesh of the Son
of man and drink his blood, you have no life in you; he
who eats my flesh and drinks my blood has eternal life, and
I will raise him up at the last day. For my flesh is food

indeed, and my blood is drink indeed. He who eats my flesh and drinks my blood abides in me, and I in him. As the living Father sent me, and I live because of the Father, so he who eats me will live because of me. This is the bread which came down from heaven, not such as the fathers ate and died; he who eats this bread will live ever." This he said in the synagogue, as he taught at Caper'na-um.

Saturday

Psalm 107:33-43 [page 748],
Psalm 108:1-6(7-13) [page 749] ❖ *Psalm 33* [page 626]

A Reading (Lesson) from the Book of Jeremiah [23:9-15]

Concerning the prophets: My heart is broken within me, all my bones shake; I am like a drunken man, like a man overcome by wine, because of the Lord and because of his holy words. For the land is full of adulterers; because of the curse the land mourns, and the pastures of the wilderness are dried up. Their course is evil, and their might is not right. "Both prophet and priest are ungodly; even in my house I have found their wickedness, says the Lord. Therefore their way shall be to them like slippery paths in the darkness, into which they shall be driven and fall; for I will bring evil upon them in the year of their punishment, says the Lord. In the prophets of Samar'ia I saw an unsavory thing: they prophesied by Ba'al and led my people Israel astray. But in the prophets of Jerusalem I have seen a horrible thing: they commit adultery and walk in lies; they strengthen the hands of evildoers, so that no one turns from his wickedness; all of them have become like Sodom to me, and its inhabitants like Gomor'rah." Therefore thus says the Lord of hosts concerning the prophets: "Behold, I will feed them with wormwood, and give them poisoned water to drink: for from the prophets of Jerusalem ungodliness has gone forth into all the land."

A Reading (Lesson) from the Letter of Paul to the Romans [9:1-18]

I am speaking the truth in Christ, I am not lying; my conscience bears me witness in the Holy Spirit, that I have great sorrow and unceasing anguish in my heart. For I could wish that I myself were accursed and cut off from Christ for the sake of my brethren, my kinsmen by race. They are Israelites, and to them belong the sonship, the glory, the convenants, the giving of the law, the worship, and the promises; to them belong the patriarchs, and of their race, according to the flesh, is the Christ. God who is over all be blessed for ever. Amen. But it is not as though the word of God had failed. For not all who are descended from Israel belong to Israel, and not all are children of Abraham because they are his descendants; but "Through Isaac shall your descendants be named." This means that it is not the children of the flesh who are the children of God, but the children of the promise are reckoned as descendants. For this is what the promise said, "About this time I will return and Sarah shall have a son." And not only so, but also when Rebecca had conceived children by one man, our forefather Isaac, though they were not yet born and had done nothing either good or bad, in order that God's purpose of election might continue, not because of works but because of his call, she was told, "The elder will serve the younger." As it is written, "Jacob I loved, but Esau I hated." What shall we say then? Is there injustice on God's part? By no means! For he says to Moses, "I will have mercy on whom I have mercy, and I will have compassion on whom I have compassion." So it depends not upon man's will or exertion, but upon God's mercy. For the scripture says to Pharoah, "I have raised you up for the very purpose of showing my power in you, so that my name may be proclaimed in all the earth." So then he has mercy upon whomever he wills, and he hardens the heart of whomever he wills.

A Reading (Lesson) from the Gospel according to John
[6:60-71]

Many of Jesus' disciples, when they heard him say, "He who eats this bread will live forever," said, "This is a hard saying; who can listen to it?" But Jesus, knowing in himself that his disciples murmured at it, said to them, "Do you take offense at this? Then what if you were to see the Son of man ascending where he was before? It is the spirit that gives life, the flesh is of no avail; the words that have spoken to you are spirit and life. But there are some of you that do not believe." For Jesus knew from the first who those were that did not believe, and who it was that would betray him. And he said, "This is why I told you that no one can come to me unless it is granted him by the Father." After this many of his disciples drew back and no longer went about with him. Jesus said to the twelve, "Do you also wish to go away?" Simon Peter answered him, "Lord, to whom shall we go? You have the words of eternal life; and we have believed, and have come to know, that you are the Holy One of God." Jesus answered them, "Did I not choose you, the twelve, and one of you is a devil?" He spoke of Judas the son of Simon Iscariot, for he, one of the twelve, was to betray him.

Week of 5 Lent

Sunday

Psalm 118 [page 760] ❖ *Psalm 145* [page 801]

A Reading (Lesson) from the Book of Jeremiah [23:16-32]

Thus says the Lord of hosts: "Do not listen to the words of the prophets who prophesy to you, filling you with vain hopes; they speak visions of their own minds, not from the mouth of the Lord. They say continually to those who despise the word of the Lord, 'It shall be well with you'; and to every one who stubbornly follows his own heart, they say, 'No evil shall come upon you.'" For who among them has stood in the council of the Lord to perceive and to hear his word, or who has given heed to his word and listened? Behold, the storm of the Lord! Wrath has gone forth, a whirling tempest; it will burst upon the head of the wicked. The anger of the Lord will not turn back until he has executed and accomplished the intents of his mind. In the latter days you will understand it clearly. "I did not send the prophets, yet they ran; I did not speak to them, yet they prophesied. But if they had stood in my council, then they would have proclaimed my words to my people, and they would have turned them from their evil way, and from the evil of their doings. Am I a God at hand, says the Lord, and not a God afar off? Can a man hide himself in secret places so that I cannot see him? says the Lord. Do I not fill heaven and earth? says the Lord. I have heard what the prophets have said who prophesy lies in my name, saying, 'I have dreamed, I have dreamed!' How long shall there be lies in the heart of the prophets who prophesy lies, and who prophesy the deceit of their own heart, who think to make my people forget my name by their dreams which they tell one another, even as their fathers forgot my name for Ba'al? Let the prophet who has a dream tell the dream, but let him who has my word speak my word faithfully. What has straw in common with wheat? says the Lord. Is not my word like fire, says the Lord, and like a hammer which breaks the rock in pieces? Therefore, behold, I am against the prophets, says the Lord, who steal my words from one another. Behold, I am against the prophets, says the Lord, who use their tongues and say, 'Says the Lord.' Behold, I am against those who prophesy lying dreams, says the Lord, and who tell them and lead my people astray by their lies and their recklessness, when I did not send them or charge them; so they do not profit this people at all, says the Lord."

A Reading (Lesson) from the First Letter of Paul to the Corinthians [9:19-27]

Though I am free from all men, I have made myself a slave to all, that I might win the more. To the Jews I became as a Jew, in order to win Jews; to those under the law I became as one under the law—though not being myself under the law—that I might win those under the law. To those outside the law I became as one outside the law—not being without law toward God but under the law of Christ—that I might win those outside the law. To the weak I became weak, that I might win the weak. I have become all things to all men, that I might by all means save some. I do it all for the sake of the gospel, that I may share in its blessings. Do you not know that in a race all the runners compete, but only one receives the prize? So run that you may obtain it. Every athlete exercises self-control in all things. They do it to receive a perishable wreath, but we an imperishable. Well, I do not run aimlessly, I do not box as one beating the air; but I pommel my body and subdue it, lest after preaching to others I myself should be disqualified.

A Reading (Lesson) from the Gospel according to Mark [8:31—9:1]

Jesus began to teach his disciples that the Son of man must suffer many things, and be rejected by the elders and the chief priests and the scribes, and be killed, and after three days rise again. And he said this plainly. And Peter took him, and began to rebuke him. But turning and seeing his disciples, he rebuked Peter, and said, "Get behind me, Satan! For you are not on the side of God, but of men." And he called to him the multitude with his disciples, and said to them, "If any man would come after me, let him deny himself and take up his cross and follow me. For whoever would save his life will lose it; and whoever loses his life for my sake and the gospel's will save it. For what does it profit a man, to gain the whole world and forfeit his life? For what can a man give in return for his life? For whoever is ashamed of me and of my words in this adulterous and sinful generation, of him will the Son of man also be ashamed, when he comes in the glory of his Father with the holy angels." And he said to them, "Truly, I say to you, there are some standing here who will not taste death before they see that the kingdom of God has come with power."

Monday

Psalm 31 [page 622] ❖ *Psalm 35* [page 629]

A Reading (Lesson) from the Book of Jeremiah [24:1-10]

After Nebuchadrez'zar king of Babylon had taken into exile from Jerusalem Jeconi'ah the son of Jehoi'akim, king of Judah, together with the princes of Judah, the craftsmen, and the smiths, and had brought them to Babylon, the Lord showed me this vision: Behold, two baskets of figs placed before the temple of the Lord. One basket had very good figs, like first-ripe figs, but the other basket had very bad figs, so bad that they could not be eaten. And the Lord said to me, "What do you see, Jeremiah?" I said, "Figs, the good figs very good, and the bad figs very bad, so bad that they cannot be eaten." Then the word of the Lord came to me: "Thus says the Lord, the God of Israel: Like these good figs, so I will regard as good the exiles from Judah, whom I have sent away from this place to the land of the Chalde'ans. I will set my eyes upon them for good, and I will bring them back to this land. I will build them up, and not tear them down; I will plant them, and not uproot them. I will give them a heart to know that I am the Lord; and they shall be my people and I will be their God, for they shall return to me with their whole heart. But thus says the Lord: Like the bad figs which are so bad they cannot be eaten, so will I treat Zedeki'ah the king of Judah, his princes, the remnant of Jerusalem who remain in this land, and those who dwell in the land of Egypt. I will make them a horror to all the kingdoms of the earth, to be a reproach, a byword, a taunt, and a curse in all the places where I shall drive them. And I will send sword, famine, and pestilence upon them, until they shall be utterly destroyed from the land which I gave to them and their fathers."

A Reading (Lesson) from the Letter of Paul to the Romans [9:19-33]

You will say to me then, "Why does he still find fault? For who can resist his will?" But who are you, a man, to answer back to God? Will what is molded say to its molder, "Why have you made me thus?" Has the potter no right over the clay, to make out of the same lump one vessel for beauty and another for menial use? What if God, desiring to show his wrath and to make known his power, has endured with much patience the vessels of wrath made for destruction, in order to make known the riches of his glory for the vessels of mercy, which he has prepared beforehand for glory, even us whom he has called, not from the Jews only but also from the Gentiles? As indeed he says in Hose'a, "Those who were not my people I will call 'my people,' and her who was not beloved I will call 'my beloved.'" "And in the very place where it was said to them, 'You are not my people,' they will be called 'sons of the living God.'" And Isaiah cries out concerning Israel: "Though the number of the sons of Israel are as the sand of the sea, only a remnant of them will be saved; for the Lord will execute his sentence upon the earth with rigor and dispatch." And as Isaiah predicted, "If the Lord of hosts had not left us children, we would have fared like Sodom and been made like Gomor'rah." What shall we say, then? That Gentiles who did not pursue righteousness have attained it, that is, righteousness through faith; but that Israel who pursued the righteousness which is based on law did not succeed in fulfilling that law. Why? Because they did not pursue it through faith, but as if it were based on works. They have stumbled over the stumbling stone, as it is written, "Behold, I am laying in Zion a stone that will make men stumble, a rock that will make them fall; and he who believes in him will not be put to shame."

A Reading (Lesson) from the Gospel according to John [9:1-17]

As he passed by, Jesus saw a man blind from his birth. And his disciples asked him, "Rabbi, who sinned, this man or his parents, that he was born blind? Jesus answered, "It was not that this man sinned, or his parents, but that the works of God might be made manifest in him. We must work the works of him who sent me, while it is day; night comes, when no one can work. As long as I am in the world, I am the light of the world." As he said this, he spat on the ground and made clay of the spittle and anointed the man's eyes with the clay, saying to him, "Go, wash in the pool of Silo'am" (which means Sent). So he went and washed and came back seeing. The neighbors and those who had seen him before as a beggar, said, "Is not this the man who used to sit and beg?" Some said, "It is he"; others said, "No, but he is like him." He said, "I am the man." They said to him, "Then how were your eyes opened?" He answered, "The man called Jesus made clay and anointed my eyes and said to me, 'Go to Silo'am and wash'; so I went and washed and received my sight." They said to him," Where is he?" He said, "I do not know." They brought to the Pharisees the man who had formerly been blind. Now it was a sabbath day when Jesus made the clay and opened his eyes. The Pharisees again asked him how he had received his sight. And he said to them, "He

put clay on my eyes, and I washed, and I see." Some of the
Pharisees said, "This man is not from God, for he does not
keep the sabbath." But others said, "How can a man who
is a sinner do such signs?" There was a division among
them. So they again said to the blind man, "What do you
say about him, since he has opened your eyes?" He said,
"He is a prophet."

Tuesday

(Psalm 120 [page 778]), *Psalm 121* [page 779],
Psalm 122 [page 779], *Psalm 123* [page 780] ❖
Psalm 124 [page 781], *Psalm 125* [page 781],
Psalm 126 [page 782], *(Psalm 127* [page 782])

A Reading (Lesson) from the Book of Jeremiah [25:8-17]

"Thus says the Lord of hosts: Because you have not obeyed
my words, behold, I will send for all the tribes of the north
says the Lord, and for Nebuchadrez'zar the king of
Babylon, my servant, and I will bring them against this
land and its inhabitants, and against all these nations
round about; I will utterly destroy them, and make them a
horror, a hissing, and an everlasting reproach. Moreover, I
will banish from them the voice of mirth and the voice of
gladness, the voice of the bridegroom and the voice of the
bride, the grinding of the millstones and the light of the
lamp. This whole land shall become a ruin and a waste,
and these nations shall serve the king of Babylon seventy
years. Then after seventy years are completed, I will punish
the king of Babylon and that nation, the land of the
Chalde'ans, for their iniquity, says the Lord, making the
land an everlasting waste. I will bring upon that land all
the words which I have uttered against it, everything
written in this book, which Jeremiah prophesied against
all the nations. For many nations and great kings shall
make slaves even of them; and I will recompense them

according to their deeds and the work of their hands."
Thus the Lord, the God of Israel, said to me: "Take from
my hand this cup of the wine of wrath, and make all the
nations to whom I send you drink it. They shall drink and
stagger and be crazed because of the sword which I am
sending among them." So I took the cup from the Lord's
hand, and made all the nations to whom the Lord sent me
drink it.

*A Reading (Lesson) from the Letter of Paul
to the Romans* [10:1-13]

Brethren, my heart's desire and prayer to God for them is
that they may be saved. I bear them witness that they have
a zeal for God, but it is not enlightened. For, being
ignorant of the righteousness that comes from God, and
seeking to establish their own, they did not submit to
God's righteousness. For Christ is the end of the law, that
every one who has faith may be justified. Moses writes that
the man who practices the righteousness which is based on
the law shall live by it. But the righteousness based on faith
says, Do not say in your heart, "Who will ascend into
heaven?" (that is, to bring Christ down) or "Who will
descend into the abyss? (that is, to bring Christ up from the
dead). But what does it say? The word is near you, on your
lips and in your heart (that is, the word of faith which we
preach); because, if you confess with your lips that Jesus is
Lord and believe in your heart that God raised him from
the dead, you will be saved. For man believes with his
heart and so is justified, and he confesses with his lips and
so is saved. The scripture says, "No one who believes in
him will be put to shame." For there is no distinction
between Jew and Greek; the same Lord is Lord of all and
bestows his riches upon all who call upon him. For, "every
one who calls upon the name of the Lord will be saved."

A Reading (Lesson) from the Gospel according to John
[9:18-41]

The Jews did not believe that the man had been blind and
had received his sight, until they called the parents of the
man who had received his sight, and asked them, "Is this
your son, who you say was born blind? How then does he
now see?" His parents answered, "We know that this is
our son, and that he was born blind; but how he now sees
we do not know, nor do we know who opened his eyes.
Ask him; he is of age, he will speak for himself." His
parents said this because they feared the Jews, for the Jews
had already agreed that if any one should confess him to be
Christ, he was to be put out of the synagogue. Therefore
his parents said, "He is of age, ask him." So for the second
time they called the man who had been blind, and said to
him, "Give God the praise; we know that this man is a
sinner." He answered, "Whether he is a sinner, I do not
know; one thing I know, that though I was blind, now I
see." They said to him, "What did he do to you? How did
he open your eyes?" He answered them, "I have told you
already, and you would not listen. Why do you want to
hear it again? Do you too want to become his disciples?"
And they reviled him, saying, "You are his disciple, but we
are disciples of Moses. We know that God has spoken to
Moses, but as for this man, we do not know where he
comes from." The man answered, "Why, this is a marvel!
You do not know where he comes from, and yet he opened
my eyes. We know that God does not listen to sinners, but
if any one is a worshiper of God and does his will, God
listens to him. Never since the world began has it been
heard that any one opened the eyes of a man born blind. If
this man were not from God, he could do nothing." They
answered him, "You were born in utter sin, and would you
teach us?" And they cast him out. Jesus heard that they
had cast him out, and having found him he said, "Do you
believe in the Son of man?" He answered, "And who is he,
sir, that I may believe in him?" Jesus said to him, "You

have seen him, and it is he who speaks to you." He said, "Lord, I believe"; and he worshiped him. Jesus said, "For judgment I came into this world, that those who do not see may see, and that those who see may become blind." Some of the Pharisees near him heard this, and they said to him, "Are we also blind?" Jesus said to them, "If you were blind, you would have no guilt; but now that you say, 'We see,' your guilt remains."

Wednesday

Psalm 119:145-176 [page 775] ❖ *Psalm 128* [page 783], *Psalm 129* [page 784], *Psalm 130* [page 784]

A Reading (Lesson) from the Book of Jeremiah [25:30-38]

"You, therefore, shall prophesy against them all these words, and say to them: 'The Lord will roar from on high, and from his holy habitation utter his voice; he will roar mightily against his fold, and shout, like those who tread grapes, against all the inhabitants of the earth. The clamor will resound to the ends of the earth, for the Lord has an indictment against the nations; he is entering into judgment with all flesh, and the wicked he will put to the sword, says the Lord.' Thus says the Lord of hosts: Behold, evil is going forth from nation to nation, and a great tempest is stirring from the farthest parts of the earth! And those slain by the Lord on that day shall extend from one end of the earth to the other. They shall not be lamented, or gathered, or buried; they shall be dung on the surface of the ground. Wail, you shepherds, and cry, and roll in ashes, you lords of the flock, for the days of your slaughter and dispersion have come, and you shall fall like choice rams. No refuge will remain for the shepherds, nor escape for the lords of the flock. Hark, the cry of the shepherds, and the wail of the lords of the flock! For the Lord is despoiling their pasture, and the peaceful folds are devastated, because of the fierce anger of the Lord. Like a lion he has left his covert, for their land has become a waste because of the sword of the oppressor, and because of his fierce anger."

A Reading (Lesson) from the Letter of Paul to the Romans [10:14-21]

How are men to call upon him in whom they have not believed? And how are they to believe in him of whom they have never heard? And how are they to hear without a preacher? And how can men preach unless they are sent? As it is written, "How beautiful are the feet of those who preach good news!" But they have not all obeyed the gospel; for Isaiah says, "Lord, who has believed what he has heard from us?" So faith comes from what is heard, and what is heard comes by the preaching of Christ. But I ask, have they not heard? Indeed they have; for "Their voice has gone out to all the earth, and their words to the ends of the world." Again I ask, did Israel not understand? First Moses says, "I will make you jealous of those who are not a nation; with a foolish nation I will make you angry." Then Isaiah is so bold as to say, "I have been found by those who did not seek me; I have shown myself to those who did not ask for me." But of Israel he says, "All day long I have held out my hands to a disobedient and contrary people."

A Reading (Lesson) from the Gospel according to John [10:1-18]

Jesus said to the Pharisees, "Truly, truly, I say to you, he who does not enter the sheepfold by the door but climbs in by another way, that man is a thief and a robber; but he who enters by the door is the shepherd of the sheep. To him the gatekeeper opens; the sheep hear his voice, and he calls his own sheep by name and leads them out. When he has brought out all his own, he goes before them, and the sheep follow him, for they know his voice. A stranger they will not follow, but they will flee from him, for they do not know the voice of strangers." This figure Jesus used with them, but they did not understand what he was saying to them. So Jesus again said to them, "Truly, truly, I say to you, I am the door of the sheep. All who came before me are thieves and robbers; but the sheep did not heed them. I am the door; if any one enters by me, he will be saved, and will go in and out and find pasture. The thief comes only to steal and kill and destroy; I came that they may have life, and have it abundantly. I am the good shepherd. The good shepherd lays down his life for the sheep. He who is a hireling and not a shepherd, whose own the sheep are not, sees the wolf coming and leaves the sheep and flees; and the wolf snatches them and scatters them. He flees because he is a hireling and cares nothing for the sheep. I am the good shepherd; I know my own and my own know me, as the Father knows me and I know the Father; and I lay down my life for the sheep. And I have other sheep, that are not of this fold; I must bring them also, and they will heed my voice. So there shall be one flock, one shepherd. For this reason the Father loves me, because I lay down my life, that I may take it again. No one takes it from me, but I lay it down of my own accord. I have power to lay it down, and I have power to take it again; this charge I have received from my Father."

Thursday

Psalm 131 [page 785], *Psalm 132* [page 785], *(Psalm 133* [page 787])* ❖ *Psalm 140* [page 796], *Psalm 142* [page 798]

A Reading (Lesson) from the Book of Jeremiah [26:1-16]

In the beginning of the reign of Jehoi′akim the son of

Josi'ah, king of Judah, this word came from the Lord, "Thus says the Lord: Stand in the court of the Lord's house, and speak to all the cities of Judah which come to worship in the house of the Lord all the words that I command you to speak to them; do not hold back a word. It may be they will listen, and every one turn from his evil way, that I may repent of the evil which I intend to do to them because of their evil doings. You shall say to them, 'Thus says the Lord: If you will not listen to me, to walk in my law which I have set before you, and to heed the words of my servants the prophets whom I send to you urgently, though you have not heeded, then I will make this house like Shiloh, and I will make this city a curse for all the nations of the earth.'" The priests and the prophets and all the people heard Jeremiah speaking these words in the house of the Lord. And when Jeremiah had finished speaking all that the Lord had commanded him to speak to all the people, then the priests and the prophets and all the people laid hold of him, saying, "You shall die! Why have you prophesied in the name of the Lord, saying, 'This house shall be like Shiloh, and this city shall be desolate, without inhabitant'?" And all the people gathered about Jeremiah in the house of the Lord. When the princes of Judah heard these things, they came up from the king's house to the house of the Lord and took their seat in the entry of the New Gate of the house of the Lord. Then the priests and the prophets said to the princes and to all the people, "This man deserves the sentence of death, because he has prophesied against this city, as you have heard with your own ears." Then Jeremiah spoke to all the princes and all the people saying, "The Lord sent me to prophesy against this house and this city all the words you have heard. Now therefore amend your ways and your doings, and obey the voice of the Lord your God, and the Lord will repent of the evil which he has pronounced against you. But as for me, behold, I am in your hands. Do with me as seems good and right to you. Only know for certain that if you put me to death, you will bring innocent blood upon yourselves and upon this city and its inhabitants, for in truth the Lord sent me to you to speak all these words in your ears." Then the princes and all the people said to the priests and the prophets, "This man does not deserve the sentence of death, for he has spoken to us in the name of the Lord our God."

A Reading (Lesson) from the Letter of Paul to the Romans [11:1-12]

I ask, then, has God rejected his people? By no means! I myself am an Israelite, a descendant of Abraham, a member of the tribe of Benjamin. God has not rejected his people whom he foreknew. Do you not know what the scripture says of Eli′jah, how he pleads with God against Israel? "Lord, they have killed thy prophets, they have demolished thy altars, and I alone am left, and they seek my life." But what is God's reply to him? "I have kept for myself seven thousand men who have not bowed the knee to Ba′al." So too at the present time there is a remnant, chosen by grace. But if it is by grace, it is no longer on the basis of works; otherwise grace would no longer be grace. What then? Israel failed to obtain what it sought. The elect obtained it, but the rest were hardened, as it is written, "God gave them a spirit of stupor, eyes that should not see and ears that should not hear, down to this very day." And David says, "Let their table become a snare and a trap, a pitfall and a retribution for them; let their eyes be darkened so that they cannot see, and bend their backs for ever." So I ask, have they stumbled so as to fall? By no means! But through their trespass salvation has come to the Gentiles, so as to make Israel jealous. Now if their trespass means riches for the world, and if their failure means riches for the Gentiles, how much more will their full inclusion mean!

A Reading (Lesson) from the Gospel according to John
[10:19-42]

There was again a division among the Jews because of
these words. Many of them said, "He has a demon, and he
is mad; why listen to him?" Others said, "These are not the
sayings of one who has a demon. Can a demon open the
eyes of the blind?" It was the feast of the Dedication at
Jerusalem; it was winter, and Jesus was walking in the
temple, in the portico of Solomon. So the Jews gathered
round him and said to him, "How long will you keep us in
suspense? If you are the Christ, tell us plainly." Jesus
answered them, "I told you, and you do not believe. The
works that I do in my Father's name, they bear witness to
me; but you do not believe, because you do not belong to
my sheep. My sheep hear my voice, and I know them, and
they follow me; and I give them eternal life, and they shall
never perish, and no one shall snatch them out of my hand.
My Father, who has given them to me, is greater than all,
and no one is able to snatch them out of the Father's hand.
I and the Father are one." The Jews took up stones again to
stone him. Jesus answered them, "I have shown you many
good works from the Father; for which of these do you
stone me?" The Jews answered him, "It is not for a good
work that we stone you but for blasphemy; because you,
being a man, make yourself God." Jesus answered them,
"Is it not written in your law, 'I said, you are gods'? If he
called them gods to whom the word of God came (and
scripture cannot be broken), do you say of him whom the
Father consecrated and sent into the world, 'You are
blaspheming,' because I said, 'I am the son of God'? If I am
not doing the works of my Father, then do not believe me;
but if I do them, even though you do not believe me,
believe the works, that you may know and understand that
the Father is in me and I am in the Father." Again they
tried to arrest him, but he escaped from their hands. He
went away again across the Jordan to the place where John

at first baptized, and there he remained. And many came to him; and they said, "John did no sign, but everything that John said about this man was true." And many believed in him there.

Friday

*Psalm 95** [page 724] & *Psalm 22* [page 610] ❖
Psalm 141 [page 797], *Psalm 143:1-11(12)* [page 798]

A Reading (Lesson) from the Book of Jeremiah [29:1,4-13]

These are the words of the letter which Jeremiah the prophet sent from Jerusalem to the elders of the exiles, and to the priests, the prophets, and all the people, whom Nebuchadne'zar had taken into exile from Jerusalem to Babylon: "Thus says the Lord of hosts, the God of Israel, to all the exiles whom I have sent into exile from Jerusalem to Babylon: Build houses and live in them; plant gardens and eat their produce. Take wives and have sons and daughters; take wives for your sons, and give your daughters in marriage, that they may bear sons and daughters; multiply there, and do not decrease. But seek the welfare of the city where I have sent you into exile, and pray to the Lord on its behalf, for in its welfare you will find your welfare. For thus says the Lord of hosts, the God of Israel: Do not let your prophets and your diviners who are among you deceive you, and do not listen to the dreams which they dream, for it is a lie which they are prophesying to you in my name; I did not send them, says the Lord. For thus says the Lord: When seventy years are completed for Babylon, I will visit you, and I will fulfil to you my promise and bring you back to this place. For I know the plans I have for you, says the Lord, plans for welfare and not for evil, to give you a future and a hope.

*For the Invitatory

Then you will call upon me and come and pray to me, and I will hear you. You will seek me and find me; when you seek me with all your heart.

A Reading (Lesson) from the Letter of Paul to the Romans [11:13-24]

Now I am speaking to you Gentiles. Inasmuch then as I am an apostle to the Gentiles, I magnify my ministry in order to make my fellow Jews jealous, and thus save some of them. For if their rejection means the reconciliation of the world, what will their acceptance mean but life from the dead? If the dough offered as first fruits is holy, so is the whole lump; and if the root is holy, so are the branches. But if some of the branches were broken off, and you, a wild olive shoot, were grafted in their place to share the richness of the olive tree, do not boast over the branches. If you do boast, remember it is not you that support the root, but the root that supports you. You will say, "Branches were broken off so that I might be grafted in." That is true. They were broken off because of their unbelief, but you stand fast only through faith. So do not become proud, but stand in awe. For if God did not spare the natural branches, neither will he spare you. Note then the kindness and the severity of God: severity toward those who have fallen, but God's kindness to you, provided you continue in his kindness; otherwise you too will be cut off. And even the others, if they do not persist in their unbelief, will be grafted in, for God has the power to graft them in again. For if you have been cut from what is by nature a wild olive tree, and grafted, contrary to nature, into a cultivated olive tree, how much more will these natural branches be grafted back into their own olive tree.

A Reading (Lesson) from the Gospel according to John [11:1-27]

Now a certain man was ill, Laz'arus of Bethany, the village

of Mary and her sister Martha. It was Mary who anointed the Lord with ointment and wiped his feet with her hair, whose brother Laz'arus was ill. So the sisters sent to him, saying, "Lord, he whom you love is ill." But when Jesus heard it he said, "This illness is not unto death; it is for the glory of God, so that the Son of God may be glorified by means of it." Now Jesus loved Martha and her sister and Laz'arus. So when he heard that he was ill, he stayed two days longer in the place where he was. Then after this he said to the disciples, "Let us go into Judea again." The disciples said to him, "Rabbi, the Jews were but now seeking to stone you, and are you going there again?" Jesus answered, "Are there not twelve hours in the day? If any one walks in the day, he does not stumble, because he sees the light of this world. But if any one walks in the night, he stumbles, because the light is not in him." Thus he spoke, and then he said to them, "Our friend Laz'arus has fallen asleep, but I go to awake him out of sleep." The disciples said to him, "Lord, if he has fallen asleep, he will recover." Now Jesus has spoken of his death, but they thought that he meant taking rest in sleep. Then Jesus told them plainly, "Laz'arus is dead; and for your sake I am glad that I was not there, so that you may believe. But let us go to him." Thomas, called the Twin, said to his fellow disciples, "Let us also go, that we may die with him." Now when Jesus came, he found that Laz'arus had already been in the tomb four days. Bethany was near Jerusalem, about two miles off, and many of the Jews had come to Martha and Mary to console them concerning their brother. When Martha heard that Jesus was coming, she went and met him, while Mary sat in the house. Martha said to Jesus, "Lord, if you had been here, my brother would not have died. And even now I know that whatever you ask from God, God will give you." Jesus said to her, "Your brother will rise again." Martha said to him, "I know that he will rise again in the resurrection at the last day." Jesus said to her, "I am the resurrection and the life; he who believes in me, though he die, yet shall he live, and whoever lives and believes in me shall never die. Do you believe this?" She said to him, "Yes, Lord; I believe that you are the Christ, the Son of God, he who is coming into the world."

or this

A Reading (Lesson) from the Gospel according to John [12:1-10]

Six days before the Passover, Jesus came to Bethany, where Laz'arus was, whom Jesus had raised from the dead. There they made him a supper; Martha served, and Laz'arus was one to those at table with him. Mary took a pound of costly ointment of pure nard and anointed the feet of Jesus and wiped his feet with her hair; and the house was filled with the fragrance of the ointment. But Judas Iscariot, one of his disciples (he who was to betray him), said, "Why was this ointment not sold for three hundred denarii and given to the poor?" This he said, not that he cared for the poor but because he was a thief, and as he had the money box he used to take what was put into it. Jesus said, "Let her alone, let her keep it for the day of my burial. The poor you always have with you, but you do not always have me." When the great crowd of the Jews learned that he was there, they came, not only on account of Jesus but also to see Laz'arus, whom he had raised from the dead. So the chief priests planned to put Laz'arus also to death.

Saturday

Psalm 137:1-6(7-9) [page 792],   *Psalm 144* [page 801]   ❖
Psalm 42 [page 643],   *Psalm 43* [page 644]

A Reading (Lesson) from the Book of Jeremiah [31:27-34]

"Behold, the days are coming, says the Lord, when I will sow the house of Israel and the house of Judah with the seed of man and the seed of beast. And it shall come to pass that as I have watched over them to pluck up and break down, to overthrow, destroy, and bring evil, so I will watch over them to build and to plant, says the Lord. In those days they shall no longer say: 'The fathers have eaten sour grapes, and the children's teeth shall be set on edge.' But every one shall die for his own sin; each man who eats sour grapes, his teeth shall be set on edge. Behold, the days are coming, says the Lord, when I will make a new covenant with the house of Israel and the house of Judah, not like the covenant which I made with their fathers when I took them by the hand to bring them out of the land of Egypt, my covenant which they broke, though I was their husband, says the Lord. But this is the covenant which I will make with the house of Israel after those days, says the Lord: I will put my law within them, and I will write it upon their hearts; and I will be their God, and they shall be my people. And no longer shall each man teach his neighbor and each his brother, saying, "Know the Lord,' for they shall all know me, from the least of them to the greatest, says the Lord; for I will forgive their iniquity, and I will remember their sin no more."

*A Reading (Lesson) from the Letter of Paul
to the Romans* [11:25-36]

Lest you be wise in your own conceits, I want you to understand this mystery, brethren: a hardening has come upon part of Israel, until the full number of the Gentiles come in, and so all Israel will be saved; as it is written, "The Deliverer will come from Zion, he will banish ungodliness from Jacob"; "and this will be my covenant with them when I take away their sins." As regards the gospel they are enemies of God, for your sake; but as regards election they are beloved for the sake of their forefathers. For the gifts and the call of God are irrevocable. Just as you were once disobedient to God but now have received mercy because of their disobedience, so they have now been disobedient in order that by the mercy shown to you they also may receive mercy. For God has consigned all men to disobedience, that he might have mercy upon all. O the depth of the riches and wisdom and knowledge of God! How unsearchable are his judgments and how inscrutable his ways! "For who has known the mind of the Lord, or who has been his counselor?" "Or who has given a gift to him that he might be repaid?" For from him and through him and to him are all things. To him be glory for ever. Amen.

A Reading (Lesson) from the Gospel according to John [11:28-44]

When Martha had said this, she went and called her sister Mary, saying quietly, "The Teacher is here and is calling for you." And when she heard it, she rose quickly and went to him. Now Jesus had not yet come to the village, but was still in the place where Martha had met him. When the Jews who were with her in the house, consoling her, saw Mary rise quickly and go out, they followed her, supposing that she was going to the tomb to weep there. Then Mary, when she came where Jesus was and saw him, fell at his feet, saying to him, "Lord, if you had been here, my brother would not have died." When Jesus saw her weeping, and the Jews who came with her also weeping, he was deeply moved in spirit and troubled; and he said, "Where have you laid him?" They said to him, "Lord, come and see." Jesus wept. So the Jews said, "See how he loved him!" But some of them said, "Could not he who opened the eyes of the blind man have kept this man from dying?" Then Jesus, deeply moved again, came to the tomb; it was a cave, and stone lay upon it. Jesus said, "Take away the stone." Martha, the sister of the dead man, said to him, "Lord, by this time there will be an odor, for he has been dead four days." Jesus said to her, "Did I not tell you that if you would believe you would see the glory of God?" So they took away the stone. And Jesus lifted up his eyes and said, "Father, I thank thee that thou hast heard me. I knew that thou hearest me always, but I have said this on account of the people standing by, that they may believe that thou didst send me." When he had said this, he cried with a loud voice, "Laz'arus, come out." The dead man came out, his hands and feet bound with bandages, and his face wrapped with a cloth. Jesus said to them, "Unbind him, and let him go."

or this

A Reading (Lesson) from the Gospel according to John
[12:37-50]

Though Jesus had done so many signs before them, yet they did not believe in him; it was that the word spoken by the prophet Isaiah might be fulfilled: "Lord, who has believed our report and to whom has the arm of the Lord been revealed?" Therefore they could not believe. For Isaiah again said, "He has blinded their eyes and hardened their heart, lest they should see with their eyes and perceive with their heart, and turn for me to heal them." Isaiah said this because he saw his glory and spoke of him. Nevertheless many even of the authorities believed in him, but for fear of the Pharisees they did not confess it, lest they should be put out of the synagogue: for they loved the praise of men more than the praise of God. And Jesus cried out and said, "He who believes in me, believes not in me but in him who sent me. And he who sees me sees him who sent me. I have come as light into the world, that whoever believes in me may not remain in darkness. If any one hears my sayings and does not keep them, I do not judge him; for I did not come to judge the world but to save the world. He who rejects me and does not receive my sayings has a judge; the word that I have spoken will be his judge on the last day. For I have not spoken on my own authority; the Father who sent me has himself given me commandment what to say and what to speak. And I know that his commandment is eternal life. What I say, therefore, I say as the Father has bidden me."

Holy Week

Palm Sunday

Psalm 24 [page 613],   *Psalm 29* [page 620]   ❖
Psalm 103 [page 733]

A Reading (Lesson) from the Book of Zechariah   [9:9-12]*

Rejoice greatly, O daughter of Zion! Shout aloud, O
daughter of Jerusalem! Lo, your king comes to you;
triumphant and victorious is he, humble and riding on an
ass, on a colt the foal of an ass. I will cut off the chariot
from E′phraim and the war horse from Jerusalem; and the
battle bow shall be cut off, and he shall command peace to
the nations; his dominion shall be from sea to sea, and
from the River to the ends of the earth. As for you also,
because of the blood of my covenant with you, I will set
your captives free from the waterless pit. Return to your
stronghold, O prisoners of hope; today I declare that I will
restore to you double.

*A Reading (Lesson) from the First Letter of Paul
to Timothy*   [6:12-16]*

Fight the good fight of the faith; take hold of the eternal
life to which you were called when you made the good
confession in the presence of many witnesses. In the
presence of God who gives life to all things, and of Christ
Jesus who in his testimony before Pontius Pilate made the
good confession, I charge you to keep the commandment
unstained and free from reproach until the appearing of
our Lord Jesus Christ; and this will be made manifest at
the proper time by the blessed and only Sovereign, the
King of kings and Lord of lords, who alone has

*Intended for use in the morning

immortality and dwells in unapproachable light, whom no man has ever seen or can see. To him be honor and eternal dominion. Amen.

A Reading (Lesson) from the Book of Zechariah
[12:9-11;13:1,7-9]†

Thus says the Lord: "On that day I will seek to destroy all the nations that come against Jerusalem. And I will pour out on the house of David and the inhabitants of Jerusalem a spirit of compassion and supplication, so that, when they look on him whom they have pierced, they shall mourn for him, as one mourns for an only child, and weep bitterly over him, as one weeps over a first-born. On that day the mourning in Jerusalem will be as great as the mourning for Hadadrim'mon in the plain of Megid'do. On that day there shall be a fountain opened for the house of David and the inhabitants of Jerusalem to cleanse them from sin and uncleanness." "Awake, O sword, against my shepherd, against the man who stands next to me," says the Lord of hosts. "Strike the shepherd, that the sheep may be scattered; I will turn my hand against the little ones. In the whole land, says the Lord, two thirds shall be cut off and perish, and one third shall be left alive. And I will put this third into the fire, and refine them as one refines silver, and test them as gold is tested. They will call on my name, and I will answer them. I will say, 'They are my people'; and they will say, 'The Lord is my God.'"

A Reading (Lesson) from the Gospel according to Matthew
[21:12-17]

Jesus entered the temple of God and drove out all who sold and bought in the temple, and he overturned the tables of the moneychangers and the seats of those who sold

†Intended for use in the evening

pigeons. He said to them, "It is written, 'My house shall be called a house of prayer'; but you make it a den of robbers." And the blind and the lame came to him in the temple, and he healed them. But when the chief priests and the scribes saw the wonderful things that he did, and the children crying out in the temple, "Hosanna to the Son of David!" they were indignant; and they said to him, "Do you hear what these are saying?" And Jesus said to them, "Yes; have you never read, 'Out of the mouth of babes and sucklings thou hast brought perfect praise'?" And leaving them, he went out of the city to Bethany and lodged there.

Monday

Psalm 51:1-18(19-20) [page 656] ❖
Psalm 69:1-23 [page 679]

A Reading (Lesson) from the Book of Jeremiah [12:1-16]

Righteous art thou, O Lord, when I complain to thee; yet would plead my case before thee. Why does the way of the wicked prosper? Why do all who are treacherous thrive? Thou plantest them, and they take root; they grow and bring forth fruit; thou art near in their mouth and far from their heart. But thou, O Lord, knowest me; thou seest me and triest my mind toward thee. Pull them out like sheep for the slaughter, and set them apart for the day of slaughter. How long will the land mourn, and the grass of every field wither? For the wickedness of those who dwell in it the beasts and the birds are swept away, because men said, "He will not see our latter end." "If you have raced with men on foot, and they have wearied you, how will you compete with horses? And if in a safe land you fall down, how will you do in the jungle of the Jordan? For even your brothers and the house of your father, even they have dealt treacherously with you; they are in full cry after you; believe them not, though they speak fair words to you." "I have forsaken my house, I have abandoned my heritage; I have given the beloved of my soul into the hands of her enemies. My heritage has become to me like a lion in the forest, she has lifted up her voice against me; therefore I hate her. Is my heritage to me like a speckled bird of prey? Are the birds of prey against her round about? Go, assemble all the wild beasts; bring them to devour. Many shepherds have destroyed my vineyard, they have trampled down my portion, they have made my pleasant portion a desolate wilderness. They have made it a desolation; desolate, it mourns to me. The whole land is made desolate, but no man lays it to heart. Upon all the bare heights in the desert destroyers have come; for the sword of the Lord devours from one end of the land to the other; no flesh has peace. They have sown wheat and have reaped thorns, they have tired themselves out but profit nothing. They shall be ashamed of their harvests because of the fierce anger of the Lord." Thus says the Lord concerning all my evil neighbors who touch the heritage which I have given my people Israel to inherit: "Behold, I will pluck them up from their land, and I will pluck up the house of Judah from among them. And after I have plucked them up, I will again have compassion on them, and I will bring them again each to his heritage and each to his land. And it shall come to pass, if they will diligently learn the ways of my people, to swear by my name, 'As the Lord lives,' even as they taught my people to swear by Ba'al, then they shall be built up in the midst of my people."

A Reading (Lesson) from the Letter of Paul to the Philippians [3:1-14]

Finally, my brethren, rejoice in the Lord. To write the same things to you is not irksome to me, and is safe for you. Look out for the dogs, look out for the evil-workers, look out for those who mutilate the flesh. For we are the true circumcision, who worship God in spirit, and glory in

Christ Jesus, and put no confidence in the flesh. Though I myself have reason for confidence in the flesh also. If any other man thinks he has reason for confidence in the flesh I have more: circumcised on the eighth day, of the people of Israel, of the tribe of Benjamin, a Hebrew born of Hebrews; as to the law a Pharisee, as to zeal a persecutor of the church, as to righteousness under the law blameless But whatever gain I had, I counted as loss for the sake of Christ. Indeed I count everything as loss because of the surpassing worth of knowing Christ Jesus my Lord. For his sake I have suffered the loss of all things, and count them as refuse, in order that I may gain Christ and be found in him, not having a righteousness of my own, based on law, but that which is through faith in Christ, the righteousness from God that depends on faith; that I may know him and the power of his resurrection, and may share his sufferings, becoming like him in his death, that i possible I may attain the resurrection from the dead. Not that I have already obtained this or am already perfect; but I press on to make it my own, because Christ Jesus has made me his own. Brethren, I do not consider that I have made it my own; but one thing I do, forgetting what lies behind and straining forward to what lies ahead, I press toward the goal for the prize of the upward call of God in Christ Jesus.

A Reading (Lesson) from the Gospel according to John
[12:9-19]

When the great crowd of the Jews learned that Jesus was there, they came, not only on account of Jesus but also to see Laz'arus, whom he had raised from the dead. So the chief priests planned to put Laz'arus also to death, because on account of him many of the Jews were going away and believing in Jesus. The next day a great crowd who had come to the feast heard that Jesus was coming to Jerusalem. So they took branches of palm trees and went out to meet him, crying "Hosanna! Blessed is he who

comes in the name of the Lord, even the King of Israel!"
And Jesus found a young ass and sat upon it; as it is
written, "Fear not, daughter of Zion; behold, your king is
coming, sitting on an ass's colt!" His disciples did not
understand this at first; but when Jesus was glorified, then
they remembered that this had been written of him and
had been done to him. The crowd that had been with him
when he called Laz'arus out of the tomb and raised him
from the dead bore witness. The reason why the crowd
went to meet him was that they heard he had done this
sign. The Pharisees then said to one another, "You see that
you can do nothing; look, the world has gone after him."

Tuesday

Psalm 6 [page 589],   *Psalm 12* [page 597]   ❖
Psalm 94 [page 722]

A Reading (Lesson) from the Book of Jeremiah [15:10-21]

Woe is me, my mother, that you bore me, a man of strife
and contention to the whole land! I have not lent, nor have
I borrowed, yet all of them curse me. So let it be, O Lord, if
I have not entreated thee for their good, if I have not
pleaded with thee on behalf of the enemy in the time of
trouble and in the time of distress! Can one break iron,
iron from the north, and bronze? "Your wealth and your
treasures I will give as spoil, without price, for all your
sins, throughout all your territory. I will make you serve
your enemies in a land which you do not know, for in my
anger a fire is kindled which shall burn for ever." O Lord,
thou knowest; remember me and visit me, and take
vengeance for me on my persecutors. In thy forbearance
take me not away; know that for thy sake I bear reproach.
Thy words were found, and I ate them, and thy words
became to me a joy and the delight of my heart; for I am
called by thy name, O Lord, God of hosts. I did not sit in

the company of merrymakers, nor did I rejoice; I sat alone
because thy hand was upon me, for thou hadst filled me
with indignation. Why is my pain unceasing, my wound
incurable, refusing to be healed? Wilt thou be to me like a
deceitful brook, like waters that fail? Therefore thus says
the Lord: "If you return, I will restore you, and you shall
stand before me. If you utter what is precious, and not
what is worthless, you shall be as my mouth. They shall
turn to you, but you shall not turn to them. And I will
make you to this people a fortified wall of bronze; they w
fight against you, but they shall not prevail over you, for I
am with you to save you and deliver you," says the Lord.
"I will deliver you out of the hand of the wicked, and
redeem you from the grasp of the ruthless."

*A Reading (Lesson) from the Letter of Paul
to the Philippians* [3:15-21]

Let those of us who are mature be thus minded; and if in
anything you are otherwise minded, God will reveal that
also to you. Only let us hold true to what we have attaine
Brethren, join in imitating me, and mark those who so liv
as you have an example in us. For many, of whom I have
often told you and now tell you even with tears, live as
enemies of the cross of Christ. Their end is destruction,
their god is the belly, and they glory in their shame, with
minds set on earthly things. But our commonwealth is in
heaven, and from it we await a Savior, the Lord Jesus
Christ, who will change our lowly body to be like his
glorious body, by the power which enables him even to
subject all things to himself.

A Reading (Lesson) from the Gospel according to John
[12:20-26]

Among those who went up to worship at the feast were
some Greeks. So these came to Philip, who was from
Beth-sa'ida in Galilee, and said to him, "Sir, we wish to se

Jesus." Philip went and told Andrew; Andrew went with Philip and they told Jesus. And Jesus answered them, "The hour has come for the Son of man to be glorified. Truly, truly, I say to you, unless a grain of wheat falls into the earth and dies, it remains alone; but if it dies, it bears much fruit. He who loves his life loses it, and he who hates his life in this world will keep it for eternal life. If any one serves me, he must follow me; and where I am, there shall my servant be also; if any one serves me, the Father will honor him."

Wednesday

Psalm 55 [page 660]   ❖   *Psalm 74* [page 689]

A Reading (Lesson) from the Book of Jeremiah
[17:5-10,14-17]

Thus says the Lord: "Cursed is the man who trusts in man and makes flesh his arm, whose heart turns away from the Lord. He is like a shrub in the desert, and shall not see any good come. He shall dwell in the parched places of the wilderness, in an uninhabited salt land. Blessed is the man who trusts in the Lord, whose trust is the Lord. He is like a tree planted by water, that sends out its roots by the stream, and does not fear when heat comes, for its leaves remain green, and is not anxious in the year of drought, for it does not cease to bear fruit." The heart is deceitful above all things, and desperately corrupt; who can understand it? "I the Lord search the mind and try the heart, to give to every man according to his ways, according to the fruit of his doings." Heal me, O Lord, and I shall be healed; save me, and I shall be saved; for thou art my praise. Behold, they say to me, "Where is the word of the Lord? Let it come!" I have not pressed thee to send evil, nor have I desired the day of disaster, thou knowest; that which came out of my lips was before thy face. Be not a terror to me; thou art my refuge in the day of evil.

*A Reading (Lesson) from the Letter of Paul
to the Philippians* [4:1-13]

Therefore, my brethren, whom I love and long for, my joy and crown, stand firm thus in the Lord, my beloved. I entreat Eu-o'dia and I entreat Syn'tyche to agree in the Lord. And I ask you also, true yokefellow, help these women, for they have labored side by side with me in the gospel together with Clement and the rest of my fellow workers, whose names are in the book of life. Rejoice in the Lord always; again I will say, Rejoice. Let all men know your forbearance. The Lord is at hand. Have no anxiety about anything, but in everything by prayer and supplication with thanksgiving let your requests be made known to God. And the peace of God, which passes all understanding, will keep your hearts and your minds in Christ Jesus. Finally, brethren, whatever is true, whatever is honorable, whatever is just, whatever is pure, whatever is lovely, whatever is gracious, if there is any excellence, if there is anything worthy of praise, think about these things. What you have learned and received and heard and seen in me, do; and the God of peace will be with you. I rejoice in the Lord greatly that now at length you have revived your concern for me; you were indeed concerned for me, but you had no opportunity. Not that I complain of want; for I have learned, in whatever state I am, to be content. I know how to be abased, and I know how to abound; in any and all circumstances I have learned the secret of facing plenty and hunger, abundance and want. I can do all things in him who strengthens me.

A Reading (Lesson) from the Gospel according to John
[12:27-36]

Jesus answered Philip and Andrew, "Now is my soul troubled. And what shall I say? 'Father, save me from this hour'? No, for this purpose I have come to this hour. Father, glorify thy name." Then a voice came from heaven,

"I have glorified it, and I will glorify it again." The crowd standing by heard it and said that it had thundered. Others said, "An angel has spoken to him." Jesus answered, "This voice has come for your sake, not for mine. Now is the judgment of this world, now shall the ruler of this world be cast out; and I, when I am lifted up from the earth, will draw all men to myself." He said this to show by what death he was to die. The crowd answered him, "We have heard from the law that the Christ remains for ever. How can you say that the Son of man must be lifted up? Who is this Son of man?" Jesus said to them, "The light is with you for a little longer. Walk while you have the light, lest the darkness overtake you; he who walks in the darkness does not know where he goes. While you have the light, believe in the light, that you may become sons of light."

Maundy Thursday

Psalm 102 [page 731] ❖ *Psalm 142* [page 798]
Psalm 143 [page 798]

A Reading (Lesson) from the Book of Jeremiah [20:7-11]

O Lord, thou hast deceived me, and I was deceived; thou art stronger than I, and thou hast prevailed. I have become a laughingstock all the day; every one mocks me. For whenever I speak, I cry out, I shout, "Violence and destruction!" For the word of the Lord has become for me a reproach and derision all day long. If I say, "I will not mention him, or speak any more in his name," there is in my heart as it were a burning fire shut up in my bones, and I am weary with holding it in, and I cannot. For I hear many whispering. Terror is on every side! "Denounce him! Let us denounce him!" say all my familiar friends, watching for my fall. "Perhaps he will be deceived, then we can overcome him, and take our revenge on him." But the Lord is with me as a dread warrior; therefore my

persecutors will stumble, they will not overcome me. They
will be greatly shamed, for they will not succeed. Their
eternal dishonor will never be forgotten.

*A Reading (Lesson) from the First Letter of Paul
to the Corinthians* [10:14-17,11:27-32]

My beloved, shun the worship of idols. I speak as to
sensible men; judge for yourselves what I say. The cup of
blessing which we bless, is it not a participation in the
blood of Christ? The bread which we break, is it not a
participation in the body of Christ? Because there is one
bread, we who are many are one body, for we all partake
of the one bread. Whoever, therefore, eats the bread or
drinks the cup of the Lord in an unworthy manner will be
guilty of profaning the body and blood of the Lord. Let a
man examine himself, and so eat of the bread and drink of
the cup. For any one who eats and drinks without
discerning the body eats and drinks judgment upon
himself. That is why many of you are weak and ill, and
some have died. But if we judged ourselves truly, we
should not be judged. But when we are judged by the Lord
we are chastened so that we may not be condemned along
with the world.

A Reading (Lesson) from the Gospel according to John
[17:1-11(12-26)]

When Jesus had spoken, he lifted up his eyes to heaven and
said, "Father, the hour has come; glorify thy Son that the
Son may glorify thee, since thou hast given him power over
all flesh, to give eternal life to all whom thou hast given
him. And this is eternal life, that they know thee the only
true God, and Jesus Christ whom thou hast sent. I glorified
thee on earth, having accomplished the work which thou
gavest me to do; and now, Father, glorify thou me in thy
own presence with the glory which I had with thee before
the world was made. I have manifested thy name to the

men whom thou gavest me out of the world; thine they were, and thou gavest them to me, and they have kept thy word. Now they know that everything that thou hast given me is from thee; for I have given them the words which thou gavest me, and they have received them and know in truth that I came from thee; and they have believed that thou didst send me. I am praying for them; I am not praying for the world but for those whom thou hast given me, for they are thine; all mine are thine, and thine are mine, and I am glorified in them. And now I am no more in the world, but they are in the world, and I am coming to thee. Holy Father, keep them in thy name, which thou hast given me, that they may be one, even as we are one.

> While I was with them, I kept them in thy name, which thou hast given me; I have guarded them, and none of them is lost but the son of perdition, that the scripture might be fulfilled. But now I am coming to thee; and these things I speak in the world, that they may have my joy fulfilled in themselves. I have given them thy word; and the world has hated them because they are not of the world, even as I am not of the world. I do not pray that thou shouldst take them out of the world, but that thou shouldst keep them from the evil one. They are not of the world, even as I am not of the world. Sanctify them in the truth; thy word is truth. As thou didst send me into the world, so I have sent them into the world. And for their sake I consecrate myself, that they also may be consecrated in truth. I do not pray for these only, but also for those who believe in me through their word, that they may all be one; even as thou, Father, art in me, and I in thee, that they also may be in us, so that the world may believe that thou hast sent me. The glory which thou hast given me I have given to them, that they may be one even as we are one, I in them and thou in me, that they may become perfectly one, so that the world may know that thou hast sent me and hast loved them even as thou hast loved me. Father, I desire that

they also, whom thou hast given me, may be with me where I am, to behold my glory which thou hast given me in thy love for me before the foundation of the world. O righteous Father, the world has not known thee, but I have known thee; and these know that thou hast sent me. I made known to them thy name, and I will make it known, that the love with which thou has loved me may be in them, and I in them."

Good Friday

*Psalm 95** [page 724]   &   *Psalm 22* [page 610]   ❖
Psalm 40:1-14(15-19) [page 640],   *Psalm 54* [page 659]

A Reading (Lesson) from the Book of Wisdom
[1:16—2:1,12-22]

Ungodly men by their words and deeds summoned death; considering him a friend, they pined away, and they made a covenant with him, because they are fit to belong to his party. For they reasoned unsoundly, saying to themselves, "Short and sorrowful is our life, and there is no remedy when a man comes to his end, and no one has been known to return from Hades. Let us lie in wait for the righteous man, because he is inconvenient to us and opposes our actions; he reproaches us for sins against the law, and accuses us of sins against our training. He professes to have knowledge of God, and calls himself a child of the Lord. He became to us a reproof of our thoughts; the very sight of him is a burden to us, because his manner of life is unlike that of others, and his ways are strange. We are considered by him as something base, and he avoids our ways as unclean; he calls the last end of the righteous happy, and boasts that God is his father. Let us see if his words are true, and let us test what will happen at the end

*For the Invitatory

of his life; for if the righteous man is God's son, he will help him, and will deliver him from the hand of his adversaries. Let us test him with insult and torture, that we may find out how gentle he is, and make trial of his forbearance. Let us condemn him to a shameful death, for, according to what he says, he will pe protected." Thus they reasoned, but they were led astray, for their wickedness blinded them, and they did not know the secret purposes of God, nor hope for the wages of holiness, nor discern the prize for blameless souls.

or this

A Reading (Lesson) from the Book of Genesis [22:1-14]

God tested Abraham, and said to him, "Abraham!" And he said, "Here am I." He said, "Take your son, your only son Isaac, whom you love, and go to the land of Mori'ah, and offer him there as a burnt offering upon one of the mountains of which I shall tell you." So Abraham rose early in the morning, saddled his ass, and took two of his young men with him, and his son Isaac; and he cut the wood for the burnt offering, and arose and went to the place of which God had told him. On the third day Abraham lifted up his eyes and saw the place afar off. Then Abraham said to his young men, "Stay here with the ass; I and the lad will go yonder and worship, and come again to you." And Abraham took the wood of the burnt offering, and laid it on Isaac his son; and he took in his hand the fire and the knife. So they went both of them together. And Isaac said to his father Abraham, "My father!" And he said, "Here am I, my son." He said, "Behold, the fire and the wood; but where is the lamb for a burnt offering?" Abraham said, "God will provide himself the lamb for a burnt offering, my son." So they went both of them together. When they came to the place of which God had told him, Abraham built an altar there, and laid the wood in order, and bound Isaac his son, and laid him on the altar, upon the wood. Then Abraham put forth his hand, and took the knife to slay his son. But the angel of the Lord called to him from heaven, and said, "Abraham, Abraham!" And he said, "Here am I." He said, "Do not lay your hand on the lad or do anything to him; for now I know that you fear God, seeing you have not withheld your son, your only son, from me." And Abraham lifted up his eyes and looked, and behold, behind him was a ram, caught in a thicket by his horns; and Abraham went and took the ram, and offered it up as a burnt offering instead of his son. So Abraham called the name of that place The Lord will provide; as it is said to this day, "On the mount of the Lord it shall be provided."

A Reading (Lesson) from the First Letter of Peter [1:10-20]

The prophets who prophesied of the grace that was to be yours searched and inquired about this salvation; they inquired what person or time was indicated by the Spirit of Christ within them when predicting the sufferings of Christ and the subsequent glory. It was revealed to them that they were serving not themselves but you, in the things which have now been announced to you by those who preached the good news to you through the Holy Spirit sent from heaven, things into which angels long to look. Therefore gird up your minds, be sober, set your hope fully upon the grace that is coming to you at the revelation of Jesus Christ. As obedient children, do not be conformed to the passions of your former ignorance, but as he who called you is holy, be holy yourselves in all your conduct; since it is written, "You shall be holy, for I am holy." And if you invoke as Father him who judges each one impartially according to his deeds, conduct yourselves with fear throughout the time of your exile. You know that you were ransomed from the futile ways inherited from your fathers, not with perishable things such as silver or gold, but with the precious blood of Christ, like that of a lamb without blemish or spot. He was destined before the foundation of the world but was made manifest at the end of the times for your sake.

A Reading (Lesson) from the Gospel according to John
[13:36-38]*

Simon Peter said to Jesus, "Lord, where are you going?" Jesus answered, "Where I am going you cannot follow me now; but you shall follow afterward." Peter said to him, "Lord, why cannot I follow you now? I will lay down my life for you." Jesus answered, "Will you lay down your life for me? Truly, truly, I say to you, the cock will not crow, till you have denied me three times."

A Reading (Lesson) from the Gospel according to John
[19:38-42]†

Joseph of Arimathe'a, who was a disciple of Jesus, but secretly, for fear of the Jews, asked Pilate that he might take away the body of Jesus, and Pilate gave him leave. So he came and took away the body. Nicode'mus also, who had at first come to him by night, came bringing a mixture of myrrh and aloes about a hundred pounds' weight. They took the body of Jesus and bound it in linen cloths with the spices, as is the burial custom of the Jews. Now in the place where he was crucified there was a garden, and in the garden a new tomb where no one had ever been laid. So because of the Jewish day of Preparation, as the tomb was close at hand, they laid Jesus there.

*Intended for use in the morning
†Intended for use in the evening

Holy Saturday

Psalm 95* [page 724] & *Psalm 88* [page 712] ❖
Psalm 27 [page 617]

A Reading (Lesson) from the Book of Job [19:12-27a]

Job answered Bildad the Shuhite: "Have pity on me, have pity on me, O you my friends, for the hand of God has touched me! Why do you, like God, pursue me? Why are you not satisfied with my flesh? Oh that my words were written! Oh that they were inscribed in a book! Oh that with an iron pen and lead they were graven in the rock for ever! For I know that my Redeemer lives, and at last he will stand upon the earth; and after my skin has been thus destroyed, then from my flesh I shall see God, whom I shall see on my side, and my eyes shall behold, and not another."

A Reading (Lesson) from the Letter to the Hebrews [4:1-16]

While the promise of entering his rest remains, let us fear lest any of you be judged to have failed to reach it. For good news came to us just as to them; but the message which they heard did not benefit them, because it did not meet with faith in the hearers. For we who have believed enter that rest, as he has said, "As I swore in my wrath, 'They shall never enter my rest,'" although his works were finished from the foundation of the world. For he has somewhere spoken of the seventh day in this way, "And God rested on the seventh day from all his works." And again in this place he said, "They shall never enter my rest." Since therefore it remains for some to enter it, and those who formerly received the good news failed to enter because of disobedience, again he sets a certain day,

---

*For the Invitatory

"Today," saying through David so long afterward, in the words already quoted, "Today, when you hear his voice, do not harden your hearts." For if Joshua had given them rest, God would not speak later of another day. So then, there remains a sabbath rest for the people of God; for whoever enters God's rest also ceases from his labors as God did from his. Let us therefore strive to enter that rest, that no one fall by the same sort of disobedience. For the word of God is living and active, sharper than any two-edged sword, piercing to the division of soul and spirit, of joints and marrow, and discerning the thoughts and intentions of the heart. And before him no creature is hidden, but all are open and laid bare to the eyes of him with whom we have to do. Since then we have a great high priest who has passed through the heavens, Jesus, the Son of God, let us hold fast our confession. For we have not a high priest who is unable to sympathize with our weaknesses, but one who in every respect has been tempted as we are, yet without sin. Let us then with confidence draw near to the throne of grace, that we may receive mercy and find grace to help in time of need.

Romans 8:1-11†   [page 322 above]

Easter Week

Easter Day

Psalm 148 [page 805],   *Psalm 149* [page 807],
Psalm 150 [page 807]   ❖   *Psalm 113* [page 756],
Psalm 114 [page 756]   *or*   *Psalm 118* [page 760]

†*Intended for use in the evening*

A Reading (Lesson) from the Book of Exodus [12:1-14]*

The Lord said to Moses and Aaron in the land of Egypt,
"This month shall be for you the beginning of months; it
shall be the first month of the year for you. Tell all the
congregation of Israel that on the tenth day of this month
they shall take every man a lamb according to their
fathers' houses, a lamb for a household; and if the
household is too small for a lamb, then a man and his
neighbor next to his house shall take according to the
number of persons; according to what each can eat you
shall make your count for the lamb. Your lamb shall be
without blemish, a male a year old; you shall take it from
the sheep or from the goats; and you shall keep it until the
fourteenth day of this month, when the whole assembly of
the congregation of Israel shall kill their lambs in the
evening. Then they shall take some of the blood, and put it
on the two doorposts and the lintel of the houses in which
they eat them. They shall eat the flesh that night, roasted;
with unleavened bread and bitter herbs they shall eat it. Do
not eat any of it raw or boiled with water, but roasted, its
head with its legs and its inner parts. And you shall let
none of it remain until the morning, anything that remains
until the morning you shall burn. In this manner you shall
eat it: your loins girded, your sandals on your feet, and
your staff in your hand; and you shall eat it in haste. It is
the Lord's passover. For I will pass through the land of
Egypt that night, and I will smite all the first-born in the
land of Egypt, both man and beast; and on all the gods of
Egypt I will execute judgments: I am the Lord. The blood
shall be a sign for you, upon the houses where you are; and
when I see the blood, I will pass over you, and no plague
shall fall upon you to destroy you, when I smite the land of

Intended for use in the morning

Egypt. This day shall be for you a memorial day, and you shall keep it as a feast to the Lord; throughout your generations you shall observe it as an ordinance for ever."

John 1:1-18 [page 251 above]

A Reading (Lesson) from the Book of Isaiah [51:9-11]†

Awake, awake, put on strength, O arm of the Lord; awake, as in days of old, the generations of long ago. Was it not thou that didst cut Rahab in pieces, that didst pierce the dragon? Was it not thou that didst dry up the sea, the waters of the great deep; that didst make the depths of the sea a way for the redeemed to pass over? And the ransomed of the Lord shall return, and come to Zion with singing; everlasting joy shall be upon their heads; they shall obtain joy and gladness, and sorrow and sighing shall flee away.

A Reading (Lesson) from the Gospel according to Luke [24:13-35]†

That very day two of them were going to a village named Emma'us, about seven miles from Jerusalem, and talking with each other about all these things that had happened. While they were talking and discussing together, Jesus himself drew near and went with them. But their eyes were kept from recognizing him. And he said to them, "What is this conversation which you are holding with each other as you walk?" And they stood still, looking sad. Then one of them, named Cle'opas, answered him, "Are you the only visitor to Jerusalem who does not know the things that have happened there in these days?" And he said to them, "What things?" And they said to him, "Concerning Jesus of Nazareth, who was a prophet mighty in deed and word

*Intended for use in the morning
†Intended for use in the evening

before God and all the people, and how our chief priests and rulers delivered him up to be condemned to death, and crucified him. But we had hoped that he was the one to redeem Israel. Yes, and besides all this, it is now the third day since this happened. Moreover, some women of our company amazed us. They were at the tomb early in the morning and did not find his body; and they came back saying that they had even seen a vision of angels, who said that he was alive. Some of those who were with us went to the tomb, and found it just as the women had said; but him they did not see." And he said to them, "O foolish men, and slow of heart to believe all that the prophets have spoken! Was it not necessary that the Christ should suffer these things and enter into his glory?" And beginning with Moses and all the prophets, he interpreted to them in all the scriptures the things concerning himself. So they drew near to the village to which they were going. He appeared to be going further, but they constrained him, saying, "Stay with us, for it is toward evening and the day is now far spent." So he went in to stay with them. When he was at table with them, he took the bread and blessed, and broke it, and gave it to them. And their eyes were opened and they recognized him; and he vanished out of their sight. They said to each other, "Did not our hearts burn within us while he talked to us on the road, while he opened to us the scriptures?" And they rose that same hour and returned to Jerusalem; and they found the eleven gathered together and those who were with them, who said, "The Lord has risen indeed, and has appeared to Simon!" Then they told what had happened on the road, and how he was known to them in the breaking of the bread.

or this

A Reading (Lesson) from the Gospel according to John
[20:19-23]†

On the evening of that day, the first day of the week, the
doors being shut where the disciples were, for fear of the
Jews, Jesus came and stood among them and said to them,
"Peace be with you." When he had said this, he showed
them his hands and his side. Then the disciples were glad
when they saw the Lord. Jesus said to them again, "Peace
be with you. As the Father has sent me, even so I send
you." And when he had said this, he breathed on them,
and said to them, "Receive the Holy Spirit. If you forgive
the sins of any, they are forgiven; if you retain the sins of
any, they are retained."

Monday

Psalm 93 [page 722],   *Psalm 98* [page 727]   ❖
Psalm 66 [page 673]

A Reading (Lesson) from the Book of Jonah [2:1-9]

Jonah prayed to the Lord his God from the belly of the
fish, saying, "I called to the Lord, out of my distress, and
he answered me; out of the belly of Sheol I cried, and thou
didst hear my voice. For thou didst cast me into the deep,
into the heart of the seas, and the flood was round about
me; all thy waves and thy billows passed over me. Then I
said, 'I am cast out from thy presence; how shall I again
look upon thy holy temple?' The waters closed in over me,
the deep was round about me; weeds were wrapped about
my head at the roots of the mountains. I went down to the
land whose bars closed upon me for ever; yet thou didst
bring up my life from the Pit, O Lord my God. When my
soul fainted within me, I remembered the Lord; and my

†*Intended for use in the evening*

prayer came to thee, into thy holy temple. those who pay regard to vain idols forsake their true loyalty. But I with the voice of thanksgiving will sacrifice to thee; what I have vowed I will pay. Deliverance belongs to the Lord!"

A Reading (Lesson) from the Acts of the Apostles
[2:14,22-32]*

Peter, standing with the eleven, lifted up his voice and addressed them, "Men of Judea and all who dwell in Jerusalem, let this be known to you, and give ear to my words. Men of Israel, hear these words: Jesus of Nazareth, a man attested to you by God with mighty works and wonders and signs which God did through him in your midst, as you yourselves know—this Jesus, delivered up according to the definite plan and foreknowledge of God, you crucified and killed by the hands of lawless men. But God raised him up, having loosed the pangs of death, because it was not possible for him to be held by it. For David says concerning him, 'I saw the Lord always before me, for he is at my right hand that I may not be shaken; therefore my heart was glad, and my tongue rejoiced; moreover my flesh will dwell in hope. For thou wilt not abandon my soul to Hades, nor let thy Holy One see corruption. Thou hast made known to me the ways of life; thou wilt make me full of gladness with thy presence.' Brethren, I may say to you confidently of the patriarch David that he both died and was buried, and his tomb is with us to this day. Being therefore a prophet, and knowing that God had sworn with an oath to him that he would set one of his descendants upon his throne, he foresaw and spoke of the resurrection of the Christ, that he was not abandoned to Hades, nor did his flesh see corruption. This Jesus God raised up, and of that we all are witnesses."

Duplicates the First Lesson at the Eucharist. Readings from Year Two may be substituted.

A Reading (Lesson) from the Gospel according to John
[14:1-14]

Jesus answered Peter and said to the disciples, "Let not your hearts be troubled; believe in God, believe also in me. In my Father's house are many rooms; if it were not so, would I have told you that I go to prepare a place for you? And when I go and prepare a place for you, I will come again and will take you to myself, that where I am you may be also. And you know the way where I am going." Thomas said to him, "Lord, we do not know where you are going; how can we know the way?" Jesus said to him, "I am the way, and the truth, and the life; no one comes to the Father, but by me. If you had known me, you would have known my Father also; henceforth you know him and have seen him." Philip said to him, "Lord, show us the Father, and we shall be satisfied." Jesus said to him, "Have I been with you so long, and yet you do not know me, Philip? He who has seen me has seen the Father; how can you say, 'Show us the Father'? Do you not believe that I am in the Father and the Father in me? The words that I say to you I do not speak on my own authority; but the Father who dwells in me does his works. Believe me that I am in the Father and the Father in me; or else believe me for the sake of the works themselves. Truly, truly, I say to you, he who believes in me will also do the works that I do; and greater works than these will he do, because I go to the Father. Whatever you ask in my name, I will do it, that the Father may be glorified in the Son; if you ask anything in my name, I will do it.

Tuesday

Psalm 103 [page 733]   ❖   *Psalm 111* [page 754],
Psalm 114 [page 756]

A Reading (Lesson) from the Book of Isaiah [30:18-21]

The Lord waits to be gracious to you; he exalts himself to show mercy to you. For the Lord is a God of justice; blessed are all those who wait for him. Yea, O people in Zion who dwell at Jerusalem; you shall weep no more. He will surely be gracious to you at the sound of your cry; when he hears it, he will answer you. And though the Lord give you the bread of adversity and the water of affliction, yet your Teacher will not hide himself any more, but your eyes shall see your Teacher. And your ears shall hear a word behind you, saying, "This is the way, walk in it," when you turn to the right or when you turn to the left.

A Reading (Lesson) from the Acts of the Apostles [2:36-41(42-47)]*

Peter, standing with the eleven, lifted up his voice and addressed them, "Let all the house of Israel therefore know assuredly that God has made him both Lord and Christ, this Jesus whom you crucified." Now when they heard this they were cut to the heart, and said to Peter and the rest of the apostles, "Brethren, what shall we do?" And Peter said to them, "Repent, and be baptized every one of you in the name of Jesus Christ for the forgiveness of your sins; and you shall receive the gift of the Holy Spirit. For the promise is to you and to your children and to all that are far off, every one whom the Lord our God calls to him." And he testified with many other words and exhorted them, saying, "Save yourselves from this crooked generation." So those who received his word were baptized, and there were added that day about three thousand souls.

*Duplicates the First Lesson at the Eucharist. Readings from Year Two may be substituted.

And they devoted themselves to the apostles' teaching and fellowship, to the breaking of bread and the prayers. And fear came upon every soul; and many wonders and signs were done through the apostles. And all who believed were together and had all things in common; and they sold their possessions and goods and distributed them to all, as any had need. And day by day, attending the temple together and breaking bread in their homes, they partook of food with glad and generous hearts, praising God and having favor with all the people. And the Lord added to their number day by day those who were being saved.

A Reading (Lesson) from the Gospel according to John [14:15-31]

Jesus said to Philip and the disciples, "If you love me, you will keep my commandments. And I will pray the Father, and he will give you another Counselor, to be with you for ever, even the Spirit of truth, whom the world cannot receive, because it neither sees him nor knows him; you know him, for he dwells with you, and will be in you. I will not leave you desolate; I will come to you. Yet a little while, and the world will see me no more, but you will see me; because I live, you will live also. In that day you will know that I am in my Father, and you in me, and I in you. He who has my commandments and keeps them, he it is who loves me; and he who loves me will be loved by my Father, and I will love him and manifest myself to him." Judas (not Iscariot) said to him, "Lord, how is it that you will manifest yourself to us, and not to the world?" Jesus answered him, "If a man loves me, he will keep my word, and my Father will love him, and we will come to him and make our home with him. He who does not love me does not keep my words; and the word which you hear is not mine but the Father's who sent me. These things I have spoken to you, while I am still with you. But the Counselor, the Holy Spirit, whom the Father will send in my name, he will teach you all things, and bring to your remembrance all that I have said to you. Peace I leave with you; my peace I give to you; not as the world gives do I give to you. Let not your hearts be troubled, neither let them be afraid. You heard me say to you, 'I go away, and I will come to you.' If you loved me, you would have rejoiced, because I go to the Father; for the Father is greater than I. And now I have told you before it takes place, so that when it does take place, you may believe. I will no longer talk much with you, for the ruler of this world is coming. He has no power over me; but I do as the Father has commanded me, so that the world may know that I love the Father. Rise, let us go hence."

Wednesday

Psalm 97 [page 726],   *Psalm 99* [page 728]   ❖
Psalm 115 [page 757]

A Reading (Lesson) from the Book of Micah [7:7-15]

As for me, I will look to the Lord, I will wait for the God of my salvation; my God will hear me. Rejoice not over me, O my enemy; when I fall, I shall rise; when I sit in darkness, the Lord will be a light to me. I will bear the indignation of the Lord because I have sinned against him, until he pleads my cause and executes judgment for me. He will bring me forth to the light; I shall behold his deliverance. Then my enemy will see, and shame will cover her who said to me, "Where is the Lord your God?" My eyes will gloat over her; now she will be trodden down like the mire of the streets. A day for the building of your walls! In that day the boundary shall be far extended. In that day they will come to you, from Assyria to Egypt, and from Egypt to the River, from sea to sea and from mountain to mountain. But the earth will be desolate because of its inhabitants, for the fruit of their doings. Shepherd thy people with thy staff, the flock of thy inheritance, who dwell alone in a forest in the midst of a garden land; let them feed in Bashan and Gilead as in the days of old. As in the days when you came out of the land of Egypt I will show them marvelous things.

A Reading (Lesson) from the Acts of the Apostles [3:1-10]*

Peter and John were going up to the temple at the hour of prayer, the ninth hour. And a man lame from birth was being carried, whom they laid daily at that gate of the temple which is called Beautiful to ask alms of those who entered the temple. Seeing Peter and John about to go into the temple, he asked for alms. And Peter directed his gaze at him, with John, and said, "Look at us." And he fixed his attention upon them, expecting to receive something from them. But Peter said, "I have no silver and gold, but I give you what I have; in the name of Jesus Christ of Nazareth, walk." And he took him by the right hand and raised him up; and immediately his feet and ankles were made strong. And leaping up he stood and walked and entered the temple with them, walking and leaping and praising God. And all the people saw him walking and praising God, and recognized him as the one who sat for alms at the Beautiful Gate of the temple; and they were filled with wonder and amazement at what had happened to him.

A Reading (Lesson) from the Gospel according to John [15:1-11]

Jesus said to his disciples, "I am the true vine, and my Father is the vinedresser. Every branch of mine that bears no fruit, he takes away, and every branch that does bear fruit he prunes, that it may bear more fruit. You are already made clean by the word which I have spoken to

*Duplicates the First Lesson at the Eucharist. Readings from Year Two may be substituted.

you. Abide in me, and I in you. As the branch cannot bear fruit by itself, unless it abides in the vine, neither can you, unless you abide in me. I am the vine, you are the branches. He who abides in me, and I in him, he it is that bears much fruit, for apart from me you can do nothing. If a man does not abide in me, he is cast forth as a branch and withers; and the branches are gathered, thrown into the fire and burned. If you abide in me, and my words abide in you, ask whatever you will, and it shall be done for you. By this my Father is glorified, that you bear much fruit, and so prove to be my disciples. As the Father has loved me, so have I loved you; abide in my love. If you keep my commandments, you will abide in my love, just as I have kept my Father's commandments and abide in his love. These things I have spoken to you, that my joy may be in you, and that your joy may be full."

Thursday

Psalm 146 [page 803],   *Psalm 147* [page 804]   ❖
Psalm 148 [page 805],   *Psalm 149* [page 807]

A Reading (Lesson) from the Book of Ezekiel [37:1-14]

The hand of the Lord was upon me, and he brought me out by the Spirit of the Lord, and set me down in the midst of the valley; it was full of bones. And he led me round among them; and behold, there were very many upon the valley; and lo, they were very dry. And he said to me, "Son of man, can these bones live?" And I answered, "O Lord God, thou knowest." Again he said to me, "Prophesy to these bones, and say to them, O dry bones, hear the word of the Lord. Thus say the Lord God to these bones: Behold, I will cause breath to enter you, and you shall live. And I will lay sinews upon you, and will cause flesh to come upon you, and cover you with skin, and put breath in you, and you shall live; and you shall know that I am the Lord." So I prophesied as I was commanded; and as I prophesied, there was a noise, and behold, a rattling; and the bones came together, bone to its bone. And as I looked, there were sinews on them, and flesh had come upon them, and skin had covered them; but there was no breath in them. Then he said to me, "Prophesy to the breath, prophesy, son of man, and say to the breath, Thus says the Lord God: Come from the four winds, O breath, and breathe upon these slain, that they may live." So I prophesied as he commanded me, and the breath came into them, and they lived, and stood upon their feet, an exceedingly great host. Then he said to me, "Son of man, these bones are the whole house of Israel. Behold, they say, 'Our bones are dried up, and our hope is lost; we are clean cut off.' Therefore prophesy and say to them, Thus says the Lord God: Behold, I will open your graves, and raise you from your graves, O my people; and I will bring you home into the land of Israel. And you shall know that I am the Lord, when I open your graves, and raise you from your graves, O my people. And I will put my Spirit within you, and you shall live, and I will place you in your own land; then you shall know that I, the Lord, have spoken, and I have done it, says the Lord."

A Reading (Lesson) from the Acts of the Apostles
[3:11-26]*

While the lame man who had been cured clung to Peter and John, all the people ran together to them in the portico called Solomon's, astounded. And when Peter saw it he addressed the people. "Men of Israel, why do you wonder at this, or why do you stare at us, as though by our own power or piety we had made him walk? The God of Abraham and of Isaac and of Jacob, the God of our fathers, glorified his servant Jesus, whom you delivered up and denied in the presence of Pilate, when he had decided

*Duplicates the First Lesson at the Eucharist. Readings from Year Two may be substituted.

to release him. But you denied the Holy and Righteous One, and asked for a murderer to be granted to you, and killed the Author of life, whom God raised from the dead To this we are witnesses. And his name, by faith in his name, has made this man strong whom you see and know and the faith which is through Jesus has given the man the perfect health in the presence of you all. And now, breathren, I know that you acted in ignorance, as did also your rulers. But what God foretold by the mouth of all the prophets, that his Christ should suffer, he thus fulfilled. Repent therefore, and turn again, that your sins may be blotted out, that times of refreshing may come from the presence of the Lord, and that he may send the Christ appointed for you, Jesus, whom heaven must receive unt the time for establishing all that God spoke by the mouth of his holy prophets from of old. Moses said, 'The Lord God will raise up for you a prophet from your brethren a he raised me up. You shall listen to him in whatever he te you. And it shall be that every soul that does not listen to that prophet shall be destroyed from the people.' And all the prophets who have spoken, from Samuel and those who came afterwards, also proclaimed these days. You a the sons of the prophets and of the convenant which God gave to your fathers, saying to Abraham, 'And in your posterity shall all the families of the earth be blessed.' God having raised up his servant, sent him to you first, to bless you in turning every one of you from your wickedness."

A Reading (Lesson) from the Gospel according to John
[15:12-27]

Jesus said to his disciples, "This is my commandment, tha you love one another as I have loved you. Greater love ha no man than this, that a man lay down his life for his friends. You are my friends if you do what I command yo No longer do I call you servants, for the servant does not know what his master is doing; but I have called you friends, for all that I have heard from my Father I have made known to you. You did not choose me, but I chose you and appointed you that you should go and bear fruit and that your fruit should abide; so that whatever you ask the Father in my name, he may give it to you. This I command you, to love one another. If the world hates you, know that it has hated me before it hated you. If you were of the world, the world would love its own; but because you are not of the world, but I chose you out of the world, therefore the world hates you. Remember the word that I said to you, 'A servant is not greater than his master.' If they persecuted me, they will persecute you; if they kept my word, they will keep yours also. But all this they will do to you on my account, because they do not know him who sent me. If I had not come and spoken to them, they would not have sin; but now they have no excuse for their sin. He who hates me hates my Father also. If I had not done among them the works which no one else did, they would not have sin; but now they have seen and hated both me and my Father. It is to fulfil the word that is written in their law, 'They hated me without a cause.' But when the Counselor comes, whom I shall send to you from the Father, even the Spirit of truth, who proceeds from the Father, he will bear witness to me; and you also are witnesses, because you have been with me from the beginning."

Friday

Psalm 136 [page 789]   ❖   *Psalm 118* [page 760]

A Reading (Lesson) from the Book of Daniel [12:1-4,13]

One having the appearance of a man said to me, "At that time shall arise Michael, the great prince who has charge of your people. And there shall be a time of trouble, such as never has been since there was a nation till that time; but at that time your people shall be delivered, every one

whose name shall be found written in the book. And man
of those who sleep in the dust of the earth shall awake,
some to everlasting life, and some to shame and everlastin
contempt. And those who are wise shall shine like the
brightness of the firmament; and those who turn many to
righteousness, like the stars for ever and ever. But you,
Daniel, shut up the words, and seal the book, until the tim
of the end. Many shall run to and fro, and knowledge sha
increase. But go your way till the end; and you shall rest,
and shall stand in your allotted place at the end of the
days."

A Reading (Lesson) from the Acts of the Apostles [4:1-12]

As Peter and John were speaking to the people, the priests
and the captain of the temple and the Sad'ducees came
upon them, annoyed because they were teaching the
people and proclaiming in Jesus the resurrection from the
dead. And they arrested them and put them in custody
until the morrow, for it was already evening. But many of
those who heard the word believed; and the number of th
men came to about five thousand. On the morrow their
rulers and elders and scribes were gathered together in
Jerusalem, with Annas the high priest and Ca'iaphas and
John and Alexander, and all who were of the high-priestly
family. And when they had set them in the midst, they
inquired, "By what power or by what name do you do
this?" Then Peter, filled with the Holy Spirit, said to them.
"Rulers of the people and elders, if we are being examined
today concerning a good deed done to a cripple, by what
means this man has been healed, be it known to you all,
and to all the people of Israel, that by the name of Jesus
Christ of Nazareth, whom you crucified, whom God raise
from the dead, by him this man is standing before you

---

*Duplicates the First Lesson at the Eucharist. Readings from Year Tw
may be substituted.*

well. This is the stone which was rejected by you builders, but which has become the head of the corner. And there is salvation in no one else, for there is no other name under heaven given among men by which we must be saved."

A Reading (Lesson) from the Gospel according to John
[16:1-15]

Jesus said to his disciples, "I have said all this to you to keep you from falling away. They will put you out of the synagogues; indeed the hour is coming when whoever kills you will think he is offering service to God. And they will do this because they have not known the Father, nor me. But I have said these things to you, that when their hour comes you may remember that I told you of them. I did not say these things to you from the beginning, because I was with you. But now I am going to him who sent me; yet none of you asks me, 'Where are you going?' But because I have said these things to you, sorrow has filled your hearts. Nevertheless I tell you the truth: it is to your advantage that I go away, for if I do not go away, the Counselor will not come to you; but if I go, I will send him to you. And when he comes, he will convince the world concerning sin and righteousness and judgment: concerning sin, because they do not believe in me; concerning righteousness, because I go to the Father, and you will see me no more; concerning judgment, because the ruler of this world is judged. I have yet many things to say to you, but you cannot bear them now. When the Spirit of truth comes, he will guide you into all the truth; for he will not speak on his own authority, but whatever he hears he will speak, and he will declare to you the things that are to come. He will glorify me, for he will take what is mine and declare it to you. All that the Father has is mine; therefore I said that he will take what is mine and declare it to you."

Saturday

Psalm 145 [page 801]   ❖   *Psalm 104* [page 735]

Isaiah 25:1-9   [page 74 above]

A Reading (Lesson) from the Acts of the Apostles
[4:13-21(22-31)]*

When the rulers and elders and scribes saw the boldness of
Peter and John, and perceived that they were uneducated,
common men, they wondered; and they recognized that
they had been with Jesus. But seeing the man that had been
healed standing beside them, they had nothing to say in
opposition. But when they had commanded them to go
aside out of the council, they conferred with one another,
saying, "What shall we do with these men? For that a
notable sign has been performed through them is manifest
to all the inhabitants of Jerusalem, and we cannot deny it.
But in order that it may spread no further among the
people, let us warn them to speak no more to any one in
this name." So they called them and charged them not to
speak or teach at all in the name of Jesus. But Peter and
John answered them, "Whether it is right in the sight of
God to listen to you rather than to God, you must judge;
for we cannot but speak of what we have seen and heard."
And when they had further threatened them, they let them
go, finding no way to punish them, because of the people;
for all men praised God for what had happened.

> For the man on whom this sign of healing was
> performed was more than forty years old. When they
> were released they went to their friends and reported
> what the chief priests and the elders had said to them.
> And when they heard it, they lifted their voices together

*Duplicates the First Lesson at the Eucharist. Readings from Year Two
may be substituted.*

to God and said, "Sovereign Lord, who didst make the heaven and the earth and the sea and everything in them, who by the mouth of our father David, thy servant, didst say by the Holy Spirit, 'Why did the Gentiles rage, and the peoples imagine vain things? The kings of the earth set themselves in array, and the rulers were gathered together, against the Lord and against his Anointed'—for truly in this city there were gathered together against thy holy servant Jesus, whom thou didst anoint, both Herod and Pontius Pilate, with the Gentiles and the peoples of Israel, to do whatever thy hand and thy plan had predestined to take place. And now, Lord, look upon their threats, and grant to thy servants to speak thy word with all boldness, while thou stretchest out thy hand to heal, and signs and wonders are performed through the name of thy holy servant Jesus. And when they had prayed, the place in which they were gathered together was shaken; and they were all filled with the Holy Spirit and spoke the word of God with boldness.

A Reading (Lesson) from the Gospel according to John
[16:16-33]

Jesus said to his disciples, "A little while, and you will see me no more; again a little while, and you will see me." Some of his disciples said to one another, "What is this that he says to us, 'A little while, and you will not see me, and again a little while, and you will see me'; and, 'because I go to the Father'?" They said, "What does he mean by 'a little while'? We do not know what he means." Jesus knew that they wanted to ask him; so he said to them, "Is this what you are asking yourselves, what I meant by saying 'A little while, and you will not see me, and again a little while, and you will see me'? Truly, truly, I say to you, you will weep and lament, but the world will rejoice; you will be sorrowful, but your sorrow will turn into joy. When a woman is in travail she has sorrow, because her hour has come; but when she is delivered of the child, she no longer remembers the anguish, for joy that a child is born into the world. So you have sorrow now, but I will see you again and your hearts will rejoice, and no one will take your joy from you. In that day you will ask nothing of me. Truly, truly, I say to you, if you ask anything of the Father, he will give it to you in my name. Hitherto you have asked nothing in my name; ask, and you will receive, that your joy may be full. I have said this to you in figures; the hour is coming when I shall no longer speak to you in figures but tell you plainly of the Father. In that day you will ask in my name; and I do not say to you that I shall pray the Father for you; for the Father himself loves you, because you have loved me and have believed that I came from the Father. I came from the Father and have come into the world; again, I am leaving the world and going to the Father." His disciples said, "Ah, now you are speaking plainly, not in any figure! Now we know that you know all things, and need none to question you; by this we believe that you came from God." Jesus answered them, "Do you now believe? The hour is coming, indeed it has come, when you will be scattered, every man to his home, and will leave me alone; yet I am not alone, for the Father is with me. I have said this to you, that in me you may have peace. In the world you have tribulation; but be of good cheer, I have overcome the world."

Week of 2 Easter

Sunday

Psalm 146 [page 803], *Psalm 147* [page 804] ❖
Psalm 111 [page 754], *Psalm 112* [page 755],
Psalm 113 [page 756]

A Reading (Lesson) from the Book of Isaiah [43:8-13]

Bring forth the people who are blind, yet have eyes, who are deaf, yet have ears! Let all the nations gather together, and let the peoples assemble. Who among them can declare this, and show us the former things? Let them bring their witnesses to justify them, and let them hear and say, It is true. "You are my witnesses," says the Lord, "and my servant whom I have chosen, that you may know and believe me and understand that I am He. Before me no god was formed, nor shall there be any after me. I, I am the Lord, and besides me there is no savior. I declared and saved and proclaimed, when there was no strange god among you; and you are my witnesses," says the Lord. "I am God, and also henceforth I am He; there is none who can deliver from my hand; I work and who can hinder it?"

A Reading (Lesson) from the First Letter of Peter [2:2-10]

Like newborn babes, long for the pure spiritual milk, that by it you may grow up to salvation; for you have tasted the kindness of the Lord. Come to him, to that living stone, rejected by men but in God's sight chosen and precious; and like living stones be yourselves built into a spiritual house, to be a holy priesthood, to offer spiritual sacrifices acceptable to God through Jesus Christ. For it stands in scripture: "Behold, I am laying in Zion a stone, a cornerstone chosen and precious, and he who believes in him will not be put to shame." To you therefore who believe, he is precious, but for those who do not believe, "The very stone which the builders rejected has become the head of the corner," and "A stone that will make men stumble, a rock that will make them fall"; for they stumble because they disobey the word, as they were destined to do. But you are a chosen race, a royal priesthood, a holy nation, God's own people, that you may declare the wonderful deeds of him who called you out of darkness

into his marvelous light. Once you were no people but now
you are God's people; once you had not received mercy but
now you have received mercy.

A Reading (Lesson) from the Gospel according to John
[14:1-7]

Jesus said to Peter and the disciples, "Let not your hearts
be troubled; believe in God, believe also in me. In my
Father's house are many rooms; if it were not so, would I
have told you that I go to prepare a place for you? And
when I go and prepare a place for you, I will come again
and will take you to myself, that were I am you may be
also. And you know the way where I am going." Thomas
said to him, "Lord, we do not know where you are going;
how can we know the way?" Jesus said to him, "I am the
way, and the truth, and the life; no one comes to the
Father, but by me. If you had known me, you would have
known my Father also; henceforth you know him and
have seen him."

Monday

Psalm 1 [page 585],   *Psalm 2* [page 586],
Psalm 3 [page 587]   ❖   *Psalm 4* [page 587],
Psalm 7 [page 590]

A Reading (Lesson) from the Book of Daniel [1:1-21]

In the third year of the reign of Jehoi'akim king of Judah,
Nebuchadnez'zar king of Babylon came to Jerusalem and
besieged it. And the Lord gave Jehoi'akim king of Judah
into his hand, with some of the vessels of the house of
God; and he brought them to the land of Shinar, to the
house of his god, and placed the vessels in the treasury of
his god. Then the king commanded Ash'penaz, his chief
eunuch, to bring some of the people of Israel, both of the

royal family and of the nobility, youths without blemish, handsome and skilful in all wisdom, endowed with knowledge, understanding learning, and competent to serve in the king's palace, and to teach them the letters and language of the Chalde'ans. The king assigned them a daily portion of the rich food which the king ate, and of the wine which he drank. They were to be educated for three years, and at the end of that time they were to stand before the king. Among these were Daniel, Hanani'ah, Mish'a-el, and Azari'ah of the tribe of Judah. And the chief of the eunuchs gave them names: Daniel he called Belteshaz'zar, Hanani'ah he called Shadrach, Mish'a-el he called Meshach, and Azari'ah he called Abed'nego. But Daniel resolved that he would not defile himself with the king's rich food, or with the wine which he drank; therefore he asked the chief of the eunuchs to allow him not to defile himself. And God gave Daniel favor and compassion in the sight of the chief of the eunuchs; and the chief of the eunuchs said to Daniel, "I fear lest my lord the king, who appointed your food and your drink, should see that you were in poorer condition than the youths who are of your own age. So you would endanger my head with the king." Then Daniel said to the steward whom the chief of the eunuchs had appointed over Daniel, Hanani'ah, Mish'a-el, and Azari'ah; "Test your servants for ten days; let us be given vegetables to eat and water to drink. Then let our appearance and the appearance of the youths who eat the king's rich food be observed by you, and according to what you see deal with your servants." So he hearkened to them in this matter, and tested them for ten days. At the end of ten days it was seen that they were better in appearance and fatter in flesh than all the youths who ate the king's rich food. So the steward took away their rich food and the wine they were to drink, and gave them vegetables. As for these four youths, God gave them learning and skill in all letters and wisdom; and Daniel had understanding in all visions and dreams. At the end of the time, when the king had commanded that they should be brought in, the chief of the eunuchs brought them in before Nebuchadnez'zar. And the king spoke with them, and among them all none was found like Daniel, Hanani'ah, Mish'a-el, and Azari'ah; therefore they stood before the king. And in every matter of wisdom and understanding concerning which the king inquired of them, he found them ten times better than all the magicians and enchanters that were in all his kingdom. And Daniel continued until the first year of King Cyrus.

A Reading (Lesson) from the First Letter of John [1:1-10]

That which was from the beginning, which we have heard, which we have seen with our eyes, which we have looked upon and touched with our hands, concerning the word of life — the life was made manifest, and we saw it, and testify to it, and proclaim to you the eternal life which was with the Father and was made manifest to us — that which we have seen and heard we proclaim also to you, so that you may have fellowship with us; and our fellowship is with the Father and with his Son Jesus Christ. And we are writing this that our joy may be complete. This is the message we have heard from him and proclaim to you, that God is light and in him is no darkness at all. If we say we have fellowship with him while we walk in darkness, we lie and do not live according to the truth; but if we walk in the light, as he is in the light, we have fellowship with one another, and the blood of Jesus his Son cleanses us from all sin. If we say we have no sin, we deceive ourselves, and truth is not in us. If we confess our sins, he is faithful and just, and will forgive our sins and cleanse us from all unrighteousness. If we say we have not sinned, we make him a liar, and his word is not in us.

A Reading (Lesson) from the Gospel according to John
[17:1-11]

When Jesus had spoken these words, he lifted up his eyes
to heaven and said, "Father , the hour has come; glorify
thy Son that the Son may glorify thee, since thou hast given
him power over all flesh, to give eternal life to all whom
thou hast given him. And this is eternal life, that they know
thee the only true God, and Jesus Christ whom thou hast
sent. I glorified thee on earth, having accomplished the
work which thou gavest me to do; and now, Father, glorify
thou me in thy own presence with the glory which I had
with thee before the world was made. I have manifested
thy name to the men whom thou gavest me out of the
world; thine they were, and thou gavest them to me, and
they have kept thy word. Now they know that everything
that thou hast given me is from thee; for I have given them
the words which thou gavest me, and they have received
them and know in truth that I came from thee; and they
have believed that thou didst send me. I am praying for
them; I am not praying for the world but for those whom
thou hast given me, for they are thine; all mine are thine,
and thine are mine, and I am glorified in them. And now I
am no more in the world, but they are in the world, and I
am coming to thee. Holy Father, keep them in thy name,
which thou hast given me, that they may be one, even as
we are one."

Tuesday

Psalm 5 [page 588], *Psalm 6* [page 589] ❖
Psalm 10 [page 594], *Psalm 11* [page 596]

A Reading (Lesson) from the Book of Daniel [2:1-16]

In the second year of the reign of Nebuchadnez′zar,
Nebuchadnez′zar had dreams; and his spirit was troubled,
and his sleep left him. Then the king commanded that the

magicians, the enchanters, the sorcerers, and the Chalde'ans be summoned, to tell the king his dreams. So they came in and stood before the king. And the king said to them, "I had a dream, and my spirit is troubled to know the dream." Then the Chalde'ans said to the king, "O king, live for ever! Tell your servants the dream, and we will show the interpretation." The king answered the Chalde'ans, "The word from me is sure; if you do not make known to me the dream and its interpretation, you shall be torn limb from limb, and your houses shall be laid in ruins. But if you show the dream and its interpretation, you shall receive from me gifts and rewards and great honor. Therefore show me the dream and its interpretation." They answered a second time, "Let the king tell his servants the dream, and we will show its interpretation." The king answered, "I know with certainty that you are trying to gain time, because you see that the word from me is sure that if you do not make the dream known to me, there is but one sentence for you. You have agreed to speak lying and corrupt words before me till the times change. Therefore tell me the dream, and I shall know that you can show me its interpretation." The Chalde'ans answered the king, "There is not a man on earth who can meet the king's demand; for no great and powerful king has asked such a thing of any magician or enchanter or Chalde'an. The thing that the king asks is difficult, and none can show it to the king except the gods, whose dwelling is not with flesh." Because of this the king was angry and very furious, and commanded that all the wise men of Babylon be destroyed. So the decree went forth that the wise men were to be slain, and they sought Daniel and his companions, to slay them. Then Daniel replied with prudence and discretion to Ar'i-och, the captain of the king's guard, who had gone out to slay the wise men of Babylon; he said to Ar'i-och, the king's captain, "Why is the decree of the king so severe?" Then Ar'i-och made the matter known to Daniel. And Daniel went in and besought the king to appoint him a time, that he might show to the king the interpretation.

A Reading (Lesson) from the First Letter of John [2:1-11]

My little children, I am writing this to you so that you may
not sin; but if any one does sin, we have an advocate with
the Father, Jesus Christ the righteous; and he is the
expiation for our sins, and not for ours only but also for
the sins of the whole world. And by this we may be sure
that we know him, if we keep his commandments. He who
says "I know him" but disobeys his commandments is a
liar, and the truth is not in him; but whoever keeps his
word, in him truly love for God is perfected. By this we
may be sure that we are in him: he who says he abides in
him ought to walk in the same way in which he walked.
Beloved, I am writing you no new commandment, but an
old commandment which you had from the beginning; the
old commandment is the word, which you have heard. Yet
I am writing you a new commandment, which is true in
him and in you, because the darkness is passing away and
the true light is already shining. He who says he is in the
light and hates his brother is in the darkness still. He who
loves his brother abides in the light, and in it there is no
cause for stumbling. But he who hates his brother is in the
darkness and walks in the darkness, and does not know
where he is going, because the darkness has blinded his
eyes.

A Reading (Lesson) from the Gospel according to John
[17:12-19]

Jesus lifted up his eyes to heaven and said, "While I was
with them, I kept them in thy name, which thou hast given
me; I have guarded them, and none of them is lost but the
son of perdition, that the scripture might be fulfilled. But
now I am coming to thee; and these things I speak in the
world, that they may have my joy fulfilled in themselves. I
have given them thy word; and the world has hated them
because they are not of the world, even as I am not of the
world. I do not pray that thou shouldst take them out of

the world, but that thou shouldst keep them from the evil
one. They are not of the world, even as I am not of the
world. Sanctify them in the truth; thy word is truth. As
thou didst send me into the world, so I have sent them into
the world. And for their sake I consecrate myself, that they
also may be consecrated in truth."

Wednesday

Psalm 119:1-24 [page 763] ❖ *Psalm 12* [page 597],
Psalm 13 [page 597],   *Psalm 14* [page 598]

A Reading (Lesson) from the Book of Daniel [2:17-30]

Daniel went to his house and made the matter known to
Hanani′ah, Mish′a-el, and Azari′ah, his companions, and
told them to seek mercy of the God of heaven concerning
this mystery, so that Daniel and his companions might not
perish with the rest of the wise men of Babylon. Then the
mystery was revealed to Daniel in a vision of the night.
Then Daniel blessed the God of heaven. Daniel said:
"Blessed be the name of God for ever and ever, to whom
belong wisdom and might. He changes times and seasons;
he removes kings and sets up kings; he gives wisdom to the
wise and knowledge to those who have understanding; he
reveals deep and mysterious things; he knows what is in
the darkness, and the light dwells with him. To thee, O
God of my fathers, I give thanks and praise, for thou hast
given me wisdom and strength, and hast now made known
to me what we asked of thee, for thou hast made known to
us the king's matter." Therefore Daniel went in to Ar′i-och,
whom the king had appointed to destroy the wise men of
Babylon; he went and said thus to him, "Do not destroy
the wise men of Babylon; bring me in before the king, and
will show the king the interpretation." Then Ar′i-och
brought in Daniel before the king in haste, and said thus to
him: "I have found among the exiles from Judah a man
who can make known to the king the interpretation." The

king said to Daniel, whose name was Belteshaz'zar, "Are you able to make known to me the dream that I have seen and its interpretation?" Daniel answered the king, "No wise men, enchanters, magicians, or astrologers can show to the king the mystery which the king has asked, but there is a God in heaven who reveals mysteries, and he has made known to King Nebuchadnez'zar what will be in the latter days. Your dream and the visions of your head as you lay in bed are these: To you, O king, as you lay in bed came thoughts of what would be hereafter, and he who reveals mysteries made known to you what is to be. But as for me, not because of any wisdom that I have more than all the living has this mystery been revealed to me, but in order that the interpretation may be known to the king, and that you may know the thoughts of your mind."

1 John 2:12-17   [page 81 above]

A Reading (Lesson) from the Gospel according to John
[17:20-26]

Jesus lifted up his eyes to heaven and said, "I do not pray for these only, but also for those who believe in me through their word, that they may all be one; even as thou, Father, art in me, and I in thee, that they also may be in us, so that the world may believe that thou hast sent me. The glory which thou hast given me I have given to them, that they may be one even as we are one, I in them and thou in me, that they may become perfectly one, so that the world may know that thou hast sent me and hast loved them even as thou hast loved me. Father, I desire that they also, whom thou hast given me, may be with me where I am, to behold my glory which thou hast given me in thy love for me before the foundation of the world. O righteous Father, the world has not known thee, but I have known thee; and these know that thou hast sent me. I made known to them thy name, and I will make it known, that the love with which thou hast loved me may be in them, and I in them."

Thursday

Psalm 18:1-20 [page 602]   ❖   *Psalm 18:21-50* [page 604]

A Reading (Lesson) from the Book of Daniel [2:31-49]

Daniel answered the king, "You saw, O king, and behold, a great image. This image, mighty and of exceeding brightness, stood before you, and its appearance was frightening. The head of this image was of fine gold, its breast and arms of silver, its belly and thighs of bronze, its legs of iron, its feet partly of iron and partly of clay. As you looked, a stone was cut out by no human hand, and it smote the image on its feet of iron and clay, and broke them in pieces; then the iron, the clay, the bronze, the silver, and the gold, all together were broken in pieces, and became like the chaff of the summer threshing floors; and the wind carried them away, so that not a trace of them could be found. But the stone that struck the image became a great mountain and filled the whole earth. This was the dream; now we will tell the king its interpretation. You, O king, the king of kings, to whom the God of heaven has given the kingdom, the power, and the might, and the glory, and into whose hand he has given, wherever they dwell, the sons of men, the beasts of the field, and the birds of the air, making you rule over them all—you are the head of gold. After you shall arise another kingdom inferior to you, and yet a third kingdom of bronze, which shall rule over all the earth. And there shall be a fourth kingdom, strong as iron, because iron breaks to pieces and shatters all things; and like iron which crushes, it shall break and crush all these. And as you saw the feet and toes partly of potter's clay and partly of iron, it shall be a divided kingdom; but some of the firmness of iron shall be in it, just as you saw iron mixed with miry clay. And as the toes of the feet were partly iron and partly clay, so the kingdom shall be partly strong and partly brittle. As you saw the iron mixed with miry clay, so they will mix with one another in marriage, but they will not hold together, just as iron does not mix with clay. And in the days of those kings the God of heaven will set up a kingdom which shall never be destroyed, nor shall its sovereignty be left to another people. It shall break in pieces all these kingdoms and bring them to an end, and it shall stand for ever; just as you saw that a stone was cut from a mountain by no human hand, and that it broke in pieces the iron, the bronze, the clay, the silver, and the gold. A great God has made known to the king what shall be hereafter. The dream is certain, and its interpretation sure." Then King Nebuchadnez'zar fell upon his face, and did homage to Daniel, and commanded that an offering and incense be offered up to him. The king said to Daniel, "Truly, your God is God of gods and Lord of kings, and a revealer of mysteries, for you have been able to reveal this mystery." Then the king gave Daniel high honors and many great gifts, and made him ruler over the whole province of Babylon, and chief prefect over all the wise men of Babylon. Daniel made request of the king, and he appointed Shadrach, Meshach, and Abed'nego over the affairs of the province of Babylon; but Daniel remained at the king's court.

A Reading (Lesson) from the First Letter of John [2:18-29]

Children, it is the last hour; and as you have heard that antichrist is coming, so now many antichrists have come; therefore we know that it is the last hour. They went out from us, but they were not of us; for if they had been of us, they would have continued with us; but they went out, that it might be plain that they all are not of us. But you have been anointed by the Holy One, and you all know. I write to you, not because you do not know the truth, but because you know it, and know that no lie is of the truth. Who is the liar but he who denies that Jesus is the Christ? This is the antichrist, he who denies the Father and the Son. No one who denies the Son has the Father. He who confesses the Son has the Father also. Let what you heard from the beginning abide in you. If what you heard from the beginning abides in you, then you will abide in the Son and in the Father. And this is what he has promised us, eternal life. I write this to you about those who would deceive you; but the anointing which you received from him abides in you, and you have no need that any one should teach you; as his anointing teaches you about everything, and is true, and is no lie, just as it has taught you, abide in him. And now, little children, abide in him, so that when he appears we may have confidence and not shrink from him in shame at his coming. If you know that he is righteous, you may be sure that every one who does right is born of him.

A Reading (Lesson) from the Gospel according to Luke
[3:1-14]

In the fifteenth year of the reign of Tibe'ri-us Caesar, Pontius Pilate being governor of Judea, and Herod being tetrarch of Galilee, and his brother Philip tetrarch of the region of Iturae'a and Trachoni'tis, and Lysa'ni-as tetrarch of Abile'ne, in the high-priesthood of Annas and Ca'iaphas, the word of God came to John the son of Zechari'ah in the wilderness; and he went into all the region about the Jordan, preaching a baptism of repentance for the forgiveness of sins. As it is written in the book of the words of Isaiah the prophet, "The voice of one crying in the wilderness: Prepare the way of the Lord, make his paths straight. Every valley shall be filled, and every mountain and hill shall be brought low, and the crooked shall be made straight, and the rough ways shall be made smooth; and all flesh shall see the salvation of God." He said therefore to the multitudes that came out to be baptized by him, "You brood of vipers! Who warned you to flee from the wrath to come? Bear fruits that befit repentance, and do not begin to say to yourselves, 'We have Abraham as our father'; for I tell you, God is able from these stones to raise up children to Abraham. Even now the axe is laid to the root of the trees; every tree therefore that does not bear good fruit is cut down and thrown into the fire." And the multitudes asked him, "What then shall we do?" And he answered them, "He who has two coats, let him share with him who has none; and he who has food, let him do likewise." Tax collectors also came to be baptized, and said to him, "Teacher, what shall we do?" And he said to them, "Collect no more than is appointed you." Soldiers also asked him, "And we, what shall we do?" And he said to them, "Rob no one by violence or false accusation, and be content with your wages."

Friday

Psalm 16 [page 599],   *Psalm 17* [page 600]   ❖
Psalm 134 [page 787],   *Psalm 135* [page 788]

A Reading (Lesson) from the Book of Daniel [3:1-18]

King Nebuchandnez'zar made an image of gold, whose height was sixty cubits and its breadth six cubits. He set it up on the plain of Dura, in the province of Babylon. Then King Nebuchadnez'zar sent to assemble the satraps, the prefects, and the governors, the counselors, the treasurers, the justices, the magistrates, and all the officials of the provinces to come to the dedication of the image which King Nebuchadnez'zar had set up. Then the satraps, the prefects, and the governors, the counselors, the treasurers, the justices, the magistrates, and all the officials of the provinces, were assembled for the dedication of the image that King Nebuchadnez'zar had set up; and they stood before the image that Nebuchadnez'zar had set up. And the herald proclaimed aloud, "You are commanded, O peoples, nations, and languages, that when you hear the sound of the horn, pipe, lyre, trigon, harp, bagpipe, and every kind of music, you are to fall down and worship the golden image that King Nebuchadnez'zar has set up; and whoever does not fall down and worship shall immediately be cast into a burning fiery furnace." Therefore, as soon as all the peoples heard the sound of the horn, pipe, lyre, trigon, harp, bagpipe, and every kind of music, all the peoples, nations, and languages fell down and worshipped the golden image which King Nebuchadnez'zar had set up. Therefore at that time certain Chalde'ans came forward and maliciously accused the Jews. They said to King Nebuchadnez'zar, "O king, live for ever! You, O king, have made a decree, that every man who hears the sound of the horn, pipe, lyre, trigon, harp, bagpipe, and every kind of music, shall fall down and worship the golden image; and whoever does not fall down and worship shall be cast into a burning fiery furnace. There are certain Jews whom you have appointed over the affairs of the province of Babylon: Shadrach, Meshach, and Abed'nego. These men, O king, pay no heed to you; they do not serve your gods or worship the golden image which you have set up." Then Nebuchadnez'zar in furious rage commanded that Shadrach, Meshach, and Abed'nego be brought. Then they brought these men before the king. Nebuchadnez'zar said to them, "Is it true, O Shadrach, Meshach, and Abed'nego, that you do not serve my gods or worship the golden image which I have set up? Now if you are ready when you hear the sound of the horn, pipe, lyre, trigon, harp, bagpipe, and every kind of music, to fall down and worship the image which I have made, well and good; but if you do not worship, you shall immediately be cast into a burning fiery furnace; and who is the god that will deliver you out of my hands?" Shadrach, Meshach, and Abed'nego answered the king, "O Nebuchadnez'zar, we have no need to answer you in this matter. If it be so, our God whom we serve is able to deliver us from burning fiery furnace; and he will deliver us out of your hand, O king. But if not, be it known to you, O king, that we will not serve your gods or worship the golden image which you have set up."

A Reading (Lesson) from the First Letter of John [3:1-10]

See what love the Father has given us, that we should be called children of God; and so we are. The reason why the world does not know us is that it did not know him. Beloved, we are God's children now; it does not yet appear what we shall be, but we know that when he appears we shall be like him, for we shall see him as he is. And every one who thus hopes in him purifies himself as he is pure. Every one who commits sin is guilty of lawlessness; sin is lawlessness. You know that he appeared to take away sins, and in him there is no sin. No one who abides in him sins; no one who sins has either seen him or known him. Little children, let no one deceive you. He who does right is righteous, as he is righteous. He who commits sin is of the devil; for the devil has sinned from the beginning. The reason the Son of God appeared was to destroy the works of the devil. No one born of God commits sin; for God's nature abides in him, and he cannot sin because he is born of God. By this it may be seen who are the children of God, and who are the children of the devil: whoever does not do right is not of God, nor he who does not love his brother.

A Reading (Lesson) from the Gospel according to Luke [3:15-22]

As the people were in expectation, and all men questioned in their hearts concerning John, whether perhaps he were the Christ, John answered them all, "I baptize you with water; but he who is mightier than I is coming, the thong of whose sandals I am not worthy to untie; he will baptize you with the Holy Spirit and with fire. His winnowing fork is in his hand, to clear his threshing floor, and to gather the wheat into his granary, but the chaff he will burn with unquenchable fire." So, with many other exhortations, he preached good news to the people. But Herod the tetrarch, who had been reproved by him for Hero'di-as, his brother's wife, and for all the evil things that Herod had done, added this to them all, that he shut up John in prison. Now when all the people were baptized, and when Jesus also had been baptized and was praying, the heaven was opened, and the Holy Spirit descended upon him in bodily form, as a dove, and a voice came from heaven, "Thou art my beloved Son; wth thee I am well pleased."

Saturday

Psalm 20 [page 608],   *Psalm 21:1-7(8-14)* [page 608]   ❖
Psalm 110:1-5(6-7) [page 753],   *Psalm 116* [page 759],
Psalm 117 [page 760]

A Reading (Lesson) from the Book of Daniel [3:19-30]

Nebuchadnez'zar was full of fury, and the expression of his face was changed against Shadrach, Meshach, and Abed'nego. He ordered the furnace heated seven times more than it was wont to be heated. And he ordered certain mighty men of his army to bind Shadrach, Meshach, and Abed'nego, and to cast them into the burning fiery furnace. Then these men were bound in their mantles, their tunics, their hats, and their other garments, and they were cast into the burning fiery furnace. Because the king's order was strict and the furnace very hot, the flame of the fire slew those men who took up Shadrach, Meshach, and Abed'nego. And these three men, Shadrach, Meshach, and Abed'nego, fell bound into the burning fiery furnace. Then King Nebuchadnez'zar was astonished and rose up in haste. He said to his counselors, "Did we not cast three men bound into the fire?" They answered the king, "True, O king." He answered, "But I see four men loose, walking in the midst of the fire, and they are not hurt; and the appearance of the fourth is like a son of the gods." Then Nebuchadnez'zar came near to the door of the burning fiery furnace and said, "Shadrach, Meshach, and Abed'nego, servants of the Most High God, come forth, and come here!" Then Shadrach, Meshach, and Abed'nego came out from the fire. And the satraps, the prefects, the governors, and the king's counselors gathered together and saw that the fire had not had any power over the bodies of those men; the hair of their heads was not singed, their mantles were not harmed, and no smell of fire had come upon them. Nebuchadnez'zar said, "Blessed be the God of Shadrach, Meshach, and Abed'nego, who has sent his angel and delivered his servants, who trusted in him, and set at nought the king's command, and yielded up their bodies rather than serve and worship any god except their own God. Therefore I make a decree: Any people, nation, or language that speaks anything against the God of Shadrach, Meshach, and Abed'nego shall be torn limb from limb, and their houses laid in ruins; for there is no other god who is able to deliver in this way." Then the king promoted Shadrach, Meshach, and Abed'nego in the province of Babylon.

A Reading (Lesson) from the First Letter of John [3:11-18]

This is the message which you have heard from the beginning, that we should love one another, and not be like Cain who was of the evil one and murdered his brother. And why did he murder him? Because his own deeds were evil and his brother's righteous. Do not wonder brethren, that the world hates you. We know that we have passed out of death into life, because we love the brethren. He who does not love abides in death. Any one who hates his brother is a murderer, and you know that no murderer has eternal life abiding in him. By this we know love, that he laid down his life for us; and we ought to lay down our lives for the brethren. But if any one has the world's goods and sees his brother in need, yet closes his heart against him, how does God's love abide in him? Little children, let us not love in word or speech but in deed and in truth.

A Reading (Lesson) from the Gospel according to Luke
[4:1-13]

Jesus, full of the Holy Spirit, returned from the Jordan, and was led by the Spirit for forty days in the wilderness, tempted by the devil. And he ate nothing in those days; and when they were ended, he was hungry. The devil said to him, "If you are the Son of God, command this stone to become bread." And Jesus answered him, "It is written, 'Man shall not live by bread alone.'" And the devil took him up, and showed him all the kingdoms of the world in a moment of time, and said to him, "To you I will give all this authority and their glory; for it has been delivered to me, and I give it to whom I will. If you, then, will worship me, it shall all be yours." And Jesus answered him, "It is written, 'You shall worship the Lord your God, and him only shall you serve.'" And he took him to Jerusalem, and set him on the pinnacle of the temple, and said to him, "If you are the Son of God, throw yourself down from here; for it is written, 'He will give his angels charge of you, to guard you,' and 'On their hands they will bear you up, lest you strike your foot against a stone.'" And Jesus answered him, "It is said, 'You shall not tempt the Lord your God.'" And when the devil had ended every temptation, he departed from him until an opportune time.

Week of 3 Easter

Sunday

Psalm 148 [page 805],   *Psalm 149* [page 807]   ❖
Psalm 150 [page 807],   *Psalm 114* [page 756],
Psalm 115 [page 757]

A Reading (Lesson) from the Book of Daniel [4:1-18]

King Nebuchadnez'zar to all peoples, nations, and

languages, that dewll in all the earth: Peace be multiplied to you! It has seemed good to me to show the signs and wonders that the Most High God has wrought toward me. How great are his signs, how mightly his wonders! His kingdom is an everlasting kingdom, and his dominion is from generation to generation. I, Nebuchadnez'zar, was at ease in my house and prospering in my palace. I had a dream which made me afraid; as I lay in bed the fancies and the visions of my head alarmed me. Therefore I made a decree that all the wise men of Babylon should be brought before me, that they might make known to me the interpretation of the dream. Then the magicians, the enchanters, the Chalde'ans, and the astrologers came in; and I told them the dream, but they could not make known to me its interpretation. At last Daniel came in before me—he who was named Belteshaz'zar after the name of my god, and in whom is the spirit of the holy gods—and I told him the dream, saying, "O Belteshaz'zar, chief of the magicians, because I know that the spirit of the holy gods is in you and that no mystery is difficult for you, here is the dream which I saw; tell me its interpretation. The visions of my head as I lay in bed were these: I saw, and behold, a tree in the midst of the earth; and its height was great. The tree grew and became strong, and its top reached to heaven, and it was visible to the end of the whole earth. Its leaves were fair and its fruit abundant, and in it was food for all. The beasts of the field found shade under it, and the birds of the air dwelt in its branches, and all flesh was fed from it. I saw in the visions of my head as I lay in bed, and behold, a watcher, a holy one, came down from heaven. He cried aloud and said thus, 'Hew down the tree and cut off its branches, strip off its leaves and scatter its fruit; let the beasts flee from under it and the birds from its branches. But leave the stump of its roots in the earth, bound with a band of iron and bronze, amid the tender grass of the field. Let him be wet with the dew of heaven; let his lot be with the beasts in the grass of the earth; let his mind be changed from a man's, and let a beast's mind be given to him; and let seven times pass over him. The sentence is by the decree of the watchers, the decision by the word of the holy ones, to the end that the living may know that the Most High rules the kingdom of men, and gives it to whom he will, and sets over it the lowliest of men.' This dream I, King Nebuchadnez′zar, saw. And you, O Belteshaz′zar, declare the interpretation, because all the wise men of my kingdom are not able to make known to me the interpretation, but you are able, for the spirit of the holy gods is in you."

A Reading (Lesson) from the First Letter of Peter [4:7-11]

The end of all things is at hand; therefore keep sane and sober for your prayers. Above all hold unfailing your love for one another, since love covers a multitude of sins. Practice hospitality ungrudgingly to one another. As each has received a gift, employ it for one another, as good stewards of God's varied grace: whoever speaks, as one who utters oracles of God; whoever renders service, as one who renders it by the strength which God supplies; in order that in everything God may be glorified through Jesus Christ. To him belong glory and dominion for ever and ever. Amen.

A Reading (Lesson) from the Gospel according to John [21:15-25]

When they had finished breakfast, Jesus said to Simon Peter, "Simon, son of John, do you love me more than these?" He said to him, "Yes, Lord; you know that I love you." He said to him, "Feed my lambs." A second time he said to him, "Simon, son of John, do you love me?" He said to him, "Yes, Lord; you know that I love you." He said to him, "Tend my sheep." He said to him the third time, "Simon, son of John, do you love me?" Peter was grieved because he said to him the third time, "Do you love me?" And he said to him, "Lord, you know everything; you know that I love you." Jesus said to him, "Feed my sheep. Truly, truly, I say to you, when you were young, you girded yourself and walked where you would; but when you are old, you will stretch out your hands, and another will gird you and carry you where you do not wish to go." (This he said to show by what death he was to glorify God.) And after this he said to him, "Follow me." Peter turned and saw following the disciple whom Jesus loved, who had lain close to his breast at the supper and had said, "Lord, who is it that is going to betray you?" When Peter saw him, he said to Jesus, "Lord, what about this man?" Jesus said to him, "If it is my will that he remain until I come, what is that to you? Follow me!" The saying spread abroad among the brethren that this disciple was not to die; yet Jesus did not say to him that he was not to die, but, "If it is my will that he remain until I come, what is that to you?" This is the disciple who is bearing witness to these things, and who has written these things; and we know that his testimony is true. But there are also many other things which Jesus did; were every one of them to be written, I suppose that the world itself could not contain the books that would be written.

Monday

Psalm 25 [page 614]   ❖   *Psalm 9* [page 593],
Psalm 15 [page 599]

A Reading (Lesson) from the Book of Daniel [4:19-27]

Daniel, whose name was Belteshaz'zar, was dismayed for a moment, and his thoughts alarmed him. The king said, "Belteshaz'zar, let not the dream or the interpretation alarm you." Belteshaz'zar answered, "My lord, may the dream be for those who hate you and its interpretation for your enemies! The tree you saw, which grew and became strong, so that its top reached to heaven, and it was visible to the end of the whole earth; whose leaves were fair and its fruit abundant, and in which was food for all; under which beasts of the field found shade, and in whose branches the birds of the air dwelt—it is you, O king, who have grown and become very strong. Your greatness has grown and reaches to heaven, and your dominion to the ends of the earth. And whereas the king saw a watcher, a holy one, coming down from heaven and saying, 'Hew down the tree and destroy it, but leave the stump of its roots in the earth, bound with a band of iron and bronze, in the tender grass of the field; and let him be wet with the dew of heaven; and let his lot be with the beasts of the field, till seven times pass over him'; this is the interpretation, O king: It is a decree of the Most High, which has come upon my lord the king, that you shall be driven from among men, and your dwelling shall be with the beasts of the field; you shall be made to eat grass like an ox, and you shall be wet with the dew of heaven, and seven times shall pass over you, till you know that the Most High rules the kingdom of men, and gives it to whom he will. And as it was commanded to leave the stump of the roots of the tree, your kingdom shall be sure for you from the time that you know that Heaven rules. Therefore, O king, let my counsel be acceptable to you; break off your sins by practicing righteousness, and your iniquities by showing mercy to the oppressed, that there may perhaps be a lengthening of your tranquility."

A Reading (Lesson) from the First Letter of John
[3:19—4:6]

By this we shall know that we are of the truth, and reassure our hearts before him whenever our hearts condemn us; for God is greater than our hearts, and he knows everything. Beloved, if our hearts do not condemn us, we have confidence before God; and we receive from him whatever we ask, because we keep his commandments and do what pleases him. And this is his commandment, that we should believe in the name of his Son Jesus Christ and love one another, just as he has commanded us. All who keep his commandments abide in him, and he in them. And by this we know that he abides in us, by the Spirit which he has given us. Beloved, do not believe every spirit, but test the spirits to see whether they are of God; for many false prophets have gone out into the world. By this you know the Spirit of God: every spirit which confesses that Jesus Christ has come in the flesh is of God, and every spirit which does not confess Jesus, is not of God. This is the spirit of antichrist, of which you heard that it was coming, and now it is in the world already. Little children, you are of God, and have overcome them; for he who is in you is greater than he who is in the world. They are of the world, therefore what they say is of the world, and the world listens to them. We are of God. Whoever knows God listens to us, and he who is not of God does not listen to us. By this we know the spirit of truth and the spirit of error.

A Reading (Lesson) from the Gospel according to Luke
[4:14-30]

Jesus returned in the power of the Spirit into Galilee, and a report concerning him went out through all the surrounding country. And he taught in their synagogues, being glorified by all. And he came to Nazareth, where he had been brought up; and he went to the synagogue, as his custom was, on the sabbath day. And he stood up to read; and there was given to him the book of the prophet Isaiah. He opened the book and found the place where it was written, "The Spirit of the Lord is upon me, because he has anointed me to preach good news to the poor. He has sent me to proclaim release to the captives and recovering of sight to the blind, to set at liberty those who are oppressed, to proclaim the acceptable year of the Lord." And he closed the book, and gave it back to the attendant, and sat down; and the eyes of all in the synagogue were fixed on him. And he began to say to them, "Today this scripture has been fulfilled in your hearing." And all spoke well of him, and wondered at the gracious words which proceeded out of his mouth; and they said, "Is not this Joseph's son?" And he said to them, "Doubtless you will quote to me this proverb, 'Physician, heal yourself; what we have heard you did at Caper'na-um, do here also in your own country.'" And he said, "Truly, I say to you, no prophet is acceptable in his own country. But in truth, I tell you, there were many widows in Israel in the days of Eli'jah, when the heaven was shut up three years and six months, when there came a great famine over all the land; and Eli'jah was sent to none of them but only to Zar'ephath, in the land of Sidon, to a woman who was a widow. And there were many lepers in Israel in the time of the prophet Eli'sha; and none of them was cleansed, but only Na'aman the Syrian." When they heard this, all in the synagogue were filled with wrath. And they rose up and put him out of the city, and led him to the brow of the hill on which their city was built, that they might throw him down headlong. But passing through the midst of them he went away.

Tuesday

Psalm 26 [page 616], *Psalm 28* [page 619] ❖
Psalm 36 [page 632], *Psalm 39* [page 638]

A Reading (Lesson) from the Book of Daniel [4:28-37]

All this came upon King Nebuchadnez'zar. At the end of twelve months he was walking on the roof of the royal palace of Babylon, and the king said, "Is not this great Babylon, which I have built by my mighty power as a royal residence and for the glory of my majesty?" While the words were still in the king's mouth, there fell a voice from heaven, "O King Nebuchadnez'zar, to you it is spoken: The kingdom has departed from you, and you shall be driven from among men and your dwelling shall be with the beasts of the field; and you shall be made to eat grass like an ox; and seven times shall pass over you, until you have learned that the Most High rules the kingdom of men and gives it to whom he will." Immediately the word was fulfilled upon Nebuchadnez'zar. He was driven from among men, and ate grass like an ox, and his body was wet with the dew of heaven till his hair grew as long as eagles' feathers, and his nails were like birds' claws. At the end of the days I, Nebuchadnez'zar, lifted my eyes to heaven, and my reason returned to me, and I blessed the Most High, and praised and honored him who lives for ever; for his dominion is an everlasting dominion, and his kingdom endures from generation to generation; all the inhabitants of the earth are accounted as nothing; and he does according to his will in the host of heaven and among the inhabitants of the earth; and none can stay his hand or say to him, "What doest thou?" At the same time my reason returned to me; and for the glory of my kingdom, my majesty and splendor returned to me. My counselors and my lords sought me, and I was established in my kingdom, and still more greatness was added to me. Now I, Nebuchadnez'zar, praise and extol and honor the King of heaven; for all his works are right and his ways are just; and those who walk in pride he is able to abase.

A Reading (Lesson) from the First Letter of John [4:7-21]

Beloved, let us love one another; for love is of God, and he who loves is born of God and knows God. He who does not love does not know God; for God is love. In this the love of God was made manifest among us, that God sent his only Son into the world, so that we might live through him. In this is love, not that we loved God but that he loved us and sent his only Son to be the expiation of our sins. Beloved, if God so loved us, we also ought to love one another. No man has ever seen God; if we love one another, God abides in us and his love is perfected in us. By this we know that we abide in him and he in us, because he has given us of his own Spirit. And we have seen and testify that the Father has sent his Son as the Savior of the world. Whoever confesses that Jesus is the Son of God, God abides in him, and he in God. So we know and believe the love God has for us. God is love, and he who abides in love abides in God, and God abides in him. In this is love perfected with us, that we may have confidence for the day of judgment, because as he is so are we in this world. There is no fear in love, but perfect love casts out fear. For fear has to do with punishment, and he who fears is not perfected in love. We love, because he first loved us. If any one says, "I love God," and hates his brother, he is a liar; for he who does not love his brother whom he has seen, cannot love God whom he has not seen. And this commandment we have from him, that he who loves God should love his brother also.

A Reading (Lesson) from the Gospel according to Luke [4:31-37]

Jesus went down to Caper'na-um, a city of Galilee. And he was teaching them on the sabbath; and they were astonished at his teaching, for his word was with authority. And in the synagogue there was a man who had the spirit of an unclean demon; and he cried out with a loud voice, "Ah! What have you to do with us, Jesus of Nazareth? Have you come to destroy us? I know who you are, the Holy One of God." But Jesus rebuked him, saying, "Be silent, and come out of him!" And when the demon had thrown him down in the midst, he came out of him, having done him no harm. And they were all amazed and said to one another, "What is this word? For with authority and power he commands the unclean spirits, and they come out." And reports of him went out into every place in the surrounding region.

Wednesday

Psalm 38 [page 636]   ❖   *Psalm 119:25-48* [page 765]

A Reading (Lesson) from the Book of Daniel [5:1-12]

King Belshaz'zar made a great feast for a thousand of his lords, and drank wine in front of the thousand. Belshaz'zar, when he tasted the wine, commanded that the vessels of gold and of silver which Nebuchadnez'zar his father had taken out of the temple in Jerusalem be brought, that the king and his lords, his wives, and his concubines might drink from them. Then they brought in the golden and silver vessels which had been taken out of the temple, the house of God in Jerusalem; and the king and his lords, his wives, and his concubines drank from them. They drank wine, and praised the gods of gold and silver, bronze, iron, wood, and stone. Immediately the fingers of a man's hand appeared and wrote on this plaster of the wall of the king's palace, opposite the lampstand; and the king saw the hand as it wrote. Then the king's color changed, and his thoughts alarmed him; his limbs gave way, and his knees knocked together. The king cried aloud to bring in the enchanters, the Chalde'ans, and the astrologers. The king said to the wise men of Babylon, "Whoever reads this writing, and shows me its interpretation, shall be clothed with purple, and have a chain of gold about his neck, and shall be the third ruler in the kingdom." Then all the king's wise men came in, but they could not read the writing or make known to the king the interpretation. Then King Belshaz'zar was greatly alarmed, and his color changed; and his lords were perplexed. The queen, because of the words of the king and his lords, came into the banqueting hall; and the queen said, "O king, live for ever! Let not your thoughts alarm you or your color change. There is in your kingdom a man in whom is the spirit of the holy gods. In the days of your father light and understanding and wisdom, like the wisdom of the gods, were found in him, and King

Nebuchadnez'zar, your father, made him chief of the
magicians, enchanters, Chalde'ans, and astrologers,
because an excellent spirit, knowledge and understanding
to interpret dreams, explain riddles, and solve problems
were found in this Daniel, whom the king named
Belteshaz'zar. Now let Daniel be called, and he will show
the interpretation."

A Reading (Lesson) from the First Letter of John [5:1-12]

Every one who believes that Jesus is the Christ is a child of
God, and every one who loves the parent loves the child.
By this we know that we love the children of God, when
we love God and obey his commandments. For this is the
love of God, that we keep his commandments. And his
commandments are not burdensome. For whatever is born
of God overcomes the world; and this is the victory that
overcomes the world, our faith. Who is it that overcomes
the world but he who believes that Jesus is the Son of God?
This is he who came by water and blood, Jesus Christ, not
with the water only but with the water and the blood. And
the Spirit is the witness, because the Spirit is the truth.
There are three witnesses, the Spirit, the water, and the
blood; and these three agree. If we receive the testimony of
men, the testimony of God is greater; for this is the
testimony of God that he has borne witness to his Son. He
who believes in the Son of God has the testimony in
himself. He who does not believe God has made him a liar,
because he has not believed in the testimony that God has
borne to his Son. And this is the testimony, that God gave
us eternal life, and this life is in his Son. He who has the
Son has life; he who has not the Son of God has not life.

A Reading (Lesson) from the Gospel according to Luke
[4:38-44]

Jesus arose and left the synagogue, and entered Simon's
house. Now Simon's mother-in-law was ill with a high

fever, and they besought him for her. And he stood over her and rebuked the fever, and it left her; and immediately she rose and served them. Now when the sun was setting, all those who had any that were sick with various diseases brought them to him; and he laid his hands on every one of them and healed them. And demons also came out of many, crying, "You are the Son of God!" But he rebuked them, and would not allow them to speak, because they knew that he was the Christ. And when it was day he departed and went into a lonely place. And the people sought him and came to him, and would have kept him from leaving them; but he said to them, "I must preach the good news of the kingdom of God to the other cities also; for I was sent for this purpose." And he was preaching in the synagogues of Judea.

Thursday

Psalm 37:1-18 [page 633]   ❖   *Psalm 37:19-42* [page 634]

A Reading (Lesson) from the Book of Daniel [5:13-30]

Daniel was brought in before the king. The king said to Daniel, "You are that Daniel, one of the exiles of Judah, whom the king my father brought from Judah. I have heard of you that the spirit of the holy gods is in you, and that light and understanding and excellent wisdom are found in you. Now the wise men, the enchanters, have been brought in before me to read this writing and make known to me its interpretation; but they could not show the interpretation of the matter. But I have heard that you can give interpretations and solve problems. Now if you can read the writing and make known to me its interpretation, you shall be clothed with purple, and have a chain of gold about your neck, and shall be the third ruler in the kingdom." Then Daniel answered before the king, "Let your gifts be for yourself, and give your rewards to another; nevertheless I will read the writing to the king and make known to him the interpretation. O king, the Most High God gave Nebuchadnez′zar your father kingship and greatness and glory and majesty; and because of the greatness that he gave him, all peoples, nations, and languages trembled and feared before him; whom he would he slew, and whom he would he kept alive; whom he would he raised up, and whom he would he put down. But when his heart was lifted up and his spirit was hardened so that he dealt proudly, he was deposed from his kingly throne, and his glory was taken from him; he was driven from among men, and his mind was made like that of a beast, and his dwelling was with the wild asses; he was fed grass like an ox, and his body was wet with the dew of heaven, until he knew that the Most High God rules the kingdom of men, and sets over it whom he will. And you his son, Belshaz′zar, have not humbled your heart, though you knew all this, but you have lifted up yourself against the Lord of heaven; and the vessels of his house have been brought in before you, and you and your lords, your wives, and your concubines have drunk wine from them; and you have praised the gods of silver and gold, of bronze, iron, wood, and stone, which do not see or hear or know, but the God in whose hand is your breath, and whose are all your ways, you have not honored. Then from his presence the hand was sent, and this writing was inscribed. And this is the writing that was inscribed: MENE, MENE, TEKEL, and PARSIN. This is the interpretation of the matter: MENE, God has numbered the days of your kingdom and brought it to an end; TEKEL, you have been weighed in the balances and found wanting; PERES, your kingdom is divided and given to the Medes and Persians." Then Belshaz′zar commanded, and Daniel was clothed with purple, a chain of gold was put about his neck, and proclamation was made concerning him, that he should be the third ruler in the kingdom. That very night Belshaz′zar the Chalde′an king was slain. And Darius the Mede received the kingdom, being about sixty-two years old.

A Reading (Lesson) from the First Letter of John
[5:13-20 (21)]

I write this to you who believe in the name of the Son of God, that you may know that you have eternal life. And this is the confidence which we have in him, that if we ask anything according to his will he hears us. And if we know that he hears us in whatever we ask, we know that we have obtained the requests made of him. If any one sees his brother committing what is not a mortal sin, he will ask, and God will give him life for those whose sin is not mortal. There is sin which is mortal; I do not say that one is to pray for that. All wrongdoing is sin, but there is sin which is not mortal. We know that any one born of God does not sin, but He who was born of God keeps him, and the evil one does not touch him. We know that we are of God, and the whole world is in the power of the evil one. And we know that the Son of God has come and has given us understanding, to know him who is true; and we are in him who is true, in his Son Jesus Christ. This is the true God and eternal life.

| Little children, keep yourselves from idols.

A Reading (Lesson) from the Gospel according to Luke
[5:1-11]

While the people pressed upon Jesus to hear the word of God, he was standing by the lake of Gennes'aret. And he saw two boats by the lake; but the fishermen had gone out of them and were washing their nets. Getting into one of the boats, which was Simon's, he asked him to put out a little from the land. And he sat down and taught the people from the boat. And when he had ceased speaking, he said to Simon, "Put out into the deep and let down your nets for a catch." And Simon answered, "Master, we toiled all night and took nothing! But at your word I will let down the nets." And when they had done this, they enclosed a great shoal of fish; and as their nets were breaking, they beckoned to their partners in the other boat to come and help them. And they came and filled both the boats, so that they began to sink. But when Simon Peter saw it, he fell down at Jesus' knees, saying, "Depart from me, for I am a sinful man, O Lord." For he was astonished, and all that were with him, at the catch of fish which they had taken; and so also were James and John, sons of Zeb'edee, who were partners with Simon. And Jesus said to Simon, "Do not be afraid; henceforth you will be catching men." And when they had brought their boats to land, they left everything and followed him.

Friday

Psalm 105:1-22 [page 738]   ❖   *Psalm 105:23-45* [page 739]

A Reading (Lesson) from the Book of Daniel [6:1-15]

It pleased Darius to set over the kingdom a hundred and twenty satraps, to be throughout the whole kingdom; and over them three presidents, of whom Daniel was one, to whom these satraps should give account, so that the king might suffer no loss. Then this Daniel became distinguished above all the other presidents and satraps, because an excellent spirit was in him; and the king planned to set him over the whole kingdom. Then the presidents and the satraps sought to find a ground for complaint against Daniel with regard to the kingdom; but they could find no ground for complaint or any fault, because he was faithful, and no error or fault was found in him. Then these men said, "We shall not find any ground for complaint against this Daniel unless we find it in connection with the law of his God." Then these presidents and satraps came by agreement to the king and said to him, "O King Darius, live for ever! All the presidents of the kingdom, the prefects and the satraps, the counselors and the governors are agreed that the king should establish an ordinance and enforce an interdict, that whoever makes petition to any god of man for thirty days, except to you, O king, shall be cast into the den of lions. Now, O king, establish the interdict and sign the document, so that it cannot be changed, according to the law of the Medes and the Persians, which cannot be revoked." Therefore King Darius signed the document and interdict. When Daniel knew that the document had been signed, he went to his house where he had windows in his upper chamber open toward Jerusalem; and he got down upon his knees three times a day and prayed and gave thanks before his God, as he had done previously. Then these men came by agreement and found Daniel making petition and supplication before his God. Then they came near and said before the king, concerning the interdict, "O king! Did you not sign an interdict, that any man who makes petition to any god or man within thirty days except to you, O king, shall be cast into the den of lions?" The king answered, "The thing stands fast, according to the law of the Medes and Persians, which cannot be revoked." Then they answered before the king, "That Daniel, who is one of the exiles from Judah, pays no heed to you, O king, or the interdict you have signed, but makes his petition three times a day." Then the king, when he heard these words, was much distressed, and set his mind to deliver Daniel; and he labored till the sun went down to rescue him. Then these men came by agreement to the king, and said to the king, "Know, O king, that it is a law of the Medes and Persians that no interdict or ordinance which the king establishes can be changed."

A Reading (Lesson) from the Second Letter of John [1-13]

The elder to the elect lady and her children, whom I love in the truth, and not only I but also all who know the truth, because of the truth which abides in us and will be with us for ever: Grace, mercy, and peace will be with us, from God the Father and from Jesus Christ the Father's Son, in truth and love. I rejoiced greatly to find some of your children following the truth, just as we have been commanded by the Father. And now I beg you, lady, not as though I were writing you a new commandment, but the one we have had from the beginning, that we love one another. And this is love, that we follow his commandments; this is the commandment, as you have heard from the beginning, that you follow love. For many deceivers have gone out into the world, men who will not acknowledge the coming of Jesus Christ in the flesh; such as one is the deceiver and the antichrist. Look to yourselves, that you may not lose what you have worked for, but may win a full reward. Any one who goes ahead and does not abide in the doctrine of Christ does not have God; he who abides in the doctrine has both the Father and the Son. If any one comes to you and does not bring this doctrine, do not receive him into the house or give him any greeting; for he who greets him shares his wicked work. Though I have much to write to you, I would rather not use paper and ink, but I hope to come to see you and talk with you face to face, so that our joy may be complete. The children of your elect sister greet you.

A Reading (Lesson) from the Gospel according to Luke
[5:12-26]

While Jesus was in one of the cities, there came a man full of leprosy; and when he saw Jesus, he fell on his face and besought him, "Lord, if you will, you can make me clean." And he stretched out his hand, and touched him, saying, " will; be clean." And immediately the leprosy left him. And he charged him to tell no one; but "go and show yourself to the priest, and make an offering for your cleansing, as Moses commanded, for a proof to the people." But so much the more the report went abroad concerning him; and great multitudes gathered to hear and to be healed of their infirmities. But he withdrew to the wilderness and prayed. On one of those days, as he was teaching, there were Pharisees and teachers of the law sitting by, who had

come from every village of Galilee and Judea and from
Jerusalem; and the power of the Lord was with him to
heal. And behold, men were bringing on a bed a man who
was paralyzed, and they sought to bring him in and lay
him before Jesus; but finding no way to bring him in,
because of the crowd, they went up on the roof and let him
down with his bed through the tiles into the midst before
Jesus. And when he saw their faith he said, "Man, your
sins are forgiven you." And the scribes and the Pharisees
began to question, saying, "Who is this that speaks
blasphemies? Who can forgive sins but God only?" When
Jesus perceived their questionings, he answered them,
"Why do you question in your hearts? Which is easier, to
say, 'Your sins are forgiven you,' or to say 'Rise and walk'?
But that you may know that the Son of man has authority
on earth to forgive sins"—he said to the man who was
paralyzed—"I say to you, rise, take up your bed and go
home." And immediately he rose before them, and took up
that on which he lay, and went home, glorifying God. And
amazement seized them all, and they glorified God and
were filled with awe, saying, "We have seen strange things
today."

Saturday

Psalm 30 [page 621], *Psalm 32* [page 624] ❖
Psalm 42 [page 643], *Psalm 43* [page 644]

A Reading (Lesson) from the Book of Daniel [6:16-28]

The king commanded, and Daniel was brought and cast
into the den of lions. The king said to Daniel, "May your
God, whom you serve continually, deliver you!" And a
stone was brought and laid upon the mouth of the den,
and the king sealed it with his own signet and with the
signet of his lords, that nothing might be changed
concerning Daniel. Then the king went to his palace, and

spent the night fasting; no diversions were brought to him, and sleep fled from him. Then, at break of day, the king arose and went in haste to the den of lions. When he came near to the den where Daniel was, he cried out in a tone of anguish and said to Daniel, "O Daniel, servant of the living God, has your God, whom you serve continually, been able to deliver you from the lions?" Then Daniel said to the king, "O king, live for ever! My God sent his angel and shut the lions' mouths, and they have not hurt me, because I was found blameless before him; and also before you, O king, I have done no wrong." Then the king was exceedingly glad, and commanded that Daniel be taken up out of the den. So Daniel was taken up out of the den, and no kind of hurt was found upon him, because he had trusted in his God. And the king commanded, and those men who had accused Daniel were brought and cast into the den of lions—they, their children, and their wives; and before they reached the bottom of the den the lions overpowered them and broke all their bones in pieces. Then King Darius wrote to all the peoples, nations, and languages that dwell in all the earth: "Peace be multiplied to you. I make a decree, that in all my royal dominion men tremble and fear before the God of Daniel, for he is the living God, enduring for ever; his kingdom shall never be destroyed, and his dominion shall be to the end. He delivers and rescues, he works signs and wonders in heaven and on earth, he who has saved Daniel from the power of the lions." So this Daniel prospered during the reign of Darius and the reign of Cyrus the Persian.

A Reading (Lesson) from the Third Letter of John [1-15]

The elder to the beloved Ga'ius, whom I love in the truth. Beloved, I pray that all may go well with you and that you may be in health, I know that it is well with your soul. For I greatly rejoiced when some of the brethren arrived and testified to the truth of your life, as indeed you do follow the truth. No greater joy can I have than this, to hear that my children follow the truth. Beloved, it is a loyal thing you do when you render any service to the brethren, especially to strangers, who have testified to your love before the church. You will do well to send them on their journey as befits God's service. For they have set out for his sake and have accepted nothing from the heathen. So we ought to support such men, that we may be fellow workers in the truth. I have written something to the church; but Diot'rephes, who likes to put himself first, does not acknowledge my authority. So if I come, I will bring up what he is doing, prating against me with evil words. And not content with that, he refuses himself to welcome the brethren, and also stops those who want to welcome them and puts them out of the church. Beloved, do not imitate evil but imitate good. He who does good is of God; he who does evil has not seen God. Deme'trius has testimony from every one, and from the truth itself; I testify to him too, and you know my testimony is true. I had much to write to you, but I would rather not write with pen and ink; I hope to see you soon, and we will talk together face to face. Peace be to you. The friends greet you. Greet the friends, every one of them.

A Reading (Lesson) from the Gospel according to Luke
[5:27-39]

After this Jesus went out, and saw a tax collector, named Levi, sitting at the tax office; and he said to him, "Follow me." And he left everything, and rose and followed him. And Levi made a great feast in his house; and there was a large company of tax collectors and others sitting at table with them. And the Pharisees and their scribes murmured against his disciples, saying, "Why do you eat and drink with tax collectors and sinners?" And Jesus answered them, "Those who are well have no need of a physician, but those who are sick; I have not come to call the righteous, but sinners to repentance." And they said to him, "The disciples of John fast often and offer prayers, and so do the disciples of the Pharisees, but yours eat and drink." And Jesus said to them, "Can you make wedding guests fast while the bridegroom is with them? The days will come, when the bridegroom is taken away from them, and then they will fast in those days." He told them a parable also: "No one tears a piece from a new garment and puts it upon an old garment; if he does, he will tear the new, and the piece from the new will not match the old. And no one puts new wine into old wineskins; if he does, the new wine will burst the skins and it will be spilled, and the skins will be destroyed. But new wine must be put into fresh wineskins. And no one after drinking old wine desires new; for he says, 'The old is good.'"

Week of 4 Easter

Sunday

Psalm 63:1-8(9-11) [page 670], *Psalm 98* [page 727] ❖
Psalm 103 [page 733]

A Reading (Lesson) from the Book of Wisdom [1:1-15]

Love righteousness, you rulers of the earth, think of the Lord with uprightness, and seek him with sincerity of heart; because he is found by those who do not put him to the test, and manifests himself to those who do not distrust him. For perverse thoughts separate men from God, and when his power is tested, it convicts the foolish; because wisdom will not enter a deceitful soul, nor dwell in a body enslaved to sin. For a holy and disciplined spirit will flee from deceit, and will rise and depart from foolish thoughts, and will be ashamed at the approach of unrighteousness. For wisdom is a kindly spirit and will not free a blasphemer from the guilt of his words; because God is witness of his inmost feelings, and a true observer of his heart, and a hearer of his tongue. Because the Spirit of the Lord has filled the world, and that which holds all things together knows what is said; therefore no one who utters unrighteous things will escape notice, and justice, when it punishes, will not pass him by. For inquiry will be made into the counsels of an ungodly man, and a report of his words will come to the Lord, to convict him of his lawless deeds; because a jealous ear hears all things, and the sound of murmurings does not go unheard. Beware then of useless murmuring, and keep your tongue from slander; because no secret word is without result, and a lying mouth destroys the soul. Do not invite death by the error of your life, nor bring on destruction by the works of your hands; because God did not make death, and he does not delight in the death of the living. For he created all things that they might exist, and the generative forces of the world are wholesome, and there is no destructive poison in them; and the dominion of Hades is not on earth. For righteousness is immortal.

A Reading (Lesson) from the First Letter of Peter [5:1-11]

I exhort the elders among you, as a fellow elder and a witness of the sufferings of Christ as well as a partaker in the glory that is to be revealed. Tend the flock of God that is your charge, not by constraint but willingly, not for shameful gain but eagerly, not as domineering over those in your charge but being examples to the flock. And when the chief Shepherd is manifested you will obtain the unfading crown of glory. Likewise you that are younger be subject to the elders. Clothe yourselves, all of you, with humility toward one another, for "God opposes the proud, but gives grace to the humble." Humble yourselves therefore under the mighty hand of God, that in due time he may exalt you. Cast all your anxieties on him, for he cares about you. Be sober, be watchful. Your adversary the devil prowls around like a roaring lion, seeking some one to devour. Resist him, firm in your faith, knowing that the same experience of suffering is required of your brotherhood throughout the world. And after you have suffered a little while, the God of all grace, who has called you to his eternal glory in Christ, will himself restore, establish, and strengthen you. To him be the dominion for ever and ever. Amen.

A Reading (Lesson) from the Gospel according to Matthew
[7:15-29]

Jesus opened his mouth and taught his disciples, saying: "Beware of false prophets, who come to you in sheep's clothing but inwardly are ravenous wolves. You will know them by their fruits. Are grapes gathered from thorns, or figs from thistles? So, every sound tree bears good fruit, but the bad tree bears evil fruit. A sound tree cannot bear evil fruit, nor can a bad tree bear good fruit. Every tree that does not bear good fruit is cut down and thrown into the fire. Thus you will know them by their fruits. Not every one who says to me, 'Lord, Lord,' shall enter the kingdom of heaven, but he who does the will of my Father who is in heaven. On that day many will say to me, 'Lord, Lord, did we not prophesy in your name, and cast out demons in your name, and do many mighty works in your name?' And then will I declare to them, 'I never knew you; depart from me, you evildoers.' Every one then who hears these words of mine and does them will be like a wise man who built his house upon the rock; and the rain fell, and the floods came, and the winds blew and beat upon that house, but it did not fall, because it had been founded on the rock. And every one who hears these words of mine and does not do them will be like a foolish man who built his house upon the sand; and the rain fell, and the floods came, and the winds blew and beat against that house, and it fell; and great was the fall of it." And when Jesus finished these sayings, the crowds were astonished at his teaching, for he taught them as one who had authority, and not as their scribes.

Monday

Psalm 41 [page 641],   *Psalm 52* [page 657] ❖
Psalm 44 [page 645]

A Reading (Lesson) from the Book of Wisdom
[1:16—2:11,21-24]

Ungodly men by their words and deeds summoned death;
considering him a friend, they pined away, and they made
a covenant with him, because they are fit to belong to his
party. For they reasoned unsoundly, saying to themselves,
"Short and sorrowful is our life, and there is no remedy
when a man comes to his end, and no one has been known
to return from Hades. Because we were born by mere
chance, and hereafter we shall be as though we had never
been; because the breath in our nostrils is smoke, and
reason is a spark kindled by the beating of our hearts.
When it is extinguished, the body will turn to ashes, and
the spirit will dissolve like empty air. Our name will be
forgotten in time, and no one will remember our works;
our life will pass away like the traces of a cloud, and be
scattered like mist that is chased by the rays of the sun and
overcome by its heat. For our allotted time is the passing of
a shadow, and there is no return from our death, because it
is sealed up and no one turns back. Come, therefore, let us
enjoy the good things that exist, and make use of the
creation to the full as in youth. Let us take our fill of costly
wine and perfumes, and let no flower of spring pass by us.
Let us crown ourselves with rosebuds before they wither.
Let none of us fail to share in our revelry, everywhere let us
leave signs of enjoyment, because this is our portion, and
this our lot. Let us oppress the righteous poor man; let us
not spare the widow nor regard the grey hairs of the aged.
But let our might be our law of right, for what is weak
proves itself to be useless." Thus they reasoned, but they
were led astray, for their wickedness blinded them, and

they did not know the secret purposes of God, nor hope
for the wages of holiness, nor discern the prize for
blameless souls; for God created man for incorruption,
and made him in the image of his own eternity, but
through the devil's envy death entered the world, and thos
who belong to his party experience it.

*A Reading (Lesson) from the Letter of Paul
to the Colossians* [1:1-14]

Paul, an apostle of Christ Jesus by the will of God, and
Timothy our brother, To the saints and faithful brethren in
Christ at Colos'sae: Grace to you and peace from God our
Father. We always thank God, the Father of our Lord Jesu
Christ, when we pray for you, because we have heard of
your faith in Christ Jesus and of the love which you have
for all the saints, because of the hope laid up for you in
heaven. Of this you have heard before in the word of the
truth, the gospel which has come to you, as indeed in the
whole world it is bearing fruit and growing—so among
yourselves, from the day you heard and understood the
grace of God in truth, as you learned it from Ep'aphras ou
beloved fellow servant. He is a faithful minister of Christ
on our behalf and has made known to us your love in the
Spirit. And so, from the day we heard of it, we have not
ceased to pray for you, asking that you may be filled with
the knowledge of his will in all spiritual wisdom and
understanding, to lead a life worthy of the Lord, fully
pleasing to him, bearing fruit in every good work and
increasing in the knowledge of God. May you be
strengthened with all power, according to his glorious
might, for all endurance and patience with joy, giving
thanks to the Father, who has qualified us to share in the
inheritance of the saints in light. He has delivered us from
the dominion of darkness and transferred us to the
kingdom of his beloved Son, in whom we have
redemption, the forgiveness of sins.

A Reading (Lesson) from the Gospel according to Luke
[6:1-11]

On a sabbath, while Jesus was going through the grainfields, his disciples plucked and ate some heads of grain, rubbing them in their hands. But some of the Pharisees said, "Why are you doing what is not lawful to do on the sabbath?" And Jesus answered, "Have you not read what David did when he was hungry, he and those who were with him: how he entered the house of God, and took and ate the bread of the Presence, which it is not lawful for any but the priests to eat, and also gave it to those with him?" And he said to them, "The Son of man is lord of the sabbath." On another sabbath, when he entered the synagogue and taught, a man was there whose right hand was withered. And the scribes and the Pharisees watched him, to see whether he would heal on the sabbath, so that they might find an accusation against him. But he knew their thoughts, and he said to the man who had the withered hand, "Come and stand here." And he rose and stood there. And Jesus said to them, "I ask you, is it lawful on the sabbath to do good or to do harm, to save life or to destroy it?" And he looked around on them all, and said to him, "Stretch out your hand." And he did so, and his hand was restored. But they were filled with fury and discussed with one another what they might do to Jesus.

Tuesday

Psalm 45 [page 647] ❖ *Psalm 47* [page 650],
Psalm 48 [page 651]

A Reading (Lesson) from the Book of Wisdom [3:1-9]

The souls of the righteous are in the hand of God, and no torment will ever touch them. In the eyes of the foolish they seemed to have died, and their departure was thought to be an affliction, and their going from us to be their destruction; but they are at peace. For though in the sight of men they were punished, their hope is full of immortality. Having disciplined a little, they will receive great good, because God tested them and found them worthy of himself; like gold in the furnace he tried them, and like a sacrificial burnt offering he accepted them. In the time of their visitation they will shine forth, and will run like sparks through the stubble. They will govern nations and rule over peoples, and the Lord will reign over them for ever. Those who trust in him will understand truth, and the faithful will abide with him in love, because grace and mercy are upon his elect, and he watches over his holy ones.

A Reading (Lesson) from the Letter of Paul to the Colossians [1:15-23]

He is the image of the invisible God, the first-born of all creation; for in him all things were created, in heaven and on earth, visible and invisible, whether thrones or dominions or principalities or authorities—all things were created through him and for him. He is before all things, and in him all things hold together. He is the head of the body, the church; he is the beginning, the first-born from the dead, that in everything he might be pre-eminent. For in him all the fulness of God was pleased to dwell, and through him to reconcile to himself all things, whether on earth or in heaven, making peace by the blood of his cross. And you, who once were estranged and hostile in mind, doing evil deeds, he has now reconciled in his body of flesh by his death, in order to present you holy and blameless and irreproachable before him, provided that you continue in the faith, stable and steadfast, not shifting from the hope of the gospel which you heard, which has been preached to every creature under heaven, and of which I, Paul, became a minister.

A Reading (Lesson) from the Gospel according to Luke
[6:12-26]

In these days Jesus went out to the mountain to pray; and
all night he continued in prayer to God. And when it was
day, he called his disciples, and chose from them twelve,
whom he named apostles; Simon, whom he named Peter,
and Andrew his brother, and James and John, and Philip,
and Bartholomew, and Matthew, and Thomas, and James
the son of Alphaeus, and Simon who was called the Zealot,
and Judas the son of James, and Judas Iscariot, who
became a traitor. And he came down with them and stood
on a level place, with a great crowd of his disciples and a
great multitude of people from all Judea and Jerusalem
and the seacoast of Tyre and Sidon, who came to hear him
and to be healed of their diseases; and those who were
troubled with unclean spirits were cured. And all the
crowd sought to touch him, for power came forth from
him and healed them all. And he lifted up his eyes on his
disciples, and said: "Blessed are you poor, for yours is the
kingdom of God. Blessed are you that hunger now, for you
shall be satisfied. Blessed are you that weep now, for you
shall laugh. Blessed are you when men hate you, and when
they exclude you and revile you, and cast out your name as
evil, on account of the Son of man! Rejoice in that day, and
leap for joy, for behold, your reward is great in heaven; for
so their fathers did to the prophets. But woe to you that are
rich, for you have received your consolation. Woe to you
that are full now, for you shall hunger. Woe to you that
laugh now, for you shall mourn and weep. Woe to you,
when all men speak well of you, for so their fathers did to
the false prophets.

Wednesday

Psalm 119:49-72 [page 767]   ❖   *Psalm 49* [page 652],
Psalm 53 [page 658]

A Reading (Lesson) from the Book of Wisdom
[4:16—5:8]

The righteous man who has died will condemn the
ungodly who are living, and youth that is quickly perfected
will condemn the prolonged old age of the unrighteous
man. For they will see the end of the wise man, and will
not understand what the Lord purposed for him, and for
what he kept him safe. They will see, and will have
contempt for him, but the Lord will laugh them to scorn.
After this they will become dishonored corpses, and an
outrage among the dead for ever; because he will dash
them speechless to the ground, and shake them from the
foundations; they will be left utterly dry and barren, and
they will suffer anguish, and the memory of them will
perish. They will come with dread when their sins are
reckoned up, and their lawless deeds will convict them to
their face. Then the righteous man will stand with great
confidence in the presence of those who have afflicted him,
and those who make light of his labors. When they see
him, they will be shaken with dreadful fear, and they will
be amazed at his unexpected salvation. They will speak to
one another in repentance, and in anguish of spirit they
will groan, and say, "This is the man whom we once held
in derision and made a byword of reproach—we fools! We
thought that his life was madness and that his end was
without honor. Why has he been numbered among the
sons of God? And why is his lot among the saints? So it
was we who strayed from the way of truth, and the light of
righteousness did not shine on us, and the sun did not rise
upon us. We took our fill of the paths of lawlessness and
destruction, and we journeyed through trackless deserts,
but the way of the Lord we have not known. What has our
arrogance profited us? And what good has our boasted
wealth brought us?"

*A Reading (Lesson) from the Letter of Paul
to the Colossians* [1:24—2:7]

I rejoice in my sufferings for your sake, and in my flesh I
complete what is lacking in Christ's afflictions for the sake
of his body, that is, the church, of which I became a
minister according to the divine office which was given to
me for you, to make the word of God fully known, the
mystery hidden for ages and generations but now made
manifest to his saints. To them God chose to make known
how great among the Gentiles are the riches of the glory of
this mystery, which is Christ in you, the hope of glory. Him
we proclaim, warning every man and teaching every man
in all wisdom, that we may present every man mature in
Christ. For this I toil, striving with all the energy which he
mightily inspires within me. For I want you to know how
greatly I strive for you, and for those at La-odice′a, and for
all who have not seen my face, that their hearts may be
encouraged as they are knit together in love, to have all the
riches of assured understanding and the knowledge of
God's mystery, of Christ, in whom are hid all the treasure
of wisdom and knowledge. I say this in order that no one
may delude you with beguiling speech. For though I am
absent in body, yet I am with you in spirit, rejoicing to see
your good order and the firmness of your faith in Christ.
As therefore you received Christ Jesus the Lord, so live in
him, rooted and built up in him and established in the
faith, just as you were taught, abounding in thanksgiving.

A Reading (Lesson) from the Gospel according to Luke
[6:27-38]

Jesus lifted up his eyes on his disciples, and said: "I say to
you that hear, Love your enemies, do good to those who
hate you, bless those who curse you, pray for those who
abuse you. To him who strikes you on the cheek, offer the
other also; and from him who takes away your coat do not
withhold even your shirt. Give to every one who begs from

you; and of him who takes away your goods, do not ask them again. And as you wish that men would do to you, do so to them. If you love those who love you, what credit is that to you? For even sinners love those who love them. And if you do good to those who do good to you, what credit is that to you? For even sinners do the same. And if you lend to those from whom you hope to receive, what credit is that to you? Even sinners lend to sinners, to receive as much again. But love your enemies, and do good, and lend, expecting nothing in return; and your reward will be great, and you will be sons of the Most High; for he is kind to the ungrateful and the selfish. Be merciful, even as your Father is merciful. Judge not, and you will not be judged; condemn not, and you will not be condemned; forgive, and you will be forgiven; give, and it will be given to you; good measure, pressed down, shaken together, running over, will be put into your lap. For the measure you give will be the measure you get back."

Thursday

Psalm 50 [page 654]   ❖   *(Psalm 59* [page 665],
Psalm 60 [page 667])   *or*   *Psalm 114* [page 756],
Psalm 115 [page 757]

A Reading (Lesson) from the Book of Wisdom [5:9-23]

"All those things have vanished like a shadow, and like a rumor that passes by; like a ship that sails through the billowy water, and when it has passed no trace can be found, nor track of its keel in the waves; or as, when a bird flies through the air, no evidence of its passage is found; the light air, lashed by the beat of its pinions and pierced by the force of its rushing flight, is traversed by the movement of its wings, and afterward no sign of its coming is found there; or as, when an arrow is shot at a target, the air, thus divided, comes together at once, so that no one knows its pathway. So we also, as soon as we were born, ceased to be, and we had no sign of virtue to show, but were consumed in our wickedness." Because the hope of the ungodly man is like chaff carried by the wind, and like a light hoarfrost driven away by a storm; it is dispersed like smoke before the wind, and it passes like the remembrance of a guest who stays but a day. But the righteous live for ever, and their reward is with the Lord; the Most High takes care of them. Therefore they will receive a glorious crown and a beautiful diadem from the hand of the Lord, because with his right hand he will cover them, and with his arm he will shield them. The Lord will take his zeal as his whole armor, and will arm all creation to repel his enemies; he will put on righteousness as a breastplate, and wear impartial justice as a helmet; he will take holiness as an invincible shield, and sharpen stern wrath for a sword, and creation will join with him to fight against the madmen. Shafts of lightning will fly with true aim, and will leap to the target as from a well-drawn bow of clouds, and hailstones full of wrath will be hurled as from a catapult; the water of the sea will rage against them, and rivers will relentlessly overwhelm them; a mighty wind will rise against them, and like a tempest it will winnow them away. Lawlessness will lay waste the whole earth, and evil-doing will overturn the thrones of rulers.

A Reading (Lesson) from the Letter of Paul to the Colossians [2:8-23]

See to it that no one makes a prey of you by philosophy and empty deceit, according to human tradition, according to the elemental spirits of the universe, and not according to Christ. For in him the whole fulness of deity dwells bodily, and you have come to fulness of life in him, who is the head of all rule and authority. In him also you were circumcised with a circumcision made without hands, by putting off the body of flesh in the circumcision of Christ; and you were buried with him in baptism, in which you were also raised with him through faith in the working of God, who raised him from the dead. And you, who were dead in trespasses and the uncircumcision of your flesh, God made alive together with him, having forgiven us all our trespasses, having canceled the bond which stood against us with its legal demands; this he set aside, nailing it to the cross. He disarmed the principalities and powers and made a public example of them, triumphing over them in him. Therefore let no one pass judgment on you in questions of food and drink or with regard to a festival or a new moon or a sabbath. These are only a shadow of what is to come; but the substance belongs to Christ. Let no one disqualify you, insisting on self-abasement and worship of angels, taking his stand on visions, puffed up without reason by his sensuous mind, and not holding fast to the Head, from whom the whole body, nourished and knit together through its joints and ligaments, grows with a growth that is from God. If with Christ you died to the elemental spirits of the universe, why do you live as if you still belonged to the world? Why do you submit to regulations, "Do not handle, Do not taste, Do not touch" (referring to things which all perish as they are used), according to human precepts and doctrines? These have indeed an appearance of wisdom in promoting rigor of devotion and self-abasement and severity to the body, but they are of no value in checking the indulgence of the flesh.

A Reading (Lesson) from the Gospel according to Luke [6:39-49]

Jesus told his disciples a parable: "Can a blind man lead a blind man? Will they not both fall into a pit? A disciple is not above his teacher, but every one when he is fully taught will be like his teacher. Why do you see the speck that is in your brother's eye, but do not notice the log that is in your own eye? Or how can you say to your brother, 'Brother, let me take out the speck that is in your eye,' when you yourself do not see the log that is in your own eye? You hypocrite, first take the log out of your own eye, and then you will see clearly to take out the speck that is in your brother's eye. For no good tree bears bad fruit, nor again does a bad tree bear good fruit; for each tree is known by its own fruit. For figs are not gathered from thorns, nor are grapes picked from a bramble bush. The good man out of the good treasure of his heart produces good, and the evil man out of his evil treasure produces evil; for out of the abundance of the heart his mouth speaks. Why do you call me 'Lord, Lord,' and not do what I tell you? Every one who comes to me and hears my words and does them, I will show you what he is like: he is like a man building a house, who dug deep, and laid the foundation upon rock; and when a flood arose, the stream broke against that house, and could not shake it, because it had been well built. But he who hears and does not do them is like a man who built a house on the ground without a foundation; against which the stream broke, and immediately it fell, and the ruin of that house was great."

Friday

Psalm 40 [page 640],   *Psalm 54* [page 659]   ❖
Psalm 51 [page 656]

A Reading (Lesson) from the Book of Wisdom [6:12—23]

Wisdom is radiant and unfading, and she is easily discerned by those who love her, and is found by those who seek her. She hastens to make herself known to those who desire her. He who rises early to seek her will have no difficulty, for he will find her sitting at his gates. To fix one's thought on her is perfect understanding, and he who is vigilant on her account will soon be free from care, because she goes about seeking those worthy of her, and she graciously appears to them in their paths, and meets them in every thought. The beginning of wisdom is the most sincere desire for instruction, and concern for instruction is love of her, and love of her is the keeping of her laws, and giving heed to her laws is assurance of immortality, and immortality brings one near to God; so the desire for wisdom leads to a kingdom. Therefore if you delight in thrones and scepters, O monarchs over the peoples, honor wisdom, that you may reign for ever. I will tell you what wisdom is and how she came to be, and I will hide no secrets from you, but I will trace her course from the beginning of creation, and make the knowledge of her clear, and I will not pass by the truth; neither will I travel in the company of sickly envy, for envy does not associate with wisdom.

A Reading (Lesson) from the Letter of Paul to the Colossians [3:1-11]

If you have been raised with Christ, seek the things that are above, where Christ is, seated at the right hand of God. Set your minds on things that are above, not on things that are on earth. For you have died, and your life is hid with Christ in God. When Christ who is our life appears, then you also will appear with him in glory. Put to death therefore what is earthly in you: fornication, impurity, passion, evil desire, and covetousness, which is idolatry. On account of these the wrath of God is coming. In these you once walked, when you lived in them. But now put them all away: anger, wrath, malice, slander, and foul talk from your mouth. Do not lie to one another, seeing that you have put off the old nature with its practices and have put on the new nature, which is being renewed in knowledge after the image of its creator. Here there cannot be Greek and Jew, circumcised and uncircumcised, barbarian, Scyth'ian, slave, free man, but Christ is all, and in all.

A Reading (Lesson) from the Gospel according to Luke
[7:1-17]

After he had ended all his sayings in the hearing of the people Jesus entered Caper'na-um. Now a centurion had a slave who was dear to him, who was sick and at the point of death. When he heard of Jesus, he sent to him elders of the Jews, asking him to come and heal his slave. And when they came to Jesus, they besought him earnestly, saying, "He is worthy to have you do this for him, for he loves our nation, and he built us our synagogue." And Jesus went with them. When he was not far from the house, the centurion sent friends to him, saying to him, "Lord, do not trouble yourself, for I am not worthy to have you come under my roof; therefore I did not presume to come to you. But say the word, and let my servant be healed. For I am a man set under authority, with soldiers under me: and I say to one, 'Go,' and he goes; and to another, 'Come,' and he comes; and to my slave, 'Do this,' and he does it." When Jesus heard this he marveled at him, and turned and said to the multitude that followed him, "I tell you, not even in Israel have I found such faith." And when those who had been sent returned to the house, they found the slave well. Soon afterward he went to a city called Na'in, and his disciples and a great crowd went with him. As he drew near to the gate of the city, behold, a man who had died was being carried out, the only son of his mother, and she was a widow; and a large crowd from the city was with her. And when the Lord saw her, he had compassion on her, and said to her, "Do not weep." And he came and touched the bier, and the bearers stood still. And he said, "Young man, I say to you, arise." And the dead man sat up, and began to speak. And he gave him to his mother. Fear seized them all; and they glorified God, saying, "A great prophet has arisen among us!" and "God has visited his people!" And this report concerning him spread through the whole of Judea and all the surrounding country.

Saturday

Psalm 55 [page 660] ❖ *Psalm 138* [page 793],
Psalm 139:1-17 (18-23) [page 794]

A Reading (Lesson) from the Book of Wisdom [7:1-14]

I also am mortal, like all men, a descendant of the
first-formed child of earth; and in the womb of a mother I
was molded into flesh, within the period of ten months,
compacted with blood, from the seed of a man and the
pleasure of marriage. And when I was born, I began to
breathe the common air, and fell upon the kindred earth,
and my first sound was a cry, like that of all. I was nursed
with care in swaddling cloths. For no king has had a
different beginning of existence; there is for all mankind
one entrance into life, and a common departure. Therefore
I prayed, and understanding was given me; I called upon
God, and the spirit of wisdom came to me. I preferred her
to scepters and thrones, and I accounted wealth as nothing
in comparison with her. Neither did I liken to her any
priceless gem, because all gold is but a little sand in her
sight, and silver will be accounted as clay before her. I
loved her more than health and beauty, and I chose to have
her rather than light, because her radiance never ceases.
All good things came to me along with her, and in her
hands uncounted wealth. I rejoiced in them all, because
wisdom leads them; but I did not know that she was their
mother. I learned without guile and I impart without
grudging; I do not hide her wealth, for it is an unfailing
treasure for men; those who get it obtain friendship with
God, commended for the gifts that come from instruction.

*A Reading (Lesson) from the Letter of Paul
to the Colossians* [3:12-17]

Put on then, as God's chosen ones, holy and beloved,
compassion, kindness, lowliness, meekness, and patience,

forbearing one another and, if one has a complaint against another, forgiving each other; as the Lord has forgiven you, so you also must forgive. And above all these put on love, which binds everything together in perfect harmony. And let the peace of Christ rule in your hearts, to which indeed you were called in the one body. And be thankful. Let the word of Christ dwell in you richly, teach and admonish one another in all wisdom, and sing psalms and hymns and spiritual songs with thankfulness in your hearts to God. And whatever you do, in word or deed, do everything in the name of the Lord Jesus, giving thanks to God the Father through him.

A Reading (Lesson) from the Gospel according to Luke
[7:18-28(29-30) 31-35]

The disciples of John told him of all these things. And John, calling to him two of his disciples, sent them to the Lord, saying, "Are you he who is to come, or shall we look for another?" And when the men had come to him, they said, "John the Baptist has sent us to you, saying, 'Are you he who is to come, or shall we look for another?'" In that hour he cured many of diseases and plagues and evil spirits, and on many that were blind he bestowed sight. And he answered them, "Go and tell John what you have seen and heard: the blind receive their sight, the lame walk, lepers are cleansed, and the deaf hear, the dead are raised up, the poor have good news preached to them. And blessed is he who takes no offense at me." When the messengers of John had gone, he began to speak to the crowds concerning John: "What did you go out into the wilderness to behold? A reed shaken by the wind? What then did you go out to see? A man clothed in soft clothing? Behold, those who are gorgeously appareled and live in luxury are in kings' courts. What then did you go out to see? A prophet? Yes, I tell you, and more than a prophet. This is he of whom it is written, 'Behold, I send my messenger before thy face, who shall prepare thy way before thee.' I tell you, among those born of women none is greater than John: yet he who is least in the kingdom of God is greater than he."

(When they heard this all the people and the tax collectors justified God, having been baptized with the baptism of John; but the Pharisees and the lawyers rejected the purpose of God for themselves, not having been baptized by him.)

"To what then shall I compare the men of this generation, and what are they like? They are like children sitting in the market place and calling to one another, 'We piped to you, and you did not dance; we wailed, and you did not weep.' For John the Baptist has come eating no bread and drinking no wine; and you say, 'He has a demon.' The Son of man has come eating and drinking; and you say, 'Behold, a glutton and a drunkard, a friend of tax collectors and sinners!' Yet wisdom is justified by all her children."

Week of 5 Easter

Sunday

Psalm 24 [page 613], *Psalm 29* [page 620] ❖
Psalm 8 [page 592], *Psalm 84* [page 707]

A Reading (Lesson) from the Book of Wisdom [7:22—8:1]

Wisdom, the fashioner of all things, taught me. For in her there is a spirit that is intelligent, holy, unique, manifold, subtle, mobile, clear, unpolluted, distinct, invulnerable, loving the good, keen, irresistible, beneficient, humane, steadfast, sure, free from anxiety, all-powerful, overseeing all, and penetrating through all spirits that are intelligent and pure and most subtle. For wisdom is more mobile than any motion; because of her pureness she pervades and penetrates all things. For she is a breath of the power of God, and a pure emanation of the glory of the Almighty; therefore nothing defiled gains entrance into her. For she is a reflection of eternal light, a spotless mirror of the working of God, as an image of his goodness. Though she is but one, she can do all things, and while remaining in herself, she renews all things; in every generation she passes into holy souls and makes them friends of God, and prophets; for God loves nothing so much as the man who lives with wisdom. For she is more beautiful than the sun, and excels every constellation of the stars. Compared with the light she is found to be superior, for it is succeeded by the night, but against wisdom evil does not prevail. She reaches mightily from one end of the earth to the other, and she orders all things well.

A Reading (Lesson) from the Second Letter of Paul to the Thessalonians [2:13-17]

We are bound to give thanks to God always for you, brethren beloved by the Lord, because God chose you from the beginning to be saved, through sanctification by the Spirit and belief in the truth. To this he called you through our gospel, so that you may obtain the glory of our Lord Jesus Christ. So then, brethren, stand firm and hold to the traditions which you were taught by us, either by word of mouth or by letter. Now may our Lord Jesus Christ himself, and God our Father, who loved us and gave us eternal comfort and good hope through grace, comfort your hearts and establish them in every good work and word.

A Reading (Lesson) from the Gospel according to Matthew [7:7-14]

Jesus opened his mouth and taught his disciples, saying: "Ask, and it will be given you; seek, and you will find; knock, and it will be opened to you. For every one who asks receives, and he who seeks finds, and to him who knocks it will be opened. Or what man of you, if his son asks him for bread, will give him a stone? Or if he asks for a fish, will give him a serpent? If you then, who are evil, know how to give good gifts to your children, how much more will your Father who is in heaven give good things to those who ask him! So whatever you wish that men would do to you, do so to them; for this is the law and the prophets. Enter by the narrow gate; for the gate is wide and the way is easy, that leads to destruction, and those who enter by it are many. For the gate is narrow and the way is hard, that leads to life, and those who find it are few."

Monday

Psalm 56 [page 662], *Psalm 57* [page 663],
(Psalm 58 [page 664]) ❖ *Psalm 64* [page 671],
Psalm 65 [page 672]

A Reading (Lesson) from the Book of Wisdom [9:1,7-18]

"O God of my fathers and Lord of mercy, who hast made all things by thy word, thou hast chosen me to be king of thy people and to be judge over thy sons and daughters. Thou hast given command to build a temple on thy holy mountain, and an altar in the city of thy habitation, a copy of the holy tent which thou didst prepare from the beginning. With thee is wisdom, who knows thy works and was present when thou didst make the world, and who understands what is pleasing in thy sight and what is right according to thy commandments. Send her forth from the holy heavens, and from the throne of thy glory send her, that she may be with me and toil, and that I may learn what is pleasing to thee. For she knows and understands all things, and she will guide me wisely in my actions and guard me with her glory. Then my works will be acceptable, and I shall judge thy people justly, and shall be worthy of the throne of my father. For what man can learn the counsel of God? Or who can discern what the Lord wills? For the reasoning of mortals is worthless, and our designs are likely to fail, for a perishable body weighs down the soul, and this earthly tent burdens the thoughtful mind. We can hardly guess at what is on earth, and what is at hand we find with labor; but who has traced out what is in the heavens? Who has learned thy counsel, unless thou hast given wisdom and sent thy Holy Spirit from on high? And thus the paths of those on earth were set right, and men were taught what pleases thee, and were saved by wisdom."

A Reading (Lesson) from the Letter of Paul to the Colossians [(3:18—4:1)2-18]

> Wives, be subject to your husbands, as is fitting in the Lord. Husbands, love your wives, and do not be harsh with them. Children, obey your parents in everything, for this pleases the Lord. Fathers, do not provoke your children, lest they become discouraged. Slaves, obey in everything those who are your earthly masters, not with eyeservice, as men-pleasers, but in singleness of heart, fearing the Lord. Whatever your task, work heartily, as serving the Lord and not men, knowing that from the Lord you will receive the inheritance as your reward; you are serving the Lord Christ. For the wrongdoer will be paid back for the wrong he has done, and there is no partiality. Masters, treat your slaves justly and fairly, knowing that you also have a Master in heaven.

Continue steadfastly in prayer, being watchful in it with thanksgiving; and pray for us also, that God may open to us a door for the word, to declare the mystery of Christ, on account of which I am in prison, that I may make it clear, as I ought to speak. Conduct yourselves wisely toward outsiders, making the most of the time. Let your speech

always be gracious, seasoned with salt, so that you may
know how you ought to answer every one. Tych'icus will
tell you all about my affairs; he is a beloved brother and
faithful minister and fellow servant in the Lord. I have sent
him to you for this very purpose, that you may know how
we are and that he may encourage your hearts, and with
him Ones'imus, the faithful and beloved brother, who is
one of yourselves. They will tell you of everything that has
taken place here. Aristar'chus my fellow prisoner greets
you, and Mark the cousin of Barnabas (concerning whom
you have received instructions—if he comes to you, receive
him), and Jesus who is called Justus. These are the only
men of the circumcision among my fellow workers for the
kingdom of God, and they have been a comfort to me.
Ep'aphras, who is one of yourselves, a servant of Christ
Jesus, greets you, always remembering you earnestly in his
prayers, that you may stand mature and fully assured in all
the will of God. For I bear him witness that he has worked
hard for you and for those in La-odice'a and in
Hi-erap'olis. Luke the beloved physician and Demas greet
you. Give my greetings to the brethren at La-odice'a and to
Nympha and the church in her house. And when this letter
has been read among you, have it read also in the church of
the La-odice'ans; and see that you read also the letter from
La-odice'a. And say to Archip'pus, "See that you fulfil the
ministry which you have received in the Lord." I, Paul,
write this greeting with my own hand. Remember my
fetters. Grace be with you.

A Reading (Lesson) from the Gospel according to Luke
[7:36-50]

One of the Pharisees asked Jesus to eat with him, and he
went into the Pharisee's house, and took his place at table.
And behold, a woman of the city, who was a sinner, when
she learned that he was at table in the Pharisee's house,
brought an alabaster flask of ointment, and standing
behind him at his feet, weeping, she began to wet his feet

with her tears, and wiped them with the hair of her head, and kissed his feet, and anointed them with the ointment. Now when the Pharisee who had invited him saw it, he said to himself, "If this man were a prophet, he would have known who and what sort of woman this is who is touching him, for she is a sinner." And Jesus answering said to him, "Simon, I have something to say to you." And he answered, "What is it, Teacher?" "A certain creditor had two debtors; one who owed five hundred denarii, and the other fifty. When they could not pay, he forgave them both. Now which of them will love him more?" Simon answered, "The one, I suppose, to whom he forgave more." And he said to him, "You have judged rightly." Then turning toward the woman he said to Simon, "Do you see this woman? I entered your house, you gave me no water for my feet, but she has wet my feet with her tears and wiped them with her hair. You gave me no kiss, but from the time I came in she has not ceased to kiss my feet. You did not anoint my head with oil, but she has anointed my feet with ointment. Therefore I tell you, her sins, which are many, are forgiven, for she loved much; but he who is forgiven little, loves little." And he said to her, "Your sins are forgiven." Then those who were at table with him began to say among themselves, "Who is this, who even forgives sins?" And he said to the woman, "Your faith has saved you; go in peace."

Tuesday

Psalm 61 [page 668],   *Psalm 62* [page 669]   ❖
Psalm 68:1-20(21-23)24-36 [page 676]

A Reading (Lesson) from the Book of Wisdom
[10:1-4(5-12)13-21]

Wisdom protected the first-formed father of the world, when he alone had been created; she delivered him from his transgression, and gave him strength to rule all things. But when an unrighteous man departed from her in his anger, he perished because in rage he slew his brother. When the earth was flooded because of him, wisdom again saved it, steering the righteous man by a paltry piece of wood.

Wisdom also, when the nations in wicked agreement had been confounded, recognized the righteous man and preserved him blameless before God, and kept him strong in the face of his compassion for his child. Wisdom rescued a righteous man when the ungodly were perishing; he escaped the fire that descended on the Five Cities. Evidence of their wickedness still remains; a continually smoking wasteland, plants bearing fruit that does not ripen, and a pillar of salt standing as a monument to an unbelieving soul. For because they passed wisdom by, they not only were hindered from recognizing the good, but also left for mankind a reminder of their folly, so that their failures could never go unnoticed. Wisdom rescued from troubles those who served her. When a righteous man fled from his brother's wrath, she guided him on straight paths; she showed him the kingdom of God, and gave him knowledge of angels; she prospered him in his labors, and increased the fruit of his toil. When his oppressors were covetous, she stood by him and made him rich. She protected him from his enemies, and kept him safe from those who lay in wait for him; in his arduous contest she gave him the victory, so that he might learn that godliness is more powerful than anything.

When a righteous man was sold, wisdom did not desert him, but delivered him from sin. She descended with him into the dungeon, and when he was in prison she did not leave him, until she brought him the scepter of a kingdom and authority over his masters. Those who accused him she showed to be false, and she gave him everlasting honor. A holy people and blameless race wisdom delivered from a nation of oppressors. She entered the soul of a servant of the Lord, and withstood dread kings with wonders and signs. She gave to holy men the reward of their labors; she guided them along a marvelous way, and became a shelter to them by day, and a starry flame through the night. She brought them over the Red Sea, and led them through deep waters; but she drowned their enemies, and cast them up from the depth of the sea. Therefore the righteous plundered the ungodly; they sang hymns, O Lord, to thy holy name, and praised with one accord thy defending hand, because wisdom opened the mouth of the dumb, and made the tongues of babes speak clearly.

A Reading (Lesson) from the Letter of Paul to the Romans [12:1-21]

I appeal to you therefore, brethren, by the mercies of God, to present your bodies as a living sacrifice, holy and acceptable to God, which is your spiritual worship. Do not be conformed to this world but be transformed by the renewal of your mind, that you may prove what is the will of God, what is good and acceptable and perfect. For by the grace given to me I bid every one among you not to think of himself more highly than he ought to think, but to think with sober judgment, each according to the measure of faith which God has assigned him. For as in one body we have many members, and all the members do not have the same function, so we, though many, are one body in Christ, and individually members one of another. Having gifts that differ according to the grace given to us, let us use them: if prophecy, in proportion to our faith; if service, in our serving; he who teaches, in his teaching; he who exhorts, in his exhortation; he who contributes, in liberality; he who gives aid, with zeal; he who does acts of mercy, with cheerfulness. Let love be genuine; hate what is evil, hold fast to what is good; love one another with brotherly affection; outdo one another in showing honor. Never flag in zeal, be aglow with the Spirit, serve the Lord. Rejoice in your hope, be patient in tribulation, be constant in prayer. Contribute to the needs of the saints, practice hospitality. Bless those who persecute you; bless and do not curse them. Rejoice with those who rejoice, weep with those who weep. Live in harmony with one another; do not be haughty, but associate with the lowly; never be conceited. Repay no one evil for evil, but take thought for what is noble in the sight of all. If possible, so far as it depends upon you, live peaceably with all. Beloved, never avenge yourselves, but leave it to the wrath of God; for it is written, "Vengeance is mine, I will repay, says the Lord." No, "if your enemy is hungry, feed him; if he is thirsty, give him drink; for by so doing you will heap burning coals upon his head." Do not be overcome by evil, but overcome evil with good.

A Reading (Lesson) from the Gospel according to Luke [8:1-15]

Soon afterward Jesus went on through cities and villages, preaching and bringing the good news of the kingdom of God. And the twelve were with him, and also some women who had been healed of evil spirits and infirmities: Mary, called Mag'dalene, from whom seven demons had gone out, and Jo-an'na, the wife of Chu'za, Herod's steward, and Susanna, and many others, who provided for them out of their means. And when a great crowd came together and people from town after town came to him, he said in a parable: "A sower went out to sow his seed; and as he sowed, some fell along the path, and was trodden under foot, and the birds of the air devoured it. And some fell on the rock, and as it grew up, it withered away, because it had no moisture. And some fell among thorns; and the thorns grew with it and choked it. And some fell into good soil and grew, and yielded a hundredfold." As he said this, he called out, "He who has ears to hear, let him hear." And when his disciples asked him what this parable meant, he said, "To you it has been given to know the secrets of the kingdom of God; but for others they are in parables, so that seeing they may not see, and hearing they may not understand. Now the parable is this: The seed is the word of God. The ones along the path are those who have heard; then the devil comes and takes away the word from their hearts, that they may not believe and be saved. And the ones on the rock are those who, when they hear the word, receive it with joy; but these have no root, they believe for a while and in time of temptation fall away. And as for what fell among the thorns, they are those who hear, but as they go on their way they are choked by the cares and riches and pleasures of life, and their fruit does not mature. And as for that in the good soil, they are those who, hearing the word, hold it fast in an honest and good heart, and bring forth fruit with patience."

Wednesday

Psalm 72 [page 685]   ❖   *Psalm 119:73-96* [page 769]

A Reading (Lesson) from the Book of Wisdom [13:1-9]

All men who were ignorant of God were foolish by nature; and they were unable from the good things that are seen to know him who exists, nor did they recognize the craftsman while paying heed to his works; but they supposed that either fire or wind or swift air, or the circle of the stars, or turbulent water, or the luminaries of heaven were the gods that rule the world. If through delight in the beauty of these things men assumed them to be gods, let them know how much better than these is their Lord, for the author of beauty created them. And if men were amazed at their power and working, let them perceive from them how much more powerful is he who formed them. For from the greatness and beauty of created things comes a corresponding perception of their Creator. Yet these men are little to be blamed, for perhaps they go astray while seeking God and desiring to find him. For as they live among his works they keep searching, and they trust in what they see, because the things that are seen are beautiful. Yet again, not even they are to be excused; for if they had the power to know so much that they could investigate the world, how did they fail to find sooner the Lord of these things?

A Reading (Lesson) from the Letter of Paul to the Romans [13:1-14]

Let every person be subject to the governing authorities. For there is no authority except from God, and those that exist have been instituted by God. Therefore he who resists the authorities resists what God has appointed, and those who resist will incur judgment. For rulers are not a terror to good conduct, but to bad. Would you have no fear of him who is in authority? Then do what is good, and you will receive his approval, for he is God's servant for your good. But if you do wrong, be afraid, for he does not bear the sword in vain; he is the servant of God to execute his wrath on the wrongdoer. Therefore one must be subject, not only to avoid God's wrath but also for the sake of conscience. For the same reason you also pay taxes, for the authorities are ministers of God, attending to this very thing. Pay all of them their dues, taxes to whom taxes are due, revenue to whom revenue is due, respect to whom respect is due, honor to whom honor is due. Owe no one anything, except to love one another; for he who loves his neighbor has fulfilled the law. The commandments, "You shall not commit adultery, You shall not kill, You shall not steal, You shall not covet," and any other commandment are summed up in this sentence, "You shall love your neighbor as yourself." Love does no wrong to a neighbor;

therefore love is the fulfilling of the law. Besides this you know what hour it is, how it is full time now for you to wake from sleep. For salvation is nearer to us now than when we first believed; the night is far gone, the day is at hand. Let us then cast off the works of darkness and put on the armor of light; let us conduct ourselves becomingly as in the day, not in reveling and drunkenness, not in debauchery and licentiousness, not in quarreling and jealousy. But put on the Lord Jesus Christ, and make no provision for the flesh, to gratify its desires.

A Reading (Lesson) from the Gospel according to Luke
[8:16-25]

Jesus said to his disciples, "No one after lighting a lamp covers it with a vessel, or puts it under a bed, but puts it on a stand, that those who enter may see the light. For nothing is hid that shall not be made manifest, nor anything secret that shall not be known and come to light. Take heed then how you hear; for to him who has will more be given, and from him who has not, even what he thinks that he has will be taken away." Then his mother and his brothers came to him, but they could not reach him for the crowd. And he was told, "Your mother and your brothers are standing outside, desiring to see you." But he said to them, "My mother and my brothers are those who hear the word of God and do it." One day he got into a boat with his disciples, and he said to them, "Let us go across to the other side of the lake." So they set out, and as they sailed he fell asleep. And a storm of wind came down on the lake, and they were filling with water, and were in danger. And they went and woke him, saying "Master, Master, we are perishing!" And he awoke and rebuked the wind and the raging waves; and they ceased, and there was a calm. He said to them, "Where is your faith?" And they were afraid, and they marveled, saying to one another, "Who then is this, that he commands even wind and water, and they obey him?"

Thursday

(Psalm 70 [page 682]),   *Psalm 71* [page 683]   ❖
Psalm 74 [page 689]

A Reading (Lesson) from the Book of Wisdom
[14:27—15:3]

The worship of idols not to be named is the beginning and
cause and end of every evil. For their worshipers either
rave in exultation, or prophesy lies, or live unrighteously,
or readily commit perjury; for because they trust in lifeless
idols they swear wicked oaths and expect to suffer no
harm. But just penalties will overtake them on two counts:
because they thought wickedly of God in devoting
themselves to idols, and because in deceit they swore
unrighteously through contempt for holiness. For it is not
the power of the things by which men swear, but the just
penalty for those who sin, that always pursues the
transgression of the unrighteous. But thou, our God, art
kind and true, patient, and ruling all things in mercy. For
even if we sin we are thine, knowing thy power, but we
will not sin, because we know that we are accounted thine.
For to know thee is complete righteousness, and to know
thy power is the root of immortality.

*A Reading (Lesson) from the Letter of Paul
to the Romans* [14:1-12]

As for the man who is weak in faith, welcome him, but not
for disputes over opinions. One believes he may eat
anything, while the weak man eats only vegetables. Let not
him who eats despise him who abstains, and let not him
who abstains pass judgment on him who eats; for God has
welcomed him. Who are you to pass judgment on the
servant of another? It is before his own master that he
stands or falls. And he will be upheld, for the Master is
able to make him stand. One man esteems one day as

better than another, while another man esteems all days alike. Let every one be fully convinced in his own mind. He who observes the day, observes it in honor of the Lord. He also who eats, eats in honor of the Lord, since he gives thanks to God; while he who abstains, abstains in honor of the Lord and gives thanks to God. None of us lives to himself, and none of us dies to himself. If we live, we live to the Lord, and if we die, we die to the Lord; so then, whether we live or whether we die, we are the Lord's. For to this end Christ died and lived again, that he might be Lord both of the dead and of the living. Why do you pass judgment on your brother? Or you, why do you despise your brother? For we shall all stand before the judgment seat of God; for it is written, "As I live, says the Lord, every knee shall bow to me, and every tongue shall give praise to God." So each of us shall give account of himself to God.

A Reading (Lesson) from the Gospel according to Luke
[8:26-39]

Jesus and his disciples arrived at the country of the Ger'asenes, which is opposite Galilee. And as he stepped out on land, there met him a man from the city who had demons; for a long time he had worn no clothes, and he lived not in a house but among the tombs. When he saw Jesus, he cried out and fell down before him, and said with a loud voice, "What have you to do with me, Jesus, Son of the Most High God? I beseech you, do not torment me." For he had commanded the unclean spirit to come out of the man. (For many a time it had seized him; he was kept under guard, and bound with chains and fetters, but he broke the bonds and was driven by the demon into the desert.) Jesus then asked him, "What is your name?" And he said, "Legion"; for many demons had entered him. And they begged him not to command them to depart into the abyss. Now a large herd of swine was feeding there on the hillside; and they begged him to let them enter these. So he gave them leave. Then the demons came out of the man and entered the swine, and the herd rushed down the steep bank into the lake and were drowned. When the herdsmen saw what had happened, they fled, and told it in the city and in the country. Then people went out to see what had happened, and they came to Jesus, and found the man from whom the demons had gone, sitting at the feet of Jesus, clothed and in his right mind; and they were afraid. And those who had seen it told them how he who had been possessed with demons was healed. Then all the people of the surrounding country of the Ger'asenes asked him to depart from them; for they were seized with great fear; so he got into the boat and returned. The man from whom the demons had gone begged that he might be with him; but he sent him away, saying, "Return to your home, and declare how much God has done for you." And he went away, proclaiming throughout the whole city how much Jesus had done for him.

Friday

Psalm 106:1-18 [page 741]   ❖   *Psalm 106:19-48* [page 743]

A Reading (Lesson) from the Book of Wisdom
[16:15—17:1]

To escape from thy hand is impossible; for the ungodly, refusing to know thee, were scourged by the strength of thy arm, pursued by unusual rains and hail and relentless storms, and utterly consumed by fire. For—most incredible of all—in the water, which quenches all things, the fire had still greater effect, for the universe defends the righteous. At one time the flame was restrained, so that it might not consume the creatures sent against the ungodly, but that seeing this they might know that they were being pursued by the judgment of God; and at another time even in the midst of water it burned more intensely than fire, to destroy the crops of the unrighteous land. Instead of these things thou didst give thy people the food of angels, and without their toil thou didst supply them from heaven with bread ready to eat, providing every pleasure and suited to every taste. For thy sustenance manifested thy sweetness toward thy children; and the bread, ministering to the desire of the one who took it, was changed to suit every one's liking. Snow and ice withstood fire without melting, so that they might know that the crops of their enemies were being destroyed by the fire that blazed in the hail and flashed in the showers of rain; whereas the fire, in order that the righteous might be fed, even forgot its native power. For the creation, serving thee who hast made it, exerts itself to punish the unrighteous, and in kindness relaxes on behalf of those who trust in thee. Therefore at that time also, changed into all forms, it served thy all-nourishing bounty, according to the desire of those who had need, so that thy sons, whom thou didst love, O Lord, might learn that it is not the production of crops that feeds man, but that thy word preserves those who trust in thee. For what was not destroyed by fire was melted when simply warmed by a fleeting ray of the sun, to make it known that one must rise before the sun to give thee thanks, and must pray to thee at the dawning of the light; for the hope of an ungrateful man will melt like wintry frost, and flow away like waste water. Great are thy judgments and hard to describe; therefore uninstructed souls have gone astray.

A Reading (Lesson) from the Letter of Paul to the Romans [14:13-23]

Let us no more pass judgment on one another, but rather decide never to put a stumbling block or hindrance in the way of a brother. I know and am persuaded in the Lord Jesus that nothing is unclean in itself; but it is unclean for any one who thinks it unclean. If your brother is being

injured by what you eat, you are no longer walking in love.
Do not let what you eat cause the ruin of one for whom
Christ died. So do not let your good be spoken of as evil.
For the kingdom of God is not food and drink but
righteousness and peace and joy in the Holy Spirit; he who
thus serves Christ is acceptable to God and approved by
men. Let us then pursue what makes for peace and for
mutual upbuilding. Do not, for the sake of food, destroy
the work of God. Everything is indeed clean, but it is
wrong for any one to make others fall by what he eats; it is
right not to eat meat or drink wine or do anything that
makes your brother stumble. The faith that you have, keep
between yourself and God; happy is he who has no reason
to judge himself for what he approves. But he who has
doubts is condemned, if he eats, because he does not act
from faith; for whatever does not proceed from faith is sin.

A Reading (Lesson) from the Gospel according to Luke
[8:40-56]

When Jesus returned, the crowd welcomed him, for they
were all waiting for him. And there came a man named
Ja'irus, who was a ruler of the synagogue; and falling at
Jesus' feet he besought him to come to his house, for he
had an only daughter, about twelve years of age, and she
was dying. As he went, the people pressed round him. And
a woman who had had a flow of blood for twelve years
and could not be healed by any one, came up behind him,
and touched the fringe of his garment; and immediately
her flow of blood ceased. And Jesus said, "Who was it that
touched me?" When all denied it, Peter said, "Master, the
multitudes surround you and press upon you!" But Jesus
said, "Some one touched me; for I perceive that power has
gone forth from me." And when the woman saw that she
was not hidden, she came trembling, and falling down
before him declared in the presence of all people why she
had touched him, and how she had been immediately

healed. And he said to her, "Daughter, your faith has made you well; go in peace." While he was still speaking, a man from the ruler's house came and said, "Your daughter is dead; do not trouble the Teacher any more." But Jesus on hearing this answered him, "Do not fear; only believe, and she shall be well." And when he came to the house, he permitted no one to enter with him, except Peter and John and James, and the father and mother of the child. And all were weeping and bewailing her; but he said, "Do not weep; for she is not dead but sleeping." And they laughed at him, knowing that she was dead. But taking her by the hand he called, saying, "Child, arise." And her spirit returned, and she got up at once; and he directed that something should be given her to eat. And her parents were amazed; but he charged them to tell no one what had happened.

Saturday

Psalm 75 [page 691], *Psalm 76* [page 692] ❖
Psalm 23 [page 612], *Psalm 27* [page 617]

A Reading (Lesson) from the Book of Wisdom
[19:1-8,18-22]

The ungodly were assailed to the end by pitiless anger, for God knew in advance even their future actions, that, though they themselves had permitted thy people to depart and hastily sent them forth, they would change their minds and pursue them. For while they were still busy at mourning, and were lamenting at the graves of their dead, they reached another foolish decision, and pursued as fugitives those whom they had begged and compelled to depart. For the fate they deserved drew them on to this end, and made them forget what had happened, in order that they might fill up the punishment which their torments still lacked, and that thy people might experience an incredible journey, but they themselves might meet a strange death. For the whole creation in its nature was fashioned anew, complying with thy commands, that thy children might be kept unharmed. The cloud was seen overshadowing the camp, and dry land emerging where water had stood before, an unhindered way out of the Red Sea, and a grassy plain out of the raging waves, where those protected by thy hand passed through as one nation after gazing on marvelous wonders. For the elements changed places with one another, as on a harp the notes vary the nature of the rhythm, while each note remains the same. This may be clearly inferred from the sight of what took place. For land animals were transformed into water creatures, and creatures that swim moved over to the land. Fire even in water retained its normal power, and water forgot its fire-quenching nature. Flames, on the contrary, failed to consume the flesh of perishable creatures that walked among them, nor did they melt the crystalline, easily melted kind of heavenly food. For in everything, O Lord, thou hast exalted and glorified thy people; and thou hast not neglected to help them at all times and in all places.

A Reading (Lesson) from the Letter of Paul to the Romans [15:1-13]

We who are strong ought to bear with the failings of the weak, and not to please ourselves; let each of us please his neighbor for his good, to edify him. For Christ did not please himself; but, as it is written, "The reproaches of those who reproached thee fell on me." For whatever was written in former days was written for our instruction, that by steadfastness and by the encouragement of the scriptures we might have hope. May the God of steadfastness and encouragement grant you to live in such harmony with one another, in accord with Christ Jesus, that together you may with one voice glorify the God and

Father of our Lord Jesus Christ. Welcome one another, therefore, as Christ has welcomed you, for the glory of God. For I tell you that Christ became a servant to the circumcised to show God's truthfulness, in order to confirm the promises given to the patriarchs, and in order that the Gentiles might glorify God for his mercy. As it is written, "Therefore I will praise thee among the Gentiles, and sing to thy name"; and again it is said, "Rejoice, O Gentiles, with his people"; and again, "Praise the Lord, all Gentiles, and let all the peoples praise him"; and further Isaiah says, "The root of Jesse shall come, he who rises to rule the Gentiles; in him shall the Gentiles hope." May the God of hope fill you with all joy and peace in believing, so that by the power of the Holy Spirit you may abound in hope.

A Reading (Lesson) from the Gospel according to Luke [9:1-17]

Jesus called the twelve together and gave them power and authority over all demons and to cure diseases, and he sent them out to preach the kingdom of God and to heal. And he said to them, "Take nothing for your journey, no staff, nor bag, nor bread, nor money; and do not have two tunics. And whatever house you enter, stay there, and from there depart. And wherever they do not receive you, when you leave that town shake off the dust from your feet as a testimony against them." And they departed and went through the villages, preaching the gospel and healing everywhere. Now Herod the tetrarch heard of all that was done, and he was perplexed, because it was said by some that John had been raised from the dead, by some that Eli′jah had appeared, and by others that one of the old prophets had risen. Herod said, "John I beheaded; but who is this about whom I hear such things?" And he sought to see him. On their return the apostles told him what they had done. And he took them and withdrew apart to a city called Beth-sa′ida. When the crowds learned it, they followed him; and he welcomed them and spoke to them of the kingdom of God, and cured those who had need of healing. Now the day began to wear away; and the twelve came and said to him, "Send the crowd away, to go into the villages and country round about, to lodge and get provisions; for we are here in a lonely place." But he said to them, "You give them something to eat." They said, "We have no more than five loaves and two fish — unless we are to go and buy food for all these people." For there were about five thousand men. And he said to his disciples, "Make them sit down in companies, about fifty each." And they did so, and made them all sit down. And taking the five loaves and the two fish he looked up to heaven, and blessed and broke them, and gave them to the disciples to set before the crowd. And all ate and were satisfied. And they took up what was left over, twelve baskets of broken pieces.

Week of 6 Easter

Sunday

Psalm 93 [page 722],   *Psalm 96* [page 725]   ❖
Psalm 34 [page 627]

A Reading (Lesson) from the Book of Ecclesiasticus
[43:1-12,27-32]

The pride of the heavenly heights is the clear firmament, the appearance of heaven in a spectacle of glory. The sun, when it appears, making proclamation as it goes forth, is a marvelous instrument, the work of the Most High. At noon it parches the land; and who can withstand its burning heat? A man tending a furnace works in burning heat, but the sun burns the mountains three times as much; it breathes out fiery vapors, and with bright beams it blinds the eyes. Great is the Lord who made it; and at his command it hastens on its course. He made the moon also, to serve in its season to mark the times and to be an everlasting sign. From the moon comes the sign for feast days, a light that wanes when it has reached the full. The month is named for the moon, increasing marvelously in its phases, an instrument of the hosts on high shining forth in the firmament of heaven. The glory of the stars is the beauty of heaven, a gleaming array in the heights of the Lord. At the command of the Holy One they stand as ordered, they never relax in their watches. Look upon the rainbow, and praise him who made it, exceedingly beautiful in its brightness. It encircles the heaven with its glorious arc; the hands of the Most High have stretched it out. Though we speak much we cannot reach the end, and the sum of the words is: "He is the all." Where shall we find strength to praise him? For he is greater than all his works. Terrible is the Lord and very great, and marvelous is his power. When you praise the Lord, exalt him as much as you can; for he will surpass even that. When you exalt him, put forth all your strength, and do not grow weary, for you cannot praise him enough. Who has seen him and can describe him? Or who can extol him as he is? Many things greater than these lie hidden, for we have seen but few of his works.

A Reading (Lesson) from the First Letter of Paul to Timothy [3:14—4:5]

I hope to come to you soon, but I am writing these instructions to you so that, if I am delayed, you may know how one ought to behave in the household of God, which is the church of the living God, the pillar and bulwark of the truth. Great indeed, we confess, is the mystery of our religion: He was manifested in the flesh, vindicated in the Spirit, seen by angels, preached among the nations, believed on in the world, taken up in glory. Now the Spirit expressly says that in later times some will depart from the faith by giving heed to deceitful spirits and doctrines of demons, through the pretensions of liars whose consciences are seared, who forbid marriage and enjoin abstinence from foods which God created to be received with thanksgiving by those who believe and know the truth. For everything created by God is good, and nothing is to be rejected if it is received with thanksgiving; for then it is consecrated by the word of God and prayer.

A Reading (Lesson) from the Gospel according to Matthew [13:24-34a]

Another parable Jesus put before the crowd saying, "The kingdom of heaven may be compared to a man who sowed good seed in his field; but while men were sleeping, his enemy came and sowed weeds among the wheat, and went away. So when the plants came up and bore grain, then the weeds appeared also. And the servants of the householder came and said to him, 'Sir, did you not sow good seed in your field? How then has it weeds?' He said to them, 'An enemy has done this.' The servants said to him, 'Then do you want us to go and gather them?' But he said, 'No; lest in gathering the weeds you root up the wheat along with them. Let both grow together until the harvest; and at harvest time I will tell the reapers, Gather the weeds first and bind them in bundles to be burned, but gather the wheat into my barn.'" Another parable he put before them, saying, "The kingdom of heaven is like a grain of mustard seed which a man took and sowed in his field; it is the smallest of all seeds, but when it has grown it is the greatest of shrubs and becomes a tree, so that the birds of the air come and make nests in its branches." He told them another parable. "The kingdom of heaven is like leaven which a woman took and hid in three measures of flour, till it was all leavened." All this Jesus said to the crowds in parables.

Monday

Psalm 80 [page 702] ❖ *Psalm 77* [page 693],
(Psalm 79 [page 701])

Deuteronomy 8:1-10   [page 264 above]

A Reading (Lesson) from the Letter of James [1:1-15]

James, a servant of God and of the Lord Jesus Christ, To the twelve tribes in the Dispersion: Greeting. Count it all joy, my brethren, when you meet various trials, for you know that the testing of your faith produces steadfastness. And let steadfastness have its full effect, that you may be perfect and complete, lacking in nothing. If any of you lacks wisdom, let him ask God, who gives to all men generously and without reproaching, and it will be given him. But let him ask in faith, with no doubting, for he who doubts is like a wave of the sea that is driven and tossed by the wind. For that person must not suppose that a double-minded man, unstable in all his ways, will receive anything from the Lord. Let the lowly brother boast in his exaltation, and the rich in his humiliation, because like the flower of the grass he will pass away. For the sun rises with its scorching heat and withers the grass; its flower falls, and its beauty perishes. So will the rich man fade away in the midst of his pursuits. Blessed is the man who endures trial, for when he has stood the test he will receive the crown of life which God has promised to those who love him. Let no one say when he is tempted, "I am tempted by God"; for God cannot be tempted with evil and he himself tempts no one; but each person is tempted when he is lured and enticed by his own desire. Then desire when it has conceived gives birth to sin; and sin when it is full-grown brings forth death.

A Reading (Lesson) from the Gospel according to Luke
[9:18-27]

Now it happened that as Jesus was praying alone the disciples were with him; and he asked them, "Who do the people say that I am?" And they answered, "John the Baptist; but others say, Eli′jah; and others, that one of the old prophets has risen." And he said to them, "But who do you say that I am?" And Peter answered, "The Christ of God." But he charged and commanded them to tell this to no one, saying, "The Son of man must suffer many things, and be rejected by the elders and chief priests and scribes, and be killed, and on the third day be raised." And he said to all, "If any man would come after me, let him deny himself and take up his cross daily and follow me. For whoever would save his life will lose it: and whoever loses his life for my sake, he will save it. For what does it profit a man if he gains the whole world and loses or forfeits himself? For whoever is ashamed of me and of my words, of him will the Son of man be ashamed when he comes in his glory and the glory of the Father and of the holy angels. But I tell you truly, there are some standing here who will not taste death before they see the kingdom of God."

Tuesday

Psalm 78:1-39 [page 694] ❖ *Psalm 78:40-72* [page 698]

Deuteronomy 8:11-20   [page 266 above]

A Reading (Lesson) from the Letter of James [1:16-27]

Do not be deceived, my beloved brethren. Every good endowment and every perfect gift is from above, coming down from the Father of lights with whom there is no variation or shadow due to change. Of his own will he brought us forth by the word of truth that we should be a kind of first fruits of his creatures. Know this, my beloved brethren. Let every man be quick to hear, slow to speak, slow to anger, for the anger of man does not work the righteousness of God. Therefore put away all filthiness and rank growth of wickedness and receive with meekness the implanted word, which is able to save your souls. But be doers of the word, and not hearers only, deceiving yourselves. For if any one is a hearer of the word and not a doer, he is like a man who observes his natural face in a mirror; for he observes himself and goes away and at once forgets what he was like. But he who looks into the perfect law, the law of liberty, and perseveres, being no hearer that forgets but a doer that acts, he shall be blessed in his doing. If any one thinks he is religious, and does not bridle his tongue but deceives his heart, this man's religion is vain. Religion that is pure and undefiled before God and the Father is this: to visit orphans and widows in their affliction, and to keep oneself unstained from the world.

A Reading (Lesson) from the Gospel according to Luke
[11:1-13]

Jesus was praying in a certain place, and when he ceased, one of his disciples said to him, "Lord, teach us to pray, as John taught his disciples." And he said to them, "When you pray, say: Father, hallowed be thy name. Thy kingdom come. Give us each day our daily bread; and forgive us our sins, for we ourselves forgive every one who is indebted to us; and lead us not into temptation." And he said to them, "Which of you who has a friend will go to him at midnight and say to him, 'Friend, lend me three loaves, for a friend of mine has arrived on a journey, and I have nothing to set before him'; and he will answer from within, 'Do not bother me; the door is now shut, and my children are with me in bed; I cannot get up and give you anything'? I tell you, though he will not get up and give him anything because he is his friend, yet because of his importunity he will rise and give him whatever he needs. And I tell you,

Ask, and it will be given you; seek, and you will find; knock, and it will be opened to you. For every one who asks receives, and he who seeks finds, and to him who knocks it will be opened. What father among you, if his son asks for a fish, will instead of a fish give him a serpent; or if he asks for an egg, will give him a scorpion? If you then, who are evil, know how to give good gifts to your children, how much more will the heavenly Father give the Holy Spirit to those who ask him!"

Wednesday

(Morning Prayer)   *Psalm 119:97-120* [page 771]

A Reading (Lesson) from the Book of Baruch [3:24-37]

O Israel, how great is the house of God! And how vast the territory that he possesses! It is great and has no bounds; it is high and immeasurable. The giants were born there, who were famous of old, great in stature, expert in war. God did not choose them, nor give them the way to knowledge; so they perished through their folly. Who has gone up into heaven, and taken her, and brought her down from the clouds? Who has gone over the sea, and found her, and will buy her for pure gold? No one knows the way to her, or is concerned about the path to her. But he who knows all things knows her, he found her by his understanding. He who prepared the earth for all time filled it with four-footed creatures; he who sends forth the light, and it goes, called it, and it obeyed him in fear; the stars shone in their watches, and were glad; he called them, and they said, "Here we are!" They shone with gladness for him who made him. This is our God; no other can be compared to him! He found the whole way to knowledge, and gave her to Jacob his servant and to Israel whom he loved. Afterward she appeared upon earth and lived among men.

A Reading (Lesson) from the Letter of James [5:13-18]

Is any one among you suffering? Let him pray. Is any cheerful? Let him sing praise. Is any among you sick? Let him call for the elders of the church, and let them pray over him, anointing him with oil in the name of the Lord; and the prayer of faith will save the sick man, and the Lord will raise him up; and if he has committed sins, he will be forgiven. Therefore confess your sins to one another, and pray for one another, that you may be healed. The prayer of a righteous man has great power in its effects. Eli'jah was a man of like nature with ourselves and he prayed fervently that it might not rain, and for three years and six months it did not rain on the earth. Then he prayed again and the heaven gave rain, and the earth brought forth its fruit.

A Reading (Lesson) from the Gospel according to Luke [12:22-31]

Jesus said to his disciples, "I tell you, do not be anxious about your life, what you shall eat, nor about your body, what you shall put on. For life is more than food, and the body more than clothing. Consider the ravens; they neither sow nor reap, they have neither storehouse nor barn, and yet God feeds them. Of how much more value are you than the birds! And which of you by being anxious can add a cubit to his span of life? If then you are not able to do as small a thing as that, why are you anxious about the rest? Consider the lilies, how they grow; they neither toil nor spin; yet I tell you, even Solomon in all his glory was not arrayed like one of these. But if God so clothes the grass which is alive in the field today and tomorrow is thrown into the oven, how much more will he clothe you, O men of little faith! And do not seek what you are to eat and what you are to drink, nor be of anxious mind. For all the nations of the world seek these things; and your Father knows that you need them. Instead, seek his kingdom, and these things shall be yours as well.

Eve of Ascension

(Evening Prayer) *Psalm 68:1-20* [page 676]

A Reading (Lesson) from the Second Book of the Kings
[2:1-15]

When the Lord was about to take Eli'jah up to heaven by a whirlwind, Eli'jah and Eli'sha were on their way from Gilgal. And Eli'jah said to Eli'sha, "Tarry here, I pray you; for the Lord has sent me as far as Bethel." But Eli'sha said, "As the Lord lives, and as you yourself live, I will not leave you." So they went down to Bethel. And the sons of the prophets who were in Bethel came out to Eli'sha, and said to him, "Do you know that today the Lord will take away your master from over you?" And he answered, "Yes, I know it; hold your peace." Eli'jah said to him, "Eli'sha, tarry here, I pray you; for the Lord has sent me to Jericho." But he said, "As the Lord lives, and as you yourself live, I will not leave you." So they came to Jericho. The sons of the prophets who were at Jericho drew near to Eli'sha, and said to him, "Do you know that today the Lord will take away your master from over you?" And he answered, "Yes, I know it; hold your peace." Then Eli'jah said to him, "Tarry here, I pray you; for the Lord has sent me to the Jordan." But he said, "As the Lord lives, and as you yourself live, I will not leave you." So the two of them went on. Fifty men of the sons of the prophets also went, and stood at some distance from them, as they both were standing by the Jordan. Then Eli'jah took his mantle, and rolled it up, and struck the water, and the water was parted to one side and to the other, till the two of them could go over on dry ground. When they had crossed, Eli'jah said to Eli'sha, "Ask what I shall do for you, before I am taken from you." And Eli'sha said, "I pray you, let me inherit a double share of your spirit." And he said, "You have asked a hard thing; yet, if you see me as I am being taken from you, it shall be so for you; but if you do not see me, it shall not be so." And as they still went on and talked, behold, a chariot of fire and horses of fire separated the two of them. And Eli'jah went up by a whirlwind into heaven. And Eli'sha saw it and he cried, "My father, my father! the chariots of Israel and its horsemen!" And he saw him no more. Then he took hold of his own clothes and rent them in two pieces. And he took up the mantle of Eli'jah that had fallen from him, and went back and stood on the bank of the Jordan. Then he took the mantle of Eli'jah that had fallen from him, and struck the water, saying, "Where is the Lord, the God of Eli'jah?" And when he had struck the water, the water was parted to the one side and to the other; and Eli'sha went over. Now when the sons of the prophets who were at Jericho saw him over against them, they said, "The spirit of Eli'jah rests on Eli'sha." And they came to meet him, and bowed to the ground before him.

A Reading (Lesson) from the Revelation to John [5:1-14]

I saw in the right hand of him who was seated on the throne a scroll written within and on the back, sealed with seven seals; and I saw a strong angel proclaiming with a loud voice, "Who is worthy to open the scroll and break its seals?" And no one in heaven or on earth or under the earth was able to open the scroll or to look into it, and I wept much that no one was found worthy to open the scroll or to look into it. Then one of the elders said to me, "Weep not; lo, the Lion of the tribe of Judah, the Root of David, has conquered, so that he can open the scroll and its seven seals." And between the throne and the four living creatures and among the elders, I saw a Lamb standing, as though it had been slain, with seven horns and with seven eyes, which are the seven spirits of God sent out into all the earth; and he went and took the scroll from the right hand of him who was seated on the throne. And when he had taken the scroll, the four living creatures and the twenty-four elders fell down before the Lamb, each holding a harp, and with golden bowls full of incense, which are the prayers of the saints; and they sang a new song, saying, "Worthy art thou to take the scroll and to open its seals, for thou wast slain and by thy blood didst ransom men for God from every tribe and tongue and people and nation, and hast made them a kingdom and priests to our God, and they shall reign on earth." Then I looked, and I heard around the throne and the living creatures and the elders the voice of many angels, numbering myriads of myriads and thousands of thousands, saying with a loud voice, "Worthy is the Lamb who was slain, to receive power and wealth and wisdom and might and honor and glory and blessing!" And I heard every creature in heaven and on earth and under the earth and in the sea, and all therein, saying, "To him who sits upon the throne and to the Lamb be blessing and honor and glory and might for ever and ever!" And the four living creatures said, "Amen!" and the elders fell down and worshiped.

Ascension Day

Psalm 8 [page 592], *Psalm 47* [page 650] ❖
Psalm 24 [page 613], *Psalm 96* [page 725]

A Reading (Lesson) from the Book of Ezekiel
[1:1-14,24-28b]

In the thirtieth year, in the fourth month, on the fifth day of the month, as I was among the exiles by the river Chebar, the heavens were opened, and I saw visions of God. On the fifth day of the month (it was the fifth year of the exile of King Jehoi'achin), the word of the Lord came to Ezekiel the priest, the son of Buzi, in the land of the Chalde'ans by the river Chebar; and the hand of the Lord was upon him there. As I looked, behold, a stormy wind came out of the north, and a great cloud, with brightness round about it, and fire flashing forth continually, and in the midst of the fire, as it were gleaming bronze. And from the midst of it came the likeness of four living creatures. And this was their appearance: they had the form of men, but each had four faces, and each of them had four wings. Their legs were straight, and the soles of their feet were like the sole of a calf's foot; and they sparkled like burnished bronze. Under their wings on their four sides they had human hands. And the four had their faces and their wings thus: their wings touched one another; they went every one straight forward, without turning as they went. As for the likeness of their faces, each had the face of a man in front; the four had the face of a lion on the right side, the four had the face of an ox on the left side, and the four had the face of an eagle at the back. Such were their faces. And their wings were spread out above; each creature had two wings, each of which touched the wing of another, while two covered their bodies. And each went straight forward; wherever the spirit would go, they went, without turning as they went. In the midst of the living creatures there was something that looked like burning coals of fire, like torches moving to and fro among the living creatures; and the fire was bright, and out of the fire went forth lightning. And the living creatures darted to and fro, like a flash of lightning. And when they went, I heard the sound of their wings like the sound of many waters, like the thunder of the Almighty, a sound of tumult like the sound of a host; when they stood still, they let down their wings. And there came a voice from above the firmament over their heads; when they stood still, they let down their wings. And above the firmament over their heads there was the likeness of a throne, in appearance like sapphire; and seated above the likeness of a throne was a likeness as it were of a human form. And upward from what had the appearance of his loins I saw as it were gleaming bronze, like the appearance of fire enclosed round about; and downward from what had the appearance of his loins I

saw as it were the appearance of fire, and there was
brightness round about him. Like the appearance of the
bow that is in the cloud on the day of rain, so was the
appearance of the brightness round about. Such was the
appearance of the likeness of the glory of the Lord.

A Reading (Lesson) from the Letter to the Hebrews
[2:5-18]

It was not to angels that God subjected the world to come,
of which we are speaking. It has been testified somewhere,
"What is man that thou art mindful of him, or the son of
man, that thou carest for him? Thou didst make him for a
little while lower than the angels, thou hast crowned him
with glory and honor, putting everything in subjection
under his feet." Now in putting everything in subjection to
him, he left nothing outside his control. As it is, we do not
yet see everything in subjection to him. But we see Jesus,
who for a little while was made lower than the angels,
crowned with glory and honor because of the suffering of
death, so that by the grace of God he might taste death for
every one. For it was fitting that he, for whom and by
whom all things exist, in bringing many sons to glory,
should make the pioneer of their salvation perfect through
suffering. For he who sanctifies and those who are
sanctified have all one origin. That is why he is not
ashamed to call them brethren, saying, "I will proclaim thy
name to my brethren, in the midst of the congregation I
will praise thee." And again, "I will put my trust in him."
And again, "Here am I, and the children God has given
me." Since therefore the children share in flesh and blood,
he himself likewise partook of the same nature, that
through death he might destroy him who has the power of
death, that is, the devil, and deliver all those who through
fear of death were subject to lifelong bondage. For surely it
is not with angels that he is concerned but with the
descendants of Abraham. Therefore he had to be made like
his brethren in every respect, so that he might become a

merciful and faithful high priest in the service of God, to make expiation for the sins of the people. For because he himself has suffered and been tempted, he is able to help those who are tempted.

A Reading (Lesson) from the Gospel according to Matthew [28:16-20]

Now the eleven disciples went to Galilee, to the mountain to which Jesus had directed them. And when they saw him they worshiped him; but some doubted. And Jesus came and said to them, "All authority in heaven and on earth has been given to me. Go therefore and make disciples of all nations, baptizing them in the name of the Father and of the Son and of the Holy Spirit, teaching them to observe all that I have commanded you; and lo, I am with you always, to the close of the age."

Friday

Psalm 85 [page 708],   *Psalm 86* [page 709]   ❖
Psalm 91 [page 719],   *Psalm 92* [page 720]

A Reading (Lesson) from the Book of Ezekiel [1:28—3:3]

Like the appearance of the bow that is in the cloud on the day of rain, so was the appearance of the brightness round about. Such was the appearance of the likeness of the glory of the Lord. And when I saw it, I fell upon my face, and I heard the voice of one speaking. And he said to me, "Son of man, stand upon your feet, and I will speak with you." And when he spoke to me, the Spirit entered into me and set me upon my feet; and I heard him speaking to me. And he said to me, "Son of man, I send you to the people of Israel, to a nation of rebels, who have rebelled against me; they and their fathers have transgressed against me to this very day. The people also are impudent and stubborn: I send you to them; and you shall say to them, 'Thus says the Lord God.' And whether they hear or refuse to hear (for they are a rebellious house) they will know that there has been a prophet among them. And you, son of man, be not afraid of them, nor be afraid of their words, though briers and thorns are with you and you sit upon scorpions; be not afraid of their words, nor be dismayed at their looks, for they are a rebellious house. And you shall speak my words to them, whether they hear or refuse to hear; for they are a rebellious house. But you, son of man, hear what I say to you; be not rebellious like that rebellious house; open your mouth, and eat what I give you." And when I looked, behold, a hand was stretched out to me, and, lo, a written scroll was in it; and he spread it before me; and it had writing on the front and on the back, and there were written on it words of lamentation and mourning and woe. And he said to me, "Son of man, eat what is offered to you; eat this scroll, and go, speak to the house of Israel." So I opened my mouth and he gave me the scroll to eat. And he said to me, "Son of man, eat this scroll that I give you and fill your stomach with it." Then I ate it; and it was in my mouth as sweet as honey.

A Reading (Lesson) from the Letter to the Hebrews
[4:14—5:6]

Since then we have a great high priest who has passed through the heavens, Jesus, the Son of God, let us hold fast our confession. For we have not a high priest who is unable to sympathize with our weaknesses, but one who in every respect has been tempted as we are, yet without sin. Let us then with confidence draw near to the throne of grace, that we may receive mercy and find grace to help in time of need. For every high priest chosen from among men is appointed to act on behalf of men in relation to God, to offer gifts and sacrifices for sins. He can deal gently with the ignorant and wayward, since he himself is beset with weakness. Because of this he is bound to offer sacrifice for his own sins as well as for those of the people. And one does not take the honor upon himself, but he is called by God, just as Aaron was. So also Christ did not exalt himself to be made a high priest, but was appointed by him who said to him, "Thou art my Son, today I have begotten thee"; as he says also in another place, "Thou art a priest for ever, after the order of Melchiz'edek."

A Reading (Lesson) from the Gospel according to Luke [9:28-36]

Now about eight days after these sayings Jesus took with him Peter and John and James, and went up on the mountain to pray. And as he was praying, the appearance of his countenance was altered, and his raiment became dazzling white. And behold, two men talked with him, Moses and Eli'jah, who appeared in glory and spoke of his departure, which he was to accomplish at Jerusalem. Now Peter and those who were with him were heavy with sleep, and when they wakened they saw his glory and the two men who stood with him. And as the men were parting from him, Peter said to Jesus, "Master, it is well that we are here; let us make three booths, one for you and one for Moses and one for Eli'jah" — not knowing what he said. As he said this, a cloud came and overshadowed them; and they were afraid as they entered the cloud. And a voice came out of the cloud, saying, "This is my Son, my Chosen; listen to him!" And when the voice had spoken, Jesus was found alone. And they kept silence and told no one in those days anything of what they had seen.

Saturday

Psalm 87 [page 711], *Psalm 90* [page 717] ❖
Psalm 136 [page 789]

A Reading (Lesson) from the Book of Ezekiel [3:4-17]

The voice of one speaking said to me, "Son of man, go, get you to the house of Israel, and speak with my words to them. For you are not sent to a people of foreign speech and a hard language, but to the house of Israel — not to many peoples of foreign speech and a hard language, whose words you cannot understand. Surely, if I sent you to such, they would listen to you. But the house of Israel will not listen to you; for they are not willing to listen to me; because all the house of Israel are of a hard forehead and of a stubborn heart. Behold, I have made your face hard against their faces, and your forehead hard against their foreheads. Like adamant harder than flint have I made your forehead; fear them not, nor be dismayed at their looks, for they are a rebellious house." Moreover he said to me, "Son of man, all my words that I shall speak to you receive in your heart, and hear with your ears. And go get you to the exiles, to your people, and say to them, 'Thus says the Lord God'; whether they hear or refuse to hear." Then the Spirit lifted me up, and as the glory of the Lord arose from its place, I heard behind me the sound of a great earthquake; it was the sound of the wings of the living creatures as they touched one another, and the sound of the wheels beside them, that sounded like a great earthquake. The Spirit lifted me up and took me away, and I went in bitterness in the heat of my spirit, the hand of the Lord being strong upon me; and I came to the exiles at Tela'bib, who dwelt by the river Chebar. And I sat there overwhelmed among them seven days. And at the end of seven days, the word of the Lord came to me: "Son of man, I have made you a watchman for the house of Israel; whenever you hear a word from my mouth, you shall give them warning from me."

A Reading (Lesson) from the Letter to the Hebrews
[5:7-14]

In the days of his flesh, Jesus offered up prayers and
supplications, with loud cries and tears, to him who was
able to save him from death, and he was heard for his
godly fear. Although he was a Son, he learned obedience
through what he suffered; and being made perfect he
became the source of eternal salvation to all who obey
him, being designated by God a high priest after the order
of Melchiz'edek. About this we have much to say which is
hard to explain, since you have become dull of hearing.
For though by this time you ought to be teachers, you need
some one to teach you again the first principles of God's
word. You need milk, not solid food; for every one who
lives on milk is unskilled in the word of righteousness, for
he is a child. But solid food is for the mature, for those who
have their faculties trained by practice to distinguish good
from evil.

A Reading (Lesson) from the Gospel according to Luke
[9:37-50]

On the next day, when Jesus, with Peter and John and
James, had come down from the mountain, a great crowd
met him. And behold, a man from the crowd cried,
"Teacher, I beg you to look upon my son, for he is my only
child; and behold, a spirit seizes him, and he suddenly cries
out; it convulses him till he foams, and shatters him, and
will hardly leave him. And I begged your disciples to cast it
out, but they could not." Jesus answered, "O faithless and
perverse generation, how long am I to be with you and
bear with you? Bring your son here." While he was
coming, the demon tore him and convulsed him. But Jesus
rebuked the unclean spirit, and healed the boy, and gave
him back to his father. And all were astonished at the
majesty of God. But while they were all marveling at
everything he did, he said to his disciples, "Let these words

sink into your ears; for the Son of man is to be delivered into the hands of men." But they did not understand this saying, and it was concealed from them, that they should not perceive it; and they were afraid to ask him about this saying. And an argument arose among them as to which of them was the greatest. But when Jesus perceived the thought of their hearts, he took a child and put him by his side, and said to them, "Whoever receives this child in my name receives me, and whoever receives me receives him who sent me; for he who is least among you all is the one who is great." John answered, "Master, we saw a man casting out demons in your name, and we forbade him, because he does not follow with us." But Jesus said to him, "Do not forbid him; for he that is not against you is for you."

Week of 7 Easter

Sunday

Psalm 66 [page 673], *Psalm 67* [page 675] ❖
Psalm 19 [page 606], *Psalm 46* [page 649]

A Reading (Lesson) from the Book of Ezekiel [3:16-27]

At the end of seven days, the word of the Lord came to me: "Son of man, I have made you a watchman for the house of Israel; whenever you hear a word from my mouth, you shall give them warning from me. If I say to the wicked, 'You shall surely die,' and you give him no warning, nor speak to warn the wicked from his wicked way, in order to save his life, that wicked man shall die in his iniquity; but his blood I will require at your hand. But if you warn the wicked, and he does not turn from his wickedness, or from his wicked way, he shall die in his iniquity; but you will have saved your life. Again, if a righteous man turns from his righteousness and commits iniquity, and I lay a stumbling block before him, he shall die; because you have not warned him, he shall die for his sin, and his righteous deeds which he has done shall not be remembered; but his blood I will require at your hand. Nevertheless if you warn the righteous man not to sin, and he does not sin, he shall surely live, because he took warning; and you will have saved your life." And the hand of the Lord was there upon me; and he said to me, "Arise, go forth into the plain, and there I will speak with you." So I arose and went forth into the plain; and, lo, the glory of the Lord stood there, like the glory which I had seen by the river Chebar; and I fell on my face. But the Spirit entered into me, and set me upon my feet; and he spoke with me and said to me, "Go, shut yourself within your house. And you, O son of man, behold, cords will be placed upon you, and you shall be bound with them, so that you cannot go out among the people; and I will make your tongue cleave to the roof of your mouth, so that you shall be dumb and unable to reprove them; for they are a rebellious house. But when I speak with you, I will open your mouth, and you shall say to them, 'Thus says the Lord God'; he that will hear, let him hear; and he that will refuse to hear, let him refuse; for they are a rebellious house."

Ephesians 2:1-10   [page 116 above]

A Reading (Lesson) from the Gospel according to Matthew
[10:24-33,40-42]

Jesus sent out the twelve, charging them, "A disciple is not above his teacher, nor a servant above his master; it is enough for the disciple to be like his teacher, and the servant like his master. If they have called the master of the house Be-el'zebul, how much more will they malign those of his household. So have no fear of them; for nothing is covered that will not be revealed, or hidden that will not be known. What I tell you in the dark, utter in the light; and what you hear whispered, proclaim upon the housetops. And do not fear those who kill the body but cannot kill the soul; rather fear him who can destroy both soul and body in hell. Are not two sparrows sold for a penny? And not one of them will fall to the ground without your Father's will. But even the hairs of your head are all numbered. Fear not, therefore; you are of more value than many sparrows. So every one who acknowledges me before men, I also will acknowledge before my Father who is in heaven; but whoever denies me before men, I also will deny before my Father who is in heaven. He who receives you receives me, and he who receives me receives him who sent me. He who receives a prophet because he is a prophet shall receive a prophet's reward, and he who receives a righteous man because he is a righteous man shall receive a righteous man's reward. And whoever gives to one of these little ones even a cup of cold water because he is a disciple, truly, I say to you, he shall not lose his reward."

Monday

Psalm 89:1-18 [page 713] ❖ *Psalm 89:19-52* [page 715]

A Reading (Lesson) from the Book of Ezekiel [4:1-17]

The Spirit spoke with me and said to me, "You, O son of man, take a brick and lay it before you, and portray upon it a city, even Jerusalem; and put siegeworks against it, and build a siege wall against it, and cast up a mound against it; set camps also against it, and plant battering rams against it round about. And take an iron plate, and place it as an iron wall between you and the city; and set your face toward it, and let it be in a state of siege, and press the siege against it. This is a sign for the house of Israel. Then lie upon your left side, and I will lay the punishment of the house of Israel upon you; for the number of the days that you lie upon it, you shall bear their punishment. For I assign to you a number of days, three hundred and ninety days, equal to the number of the years of their punishment; so long shall you bear the punishment of the house of Israel. And when you have completed these, you shall lie down a second time, but on your right side, and bear the punishment of the house of Judah; forty days I assign you, a day for each year. And you shall set your face toward the siege of Jerusalem, with your arm bared; and you shall prophesy against the city. And, behold, I will put cords upon you, so that you cannot turn from one side to the other, till you have completed the days of your siege. And you, take wheat and barley, beans and lentils, millet and spelt, and put them into a single vessel, and make bread of them. During the number of days that you lie upon your side, three hundred and ninety days, you shall eat it. And the food which you eat shall be by weight, twenty shekels a day; once a day you shall eat it. And water you shall drink by measure, the sixth part of a hin; once a day you shall drink. And you shall eat it as a barley cake, baking it in their sight on human dung." And the Lord said, "Thus shall the people of Israel eat their bread unclean, among the nations whither I will drive them." Then I said, "Ah Lord God! behold, I have never defiled myself; from my youth up to now I have never eaten what died of itself or was torn by beasts, nor has foul flesh come into my mouth." Then he said to me, "See, I will let you have cow's dung instead of human dung, on which you may prepare your bread." Moreover he said to me, "Son of man, behold, I will break the staff of bread in Jerusalem; they shall eat bread by weight and with fearfulness; and they shall drink water by measure and in dismay. I will do this that they may lack bread and water, and look at one another in dismay, and waste away under their punishment."

A Reading (Lesson) from the Letter to the Hebrews
[6:1-12]

Let us leave the elementary doctrine of Christ and go on to
maturity, not laying again a foundation of repentance from
dead works and of faith toward God, with instruction
about ablutions, the laying on of hands, the resurrection of
the dead, and eternal judgment. And this we will do if God
permits. For it is impossible to restore again to repentance
those who have once been enlightened, who have tasted
the heavenly gift, and have become partakers of the Holy
Spirit, and have tasted the goodness of the word of God
and the powers of the age to come, if they then commit
apostasy, since they crucify the Son of God on their own
account and hold him up to contempt. For land which has
drunk the rain that often falls upon it, and brings forth
vegetation useful to those for whose sake it is cultivated,
receives a blessing from God. But if it bears thorns and
thistles, it is worthless and near to being cursed; its end is
to be burned. Though we speak thus, yet in your case,
beloved, we feel sure of better things that belong to
salvation. For God is not so unjust as to overlook your
work and the love which you showed for his sake in
serving the saints, as you still do. And we desire each one
of you to show the same earnestness in realizing the full
assurance of hope until the end, so that you may not be
sluggish, but imitators of those who through faith and
patience inherit the promises.

A Reading (Lesson) from the Gospel according to Luke
[9:51-62]

When the days drew near for him to be received up, Jesus
set his face to go to Jerusalem. And he sent messengers
ahead of him, who sent and entered a village of the
Samaritans, to make ready for him; but the people would
not receive him, because his face was set toward
Jerusalem. And when his disciples, James and John saw it,

they said, "Lord, do you want us to bid fire come down from heaven and consume them?" But he turned and rebuked them. And they went on to another village. As they were going along the road, a man said to him, "I will follow you wherever you go." And Jesus said to him, "Foxes have holes, and birds of the air have nests; but the Son of man has nowhere to lay his head." To another he said, "Follow me." But he said, "Lord, let me first go and bury my father." But he said to him, "Leave the dead to bury their own dead; but as for you, go and proclaim the kingdom of God." Another said, "I will follow you, Lord; but let me first say farewell to those at my home." Jesus said to him, "No one who puts his hand to the plow and looks back is fit for the kingdom of God."

Tuesday

Psalm 97 [page 726], *Psalm 99* [page 728],
(Psalm 100 [page 729]) ❖ *Psalm 94* [page 722],
(Psalm 95 [page 724])

A Reading (Lesson) from the Book of Ezekiel
[7:10-15,23b-27]

The word of the Lord came to me: "Behold, the day! Behold, it comes! Your doom has come, injustice has blossomed, pride has budded. Violence has grown up into a rod of wickedness; none of them shall remain, nor their abundance, nor their wealth; neither shall there be preeminence among them. The time has come, the day draws near. Let not the buyer rejoice, nor the seller mourn, for wrath is upon all their multitude. For the seller shall not return to what he has said, while they live. For wrath is upon all their multitude; it shall not turn back; and because of his iniquity, none can maintain his life. They have blown the trumpet and made all ready; but none goes to battle, for my wrath is upon all their multitude. The sword is without, pestilence and famine are within; he that is in the field dies by the sword; and him that is in the city famine and pestilence devour. Because the land is full of bloody crimes and the city is full of violence, I will bring the worst of the nations to take possession of their houses; I will put an end to their proud might, and their holy place shall be profaned. When anguish comes, they will seek peace, but there shall be none. Disaster comes upon disaster, rumor follows rumor; they seek a vision from the prophet, but the law perishes from the priest, and counsel from the elders. The king mourns, the prince is wrapped in despair, and the hands of the people of the land are palsied by terror. According to their way I will do to them, and according to their own judgments I will judge them; and they shall know that I am the Lord."

A Reading (Lesson) from the Letter to the Hebrews
[6:13-20]

When God made a promise to Abraham, since he had no one greater by whom to swear, he swore by himself, saying, "Surely I will bless you and multiply you." And thus Abraham, having patiently endured, obtained the promise. Men indeed swear by a greater than themselves, and in all their disputes an oath is final for confirmation. So when God desired to show more convincingly to the heirs of the promise the unchangeable character of his purpose, he interposed with an oath, so that through two unchangeable things, in which it is impossible that God should prove false, we who have fled for refuge might have strong encouragement to seize the hope set before us. We have this as a sure and steadfast anchor of the soul, a hope that centers into the inner shrine behind the curtain, where Jesus has gone as a forerunner on our behalf, having become a high priest for ever after the order of Melchiz'edek.

A Reading (Lesson) from the Gospel according to Luke
[10:1-17]

After this the Lord appointed seventy others, and sent them on ahead of him, two by two, into every town and place where he himself was about to come. And he said to them, "The harvest is plentiful, but the laborers are few; pray therefore the Lord of the harvest to send out laborers into his harvest. Go your way; behold, I send you out as lambs in the midst of wolves. Carry no purse, no bag, no sandals; and salute no one on the road. Whatever house you enter, first say, 'Peace be to this house!' And if a son of peace is there, your peace shall rest upon him; but if not, it shall return to you. And remain in the same house, eating and drinking what they provide, for the laborer deserves his wages; do not go from house to house. Whenever you enter a town and they receive you, eat what is set before you; heal the sick in it and say to them, 'The kingdom of God has come near to you.' But whenever you enter a town and they do not receive you, go into its streets and say, 'Even the dust of your town that clings to our feet, we wipe off against you; nevertheless know this, that the kingdom of God has come near.' I tell you, it shall be more tolerable on that day for Sodom than for that town. Woe to you, Chora'zin! woe to you, Beth-sa'ida! for if the mighty works done in you had been done in Tyre and Sidon, they would have repented long ago, sitting in sackcloth and ashes. But it shall be more tolerable in the judgment for Tyre and Sidon than for you. And you, Caper'na-um, will you be exalted to heaven? You shall be brought down to Hades. He who hears you hears me, and he who rejects you rejects me, and he who rejects me rejects him who sent me." The seventy returned with joy, saying, "Lord, even the demons are subject to us in your name!"

Wednesday

Psalm 101 [page 730], *Psalm 109:1-4(5-19)20-30* [page 75(
❖ *Psalm 119:121-144* [page 773]

A Reading (Lesson) from the Book of Ezekiel [11:14-25]

The word of the Lord came to me: "Son of man, your
brethren, even your brethren, your fellow exiles, the whole
house of Israel, all of them, are those of whom the
inhabitants of Jerusalem have said, 'They have gone far
from the Lord; to us this land is given for a possession.'
Therefore say, 'Thus says the Lord God: Though I
removed them far off among the nations, and though I
scattered them among the countries, yet I have been a
sanctuary to them for a while in the countries where they
have gone.' Therefore say, 'Thus says the Lord God: I will
gather you from the peoples, and assemble you out of the
countries where you have been scattered, and I will give
you the land of Israel.' And when they come there, they
will remove from it all its detestable things and all its
abominations. And I will give them one heart, and put a
new spirit within them; I will take the stony heart out of
their flesh and give them a heart of flesh, that they may
walk in my statutes and keep my ordinances and obey
them; and they shall be my people, and I will be their God.
But as for those whose heart goes after their detestable
things and their abominations, I will requite their deeds
upon their own heads, says the Lord God." Then the
cherubim lifted up their wings, with the wheels beside
them; and the glory of the God of Israel was over them.
And the glory of the Lord went up from the midst of the
city, and stood upon the mountain which is on the east side
of the city. And the Spirit lifted me up and brought me in
the vision by the Spirit of God into Chalde'a, to the exiles.
Then the vision that I had seen went up from me. And I
told the exiles all the things that the Lord had showed me.

A Reading (Lesson) from the Letter to the Hebrews
[7:1-17]

This Melchiz'edek, king of Salem, priest of the Most High God, met Abraham returning from the slaughter of the kings and blessed him; and to him Abraham apportioned a tenth part of everything. He is first, by translation of his name, king of righteousness, and then he is also king of Salem, that is, king of peace. He is without father or mother or genealogy, and has neither beginning of days nor end of life, but resembling the Son of God he continues a priest for ever. See how great he is! Abraham the patriarch gave him a tithe of the spoils. And those descendants of Levi who receive the priestly office have a commandment in the law to take tithes from the people, that is, from their brethren, though these also are descended from Abraham. But this man who has not their geneaology received tithes from Abraham and blessed him who had the promises. It is beyond dispute that the inferior is blessed by the superior. Here tithes are received by mortal men; there, by one of whom it is testified that he lives. One might even say that Levi himself, who receives tithes, paid tithes through Abraham, for he was still in the loins of his ancestor when Melchiz'edek met him. Now if perfection had been attainable through the Levitical priesthood (for under it the people received the law), what further need would there have been for another priest to arise after the order of Melchiz'edek, rather than one named after the order of Aaron? For when there is a change in the priesthood, there is necessarily a change in the law as well. For the one of whom these things are spoken belonged to another tribe, from which no one has ever served at the altar. For it is evident that our Lord was descended from Judah, and in connection with that tribe Moses said nothing about priests. This becomes even more evident when another priest arises in the likeness of Melchiz'edek, who has become a priest, not according to a legal requirement concerning bodily descent but by the power of an indestructible life. For it is witnessed of him, "Thou art a priest for ever, after the order of Melchiz'edek."

A Reading (Lesson) from the Gospel according to Luke [10:17-24]

The seventy returned with joy, saying, "Lord, even the demons are subject to us in your name!" And he said to them, "I saw Satan fall like lightning from heaven. Behold, I have given you authority to tread upon serpents and scorpions, and over all the power of the enemy; and nothing shall hurt you. Nevertheless do not rejoice in this, that the spirits are subject to you; but rejoice that your names are written in heaven." In that same hour he rejoiced in the Holy Spirit and said, "I thank thee, Father, Lord of heaven and earth, that thou hast hidden these things from the wise and understanding and revealed them to babes; yea, Father, for such was thy gracious will. All things have been delivered to me by my Father; and no one knows who the Son is except the Father, or who the Father is except the Son and any one to whom the Son chooses to reveal him." Then turning to the disciples he said privately, "Blessed are the eyes which see what you see! For I tell you that many prophets and kings desired to see what you see, and did not see it, and to hear what you hear, and did not hear it."

Thursday

Psalm 105:1-22 [page 738]   ❖   *Psalm 105:23-45* [page 739]

A Reading (Lesson) from the Book of Ezekiel [18:1-4,19-32]

The word of the Lord came to me again: "What do you mean by repeating this proverb concerning the land of Israel, 'The fathers have eaten sour grapes, and the children's teeth are set on edge'? As I live, says the Lord

God, this proverb shall no more be used by you in Israel. Behold, all souls are mine; the soul of the father as well as the soul of the son is mine: the soul that sins shall die. Yet you say, 'Why should not the son suffer for the iniquity of the father?' When the son has done what is lawful and right, and has been careful to observe all my statutes, he shall surely live. The soul that sins shall die. The son shall not suffer for the iniquity of the father, nor the father suffer for the iniquity of the son; the righteousness of the righteous shall be upon himself, and the wickedness of the wicked shall be upon himself. But if a wicked man turns away from all his sins which he has committed and keeps all my statutes and does what is lawful and right, he shall surely live; he shall not die. None of the transgressions which he has committed shall be remembered against him; for the righteousness which he has done he shall live. Have I any pleasure in the death of the wicked, says the Lord God, and not rather that he should turn from his way and live? But when a righteous man turns away from his righteousness and commits iniquity and does the same abominable things that the wicked man does, shall he live? None of the righteous deeds which he has done shall be remembered; for the treachery of which he is guilty and the sin he has committed, he shall die. Yet you say, 'The way of the Lord is not just.' Hear now, O house of Israel: Is my way not just? Is it not your ways that are not just? When a righteous man turns away from his righteousness and commits iniquity, he shall die for it; for the iniquity which he has committed he shall die. Again, when a wicked man turns away from the wickedness he has committed and does what is lawful and right, he shall save his life. Because he considered and turned away from all the transgressions which he had committed, he shall surely live, he shall not die. Yet the house of Israel says, 'The way of the Lord is not just.' O house of Israel, are my ways not just? Is it not your ways that are not just? Therefore I will judge you, O house of Israel, every one according to his ways, says the Lord God. Repent and turn from all your transgressions, lest iniquity be your ruin. Cast away from you all the transgressions which you have committed against me, and get yourselves a new heart and a new spirit! Why will you die, O house of Israel? For I have no pleasure in the death of any one, says the Lord God; so turn, and live."

A Reading (Lesson) from the Letter to the Hebrews
[7:18-28]

On the one hand, a former commandment is set aside because of its weakness and uselessness (for the law made nothing perfect); on the other hand, a better hope is introduced, through which we draw near to God. And it was not without an oath. Those who formerly became priests took their office without an oath, but this one was addressed with an oath, "The Lord has sworn and will not change his mind, 'Thou art a priest for ever.'" This makes Jesus the surety of a better covenant. The former priests were many in number, because they were prevented by death from continuing in office; but he holds his priesthood permanently, because he continues for ever. Consequently he is able for all time to save those who draw near to God through him, since he always lives to make intercession for them. For it was fitting that we should have such a high priest, holy, blameless, unstained, separated from sinners, exalted above the heavens. He has no need, like those high priests, to offer sacrifices daily, first for his own sins and then for those of the people; he did this once for all when he offered up himself. Indeed, the law appoints men in their weakness as high priests, but the word of the oath, which came later than the law, appoints a Son who has been made perfect for ever.

A Reading (Lesson) from the Gospel according to Luke
[10:25-37]

Behold, a lawyer stood up to put Jesus to the test, saying, "Teacher, what shall I do to inherit eternal life?" He said to him, "What is written in the law? How do you read?" And he answered, "You shall love the Lord your God with all your heart, and with all your soul, and with all your strength, and with all your mind; and your neighbor as yourself." And he said to him, "You have answered right; do this, and you will live." But he, desiring to justify himself, said to Jesus, "And who is my neighbor?" Jesus replied, "A man was going down from Jerusalem to Jericho, and he fell among robbers, who stripped him and beat him, and departed, leaving him half dead. Now by chance a priest was going down that road; and when he saw him he passed by on the other side. So likewise a Levite, when he came to the place and saw him, passed by on the other side. But a Samaritan, as he journeyed, came to where he was; and when he saw him, he had compassion, and went to him and bound up his wounds, pouring on oil and wine; then he set him on his own beast and brought him to an inn, and took care of him. And the next day he took out two denarii and gave them to the innkeeper, saying, 'Take care of him; and whatever more you spend, I will repay you when I come back.' Which of these three, do you think, proved neighbor to the man who fell among the robbers?" He said, "The one who showed mercy on him." And Jesus said to him, "Go and do likewise."

Friday

Psalm 102 [page 731]   ❖   *Psalm 107:1-32* [page 746]

A Reading (Lesson) from the Book of Ezekiel [34:17-31]

The word of the Lord came to me: "And as for you, my

flock, thus says the Lord God: Behold, I judge between sheep and sheep, rams and he-goats. Is it not enough for you to feed on the good pasture, that you must tread down with your feet the rest of your pasture; and to drink of clear water, that you must foul the rest with your feet? And must my sheep eat what you have trodden with your feet, and drink what you have fouled with your feet? Therefore thus says the Lord God to them: Behold, I, I myself will judge between the fat sheep and the lean sheep. Because you push with side and shoulder, and thrust at all the weak with your horns, till you have scattered them abroad, I will save my flock, they shall no longer be a prey; and I will judge between sheep and sheep. And I will set up over them one shepherd, my servant David, and he shall feed them: he shall feed them and be their shepherd. And I, the Lord, will be their God, and my servant David shall be prince among them; I, the Lord, have spoken. I will make with them a covenant of peace and banish wild beasts from the land, so that they may dwell securely in the wilderness and sleep in the woods. And I will make them and the places round about my hill a blessing; and I will send down the showers in their season; they shall be showers of blessing. And the trees of the field shall yield their fruit, and the earth shall yield its increase, and they shall be secure in their land; and they shall know that I am the Lord, when I break the bars of their yoke, and deliver them from the hand of those who enslaved them. They shall no more be a prey to the nations, nor shall the beasts of the land devour them; they shall dwell securely, and none shall make them afraid. And I will provide for them prosperous plantations so that they shall no more be consumed with hunger in the land, and no longer suffer the reproach of the nations. And they shall know that I, the Lord their God, am with them, and that they, the house of Israel, are my people, says the Lord God. And you are my sheep, the sheep of my pasture, and I am your God, says the Lord God."

A Reading (Lesson) from the Letter to the Hebrews
[8:1-13]

The point in what we are saying is this: we have such a high priest, one who is seated at the right hand of the throne of the Majesty in heaven, a minister in the sanctuary and the true tent which is set up not by man but by the Lord. For every high priest is appointed to offer gifts and sacrifices; hence it is necessary for this priest also to have something to offer. Now if he were on earth, he would not be a priest at all, since there are priests who offer gifts according to the law. They serve a copy and a shadow of the heavenly sanctuary; for when Moses was about to erect the tent, he was instructed by God, saying, "See that you make everything according to the pattern which was shown you on the mountain." But as it is, Christ has obtained a ministry which is as much more excellent than the old as the covenant he mediates is better, since it is enacted on better promises. For if that first covenant had been faultless, there would have been no occasion for a second. For he finds fault with them when he says: "The days will come, says the Lord, when I will establish a new covenant with the house of Israel and with the house of Judah; not like the covenant that I made with their fathers on the day when I took them by the hand to lead them out of the land of Egypt; for they did not continue in my covenant, and so I paid no heed to them, says the Lord. This is the covenant that I will make with the house of Israel after those days, says the Lord: I will put my laws into their minds, and write them on their hearts, and I will be their God, and they shall be my people. And they shall not teach every one his fellow or every one his brother, saying, 'Know the Lord,' for all shall know me, from the least of them to the greatest. For I will be merciful toward their iniquities, and I will remember their sins no more." In speaking of a new covenant he treats the first as obsolete. And what is becoming obsolete and growing old is ready to vanish away.

A Reading (Lesson) from the Gospel according to Luke
[10:38-42]

As they went on their way, Jesus entered a village; and a woman named Martha received him into her house. And she had a sister called Mary, who sat at the Lord's feet and listened to his teaching. But Martha was distracted with much serving; and she went to him and said, "Lord, do you not care that my sister has left me to serve alone? Tell her then to help me." But the Lord answered her, "Martha, Martha, you are anxious and troubled about many things; one thing is needful. Mary has chosen the good portion, which shall not be taken away from her."

Saturday

(Morning Prayer)
Psalm 107:33-43 [page 748],
Psalm 108:1-6(7-13) [page 749]

A Reading (Lesson) from the Book of Ezekiel [43:1-12]

A man, whose appearance was like bronze, brought me to the gate, the gate facing east. And behold, the glory of the God of Israel came from the east; and the sound of his coming was like the sound of many waters; and the earth shone with his glory. And the vision I saw was like the vision which I had seen when he came to destroy the city, and like the vision which I had seen by the river Chebar; and I fell upon my face. As the glory of the Lord entered the temple by the gate facing east, the Spirit lifted me up, and brought me into the inner court; and behold, the glory of the Lord filled the temple. While the man was standing beside me, I heard one speaking to me out of the temple; and he said to me, "Son of man, this is the place of my throne and the place of the soles of my feet, where I will dwell in the midst of the people of Israel for ever. And the house of Israel shall no more defile my holy name, neither they, nor their kings, by their harlotry, and by the dead bodies of their kings, by setting their threshold by my threshold and their doorposts beside my doorposts, with only a wall between me and them. They have defiled my holy name by their abominations which they have committed, so I have consumed them in my anger. Now let them put away their idolatry and the dead bodies of their kings far from me, and I will dwell in their midst for ever. And you, son of man, describe to the house of Israel the temple and its appearance and plan, that they may be ashamed of their iniquities. And if they are ashamed of all that they have done, portray the temple, its arrangement, its exits and its entrances, and its whole form; and make known to them all its ordinances and all its laws; and write it down in their sight, so that they may observe and perform all its laws and all its ordinances. This is the law of the temple: the whole territory round about upon the top of the mountain shall be most holy. Behold, this is the law of the temple."

A Reading (Lesson) from the Letter to the Hebrews
[9:1-14]

Even the first covenant had regulations for worship and an earthly sanctuary. For a tent was prepared, the outer one, in which were the lampstand and the table and the bread of the Presence; it is called the Holy Place. Behind the second curtain stood a tent called the Holy of Holies, having the golden altar of incense and the ark of the covenant covered on all sides with gold, which contained a golden urn holding the manna, and Aaron's rod that budded, and the tables of the covenant; above it were the cherubim of glory overshadowing the mercy seat. Of these things we cannot now speak in detail. These preparations having thus been made, the priests go continually into the outer tent, performing their ritual duties; but into the second only the high priest goes, and he but once a year, and not without taking blood which he offers for himself and for the errors of the people. By this the Holy Spirit indicates that the way into the sanctuary is not yet opened as long as the outer tent is still standing (which is symbolic for the present age). According to this arrangement, gifts and sacrifices are offered which cannot perfect the conscience of the worshiper, but deal only with food and drink and various ablutions, regulations for the body imposed until the time of reformation. But when Christ appeared as a high priest of the good things that have come, then through the greater and more perfect tent (not made with hands, that is, not of this creation) he entered once for all into the Holy Place, taking not the blood of goats and calves but his own blood, thus securing an eternal redemption. For if the sprinkling of defiled persons with the blood of goats and bulls and with the ashes of a heifer sanctifies for the purification of the flesh, how much more shall the blood of Christ, who through the eternal Spirit offered himself without blemish to God, purify your conscience from dead works to serve the living God.

A Reading (Lesson) from the Gospel according to Luke
[11:14-23]

Jesus was casting out a demon that was dumb; when the demon had gone out, the dumb man spoke, and the people marveled. But some of them said, "He casts out demons by Be-el′zebul, the prince of demons"; while others, to test him, sought from him a sign from heaven. But he, knowing their thoughts, said to them, "Every kingdom divided against itself is laid waste, and a divided household falls. And if Satan also is divided against himself, how will his kingdom stand? For you say that I cast out demons by Be-el′zebul. And if I cast out demons by Be-el′zebul, by whom do your sons cast them out? Therefore they shall be your judges. But if it is by the finger of God that I cast out demons, then the kingdom of God has come upon you.

When a strong man, fully armed, guards his own palace, his goods are in peace; but when one stronger than he assails him and overcomes him, he takes away his armor in which he trusted, and divides his spoil. He who is not with me is against me, and he who does not gather with me scatters."

Eve of Pentecost

(Evening Prayer)   *Psalm 33* [page 626]

A Reading (Lesson) from the Book of Exodus
[19:3-8a, 16-20]

Moses went up to God, and the Lord called to him out of the mountain, saying, "Thus you shall say to the house of Jacob, and tell the people of Israel: You have seen what I did to the Egyptians, and how I bore you on eagles' wings and brought you to myself. Now therefore, if you will obey my voice and keep my covenant, you shall be my own possession among all peoples; for all the earth is mine, and you shall be to me a kingdom of priests and a holy nation. These are the words which you shall speak to the children of Israel." So Moses came and called the elders of the people, and set before them all these words which the Lord had commanded him. And all the people answered together and said, "All that the Lord has spoken we will do." On the morning of the third day there were thunders and lightnings, and a thick cloud upon the mountain, and a very loud trumpet blast, so that all the people who were in the camp trembled. Then Moses brought the people out of the camp to meet God; and they took their stand at the foot of the mountain. And Mount Sinai was wrapped in smoke, because the Lord descended upon it in fire; and the smoke of it went up like the smoke of a kiln, and the whole mountain quaked greatly. And as the sound of the trumpet grew louder and louder, Moses spoke, and God answered him in thunder. And the Lord came down upon Mount

Sinai, to the top of the mountain; and the Lord called
Moses to the top of the mountain and Moses went up.

A Reading (Lesson) from the First Letter of Peter [2:4-10]

Come to him, to that living stone, rejected by men but in
God's sight chosen and precious; and like living stones be
yourselves built into a spiritual house, to be a holy
priesthood, to offer spiritual sacrifices acceptable to God
through Jesus Christ. For it stands in scripture: "Behold, I
am laying in Zion a stone, a cornerstone chosen and
precious, and he who believes in him will not be put to
shame." To you therefore who believe, he is precious, but
for those who do not believe, "The very stone which the
builders rejected has become the head of the corner," and
"A stone that will make men stumble, a rock that will make
them fall"; for they stumble because they disobey the
word, as they were destined to do. But you are a chosen
race, a royal priesthood, a holy nation, God's own people,
that you may declare the wonderful deeds of him who
called you out of darkness into his marvelous light. Once
you were no people but now you are God's people; once
you had not received mercy but now you have received
mercy.

The Day of Pentecost

Psalm 118 [page 760] ❖ *Psalm 145* [page 801]

Isaiah 11:1-9 [page 53 above]

*A Reading (Lesson) from the First Letter of Paul
to the Corinthians* [2:1-13]

When I came to you, brethren, I did not come proclaiming
to you the testimony of God in lofty words or wisdom. For
I decided to know nothing among you except Jesus Christ
and him crucified. And I was with you in weakness and in

much fear and trembling; and my speech and my message were not in plausible words of wisdom, but in demonstration of the Spirit and of power, that your faith might not rest in the wisdom of men but in the power of God. Yet among the mature we do impart wisdom, although it is not a wisdom of this age or of the rulers of this age, who are doomed to pass away. But we impart a secret and hidden wisdom of God, which God decreed before the ages for our glorification. None of the rulers of this age understand this; for if they had, they would not have crucified the Lord of glory. But, as it is written, "What no eye has seen, nor ear heard, nor the heart of man conceived, what God has prepared for those who love him," God has revealed to us through the Spirit. For the Spirit searches everything, even the depths of God. For what person knows a man's thoughts except the spirit of the man which is in him? So also no one comprehends the thoughts of God except the Spirit of God. Now we have received not the spirit of the world, but the Spirit which is from God, that we might understand the gifts bestowed on us by God. And we impart this in words not taught by human wisdom but taught by the Spirit, interpreting spiritual truths to those who possess the Spirit.

A Reading (Lesson) from the Gospel according to John
[14:21-29]

Jesus said to Philip, "He who has my commandments and keeps them, he it is who loves me; and he who loves me will be loved by my Father, and I will love him and manifest myself to him." Judas (not Iscariot) said to him, "Lord, how is it that you will manifest yourself to us, and not to the world?" Jesus answered him, "If a man loves me, he will keep my word, and my Father will love him, and we will come to him and make our home with him. He who does not love me does not keep my words; and the word which you hear is not mine but the Father's who sent me. These things I have spoken to you, while I am still with you. But the Counselor, the Holy Spirit, whom the Father will send in my name, he will teach you all things, and bring to your remembrance all that I have said to you. Peace I leave with you; my peace I give to you; not as the world gives do I give to you. Let not your hearts be troubled, neither let them be afraid. You heard me say to you, 'I go away, and I will come to you.' If you loved me, you would have rejoiced, because I go to the Father; for the Father is greater than I. And now I have told you before it takes place, so that when it does take place, you may believe."

On the weekdays which follow, the Readings are taken from the numbered Proper (one through six: Daily Office Readings, Year One, Volume 2) *which corresponds most closely to the date of Pentecost.*

Eve of Trinity Sunday

(Evening Prayer)   *Psalm 104* [page 735]

A Reading (Lesson) from the Book of Ecclesiasticus
[42:15-25]

I will now call to mind the works of the Lord, and will declare what I have seen. By the words of the Lord his works are done. The sun looks down on everything with its light, and the work of the Lord is full of his glory. The Lord has not enabled his holy ones to recount all his marvelous works, which the Lord the Almighty has established that the universe may stand firm in his glory. He searches out the abyss, and the hearts of men, and considers their crafty devices. For the Most High knows all that may be known, and he looks into the signs of the age. He declares what has been and what is to be, and he reveals the tracks of hidden things. No thought escapes him, and not one word is hidden from him. He has ordained the splendors of his wisdom, and he is from everlasting and to everlasting. Nothing can be added or taken away, and he needs no one to be his counselor. How greatly to be desired are all his works, and how sparkling they are to see! All these things live and remain for ever for every need, and are all obedient. All things are twofold, one opposite the other, and he has made nothing incomplete. One confirms the good things of the other, and who can have enough of beholding his glory?

Ephesians 3:14-21   [page 124 above]

Trinity Sunday

Psalm 146 [page 803],   *Psalm 147* [page 804]   ❖
Psalm 111 [page 754],   *Psalm 112* [page 755],
Psalm 113 [page 756]

A Reading (Lesson) from the Book of Ecclesiasticus
[43:1-12(27-33)]

The pride of the heavenly heights is the clear firmament, the appearance of heaven in a spectacle of glory. The sun, when it appears, making proclamation as it goes forth, is a marvelous instrument, the work of the Most High. At noon it parches the land; and who can withstand its burning heat? A man tending a furnace works in the burning heat, but the sun burns the mountains three times as much; it breathes out fiery vapors, and with bright beams it blinds the eyes. Great is the Lord who made it; and at his command it hastens on its course. He made the moon also, to serve in its season to mark the times and to be an everlasting sign. From the moon comes the sign for feast days, a light that wanes when it has reached the full. The month is named for the moon, increasing marvelously in its phases, an instrument of the hosts on high shining forth in the firmament of heaven. The glory of the stars is the beauty of heaven, a gleaming array in the heights of the Lord. At the command of the Holy One they stand as ordered, they never relax in their watches. Look upon the rainbow, and praise him who made it, exceedingly beautiful in its brightness. It encircles the heaven with its glorious arc; the hands of the Most High have stretched it out.

> Though we speak much we cannot reach the end, and the sum of all our words is: "He is the all." Where shall we find strength to praise him? For he is greater than all his works. Terrible is the Lord and very great, and marvelous is his power. When you praise the Lord, exalt him as much as you can; for he will surpass even that. When you exalt him, put forth all your strength, and do not grow weary, for you cannot praise him enough. Who has seen him and can describe him? Or who can extol him as he is? Many things greater than these lie hidden, for we have seen but few of his works. For the Lord has made all things, and to the godly he has granted wisdom.

Ephesians 4:1-16   [page 129 above]

John 1:1-18   [page 251 above]

On the weekdays which follow, the Readings are taken from the numbered Proper (two through seven: Daily Office Readings, Year One, Volume 2) which corresponds most closely to the date of Trinity Sunday

Holy Days

St. Andrew   *November 30*

(Morning Prayer)   *Psalm 34* [page 627]

A Reading (Lesson) from the Book of Isaiah   [49:1-6]

Listen to me, O coastlands, and hearken, you peoples

from afar. The Lord called me from the womb, from the body of my mother he named my name. He made my mouth like a sharp sword, in the shadow of his hand he hid me; he made me a polished arrow, in his quiver he hid me away. And he said to me, "You are my servant, Israel, in whom I will be glorified." But I said, "I have labored in vain, I have spent my strength for nothing and vanity; yet surely my right is with the Lord, and my recompense with my God." And now the Lord says, who formed me from the womb to be his servant, to bring Jacob back to him, and that Israel might be gathered to him, for I am honored in the eyes of the Lord, and my God has become my strength—he says: "It is too light a thing that you should be my servant to raise up the tribes of Jacob and to restore the preserved of Israel; I will give you as a light to the nations, that my salvation may reach to the end of the earth."

A Reading (Lesson) from the First Letter of Paul to the Corinthians [4:1-16]

This is how one should regard us, as servants of Christ and stewards of the mysteries of God. Moreover it is required of stewards that they be found trustworthy. But with me it is a very small thing that I should be judged by you or by any human court. I do not even judge myself. I am not aware of anything against myself, but I am not thereby acquitted. It is the Lord who judges me. Therefore do not pronounce judgment before the time, before the Lord comes, who will bring to light the things now hidden in darkness and will disclose the purposes of the heart. Then every man will receive his commendation from God. I have applied all this to myself and Apol'los for your benefit, brethren, that you may learn by us not to go beyond what is written, that none of you may be puffed up in favor of one against another. For who sees anything different in you? What have you that you did not receive? If then you received it, why do you boast as if it were not a gift? Already you are filled! Already you have become rich! Without us you have become kings! And would that you did reign, so that we might share the rule with you! For I think that God has exhibited us apostles as last of all, like men sentenced to death; because we have become a spectacle to the world, to angels and to men. We are fools for Christ's sake, but you are wise in Christ. We are weak, but you are strong. You are held in honor, but we in disrepute. To the present hour we hunger and thirst, we are ill-clad and buffeted and homeless, and we labor, working with our own hands. When reviled, we bless; when persecuted, we endure; when slandered, we try to conciliate; we have become, and are now, as the refuse of the world, the offscouring of all things. I do not write this to make you ashamed, but to admonish you as my beloved children. For though you have countless guides in Christ, you do not have many fathers. For I became your father in Christ Jesus through the gospel. I urge you, then, be imitators of me.

(Evening Prayer)
Psalm 96 [page 725],   *Psalm 100* [page 729]

A Reading (Lesson) from the Book of Isaiah [55:1-5]

"Ho, every one who thirsts, come to the waters; and he who has no money, come, buy and eat! Come, buy wine and milk without money and without price. Why do you spend your money for that which is not bread, and your labor for that which does not satisfy? Hearken diligently to me, and eat what is good, and delight yourselves in fatness. Incline your ear, and come to me; hear, that your soul may live; and I will make with you an everlasting covenant, my steadfast, sure love for David. Behold, I made him a witness to the peoples, a leader and commander for the peoples. Behold, you shall call nations that you know not, and nations that knew you not shall run to you, because of the Lord your God, and of the Holy One of Israel, for he has glorified you."

John 1:35-42   [page 260 above]

St. Thomas   *December 21*

(Morning Prayer)
Psalm 23 [page 612],   *Psalm 121* [page 779]

A Reading (Lesson) from the Book of Job   [42:1-6]

Job answered the Lord: "I know that thou canst do all things, and that no purpose of thine can be thwarted. 'Who is this that hides counsel without knowledge?' Therefore I have uttered what I did not understand, things too wonderful for me, which I did not know. 'Hear, and I will speak; I will question you, and you declare to me.' I had heard of thee by the hearing of the ear, but now my eye sees thee; therefore I despise myself, and repent in dust and ashes."

A Reading (Lesson) from the First Letter of Peter   [1:3-9]

Blessed be the God and Father of our Lord Jesus Christ! By his great mercy we have been born anew to a living hope through the resurrection of Jesus Christ from the dead, and to an inheritance which is imperishable, undefiled, and unfading, kept in heaven for you, who by God's power are guarded through faith for a salvation ready to be revealed in the last time. In this you rejoice, though now for a little while you may have to suffer various trials, so that the genuineness of your faith, more precious than gold which though perishable is tested by fire, may redound to praise and glory and honor at the revelation of Jesus Christ. Without having seen him you love him; though you do not now see him you believe in him and rejoice with unutterable and exalted joy. As the outcome of your faith you obtain the salvation of your souls.

(Evening Prayer)   *Psalm 27* [page 617]

Isaiah 43:8-13   [page 389 above]

John 14:1-7   [page 390 above]

St. Stephen   *December 26*

(Morning Prayer)   *Psalm 28* [page 619],   *Psalm 30* [page 621]

A Reading (Lesson) from the Second Book of Chronicles [24:17-22]

Now after the death of Jehoi′ada the princes of Judah came and did obeisance to the king; then the king hearkened to them. And they forsook the house of the Lord, the God of their fathers, and served the Ashe′rim and the idols. And wrath came upon Judah and Jerusalem for this their guilt. Yet he sent prophets among them to bring them back to the Lord; these testified against them, but they would not give heed. Then the Spirit of God took possession of Zechari′ah the son of Jehoi′ada the priest; and he stood above the people, and said to them, "Thus says God, 'Why do you trangress the commandments of the Lord, so that you cannot prosper? Because you have forsaken the Lord, he has forsaken you.'" But they conspired against him, and by command of the king they stoned him with stones in the court of the house of the Lord. Thus Jo′ash the king did not remember the kindness which Jehoi′ada, Zechari′ah's father, had shown him, but killed his son. And when he was dying, he said, "May the Lord see and avenge!"

A Reading (Lesson) from the Acts of the Apostles [6:1-7]

Now in these days when the disciples were increasing in number, the Hellenists murmured against the Hebrews because their widows were neglected in the daily distribution. And the twelve summoned the body of the disciples and said, "It is not right that we should give up preaching the word of God to serve tables. Therefore, brethren, pick out from among you seven men of good repute, full of the Spirit and of wisdom, whom we may appoint to this duty. But we will devote ourselves to prayer and to the ministry of the word." And what they said pleased the whole multitude, and they chose Stephen, a man full of faith and of the Holy Spirit, and Philip, and Proch'orus, and Nica'nor, and Timon, and Par'menas, and Nicola'us, a proselyte of Antioch. These they set before the apostles, and they prayed and laid their hands upon them. And the word of God increased; and the number of the disciples multiplied greatly in Jerusalem and a great many of the priests were obedient to the faith.

(Evening Prayer)   *Psalm 118* [page 760]

A Reading (Lesson) from the Book of Wisdom [4:7-15]

The righteous man, though he die early, will be at rest. For old age is not honored for length of time, nor measured by number of years; but understanding is grey hair for men, and a blameless life is ripe old age. There was one who pleased God and was loved by him, and while living among sinners he was taken up. He was caught up lest evil change his understanding or guile deceive his soul. For the fascination of wickedness obscures what is good, and roving desire perverts the innocent mind. Being perfected in a short time, he fulfilled long years; for his soul was pleasing to the Lord, therefore he took him quickly from the midst of wickedness. Yet the peoples saw and did not understand, nor take such a thing to heart, that God's grace and mercy are with his elect, and he watches over his holy ones.

A Reading (Lesson) from the Acts of the Apostles
[7:59—8:8]

As they were stoning Stephen, he prayed, "Lord Jesus, receive my spirit." And he knelt down and cried with a loud voice, "Lord, do not hold this sin against them." And when he had said this, he fell asleep. And Saul was consenting to his death. And on that day a great persecution arose against the church in Jerusalem; and they were all scattered throughout the region of Judea and Samar'ia, except the apostles. Devout men buried Stephen, and made great lamentation over him. But Saul was ravaging the church, and entering house after house, he dragged off men and women and committed them to prison. Now those who were scattered went about preaching the word. Philip went down to a city of Samar'ia, and proclaimed to them the Christ. And the multitudes with one accord gave heed to what was said by Philip, when they heard him and saw the signs which he did. For unclean spirits came out of many who were possessed, crying with a loud voice; and many who were paralyzed or lame were healed. So there was much joy in that city.

St. John December 27

(Morning Prayer) *Psalm 97* [page 726], *Psalm 98* [page 727]

A Reading (Lesson) from the Book of Proverbs [8:22-30]

The Lord created me at the beginning of his work, the first of his acts of old. Ages ago I was set up, at the first, before the beginning of the earth. When there were no depths I was brought forth, when there were no springs abounding with water. Before the mountains had been shaped, before the hills, I was brought forth; before he made the earth with its fields, or the first of the dust of the world. When he established the heavens, I was there, when he drew a circle on the face of the deep, when he made firm the skies above, when he established the fountains of the deep, when he assigned to the sea its limit, so that the waters might not transgress his command, when he marked out the foundations of the earth, then I was beside him, like a master workman; and I was daily his delight, rejoicing before him always.

A Reading (Lesson) from the Gospel according to John
[13:20-35]

Jesus said to the disciples, "Truly, truly, I say to you, he who receives any one whom I send receives me; and he who receives me receives him who sent me." When Jesus had thus spoken, he was troubled in spirit, and testified, "Truly, truly, I say to you, one of you will betray me." The disciples looked at one another, uncertain of whom he spoke. One of his disciples, whom Jesus loved, was lying close to the breast of Jesus; so Simon Peter beckoned to him and said, "Tell us who it is of whom he speaks." So lying thus, close to the breast of Jesus, he said to him, "Lord, who is it?" Jesus answered, "It is he to whom I shall give this morsel when I have dipped it." So when he had dipped the morsel, he gave it to Judas, the son of Simon Iscariot. Then after the morsel, Satan entered into him. Jesus said to him, "What you are going to do, do quickly." Now no one at the table knew why he said this to him. Some thought that, because Judas had the money box, Jesus was telling him, "Buy what we need for the feast"; or, that he should give something to the poor. So, after receiving the morsel, he immediately went out; and it was night.

(Evening Prayer) *Psalm 145* [page 801]

A Reading (Lesson) from the Book of Isaiah [44:1-8]

Thus says the Lord, your Redeemer, the Holy One of Israel: "But now hear, O Jacob my servant, Israel whom I have chosen! Thus says the Lord who made you, who formed you from the womb and will help you: Fear not, O Jacob my servant, Jesh'urun whom I have chosen. For I will pour water on the thirsty land, and streams on the dry ground; I will pour my Spirit upon your descendants, and my blessing on your offspring. They shall spring up like grass amid waters, like willows by flowing streams. This one will say, 'I am the Lord's,' another will call himself by the name of Jacob, and another will write on his hand, 'The Lord's,' and surname himself by the name of Israel." Thus says the Lord, the King of Israel and his Redeemer, the Lord of hosts: "I am the first and I am the last; besides me there is no god. Who is like me? Let him proclaim it, let him declare and set it forth before me. Who has announced from of old the things to come? Let them tell us what is yet to be. Fear not, nor be afraid; have I not told you from of old and declared it? And you are my witnesses! Is there a God besides me? There is no Rock; I know not any."

1 John 5:1-12   [page 416 above]

Holy Innocents   *December 28*

(Morning Prayer) *Psalm 2* [page 586], *Psalm 26* [page 616]

Isaiah 49:13-23   [page 156 above]

A Reading (Lesson) from the Gospel according to Matthew [18:1-14]

At that time the disciples came to Jesus, saying, "Who is the greatest in the kingdom of heaven?" And calling to him a child, he put him in the midst of them, and said, "Truly, I say to you, unless you turn and become like children, you will never enter the kingdom of heaven. Whoever humbles himself like this child, he is the greatest in the kingdom of heaven. Whoever receives one such child in my name receives me; but whoever causes one of these little ones who believe in me to sin, it would be better for him to have a great millstone fastened round his neck and to be drowned in the depth of the sea. Woe to the world for temptations to sin! For it is necessary that temptations come, but woe to the man by whom the temptation comes! And if your hand or your foot causes you to sin, cut it off and throw it away; it is better for you to enter life maimed or lame than with two hands or two feet to be thrown into the eternal fire. And if your eye causes you to sin, pluck it out and throw it away; it is better for you to enter life with one eye than with two eyes to be thrown into the hell of fire. See that you do not despise one of these little ones; for I tell you that in heaven their angels always behold the face of my Father who is in heaven. What do you think? If a man has a hundred sheep, and one of them has gone astray, does he not leave the ninety-nine on the mountains and go in search of the one that went astray? And if he finds it, truly, I say to you, he rejoices over it more than over the ninety-nine that never went astray. So it is not the will of my Father who is in heaven that one of these little ones should perish."

(Evening Prayer) *Psalm 19* [page 606], *Psalm 126* [page 782]

A Reading (Lesson) from the Book of Isaiah [54:1-13]

"Sing, O barren one, who did not bear; break forth into singing and cry aloud, you who have not been in travail! For the children of the desolate one will be more than the children of her that is married, says the Lord. Enlarge the place of your tent, and let the curtains of your habitations be stretched out; hold not back, lengthen your cords and strengthen your stakes. For you will spread abroad to the right and to the left, and your descendants will possess the nations and will people the desolate cities. Fear not, for you will not be ashamed; be not confounded, for you will not be put to shame; for you will forget the shame of your youth, and the reproach of your widowhood you will remember no more. For your Maker is your husband, the Lord of hosts is his name; and the Holy One of Israel is your Redeemer, the God of the whole earth he is called. For the Lord has called you like a wife forsaken and grieved in spirit, like a wife of youth when she is cast off, says your God. For a brief moment I forsook you, but with great compassion I will gather you. In overflowing wrath for a moment I hid my face from you, but with everlasting love I will have compassion on you, says the Lord, your Redeemer. For this is like the days of Noah to me: as I swore that the waters of Noah should no more go over the earth, so I have sworn that I will not be angry with you and will not rebuke you. For the mountains may depart and the hills be removed, but my steadfast love shall not depart from you, and my covenant of peace shall not be removed, says the Lord, who has compassion on you. O afflicted one, storm-tossed, and not comforted, behold, I will set your stones in antimony, and lay your foundations with sapphires. I will make your pinnacles of agate, your gates of carbuncles, and all your wall of precious stones. All your sons shall be taught by the Lord, and great shall be the prosperity of your sons."

A Reading (Lesson) from the Gospel according to Mark [10:13-16]

The people were bringing children to Jesus, that he might touch them; and the disciples rebuked them. But when Jesus saw it he was indignant, and said to them, "Let the children come to me, do not hinder them; for to such belongs the kingdom of God. Truly, I say to you, whoever does not receive the kingdom of God like a child shall not enter it." And he took them in his arms and blessed them, laying his hands upon them.

Confession of St. Peter *January 18*

(Morning Prayer) *Psalm 66* [page 673], *Psalm 67* [page 675]

A Reading (Lesson) from the Book of Ezekiel [3:4-11]

He said to me, "Son of man, go, get you to the house of Israel, and speak with my words to them. For you are not sent to a people of foreign speech and a hard language, but to the house of Israel—not to many peoples of foreign speech and a hard language, whose words you cannot understand. Surely, if I sent you to such, they would listen to you. But the house of Israel will not listen to you; for they are not willing to listen to me; because all the house of Israel are of a hard forehead and of a stubborn heart. Behold, I have made your face hard against their faces, and your forehead hard against their foreheads. Like adamant harder than flint have I made your forehead; fear them not, nor be dismayed at their looks, for they are a rebellious house." Moreover he said to me, "Son of man, all my words that I shall speak to you receive in your heart, and hear with your ears. And go, get you to the exiles, to your people, and say to them, 'Thus says the Lord God'; whether they hear or refuse to hear."

A Reading (Lesson) from the Acts of the Apostles [10:34-44]

Peter opened his mouth and said: "Truly I perceive that God shows no partiality, but in every nation any one who fears him and does what is right is acceptable to him. You know the word which he sent to Israel, preaching good news of peace by Jesus Christ (he is Lord of all), the word which was proclaimed throughout all Judea, beginning from Galilee after the baptism which John preached: how God anointed Jesus of Nazareth with the Holy Spirit and with power; how he went about doing good and healing all that were oppressed by the devil, for God was with him. And we are witnesses to all that he did both in the country of the Jews and in Jerusalem. They put him to death by hanging him on a tree; but God raised him on the third day and made him manifest; not to all the people but to us who were chosen by God as witnesses, who ate and drank with him after he rose from the dead. And he commanded us to preach to the people, and to testify that he is the one ordained by God to be judge of the living and the dead. To him all the prophets bear witness that every one who believes in him receives forgiveness of sins through his name." While Peter was still saying this, the Holy Spirit fell on all who heard the word.

(Evening Prayer)   *Psalm 118* [page 760]

A Reading (Lesson) from the Book of Ezekiel [34:11-16]

The word of the Lord came to me: "For thus says the Lord God: Behold, I, I myself will search for my sheep, and will seek them out. As a shepherd seeks out his flock when some of his sheep have been scattered abroad, so will I seek out my sheep; and I will rescue them from all places where they have been scattered on a day of clouds and thick darkness. And I will bring them out from the peoples, and gather them from the countries, and will bring them into their own land; and I will feed them on the mountains of Israel, by the fountains, and in all the inhabited places of the country. I will feed them with good pasture, and upon the mountain heights of Israel shall be their pasture; there they shall lie down in good grazing land, and on fat pasture they shall feed on the mountains of Israel. I myself will be the shepherd of my sheep, and I will make them lie down, says the Lord God. I will seek the lost, and I will bring back the strayed, and I will bind up the crippled, and I will strengthen the weak, and the fat and the strong I will watch over; I will feed them in justice."

A Reading (Lesson) from the Gospel according to John
[21:15-22]

When they had finished breakfast, Jesus said to Simon Peter, "Simon, son of John, do you love me more than these?" He said to him, "Yes, Lord; you know that I love you." He said to him, "Feed my lambs." A second time he said to him, "Simon, son of John, do you love me?" He said to him, "Yes, Lord; you know that I love you." He said to him, "Tend my sheep." He said to him the third time, "Simon, son of John, do you love me?" Peter was grieved because he said to him the third time, "Do you love me?" And he said to him, "Lord, you know everything; you know that I love you." Jesus said to him, "Feed my sheep. Truly, truly, I say to you, when you were young, you girded yourself and walked where you would; but when you are old, you will stretch out your hands, and another will gird you and carry you where you do not wish to go." (This he said to show by what death he was to glorify God.) And after this he said to him, "Follow me." Peter turned and saw following them the disciple whom Jesus loved, who had lain close to his breast at the supper and had said, "Lord, who is it that is going to betray you?" When Peter saw him, he said to Jesus, "Lord, what about this man?" Jesus said to him, "If it is my will that he remain until I come, what is that to you? Follow me!"

Conversion of St. Paul   *January 25*

(Morning Prayer)   *Psalm 19* [page 606]

Isaiah 45:18-25   [page 139 above]

*A Reading (Lesson) from the the Letter of Paul
to the Philippians* [3:4b-11]

If any other man thinks he has reason for confidence in
the flesh, I have more: circumcised on the eighth day, of
the people of Israel, of the tribe of Benjamin, a Hebrew
born of Hebrews; as to the law a Pharisee, as to zeal a
persecutor of the church, as to righteousness under the
law blameless. But whatever gain I had, I counted as loss
for the sake of Christ. Indeed I count everything as loss
because of the surpassing worth of knowing Christ Jesus
my Lord. For his sake I have suffered the loss of all
things, and count them as refuse, in order that I may gain
Christ and be found in him, not having a righteousness
of my own, based on the law, but that which is through
faith in Christ, the righteousness from God that depends
on faith; that I may know him and the power of his
resurrection, and may share his sufferings, becoming like
him in his death, that if possible I may attain the
resurrection from the dead.

(Evening Prayer)   *Psalm 119:89-112* [page 770]

A Reading (Lesson) from the Book of Ecclesiasticus
[39:1-10]

On the other hand he who devotes himself to the study of
the law of the Most High will seek out the wisdom of all
the ancients, and will be concerned with prophecies; he
will preserve the discourse of notable men and penetrate
the subtleties of parables; he will seek out the hidden
meanings of proverbs and be at home with the
obscurities of parables. He will serve among great men
and appear before rulers; he will travel through the lands

of foreign nations, for he tests the good and the evil among men. He will set his heart to rise early to seek the Lord who made him, and he will make supplication before the Most High; he will open his mouth in prayer and make supplication for his sins. If the great Lord is willing, he will be filled with the spirit of understanding; he will pour forth words of wisdom and give thanks to the Lord in prayer. He will direct his counsel and knowledge aright, and meditate on his secrets. He will reveal instruction in his teaching, and will glory in the law of the Lord's covenant. Many will praise his understanding, and it will never be blotted out; his memory will not disappear, and his name will live through all generations. Nations will declare his wisdom, and the congregation will proclaim his praise.

A Reading (Lesson) from the Acts of the Apostles [9:1-22]

Saul, still breathing threats and murder against the disciples of the Lord, went to the high priest and asked him for letters to the synagogues at Damascus, so that if he found any belonging to the Way, men or women, he might bring them bound to Jerusalem. Now as he journeyed he approached Damascus, and suddenly a light from heaven flashed about him. And he fell to the ground and heard a voice saying to him, "Saul, Saul, why do you persecute me?" And he said, "Who are you, Lord?" And he said, "I am Jesus, whom you are persecuting; but rise and enter the city, and you will be told what you are to do." The men who were traveling with him stood speechless, hearing the voice but seeing no one. Saul arose from the ground; and when his eyes were opened, he could see nothing; so they led him by the hand and brought him into Damascus. And for three days he was without sight, and neither ate nor drank. Now there was a disciple at Damascus named Anani'as. The Lord said to him in a vision, "Anani'as." And he said, "Here I am , Lord." And the Lord said to him,

"Rise and go to the street called Straight, and inquire in the house of Judas for a man of Tarsus named Saul; for behold, he is praying, and he has seen a man named Anani′as come in and lay his hands on him so t⌐ ⌐ he might regain his sight." But Anani′as answered, "Lord, I have heard from many about this man, how much evil he has done to thy saints at Jerusalem; and here he has authority from the chief priests to bind all who call upon thy name." But the Lord said to him, "Go, for he is a chosen instrument of mine to carry my name before the Gentiles and kings and the sons of Israel; for I will show him how much he must suffer for the sake of my name." So Anani′as departed and entered the house. And laying his hands on him he said, "Brother Saul, the Lord Jesus who appeared to you on the road by which you came, has sent me that you may regain your sight and be filled with the Holy Spirit." And immediately something like scales fell from his eyes and he regained his sight. Then he rose and was baptized, and took food and was strengthened. For several days he was with the disciples at Damascus. And in the synagogues immediately he proclaimed Jesus, saying, "He is the Son of God." And all who heard him were amazed, and said, "Is not this the man who made havoc in Jerusalem of those who called on this name? And he has come here for this purpose, to bring them bound before the chief priests." But Saul increased all the more in strength, and confounded the Jews who lived in Damascus by proving that Jesus was the Christ.

Eve of the Presentation   *February 1*

(Evening Prayer)   *Psalm 113* [page 756],   *Psalm 122* [page 779]

A Reading (Lesson) from the First Book of Samuel
[1:20-28a]

In due time Hannah conceived and bore a son, and she

called his name Samuel, for she said, "I have asked him of the Lord." And the man Elka'nah and all his house went up to offer to the Lord the yearly sacrifice, and to pay his vow. But Hannah did not go up, for she said to her husband, "As soon as the child is weaned, I will bring him, that he may appear in the presence of the Lord, and abide there for ever." Elka'nah her husband said to her, "Do what seems best to you, wait until you have weaned him; only, may the Lord establish his word." So the woman remained and nursed her son, until she weaned him. And when she had weaned him, she took him up with her, along with a three-year-old bull, an ephah of flour, and a skin of wine; and she brought him to the house of the Lord at Shiloh; and the child was young. Then they slew the bull, and they brought the child to Eli. And she said, "Oh, my lord! As you live, my lord, I am the woman who was standing here in your presence, praying to the Lord. For this child I prayed; and the Lord has granted me my petition which I made to him. Therefore I have lent him to the Lord; as long as he lives, he is lent to the Lord."

A Reading (Lesson) from the Letter of Paul to the Romans [8:14-21]

For all who are led by the Spirit of God are sons of God. For you did not receive the spirit of slavery to fall back into fear, but you have received the spirit of sonship. When we cry, "Abba! Father!" it is the Spirit himself bearing witness with our spirit that we are children of God, and if children, then heirs, heirs of God and fellow heirs with Christ, provided we suffer with him in order that we may also be glorified with him. I consider that the sufferings of this present time are not worth comparing with the glory that is to be revealed to us. For the creation waits with eager longing for the revealing of the sons of god; for the creation was subjected to futility, not of its own will but by the will of him who subjected it in hope; because the creation itself will be set free from its bondage to decay and obtain the glorious liberty of the children of God.

The Presentation   *February 2*

(Morning Prayer)   *Psalm 42* [page 643],   *Psalm 43* [page 644]

A Reading (Lesson) from the First Book of Samuel
[2:1-10]

Elka'nah and Hannah worshiped at Shiloh. Hannah also prayed and said, "My heart exults in the Lord; my strength is exalted in the Lord. My mouth derides my enemies, because I rejoice in thy salvation. There is none holy like the Lord, there is none besides thee; there is no rock like our God. Talk no more so very proudly, let not arrogance come from your mouth; for the Lord is a God of knowledge, and by him actions are weighed. The bows of the mighty are broken, but the feeble gird on strength. Those who were full have hired themselves out for bread, but those who were hungry have ceased to hunger. The barren have borne seven, but she who has many children is forlorn. The Lord kills and brings to life; he brings down to Sheol and raises up. The Lord makes poor and makes rich; he brings low, he also exalts. He raises up the poor from the dust; he lifts the needy from the ash heap, to make them sit with princes and inherit a seat of honor. For the pillars of the earth are the Lord's, and on them he has set the world. He will guard the feet of his faithful ones; but the wicked shall be cut off in darkness; for not by might shall a man prevail. The adversaries of the Lord shall be broken to pieces; against them he will thunder in heaven. The Lord will judge the ends of the earth; he will give strength to his king, and exalt the power of his anointed."

A Reading (Lesson) from the Gospel according to John
[8:31-36]

Jesus said to the Jews who had believed in him, "If you
continue in my word, you are truly my disciples, and you
will know the truth, and the truth will make you free."
They answered him, "We are descendants of Abraham,
and have never been in bondage to any one. How is it
that you say, 'You will be made free'?" Jesus answered
them, "Truly, truly, I say to you, every one who commits
sin is a slave to sin. The slave does not continue in the
house for ever; the son continues for ever. So if the Son
makes you free, you will be free indeed."

(Evening Prayer)   *Psalm 48* [page 651],   *Psalm 87* [page 711]

A Reading (Lesson) from the Book of Haggai [2:1-9]

In the second year of Darius the king, in the seventh
month, on the twenty-first day of the month, the word of
the Lord came by Haggai the prophet, "Speak now to
Zerub'babel the son of She-al'ti-el, governor of Judah, and
to Joshua the son of Jehoz'adak, the high priest, and to all
the remnant of the people, and say, 'Who is left among you
that saw this house in its former glory? How do you see it
now? Is it not in your sight as nothing? Yet now take
courage, O Zerub'babel, says the Lord; take courage, O
Joshua, son of Jehoz'adak, the high priest; take courage, all
you people of the land, says the Lord; work, for I am with
you, says the Lord of hosts, according to the promise that I
made you when you came out of Egypt. My Spirit abides
among you; fear not. For thus says the Lord of hosts: Once
again, in a little while, I will shake the heavens and the
earth and the sea and the dry land; and I will shake all
nations, so that the treasures of all nations shall come in,
and I will fill this house with spendor, says the Lord of
hosts. The silver is mine, and the gold is mine, says the
Lord of hosts. The latter spendor of this house shall be

greater than the former, says the Lord of hosts; and in this place I will give prosperity, says the Lord of hosts.'"

A Reading (Lesson) from the First Letter of John [3:1-8]

See what love the Father has given us, that we should be called the children of God; and so we are. The reason why the world does not know us is that it did not know him. Beloved, we are God's children now; it does not yet appear what we shall be, but we know that when he appears we shall be like him, for we shall see him as he is. And every one who thus hopes in him purifies himself as he is pure. Every one who commits sin is guilty of lawlessness; sin is lawlessness. You know that he appeared to take away sins, and in him there is no sin. No one who abides in him sins; no one who sins has either seen him or known him. Little children, let no one deceive you. He who does right is righteous, as he is righteous. He who commits sin is of the devil; for the devil has sinned from the beginning. The reason the Son of God appeared was to destroy the works of the devil.

St. Matthias *February 24*

(Morning Prayer) *Psalm 80* [page 702]

A Reading (Lesson) from the First Book of Samuel [16:1-13]

The Lord said to Samuel, "How long will you grieve over Saul, seeing I have rejected him from being king over Israel? Fill your horn with oil, and go; I will send you to Jesse the Bethlehemite, for I have provided for myself a king among his sons." And Samuel said, "How can I go? If Saul hears it, he will kill me." And the Lord said, "Take a heifer with you, and say, 'I have come to sacrifice to the Lord.' And invite Jesse to the sacrifice, and I will show you what you shall do; and you shall anoint for me him whom I name to you." Samuel did what the Lord commanded, and came to Bethlehem. The elders of the city came to meet him trembling, and said, "Do you come peaceably?" And he said, "Peaceably; I have come to sacrifice to the Lord; consecrate yourselves, and come with me to the sacrifice." And he consecrated Jesse and his sons, and invited them to the sacrifice. When they came, he looked on Eli′ab and thought, "Surely the Lord's anointed is before him." But the Lord said to Samuel, "Do not look on his appearance or on the height of his stature, because I have rejected him; for the Lord sees not as man sees; man looks on the outward appearance, but the Lord looks on the heart." Then Jesse called Abin′adab, and made him pass before Samuel. And he said, "Neither has the Lord chosen this one." And Jesse made seven of his sons pass before Samuel. And Samuel said to Jesse, "The Lord has not chosen these." And Samuel said to Jesse, "Are all your sons here?" And he said, "There remains yet the youngest, but behold, he is keeping the sheep." And Samuel said to Jesse, "Send and fetch him; for we will not sit down till he comes here." And he sent, and brought him in. Now he was ruddy, and had beautiful eyes, and was handsome. And the Lord said, "Arise, anoint him; for this is he." Then Samuel took the horn of oil, and anointed him in the midst of his brothers; and the Spirit of the Lord came mightily upon David from that day forward. And Samuel rose up, and went to Ramah.

A Reading (Lesson) from the First Letter of John [2:18-25]

Children, it is the last hour; and as you have heard that antichrist is coming, so now many antichrists have come; therefore we know that it is the last hour. They went out from us, but they were not of us; for if they had been of us, they would have continued with us; but they went out, that it might be plain that they all are not of us. But you have been anointed by the Holy One, and you all know. I write to you, not because you do not know the truth, but because you know it, and know that no lie is of the truth. Who is the liar but he who denies that Jesus is the Christ? This is the antichrist, he who denies the Father and the Son. No one who denies the Son has the Father. He who confesses the Son has the Father also. Let what you heard from the beginning abide in you. If what you heard from the beginning abides in you, then you will abide in the Son and in the Father. And this is what he has promised us, eternal life.

(Evening Prayer) *Psalm 33* [page 626]

A Reading (Lesson) from the First Book of Samuel [12:1-5]

Samuel said to all Israel, "Behold, I have hearkened to your voice in all that you have said to me, and have made a king over you. And now, behold, the king walks before you; and I am old and gray, and behold, my sons are with you; and I have walked before you from my youth until this day. Here I am; testify against me before the Lord and before his anointed. Whose ox have I taken? Or whose ass have I taken? Or whom have I defrauded? Whom have I oppressed? Or from whose hand have I taken a bribe to blind my eyes with it? Testify against me and I will restore it to you." They said, "You have not defrauded us or oppressed us or taken anything from any man's hand." And he said to them, "The Lord is witness this day, that you have not found anything in my hand." And they said, "He is witness."

A Reading (Lesson) from the Acts of the Apostles [20:17-35]

From Mile'tus Paul sent to Ephesus and called to him the elders of the church. And when they came to him, he said to them: "You yourselves know how I lived among you all the time from the first day that I set foot in Asia, serving the Lord with all humility and with tears and with trials which befell me through the plots of the Jews; how I did not shrink from declaring to you anything that was profitable, and teaching you in public and from house to house, testifying both to Jews and to Greeks of repentance to God and of faith in our Lord Jesus Christ. And now, behold, I am going to Jerusalem, bound in the Spirit, not knowing what shall befall me there; except that the Holy Spirit testifies to me in every city that imprisonment and afflictions await me. But I do not account my life of any value nor as precious to myself, if only I may accomplish my course and the ministry which I received from the Lord Jesus, to testify to the gospel of the grace of God. And now, behold, I know that all you among whom I have gone preaching the kingdom will see my face no more. Therefore I testify to you this day that I am innocent of the blood of all of you, for I did not shrink from declaring to you the whole counsel of God. Take heed to yourselves and to all the flock, in which the Holy Spirit has made you overseers, to care for the church of God which he obtained with the blood of his own Son. I know that after my departure fierce wolves will come in among you, not sparing the flock; and from among your own selves will arise men speaking perverse things, to draw away the disciples after them. Therefore be alert, remembering that for three years I did not cease night or day to admonish every one with tears. And now I commend you to God, and to the word of his grace, which is able to build you up and to give you the inheritance among all those who are sanctified. I coveted no one's silver or gold or apparel. You yourselves know that these hands ministered to my necessities, and to those who were with me. In all things I have shown you that by so toiling one must help the weak, remembering the words of the Lord Jesus, how he said, 'It is more blessed to give than to receive.'"

St. Joseph *March 19*

(Morning Prayer) *Psalm 132* [page 785]

A Reading (Lesson) from the Book of Isaiah [63:7-16]

I will recount the steadfast love of the Lord, the praises of the Lord, according to all that the Lord has granted us, and the great goodness to the house of Israel which he has granted them according to his mercy, according to the abundance of his steadfast love. For he said, Surely they are my people, sons who will not deal falsely; and he became their Savior. In all their affliction he was afflicted, and the angel of his presence saved them; in his love and in his pity he redeemed them; he lifted them up and carried them all the days of old. But they rebelled and grieved his holy Spirit; therefore he turned to be their enemy, and himself fought against them. Then he remembered the days of old, of Moses his servant. Where is he who brought up out of the sea the shepherds of his flock? Where is he who put in the midst of them his holy Spirit, who caused his glorious arm to go at the right hand of Moses, who divided the waters before them to make for himself an everlasting name, who led them through the depths? Like a horse in the desert, they did not stumble. Like cattle that go down into the valley, the Spirit of the Lord gave them rest. So thou didst lead thy people, to make for thyself a glorious name. Look down from heaven and see, from thy holy and glorious habitation. Where are thy zeal and thy might? The yearning of thy heart and thy compassion are withheld from me. For thou art our Father, though Abraham does not know us and Israel does not acknowledge us; thou, O Lord, art our Father, our Redeemer from of old is thy name.

Matthew 1:18-25 [page 71 above]

(Evening Prayer) *Psalm 34* [page 627]

A Reading (Lesson) from the Second Book of Chronicles
[6:12-17]

Solomon stood before the altar of the Lord in the presence of all the assembly of Israel, and spread forth his hands. Solomon had made a bronze platform five cubits long, five cubits wide, and three cubits high, and had set it in the court; and he stood upon it. Then he knelt upon his knees in the presence of all the assembly of Israel, and spread forth his hands toward heaven; and said, "O Lord, God of Israel, there is no God like thee, in heaven or on earth, keeping covenant and showing steadfast love to thy servants who walk before thee with all their heart; who hast kept with thy servant David my father what thou didst declare to him; yea, thou didst speak with thy mouth, and with thy hand hast fulfilled it this day. Now therefore, O Lord, God of Israel, keep with thy servant David my father what thou hast promised him, saying, 'There shall never fail you a man before me to sit upon the throne of Israel, if only your sons take heed to their way, to walk in my law as you have walked before me.' Now therefore, O Lord, God of Israel, let thy word be confirmed, which thou hast spoken to thy servant David."

Ephesians 3:14-21 [page 124 above]

Eve of the Annunciation *March 24*

(Evening Prayer) *Psalm 8* [page 592], *Psalm 138* [page 793]

A Reading (Lesson) from the Book of Genesis [3:1-15]

The serpent was more subtle than any other wild creature that the Lord God had made. He said to the woman, "Did God say, 'You shall not eat of any tree of the garden'?" And the woman said to the serpent, "We may eat of the fruit of the trees of the garden; but God said, 'You shall not eat of the fruit of the tree which is in the midst of the garden, neither shall you touch it, lest you die.'" But the serpent said to the woman, "You will not die. For God knows that when you eat of it your eyes will be opened, and you will be like God, knowing good and evil." So when the woman saw that the tree was good for food, and that it was a delight to the eyes, and that the tree was to be desired to make one wise, she took of its fruit and ate; and she also gave some to her husband, and he ate. Then the eyes of both were opened, and they knew that they were naked; and they sewed fig leaves together and made themselves aprons. And they heard the sound of the Lord God walking in the garden in the cool of the day, and the man and his wife hid themselves from the presence of the Lord God among the trees of the garden. But the Lord God called to the man, and said to him, "Where are you?" And he said, "I heard the sound of thee in the garden, and I was afraid, because I was naked; and I hid myself." He said, "Who told you that you were naked? Have you eaten of the tree of which I commanded you not to eat?" The man said, "The woman whom thou gavest to be with me, she gave me fruit of the tree, and I ate." Then the Lord God said to the woman, "What is this that you have done?" The woman said, "The serpent beguiled me, and I ate." The Lord God said to the serpent, "Because you have done this, cursed are you above all cattle, and above all wild animals; upon your belly you shall go, and dust you shall eat all the days of your life. I will put enmity between you and the woman, and between your seed and her seed; he shall bruise your head, and you shall bruise his heel."

Romans 5:12-21   [page 306 above]

or this

*A Reading (Lesson) from the Letter of Paul
to the Galatians* [4:1-7]

I mean that the heir, as long as he is a child, is no better
than a slave, though he is the owner of all the estate; but
he is under guardians and trustees until the date set by
the father. So with us; when we were children, we were
slaves to the elemental spirits of the universe. But when
the time had fully come, God sent forth his Son, born of
woman, born under the law, to redeem those who were
under the law, so that we might receive adoption as sons.
And because you are sons, God has sent the Spirit of his
Son into our hearts, crying, "Abba! Father!" So through
God you are no longer a slave but a son, and if a son then
an heir.

Annunciation   *March 25*

(Morning Prayer)   *Psalm 85* [page 708],   *Psalm 87* [page 711]

A Reading (Lesson) from the Book of Isaiah [52:7-12]

How beautiful upon the mountains are the feet of him
who brings good tidings, who publishes peace, who
brings good tidings of good, who publishes salvation,
who says to Zion, "Your God reigns." Hark, your
watchmen lift up their voice, together they sing for joy;
for eye to eye they see the return of the Lord to Zion.
Break forth together into singing, you waste places of
Jerusalem; for the Lord has comforted his people, he has
redeemed Jerusalem. The Lord has bared his holy arm
before the eyes of all the nations; and all the ends of the
earth shall see the salvation of our God. Depart, depart,
go out thence, touch no unclean thing; go out from the
midst of her, purify yourselves, you who bear the vessels
of the Lord. For you shall not go out in haste, and you
shall not go in flight, for the Lord will go before you, and
the God of Israel will be your rear guard.

A Reading (Lesson) from the Letter to the Hebrews
[2:5-10]

For it was not to angels that God subjected the world to come, of which we are speaking. It has been testified somewhere, "What is man that thou are mindful of him, or the son of man, that thou carest for him? Thou didst make him for a little while lower than the angels, thou hast crowned him with glory and honor, putting everything in subjection under his feet." Now in putting everything in subjection to him, he left nothing outside his control. As it is, we do not yet see everything in subjection to him. But we see Jesus, who for a little while was made lower than the angels, crowned with glory and honor because of the suffering of death, so that by the grace of God he might taste death for every one. For it was fitting that he, for whom and by whom all things exist, in bringing many sons to glory, should make the pioneer of their salvation perfect through suffering.

(Evening Prayer)
Psalm 110:1-5(6-7) [page 753], *Psalm 132* [page 785]

A Reading (Lesson) from the Book of Wisdom [9:1-12]

With my whole heart I said: "O God of my fathers and Lord of mercy, who hast made all things by thy word, and by thy wisdom hast formed man, to have dominion over the creatures thou hast made, and rule the world in holiness and righteousness, and pronounce judgment in uprightness of soul, give me the wisdom that sits by thy throne, and do not reject me from among thy servants. For I am thy slave and the son of thy maidservant, a man who is weak and short-lived, with little understanding of judgment and laws; for even if one is perfect among the sons of men, yet without the wisdom that comes from thee he will be regarded as nothing. Thou hast chosen me to be king of thy people and to be judge over thy sons and daughters. Thou hast given command to build a temple on thy holy mountain, and an altar in the city of thy habitation, a copy of the holy tent which thou didst prepare from the beginning. With thee is wisdom, who knows thy works and was present when thou didst make the world, and who understands what is pleasing in thy sight and what is right according to thy commandments. Send her forth from the holy heavens, and from the throne of thy glory send her, that she may be with me and toil, and that I may learn what is pleasing to thee. For she knows and understands all things, and she will guide me wisely in my actions and guard me with her glory. Then my works will be acceptable, and I shall judge thy people justly, and shall be worthy of the throne of my father."

A Reading (Lesson) from the Gospel according to John [1:9-14]

The true light that enlightens every man was coming into the world. He was in the world, and the world was made through him, yet the world knew him not. He came to his own home, and his own people received him not. But to all who received him, who believed in his name, he gave power to become children of God; who were born, not of blood nor of the will of the flesh nor of the will of man, but of God. And the Word became flesh and dwelt among us, full of grace and truth; we have beheld his glory, glory as of the only Son from the Father.

St. Mark   April 25

(Morning Prayer)   *Psalm 145* [page 801]

A Reading (Lesson) from the Book of Ecclesiasticus [2:1-11]

My son, if you come forward to serve the Lord, prepare yourself for temptation. Set your heart right and be

steadfast, and do not be hasty in time of calamity. Cleave
to him and do not depart, that you may be honored at
the end of your life. Accept whatever is brought upon
you, and in changes that humble you be patient. For gold
is tested in the fire, and acceptable men in the furnace of
humiliation. Trust in him, and he will help you; make
your ways straight, and hope in him. You who fear the
Lord, wait for his mercy; and turn not aside, lest you fall.
You who fear the Lord, trust in him, and your reward
will not fail; you who fear the Lord, hope for good
things, for everlasting joy and mercy. Consider the
ancient generations and see: who ever trusted in the Lord
and was put to shame? Or who ever presevered in the
fear of the Lord and was forsaken? Or who ever called
upon him and was overlooked? For the Lord is
compassionate and merciful; he forgives sins and
saves in time of affliction.

A Reading (Lesson) from the Acts of the Apostles
[12:25—13:3]

Barnabas and Saul returned from Jerusalem when they
had fulfilled their mission, bringing with them John
whose other name was Mark. Now in the church at
Antioch there were prophets and teachers, Barnabas,
Simeon who was called Niger, Lucius of Cyre'ne,
Man'a-en a member of the court of Herod the tetrarch,
and Saul. While they were worshiping the Lord and
fasting, the Holy Spirit said, "Set apart for me Barnabas
and Saul for the work to which I have called them." Then
after fasting and praying they laid their hands on them
and sent them off.

(Evening Prayer)　　*Psalm 67* [page 675],　　*Psalm 96* [page 725]

Isaiah 62:6-12　　[page 196 above]

*A Reading (Lesson) from the Second Letter of Paul
to Timothy* [4:1-11]

I charge you in the presence of God and of Christ Jesus
who is to judge the living and the dead, and by his
appearing and his kingdom: preach the word, be urgent
in season and out of season, convince, rebuke, and
exhort, be unfailing in patience and in teaching. For the
time is coming when people will not endure sound
teaching, but having itching ears they will accumulate for
themselves teachers to suit their own likings, and will
turn away from listening to the truth and wander into
myths. As for you, always be steady, endure suffering, do
the work of an evangelist, fulfil your ministry. For I am
already on the point of being sacrificed; the time of my
departure has come. I have fought the good fight, I have
finished the race, I have kept the faith. Henceforth there
is laid up for me the crown of righteousness, which the
Lord, the righteous judge, will award to me on that Day,
and not only to me but also to all who have loved his
appearing. Do your best to come to me soon. For Demas,
in love with this present world, has deserted me and gone
to Thessaloni'ca; Crescens has gone to Galatia, Titus to
Dalmatia. Luke alone is with me. Get Mark and bring
him with you; for he is very useful in serving me.

SS. Philip & James *May 1*

(Morning Prayer) *Psalm 119:137-160* [page 774]

A Reading (Lesson) from the Book of Job [23:1-12]

Job answered El'iphaz the Te'manite: "Today also my
complaint is bitter, his hand is heavy in spite of my
groaning. Oh, that I knew where I might find him, that I
might come even to his seat! I would lay my case before
him and fill my mouth with arguments. I would learn
what he would answer me, and understand what he
would say to me. Would he contend with me in the

greatness of his power? No; he would give heed to me. There an upright man could reason with him, and I should be acquitted for ever by my judge. Behold, I go forward, but he is not there; and backward, but I cannot perceive him; on the left hand I seek him, but I cannot behold him; I turn to the right hand, but I cannot see him. But he knows the way that I take; when he has tried me, I shall come forth as gold. My foot has held fast to his steps; I have kept his way and have not turned aside. I have not departed from the commandment of his lips; I have treasured in my bosom the words of his mouth."

John 1:43-51   [page 263 above]

(Evening Prayer)   *Psalm 139* [page 794]

A Reading (Lesson) from the Book of Proverbs [4:7-18]

My father taught me, and said to me, "The beginning of wisdom is this: Get wisdom, and whatever you get, get insight. Prize her highly, and she will exalt you; she will honor you if you embrace her. She will place on your head a fair garland; she will bestow on you a beautiful crown." Hear, my son, and accept my words, that the years of your life may be many. I have taught you the way of wisdom; I have led you in the paths of uprightness. When you walk, your step will not be hampered; and if you run, you will not stumble. Keep hold of instruction, do not let go; guard her, for she is your life. Do not enter the path of the wicked, and do not walk in the way of evil men. Avoid it; do not go on it; turn away from it and pass on. For they cannot sleep unless they have done wrong; they are robbed of sleep unless they have made some one stumble. For they eat the bread of wickedness and drink the wine of violence. But the path of the righteous is like the light of dawn, which shines brighter and brighter until full day.

John 12:20-26   [page 358 above]

Eve of the Visitation   *May* 30

(Evening Prayer)   *Psalm 132* [page 785]

A Reading (Lesson) from the Book of Isaiah   [11:1-10]

There shall come forth a shoot from the stump of Jesse, and a branch shall grow out of his roots. And the Spirit of the Lord shall rest upon him, the spirit of wisdom and understanding, the spirit of counsel and might, the spirit of knowledge and the fear of the Lord. And his delight shall be in the fear of the Lord. He shall not judge by what his eyes see, or decide by what his ears hear; but with righteousness he shall judge the poor, and decide with equity for the meek of the earth; and he shall smite the earth with the rod of his mouth, and with the breath of his lips he shall slay the wicked. Righteousness shall be the girdle of his waist, and faithfulness the girdle of his loins. The wolf shall dwell with the lamb, and the leopard shall lie down with the kid, and the calf and the lion and the fatling together, and a little child shall lead them. The cow and the bear shall feed; their young shall lie down together; and the lion shall eat straw like the ox. The sucking child shall play over the hole of the asp, and the weaned child shall put his hand on the adder's den. They shall not hurt or destroy in all my holy mountain; for the earth shall be full of the knowledge of the Lord as the waters cover the sea. In that day the root of Jesse shall stand as an ensign to the peoples; him shall the nations seek, and his dwellings shall be glorious.

Hebrews 2:11-18   [page 267 above]

The Visitation   *May* 31

(Morning Prayer)   *Psalm 72* [page 685]

A Reading (Lesson) from the First Book of Samuel
[1:1-20]

There was a certain man of Ramatha'im-zo'phim of the hill country of E'phraim, whose name was Elka'nah the son of Jero'ham, son of Eli'hu, son of Tohu, son of Zuph, an E'phraimite. He had two wives; the name of the one was Hannah, and the name of the other Penin'nah. And Penin'nah had children, but Hannah had no children. Now this man used to go up year by year from his city to worship and to sacrifice to the Lord of hosts at Shiloh, where the two sons of Eli, Hophni and Phin'ehas, were priests of the Lord. On the day when Elka'nah sacrificed, he would give portions to Penin'nah his wife and to all her sons and daughters; and, although he loved Hannah, he would give Hannah only one portion, because the Lord had closed her womb. And her rival used to provoke her sorely, to irritate her, because the Lord had closed her womb. So it went on year by year; as often as she went up to the house of the Lord, she used to provoke her. Therefore Hannah wept and would not eat. And Elka'nah, her husband said to her, "Hannah, why do you weep? And why do you not eat? And why is your heart sad? Am I not more to you than ten sons?" After they had eaten and drunk in Shiloh, Hannah rose. Now Eli the priest was sitting on the seat beside the doorpost of the temple of the Lord. She was deeply distressed and prayed to the Lord, and wept bitterly. And she vowed a vow and said, "O Lord of hosts, if thou wilt indeed look on the affliction of thy maidservant, and remember me, and not forget thy maidservant, but wilt give to thy maidservant a son, then I will give him to the Lord all the days of his life, and no razor shall touch his head." As she continued praying before the Lord, Eli observed her mouth. Hannah was speaking in her heart; only her lips moved, and her voice was not heard; therefore Eli took her to be a drunken woman. And Eli said to her, "How long will you be drunken? Put away your wine from you." But Hannah answered, "No, my lord, I am a woman sorely troubled; I have drunk neither wine nor strong drink, but I have been pouring out my soul before the Lord. Do not regard your maidservant as a base woman, for all along I have been speaking out of my great anxiety and vexation." Then Eli answered, "Go in peace, and the God of Israel grant your petition which you have made to him." And she said, "Let your maidservant find favor in your eyes." Then the woman went her way and ate, and her countenance was no longer sad. They rose early in the morning and worshiped before the Lord; then they went back to their house at Ramah. And Elka'nah knew Hannah his wife, and the Lord remembered her; and in due time Hannah conceived and bore a son, and she called his name Samuel, for she said, "I have asked him of the Lord."

A Reading (Lesson) from the Letter to the Hebrews
[3:1-6]

Therefore, holy brethren, who share in a heavenly call, consider Jesus, the apostle and high priest of our confession. He was faithful to him who appointed him, just as Moses also was faithful in God's house. Yet Jesus has been counted worthy of as much more glory than Moses as the builder of a house has more honor than the house. (For every house is built by some one, but the builder of all things is God.) Now Moses was faithful in all God's house as a servant, to testify to the things that were to be spoken later, but Christ was faithful over God's house as a son. And we are his house if we hold fast our confidence and pride in our hope.

(Evening Prayer)   *Psalm 146* [page 803],   *Psalm 147* [page 804]

Zechariah 2:10-13   [page 69 above]

Thus says the Lord of hosts, "Sing and rejoice, O daughter of Zion; for lo, I come and I will dwell in the midst of you, says the Lord. And many nations shall join themselves to the Lord in that day, and shall be my people; and I will dwell in the midst of you, and you shall know that the Lord of hosts has sent me to you. And the Lord will inherit Judah as his portion in the holy land, and will again choose Jerusalem." Be silent, all flesh, before the Lord; for he has roused himself from his holy dwelling.

A Reading (Lesson) from the Gospel according to John [3:25-30]

A discussion arose between John's disciples and a Jew over purifying. And they came to John, and said to him, "Rabbi, he who was with you beyond the Jordan, to whom you bore witness, here he is, baptizing, and all are going to him." John answered, "No one can receive anything except what is given him from heaven. You yourselves bear me witness, that I said, I am not the Christ, but I have been sent before him. He who has the bride is the bridegroom; the friend of the bridegroom, who stands and hears him, rejoices greatly at the bridegroom's voice; therefore this joy of mine is now full. He must increase, but I must decrease."

St. Barnabas *June 11*

(Morning Prayer) *Psalm 15* [page 599], *Psalm 67* [page 675]

A Reading (Lesson) from the Book of Ecclesiasticus [31:3-11]

The rich man toils as his wealth accumulates, and when he rests he fills himself with his dainties. The poor man toils as his livelihood diminishes, and when he rests he becomes needy. He who loves gold will not be justified, and he who pursues money will be led astray by it. Many have come to ruin because of gold, and their destruction has met them face to face. It is a stumbling block to those who are devoted to it, and every fool will be taken captive by it. Blessed is the rich man who is found blameless, and who does not go after gold. Who is he? And we will call him blessed, for he has done wonderful things among his people. Who has been tested by it and been found perfect? Let it be for him a ground for boasting. Who has had the power to transgress and did not transgress, and to do evil and did not do it? His prosperity will be established, and the assembly will relate his acts of charity.

A Reading (Lesson) from the Acts of the Apostles
[4:32-37]

The company of those who believed were of one heart and soul, and no one said that any of the things which he possessed was his own, but they had everything in common. And with great power the apostles gave their testimony to the resurrection of the Lord Jesus, and great grace was upon them all. There was not a needy person among them, for as many as were possessors of lands or houses sold them, and brought the proceeds of what was sold and laid it at the apostles' feet; and distribution was made to each as any had need. Thus Joseph who was surnamed by the apostles Barnabas (which means, Son of encouragement), a Levite, a native of Cyprus, sold a field which belonged to him, and brought the money and laid it at the apostles' feet.

(Evening Prayer)   *Psalm 19* [page 606],   *Psalm 146* [page 803]

A Reading (Lesson) from the Book of Job [29:1-16]

Job again took up his discourse, and said: "Oh, that I were as in the months of old, as in the days when God watched over me; when his lamp shone upon my head, and by his light I walked through darkness; as I was in my autumn days, when the friendship of God was upon my tent; when the Almighty was yet with me, when my children were about me; when my steps were washed with milk, and the rock poured out for me streams of oil! When I went out to the gate of the city, when I prepared my seat in the square, the young men saw me and withdrew, and the aged rose and stood; the princes refrained from talking, and laid their hand on their mouth; the voice of the nobles were hushed, and their tongue cleaved to the roof of their mouth. When the ear heard, it called me blessed, and when the eye saw, it approved; because I delivered the poor who cried, and the fatherless who had none to help him. The blessing of him who was about to perish came upon me, and I caused the widow's heart to sing for joy. I put on righteousness, and it clothed me; my justice was like a robe and a turban. I was eyes to the blind, and feet to the lame. I was father to the poor, and I searched out the cause of him whom I did not know.

A Reading (Lesson) from the Acts of the Apostles
[9:26-31]

When Paul had come to Jerusalem he attempted to join the disciples; and they were all afraid of him, for they did not believe that he was a disciple. But Barnabas took him, and brought him to the apostles, and declared to them how on the road he had seen the Lord, who spoke to him, and how at Damascus he had preached boldly in the name of Jesus. So he went in and out among them at Jerusalem, preaching boldly in the name of the Lord. And he spoke and disputed against the Hellenists; but they were seeking to kill him. And when the brethren knew it, they brought him down to Caesare'a, and sent him off to Tarsus. So the church throughout all Judea and Galilee and Samar'ia had peace and was built up; and walking in the fear of the Lord and in the comfort of the Holy Spirit it was multiplied.